A HISTORY OF
French Literature

A HISTORY OF
French Literature

BY

L. CAZAMIAN

OXFORD
AT THE CLARENDON PRESS

Oxford University Press, Amen House, London E.C.4

GLASGOW NEW YORK TORONTO MELBOURNE WELLINGTON
BOMBAY CALCUTTA MADRAS KARACHI LAHORE DACCA
CAPE TOWN SALISBURY NAIROBI IBADAN
KUALA LUMPUR HONG KONG

FIRST PUBLISHED 1955
REPRINTED LITHOGRAPHICALLY IN GREAT BRITAIN
AT THE UNIVERSITY PRESS, OXFORD
BY VIVIAN RIDLER, PRINTER TO THE UNIVERSITY
FROM CORRECTED SHEETS OF THE FIRST EDITION
1959, 1964, 1965

PREFACE

I OWE thanks to the authorities of the Oxford University Press, at whose request this book has been written. They have encouraged me under a sense of the special difficulty of a work that took me out of my accustomed field. Whether the offer was wisely made, and accepted, I shall not presume to say. But the years devoted to that undertaking have given me happiness in constant exertion. I have further to apologize for writing in a language not my own. Lastly, the limited scope of the survey implies a general reduction of scale, and many omissions.

The short biographical and bibliographical notes, summing up the writers' lives and their output, may be found of some use; more detailed information it was not possible to supply. Again, anything like a bibliography, however simplified, of the work done by so many scholars and critics on the literature of France, was out of the question. The student may be referred to the generally full and up-to-date lists given by the Bédier-Hazard *Littérature française*, 2 volumes, new edition, 1949. My many obligations of all kinds cannot be properly acknowledged. Besides the above there are two books I should like to mention, among a number of serviceable histories: *Histoire de la littérature française*, by Philippe Van Tieghem, 1949; and *Histoire de la littérature française du symbolisme à nos jours*, by Henri Clouard, 2 volumes: 'de 1885 à 1914' and 'de 1915 à 1940', 1947 and 1949.

L. C.

CONTENTS

PART I

Medieval Literature (ninth–fifteenth centuries)

PART II

The Renaissance (1491–1590)[1]

[1] These dates are purely symbolical: 1491 is the beginning of the personal government of Charles VIII; by 1590 the advent of Henri IV to the throne of France was very probable. The last decades of the fifteenth and of the sixteenth centuries were both harbingers of the coming periods.

PART III

Pre-Classicism (1590–1660)

PART IV

The Classical Age (1660–1715)

PART V

The Enlightenment (1715–60)

PART VI

Pre-Romanticism (1760–1820)

PART VII

Romantic Literature (1820–50)

PART VIII

Realism (1850–85)

PART IX

Symbolism (1885–1914)

PART X

Transition (1914–50)

PART I

MEDIEVAL LITERATURE

CHAPTER I

The Background

I. THE ELEMENTS OF FRENCH NATIONALITY

THE national personality that was to express itself through French literature awoke by degrees and stirred dimly before it grew to full consciousness. Its rise is a problem in itself which must be left to the specialists for discussion. Let it be said merely that an attempt to define the question in terms of race could nowhere else be more ill advised. The decisive element in the birth of the French people seems rather, when all is considered, to have been of a psychological nature; it lay in a sense of community that emerged among various groups and an instinctive will to live under one law. In the country that was to be France history shows us a mixture of different stocks. What proportion of the earliest recognizable one—the dark-haired, round-headed type that still crops up in large areas, especially of the centre, the south-east, and south-west—survived under the tidal wave of the Celtic invasions; what relation the Gauls themselves bore to these, to the Belgians, and the Germanic tribes along the Rhine, and whether the Gauls were to any extent permeated and modified, in more than their language and culture, by the Roman conquest, with its implanted colonies, its network of administrators and magistrates; what was exactly the outcome of the Frankish invasions, and how far in their turn, before a fusion was accomplished, the Franks superimposed more than a thin layer of military and political rulers; these, and sundry other issues—like the settling of

B

Burgundians in the east and north and Wisigoths in the south; of
Scandinavians not only in Normandy but over the northern half of
the country; of Greeks in the south-east, British immigrants in
Brittany, Saracens and Moors in the south, Basques in the south-
west—are not to be easily and lightly dismissed. The problems remain, even if the main body of contemporary opinion has come
round to agree that among all these strains the contribution of the
Gauls themselves remained by far the most substantial. But what
the Gauls were ethnically, and how related to this or that stock, is
still a moot point. A single assurance persists in the mind of the layman: the French as a race are the creation of historical ages; and by
the purity of the French blood nothing can be meant but a synthesis,
a composite temperament evolved through the centuries of a civilization that found and elaborated itself continuously.

Another physical factor, however, entered largely into the relative
unity of that civilization. Deeper even than racial determinations is
the influence that no race can long resist, and which is probably the
chief origin of race itself: the land. In it lay the genuine substratum
of French nationality. Of many conflicting elements it did most to
shape the French spirit, and through that French thought and literature. By its slow but unceasing action widely different trends were
brought to converge. Nature had laid the cradle of a nation in the
gently hollowed-out basin whose centre is Paris. She had not made
her wish quite obvious, had not given what was to be France the
all-round individuality of island Britain; but two high mountain
walls, the Alps and the Pyrenees, and three ocean seaboards did
plainly mark five sides of a hexagonal figure, of which only the
sixth, to the north-east, rested on a conventional and a disputed
basis.

Within this regular, almost geometrical frame the genius of the
earth and sky helped a mind to evolve that was also clear and logical.
With its situation, its main aspects, and its nicely balanced physical
configuration, the land is neither strongly northern nor overwhelm-
ingly southern; it keeps in a temperate, intermediate zone. A
sense of measure seems to emanate from the just distribution of the
high and low grounds, from the symmetrical courses of the four
big rivers through the plains spreading from the central uplands. The
French landscape has its regions of ruggedness; it can be excessive

and, as it were, arbitrary; but it is mainly characterized by its moderation, its humanity, the environment having been adapted to man as man was to the environment; by the smoothing away of irregular features, and the natural grouping of perspectives into wholes, sobered and unified beneath the patina of time. Above all it is privileged in the quality of its light. This is rarely blinding, rarely quite obscured by fogs, but for the most part spreads a gentle brilliance, and seems to sink of itself into the deeper strata of the mind, making clarity of thought a pleasure and a need. Clouds will often darken the day in the west and north, the strong sun of the south will burn at times with African fierceness; but the luminous sky of France normally has some of that purity and transparency which were to the Greeks a familiar experience and a suggestion of the joy of living.

The mind that grew in intimate and constant association with this setting developed a peculiar quality, of which some traces can be descried from the first; it evolved with a kind of dimly conscious persistence, and incorporated the adverse influences that the events of history brought to bear upon it. The human elements that had been longest in contact with the soil—the pre-Celtic and Celtic tribes—remained the core of French nationality; and the character given to them all, under the common name of Gauls, by ancient writers shows a distinct analogy to the temper of the modern French. With a continuity that persisted in spite of all accidents France emerged among the formations of early medieval Europe and her civilization began to shine with a lustre of its own. Through violent struggles, periods of expansion and retraction, she managed to survive, whilst the French monarchy, after the breakdown of Charlemagne's empire, was rising steadily above the great barons of the realm. Fresh provinces, again and again added to the monarchy's possessions, gradually followed the same lines of development; they may have momentarily altered the balance of the kingdom, but they never upset for good the tenor of the national personality. The law of its being was already too definite; and the French mind had entered, with a sureness which seems almost to reveal some groping knowledge and concurrence, upon the course of its destiny.

Still, however unified the genius of France may have been from the beginning of its conscious life, its very wealth of tendencies implied the presence of divers strains, and seeds of a positive duality were deeply implanted in it. Literary history seems to support these views. The temper of French poetry during the last 150 years, for instance, has undergone a change which cannot be entirely explained in terms of previous tradition. That romanticism should have struck such roots in the land which had identified itself with the classical ideal would tend to show that the roots of romanticism pre-existed, even if they had long seemed abortive. An irresistible inference is that what may be called the 'Latin' or 'Romance' elements in French culture did take the lead, and were pre-eminently active in moulding and shaping the personality of France; but that other elements, not completely fused with the former, remained present and obscurely effective in the progress of that personality, making themselves felt at intervals, and asserting themselves more strongly after the great intellectual change of the late eighteenth century. The thought, inspiration, and feeling which welled up in Rousseau and have more or less influenced the work of most great French writers ever since must be connected with virtualities of the French mind itself which had mostly lain dormant, although they can be traced or divined not a few times during the previous 800 years.

How should these other elements be identified and named? Bearing in mind the arbitrariness and fragility of all racial labels, one is driven to admit that the least misleading epithet that can be applied is a purely geographical one—let us say 'northern'. Just as the original genius of the English people and English literature grew from a mixture of races and a cultural graft that mingled Mediterranean influences with the predominant Teutonic stock, the no less original spirit of French literature derived from a similar fusion, in which the proportions of the components are reversed. It cannot be forgotten or ignored that however rapidly the Franks, Belgians, and Burgundians may have been assimilated by the Christian religion and the superior civilization of the romanized Gauls, they brought with them energies and instincts that made and kept them different through all the cross-breeding of the national life. This distinction between the south and the north of France, with all that it has implied and still implies socially, morally, and artistically, must never be lost sight of when the political or literary history of the people is interpreted. A stronger proportion of the various post-Celtic and northern invaders settled in the north and east, where they preserved rather more of their ethnical individuality. The fact, even after so many centuries, is still visible in the features of these provinces. Besides, when all is said, the 'Celtic genius' is itself rich, with a wide range of faculties and powers. From that decisive complexity all attempts to interpret the variegated course of the intellectual evolution of France must draw some of the main data on which their conclusions can be based.

The light of these remarks may perhaps be turned with some profit on the broader periods and changes in the development of French literature. But any effort to associate the characteristics of this or that individual writer with the several influences of this and that strain is bound to be adventurous and unsafe. The facts of collective psychology, in so far as they may be acknowledged at all, must intervene only, and then with the utmost caution, in the discussion of general movements. With this proviso it can be pointed out that the feudal system had its roots very largely in the habits and manners of the northern invaders; so that the *chansons de geste*, steeped as they are in the ideals and feelings of the feudal age, and however essentially French they may be in their spirit, were none the less originally related to the Germanic elements of the nationality in the making. This leaves the *Chanson de Roland* as it was and should remain, the focus of the moral and the literary personalities of early France.

Still, we must return to the point from which we started. If, wishing to study the literature of France, one tries to reach the accessible elements of her national originality, they are to be looked for in the world not of blood but of mind. The data in the former are merely conjectural; in the latter, though elusive they are concrete and open to direct observation. French writers from the first can be regarded as falling approximately into two main intellectual groups, seldom found in their exclusive wholeness but clearly defined and easily deduced from literary facts. The individuals themselves belong in varying degrees to both groups; a perfect singleness of allegiance to one, a perfect union and balance of the two, are not unexampled, though very rare. The spiritual history of France in far the longer part of her past shows the greater frequency and normality of a temper which is primarily intellectual, with the imagination and feeling under control; able to wield logical argument, and finding pleasure in its effectiveness; fond of the rational ordering of ideas and things. The writers of this type will aim preferably at clearness of expression, neatness of form, and coherence of structure; at a hierarchy of qualities in which emotion itself and the imagination will be checked and subjected to measure. It need hardly be said that this is the inner reality from which the instinctive addiction of French literature to the classical ideal grew and was long confirmed. That another temperament, however, from the first existed among the French, in which the main tendency was reversed, with a subjection of intelligence to imagination and feeling; that for long it asserted itself in occasional and erratic ways; that it was eventually liberated, when it revelled and rioted in its freedom and assumed superiority and command—all these facts coalesce into a psychological rendering of the outstanding events in the history of French literature. In the intermittent ascendancy of this complementary temper some of the substance of the periods from the origins to the later eighteenth century, and in its growing supremacy much more of all that followed can be interpreted, if not actually explained. Explanations, properly so called, are of course not conceivable in such a field; our generalizations do not lend themselves to deductive use. They serve rather to illumine the course of literary history and should be kept in the background; a potential aid to interpretation.

Yet emphasis should be laid here on the fact that the importance of the Celtic strand in the early growth of France is not so lightly dismissed today as it used to be; and that the Celtic spirit itself, though distinct and different from that of the other northern invaders, and despite the persistent obscurity of the whole problem, bears after all more affinity to the northern than to the southern element. This may add weight to the view of a modern critic,[1] who considers that the symbolist movement owed more, in its deeper inspiration, to Celtic than to English or German influences.

---

[1] John Charpentier, *Le Symbolisme*, 1927.

2. THE LANGUAGE

The first extant monuments of the language and the literature of France are to be viewed against the background of this organic growth and must be interpreted in terms of it, for they are themselves among its most significant tokens.

The development of the French language shows no such dramatic incident and disturbing influence as the Norman Conquest, with its linguistic consequences, did in the history of English. The popular Latin that the Romans implanted in Gaul did not mix with the native stock. It underwent a process of spontaneous evolution and change which obeyed only phonetic forces; and the number of Celtic or Germanic words that found their way into the vocabulary being relatively small, their presence did not tell on the very structure of what remained thoroughly a Romance language. The process of transformation was slow enough to evince some measure of regularity and to bear the imprint of those mental needs which from an early date had characterized the growing nation. The undoubted confusion of what may be called 'middle French' in the fourteenth and fifteenth centuries is hardly comparable with the chaotic features of the corresponding period in the evolution of English.

There was, however, from the first a duality in the spontaneous development of the French language which might have proved an awkward hindrance to its organic growth. In the southern provinces —a generous epithet here, which includes a large part of the centre, and reaches as far north as the River Loire—the Latin stock gave birth to dialects with a more marked rhythm; and this family, called *langue d'oc* or, from the name of one of its branches, *provençal*, though *limousin* would be historically more accurate, produced a literature that for more than a century appeared to be the main expression of French culture. But various historical influences, and an inner decay, for which an explanation must be found in collective psychology, caused a gradual blight to settle on the promises of the south and the focus of French civilization to shift decisively to the north. When, about the fifteenth century, the French of Paris spread finally over the southern provinces, the defeat of the *langue d'oc* had been for some time a foregone conclusion; political ascendancy, and the self-consciousness of the national mind, had concurred in making the northern limb the trunk of the tree. The first periods of French literature are to be studied, without unfairness, in the light of this decision of fate; and in a short survey only the brilliant but transitory poetical achievement of the troubadours can be mentioned.

The dialects of the north (*francien, bourguignon, lorrain, champenois, picard, wallon, normand,* &c.) were rather less musical; but from the first they evinced a distinct and vigorous tendency to make speech a convenient means for the communication of thought. A major impulse was pretty uniformly at work, serving an instinctive need for clearness and simplification. The syntax moved away from the synthetic genius of Latin towards a more and more analytic form. Just as French words dropped their endings, to the advantage of the originally accented syllable, even the reduced declension which had only two cases disappeared in the generalized use of prepositions. The various dialects gradually yielded precedence to that of the 'Île de France' or 'français' (*francien*) properly so called, which, centring round the Paris region, shared naturally in the advance of the unifying authority of the kings.

What the qualities of the instrument were the future was to show. But the progress of the language down to the seventeenth century, whatever it may have owed in the Renaissance period to writers, grammarians, and critics, was largely the work of the people itself, seeking a form of expression that satisfied its craving for directness. The diseases of affectation, mannerism, or exuberance which again and again interrupted this growth had their seeds in the misguided zeal of theorists and coteries; the masses possessed from the first an intuitive sense of the sobriety which was the final achievement of the classical age. The fight waged by Malherbe and his successors was won because it was backed by the silent preference of a whole nation. On the plain but logical texture that was being fabricated by the anonymous centuries the great artists could superimpose the beauty of individual style.

The starting-point of this long development, the first text in early French known to us, is the *Serment de Strasbourg* (842, but transmitted by a later manuscript). It still looks very close to Latin, perhaps unavoidably so, as it is a pure document, rather stiff, with little promise of the light ease that French was to pursue, and gradually achieve,

as its supreme value. No wonder that eight centuries were needed
to shape this extremely rough tool into a fine and polished means of
literary expression. . . . But it is no illusion to perceive some slight
advance as early as the end of the ninth century, in the *Cantilène de
Sainte Eulalie*; and a sense of beauty is clearly active in the *Chanson
de Saint Alexis* (probably from the latter part of the eleventh century), with the ascetic fervour that raises and animates its softly
sounding lines.

The common literary language of the French had to win its
ascendancy over the rival dialects; but another and a harder struggle
was taking place all through this transitional age: the newfangled
tongue was to assert itself, to establish its right and conquer its
heritage, against a formidable enemy in possession of the whole
vantage ground—the Latin of the Church. For several centuries,
while the unceasin progress of French can be observed and
measured, Latin was so secure in its many strongholds that it did not
seem to lose what its young competitor was gaining. Not only the
clerics but most of the lay writers, who had been trained on the
ancient language, gave it almost as a matter of course their most
earnest work and most serious thought. Besides theology, ethics,
philosophy, law, rhetoric, grammar, the chronicles of the past, and
the rudiments of the sciences, many literary subjects as well were
treated in Latin. Latin poems were written in verse that was not
built on the classical prosody but on the new syllabic rhythm, with
the addition of rhyme. This school of humanist expression, which
lived and throve through the Renaissance and lingered into the
seventeenth century, produced during the medieval period a very
large body of literature in which the incipient traits of the French
intellectual temper can be plainly traced, and which was often translated into the vernacular, sometimes by the authors themselves. If
this abundant treasure were taken into account the Middle Ages
would have an even better claim to be regarded as what they were,
a highly creative period in the history of letters.

3. EARLY FLOWERING

It is indeed a characteristic trait of French literature that it should
have begun to flower at a relatively early stage in the development

of the nationality that nourished it and the language in which it was expressed. Neither Italy nor Spain can show quite so forward a growth; in both countries the influence of the French *chansons de geste* contributed to foster the development of a native poetry. If the test of conscious artistic quality is granted its due importance, Europe had nothing by the beginning of the twelfth century, outside the field of such classical works as survived, that could compare with the *Chanson de Roland*. In England, the first two writings in which an artistic intent is brilliantly active, *The Owl and the Nightingale* and *Pearl*, belong one to the thirteenth, the other to the fourteenth century; but with the latter we reach the age of Chaucer, when in several domains a glorious compensation was reaped for the delay.

In what concerns England delay was, of course, due to the dramatic fate that disrupted her natural growth, and with the Norman Conquest implanted a usurping culture and tongue in her soil. France at that period had long outlived her own invasions, and evolved her original civilization out of equally mixed materials. All through the era of the Crusades she was an expanding force, the strongest among the fresh-born nations of medieval Europe, diffusing her genius and spirit over the neighbouring lands and peoples. The smoother course of her history during those centuries cannot by itself, however, account for her more rapid progress towards clear, orderly, and artistic self-expression. It cannot be simply, on the other hand, that she belongs rather to the Mediterranean area, and that the south in almost everything grows more quickly than the north, since Italy and Spain, although more southern, did not outrun her. This factor is probably of some importance, but the main cause must be sought elsewhere.

One falls back upon the deeply rooted individualism of the French mind; an attitude in which the clear consciousness of one's distinct being and of one's faculties is implied; with this self-consciousness, again, the activity of the mental powers is more or less bound up. These features have been from the first its proper attributes, and together form that unique complex, a national character, something almost as definite as that of the individual being. Precociousness, prompt impressions, vivacious reactions were part and parcel of the earliest temper of France, both physical and intellectual, and were to remain so through her long history. The trait links up with the eagerness of judgement, feeling, and action which has so often been noticed and is itself responsible for some of the best, and some of the worst, French qualities—the impatience and fiery lack of control, for instance, that drove the scornful knights of Philippe and Jean against the unbreakable wall of English archers at more than one momentous fight, and that still make the political life of their descendants unstable and eventful.

Such facts of elementary folk-psychology are well known. It is impossible not to trace their influence in the literary leadership which France so distinctly assumed among the slower cultures of western and central Europe from the eleventh to the fourteenth century. For the better part of 300 years she was in a position of brilliance and authority more undisputed in the field of civilization than anything she may have known later. The seeds were there; nature had sown them and they grew more rapidly than in human groups where the possibilities were no less rich but the corresponding development was more tardy. A biologist might suggest that with the *serajuventas* of the northern stocks—Scandinavian, Teutonic, or English—the promise of a deeper-rooted and more lasting creativeness was involved. But the implied criticism so far has not proved valid; groups may not be ruled by the same laws as individuals; and the French genius, after ten centuries, does not seem to be threatened with exhaustion.

Whatever the future may hold for that genius, an outstanding fact of its past is that the season of its flowering was early and luxuriant, an intellectual and artistic expansion in which all western Europe shared, indeed, but the example and encouragement of which had their focal point in France. Some allowance must be made, of course, for the favouring circumstance that the kings of the 'Capétien' dynasty, from Louis VI to Philippe le Bel, were efficient agents of the cause of national aggrandisement, which they served with a persistent will, and most of them, no doubt, with self-interested ambition. But it can still be maintained without illusion that French culture itself, in close touch with the process which moulded French political unity, was reaching a high degree of intensity and variety. The medieval system as a whole knew an organic integrity and a well-rounded definiteness of outline during the twelfth and thirteenth centuries; and although our social as well as our ethical sense today will be shocked by not a few of its crude or revolting features we must grant that in many respects it *was* a system, while thought and art did hallow it with the sanctions of genuine spirituality. Paris had the second-oldest university in Europe and attracted thousands of students and scholars from abroad; the Romanesque and later the Gothic style of religious architecture covered the soil of France with shrines whose beauty has not been surpassed; the *roman breton* soothed the imaginative craving for adventure and wonder; the 'Mystères' gave its first expression to the awakening dramatic instinct; the intoxication of refined intellectual love sustained the upsurge of lyrical poetry; the allegory flourished in vast and bold structures; while the philosophy of the schools and the eagerness of clerical or lay thinkers made the period what has often been called an earlier Renaissance. This fire did not burn selfishly within the as yet narrow bounds of one nationality; other flames were emulating and reflecting it beyond frontiers which were less fixed and solid at that time than they were to become; and all western Europe was involved in the glow and enthusiasm of a cosmopolitan age whose common Christian faith was the deepest principle of its moral harmony.

CHAPTER II

Epic Poetry

IN spite of inevitable corrections, Joseph Bédier's view of the main origin of the *chansons de geste* still holds the field. The collective element in the growth of the texts we possess lies in the influence of the monks whose sanctuaries, dotting the pilgrims' roads, naturally suggested the celebration of episodes redounding to the honour of the local saint or patron; while the poems themselves, with their organic unity, were conceived as wholes and put together by individual artists. This does not preclude the thesis that short popular poems on the deeds of famous heroes or on the lives and miracles of saints —we have many records of such—may, through their spirit, tone, and style have opened the way to more ambitious efforts. What seems to be ruled out is the half-mystical belief that somehow folk-songs of a distant past coalesced into full-grown epics.

The *chansons de geste* (or songs of the doings of yore) were written for oral delivery and recited, or rather intoned, at wakes, feasts, and fairs either by the *trouvères* who had composed them or more often by itinerant minstrels, the *jongleurs* (jugglery was part of their talents, and often of their programmes), who would accompany their voices on a *vielle* or simple string instrument. Though primitive indeed, the musical character of the performance was unmistakable. The poem was divided, according as each aspect of the theme had more or less amplitude, into stanzas of unequal length called *laisses*; the lines, generally of ten syllables, with a well-marked inner division (four and six), were bound together by the chain of 'assonance'—or identity of the last tonic vowel in the line. Rhymes properly so called appeared only in the later chansons. With their frequent repetitions, their naïve and open appeal to set effects, and their use of stereotyped turns of phrase, these songs answered much the same cravings of imagination and feeling as the English ballads on historical subjects. Their inspiration is strongly suffused with religious fervour, which does not connote unfailing respect for ecclesiastical characters. Their ideals were distinctly coloured by the aristocratic conception of chivalry, but barons and low-born alike would assemble to hear them.

These epic compositions can be ordered, as they were gradually by later poets, into three main groups or cycles: the *geste du Roi* (practically of Charlemagne), that of *Garin de Monglane* (where the central figure is Guillaume d'Orange), and that of *Doon de Mayence*, in which the unity is rather of a spiritual order. They are sufficiently alike in spirit and atmosphere for a very brief survey to consider them together.

Of these cycles the best known, the *Chanson de Roland*, enjoyed pre-eminence in all Europe through the Middle Ages but was forgotten during the classical centuries. In 1837 it was rediscovered and published from a manuscript which is one of the treasures of Oxford. The date of this Anglo-Norman text is about 1140–50; the best judges place the writing of the poem in the earliest years of the twelfth century.

The interval of time that separates it from the Old English epic, *Beowulf*—conjecturally assigned to the tenth century—is thus relatively short if one takes into account the radical differences that make a comparison quite irrelevant. We have here another world. Instead of the weird, fierce atmosphere of the Saxon poem, with its savage northern primitiveness, an infinitely more gentle light bathes a southern civilization, much farther advanced towards a degree of refinement and culture. No doubt there are many indications of manners that are still rough and cruel, and, by present-day standards, the tones of the *Song of Roland* are grand and grim. The prowess of physical force is the supreme test, the punishment of Ganelon the traitor is fearful. But in a picture of Charlemagne's age the poet, unconscious of any anachronism, gives us the setting of a completely developed feudal order. Values have arisen that are created by the soul of man. A human strain of tenderness, for instance, softens the edge of heroism; the King and his knights are moved to tears; a manly friendship unites Roland and Olivier; feminine love appears in the brief and touching episode of Aude, Roland's bride, who silently dies at the news of his death. Again, all Christian lives are ready for the sacrifice which the service of God demands; the cult of the fatherland is already a deep-laid feeling, and although the ideal figure of France has not yet assumed its fully developed features, she is to all her sons their 'sweet' mother.

Indeed, a decidedly national temper is stamped on the whole narrative, but along with this common basis of character an instinct of individual variety is at work. Roland is the typical ancestor of the proud knights who rode blindly to their death at Agincourt. His repeated refusal to blow his horn and ask for help is the direct cause of the common disaster. But he is in every way a pattern of scrupulous selflessness, showing a strong and gentle nobleness worthy of King Arthur's companions. Charles, the old emperor, is a pathetic figure in the solitariness of his fate. Olivier is convincing and attractive in his sober courage and chivalrous acceptance; and Turpin, the fighting archbishop, who does great execution on the heathen and deals out to his friends generous promises of Paradise, is a most picturesque creation. The poet's instinctive art is manifest in this fine sense of construction and skilful handling of a theme which unites dramatic force with truly epic grandeur. The technique is aware of classical precedents; Homer and Virgil are mentioned; enumeration plays a large part in the narrative; general episodes and single fights alternate. The language is clear and shows a natural gift for neat, effective expression. The verse is genuinely rhythmic, in spite of its monotony.

The reader's final impression is of a singularly modern monument of primitive greatness. The inner tragedy, in the unbreakable resolve of a few doomed men, is consistently emphasized. But the poetry of dramatic circumstance and of the natural setting is not ignored:

> Halt sunt li pui e li val tenebrus,
> Les roches bises, les destreiz merveillus.
> Le jur passerent Franceis a grant dulur.
> De .XV. liues en ot hom la rimur.
> Puis que il venent a la Tere Majur,
> Virent Guascuigne, la tere lur seignur;
> Dunc lur remembret des fius et des honurs,
> E des pulcele e des gentilz oixurs:
> Cel nen i ad ki de pitet ne plurt.
> Sur tuz les altres est Carles anguissus:
> As porz d'Espaigne ad lesset sun nevold.
> Pitet l'en prent, ne poet muer n'en plurt.[1]

---

[1] High are the mountains, and gloomy the vales; dark the rocks, sinister the gorges. This day the French crossed them in great sorrow. Fifteen miles away the rumour of

Moreover, although Roland's proud obstinacy is the main cause of disaster, our sense of impending fate is fed, at a deeper level, with less tangible hints. Both Charlemagne and Roland have premonitions of the treason that is hatching, but elect to follow their predetermined courses. This is not fatalism but an obscure abandonment to Providence and a refusal to let a high purpose be checked by weak, unworthy fears. Browning may have had this in his subconscious mind when he showed his Knight, 'quiet as despair', riding to meet what in his heart he knows to be the inevitable (*Childe Roland*).

The episodes of the fighting itself obey a kind of rhythm and are not free from convention and monotony. They do not linger so long in our memory as the intervals and pauses of the main action—such as that when Roland at the point of death mourns over his dead friends, and in a desperate effort carries their bodies successively to the dying archbishop, who absolves and blesses them with his last breath. Throughout the scene, human pathos and religious fervour are fused into a quality of sombre sublimity which the quiet wording does much to enhance.

Altogether the *Chanson de Roland* is worthy of its position as the first signal work of a great literature. It outlines with a noble simplicity the image of a national genius just entering upon its conscious career. While not equalling the sheer imaginative impressiveness of some other early epics, it stands fitly for a human world with which our minds can efficiently cope. The supernatural is close at hand; an angel and saints take Roland's soul to heaven; but the subject works itself out on a plane of mixed history and legend which an unsophisticated audience—and the author—thoroughly accept. An intuitive tendency to the classicism of the future is perceptible in the progression and balance of the poem, its incipient study of character, and its sustained force and dignity.

The pathos and grandeur of *Roland* are in no wise exceptional among the *chansons de geste*; but the poet's unrelieved singleness of note is unique. The dramatic elements elsewhere are generally toned

their march is heard. When they reach the country of their fathers, and see Gascony, the land of their lord, they bethink themselves of their estates and honours, of their maiden daughters and their noble wives: none is there but weeps from the pity of it. More than all the others is Charles full of anguish: at the passes from Spain he has left his nephew. Grief seizes upon him, he cannot help shedding tears.

down with all the shades of a wide interest in life which is often familiar and does not even exclude humour.

In *Aymeri de Narbonne* (beginning of the thirteenth century) the young hero, whose precocious, modest valour suggested to Victor Hugo a well-known piece of the *Légende des siècles*, has set his heart on a 'Princesse Lointaine', and as luck will have it the mere rumour of his exploits has been enough to awaken a corresponding passion in her. The meeting of the two lovers is told with charming naïveté, which may be slyness:

> A la pucelle a ses bras au cou mis,
> Car moult fut bien enseigné et appris.

Le Couronnement de Louis is another romantic tale, in which the heroes encounter blood-curdling perils. The fearful monster Corsolt slices off the tip of Guillaume's nose, thus adding to the fame of the latter's feats a further assurance of popularity:

> Sauf que mon nez est un peu raccourci,
> Sais que mon nom en sera allongé. . . .

Just because faith is a matter of course, the Church is treated unconventionally. The Pope, wishing Guillaume to defend Rome against the heathens, offers him full permission to eat flesh every day,

> Et femme prendre autant qu'il te plaira.

Such accidents, or flutters of a relaxed mood, are frequent enough. But it would be wrong to lay stress upon what remains a secondary aspect of the subject. The body of these poems is serious, as it is intensely religious. Most of the stories grouped under the label of *Doon de Mayence*, as, for example, *La Chevalerie Ogier*, *Renaud de Montauban*, *Girart de Roussillon*, tell of violence, resentment, revolt, and war finally conquered and harmonized by faith, repentance, and meekness. Within the *Monglane* cycle the *Chanson de Guillaume* (early twelfth century) is almost as old as *Roland*, and not unworthy of comparison with it through the austerity of its appeal to the emotions.

The shades of feeling, of course, are far from uniform. Pathos assumes a softer and more touching quality in the incident of young Vivien's death (*Aliscans*, middle of the twelfth century); or in the triumph of resurgent friendship at the end of Roland's and Olivier's deadly fight (*Girart de Viane*, early thirteenth century). On the contrary the fearful intensity, the violence of passions that still suggest an untamed civilization reappear often enough, as in the passage where Charlemagne, in his wrath, threatens young Ogier with a most cruel death (*La Chevalerie Ogier*, twelfth century).

The fact is that the *chansons de geste* gather much of the variety of human experience into their vast embrace. The inventiveness and ingenuity of the anonymous writers are boundless. Most of the main subjects branch off into numerous themes, a mode of growth made easier by the common device of uniting the heroes of different tales through links of blood. Such connexions have been established, sometimes as an afterthought, by the poets of the *Doon* cycle; in that of *Garin de Monglane* the stories hang together like one of the modern sagas in which the fate of one family is told by means of several novels.

Two *chansons* have pronounced peculiarities which are probably accidental. In the amusing trifle *Le Pelerinage de Charlemagne* (one of the oldest), a background of romance is diversified with such anticlimaxes of realistic fun that a suspicion of parody has sometimes been attached to the whole poem. In *Huon de Bordeaux* (end of the twelfth century) the part played by Oberon, and the prominent vein of the marvellous, reveal yet another tendency towards the fanciful and the supernatural which would link up with the characteristics of the *roman courtois*.

Through the late thirteenth and the fourteenth centuries the decay of the great creative impulse that had produced these epic cycles is revealed by the many rehashings, rehandlings, and continuations where the same or similar themes are treated, in verse or in prose, at endless length, in a pointless and perfunctory manner. The pleasure the authors cater for now is mostly the satisfaction of curiosity or of the taste for adventure. The single narrative that should always be excepted is *Baudouin de Sebourg*, a frankly popular, satirical, and realistic piece.

Together the *chansons de geste* constitute the rough body of a whole literature, limited possibly in the relative simplicity of its artistic devices, but rich with a substance upon which the further development of writing was to live for centuries, even when the original poems themselves had fallen into neglect.

CHAPTER III

The Roman Courtois[1]

THE *roman courtois* flourished almost as early as the *chansons de geste*, its verse form developing in the latter half of the twelfth century and its prose form in the thirteenth. Contacts have existed and analogies can be found between the epic and the romance, but they did not really appeal to the same public nor answer the same mental needs. Something universal about the epic could and did reach all classes. The success of the *roman* in its infancy was due to the influence of a more exclusive social set; women of birth and culture patronized it, and there clung to it a refined, aristocratic flavour.

As literature, it ministered frankly to the imagination and fancy; the claims of clarity might be ignored for the sake of the thrills awakened by marvellous episodes and the endless surprises of un-expected events. No longer declaimed on the sing-song of the juggler's set tone but carried forward more nimbly on the tripping rhymed couplet of eight syllables, the *romans* let themselves go, and reached inordinate length. They catered for tastes which the law-givers of classicism in France were consistently to prune, or to condemn, with ever-incomplete success. A distinct infusion of the values which our mind usually associates with the 'Celtic genius' creates an atmosphere that can be described without exaggeration as 'romantic'. It has already been pointed out that several of the thir-teenth-century epics, with their freer manner, shared somewhat in the same spirit.

Among the romances several groups are recognized, according to the nature of the subjects. Four cycles can broadly be distinguished. It is interesting, though only natural, that the earliest appeals to the intellectual sense of wonder should have gathered round the figures of classical antiquity, invested with a halo by the distance in time. To the medieval mind no memories were more moving, and no scruples of historical accuracy interfered with their attraction. The

---

[1] For the meaning of *courtois* in this connexion see below, Chapter IV.

romances of *Aeneas*, of *Troy* (by Benoit de Sainte Maure), of *Thebes*; and, as no limit was set to the shading off of ancient times into modern ages, the *Eracle* by Gautier d'Arras (end of the twelfth century) are cases in point; they were all signally successful.

The origins of the second cycle, that of the *romans bretons*, are wrapped in obscurity. Were the Celtic themes introduced to French writers from Brittany (where Celtic tribes had settled in the fifth century, when the Saxons conquered the British Isles), or from Britain, where the traditions and songs of Cornwall and Wales lay within easy reach of the Anglo-Norman poets? Whatever may have been the case, one central conclusion seems safely established: here again, what first stirred the imagination of the Middle Ages was its own inner needs, an aura of grandeur with which it glorified some privileged images. As was to happen six centuries later at the dawn of romanticism, the actuality of fact proved quite external and irrelevant to the fertility of artistic suggestion. It is well known that the mythical descent of the Briton princes from Trojan heroes was the focal point in an entanglement of innocent fiction, wishful thinking, and pious frauds. How Geoffrey of Monmouth's *Historia regum Britanniae* (1135) was translated into French by Wace, a Norman monk, and improved upon in his own *Brut*, has been often and properly emphasized. That the vitality of Breton romance expanded into those two groups, the Tristram cycle and that of the Round Table, is no less well known. But what has perhaps been insufficiently stressed is that the development of the beautiful Tristram saga, however germinal the Celtic inspiration may have been, appears to us historically in indissoluble association with and dependence upon the spirit of French literature. The story of love and death and of a nobly accepted dedication to pain is steeped in the sense of tragic fate that is the soul of all the 'Deirdres of the Sorrows'; but from the beginning it was indebted to the cherishing and fostering influence of French sensibility and art. Bédier's miraculously faithful rendering of the legend is based on the reconstruction of the archetype through the Anglo-Norman text of Thomas, and on the equally incomplete poem of a Norman *trouvère*, Béroul; several unidentified French authors, a great poet from Champagne, Chrétien de Troyes, and a French-born poetess, Marie de France, are variously connected with the spread of the theme, which radiated over western Europe through a number of translations. Very much in the same way innumerable romances were responsible for the hold which the figures of King Arthur and his knights took upon the medieval mind. Sir Thomas Malory's *Le Morte d'Arthur* gives itself out for what it is, mostly a medley of French originals; Tennyson's *Idylls of the King*, several other modern poems of note, English or American, and the world of morbid enchantment which Wagner's music has called to life, all derive from a great fascination, the spell of which was drawn from the dream and drama in the Celtic blood, but woven by French writers into a group of symbolical stories that is at the very core of man's spiritual heritage.

A third group would be made up of the *lais*, or very short romances in verse, most of which can be traced to Marie de France,[1] the gifted poetess who probably united two nationalities in her culture, French and English. The fourth may be classed under the convenient label of *roman d'aventures*, and will be dealt with last.

Of the authors of these romances not all the names are known, and little is known apart from these. It was only from a somewhat later period that the creative instinct in literature grew conscious of its claim to individual recognition; during the twelfth century writing is still often anonymous, like the handicraft of the stone-cutter of the cathedrals. Our knowledge of the outstanding personality of that literary period, Chrétien de Troyes,[2] is no less scanty.

His full importance has only been gradually recognized. He stands at the source of several movements, or fashions, that shaped the course of fiction directly during his age, and indirectly throughout the whole subsequent history of the novel. In his main works he takes the lead towards new motives of interest. He was not the first author to realize what pleasure his readers can derive from following an eventful story through the endless intricacies of a moving plot. All the tellers of tales, in verse or prose, since the world began had exploited it instinctively. Chrétien's narratives in verse, gliding swiftly along with his light eight-syllabled lines, are cleverly managed

---

[1] The name rests on her own claim that, living in England, she was *de France*, i.e., French-born.

[2] The active period of his life was from before 1160 to about 1185. He was protected by the comte de Champagne and his wife Marie, the daughter of Eleanor of Aquitaine. He lived for some time at the court of Philippe, comte de Flandre, and seems to have visited England.

to satisfy unsated appetites; as he went on his scenes of life-like realism made more and more room for marvellous episodes, adding to the excitement of adventure the glamour of fairy tales. The groundwork of his stories is not free from elements which the *chansons de geste* were making commonplace; but his matter is varied, and although the great fights from which heroes emerge duly victorious are still more than frequent, he shows some awareness of the risk of monotony.

His signal departures from the beaten track were, first, the introduction of the 'Breton' themes, with their wealth of circumstances, setting, and individualized figures. The *Tristan* which was, we know, his second romance, has been lost; the next, *Erec et Enide* (after 1160), brings in the Round Table, the island of Avalon, *la fée Morgue*, and the scene shifts from and back to Arthur's court, the King himself preserving a dignified but rather passive attitude. Again, Chrétien makes his tale point a moral and is thus in a way the originator of the novel with a purpose. *Lancelot, ou le chevalier de la Charrette* (after 1164) deals again with the romantic Breton subject, but in this text one more innovation is paramount—the author's complete allegiance to the principles, viewpoint, and maxims of the *amour courtois*. The wheel had now come full circle from the legend of Tristan and Yseut, in which the claims of true love had been magnified beyond the sacredness of conjugal ties. Lancelot grievously sins against his love, because he hesitates one moment before consenting to demean himself, at Guenevere's injunction, by climbing on to a rustic cart, no horse being available. The commands of one's lady-love now take precedence over honour itself. Chrétien's last efforts, *Yvain ou le Chevalier au Lion* (before 1174), and *Perceval ou le Conte del Graal* (before 1185) are the most interesting. The latter especially indulges the mystic tendency that was from the first potential·in the Arthurian cycle; the emblem of the Grail, whose fortune was to be so brilliant, is already present in an alluring though somewhat puzzling light; and while it is permissible to say that Chrétien makes only limited use of the opportunities of the theme, he stands none the less as the introducer to French thought, and through it to that of Europe, of one of the major keys to literary and artistic symbolism. This symbolism was stressed further in Robert de Boron's *Roman du Saint Graal* (late twelfth or early thirteenth century), and in the *Lancelot du Lac* series of prose romances (early thirteenth century).

As has been said above, a distinct branch of the *roman courtois* is the *roman d'aventures*—tales which, in spite of their free appeal to the imagination, take their stand on the actuality of existing manners, and give us in many respects a suggestive picture of the time. This vein of writing is richly represented in the texts that have come down to us. Most of them are anonymous; but several can be traced safely to one man, Jean Renart, the gifted author of *Guillaume de Dole* and the *Lai de l'ombre*. Even more delightful are two stories of the trials of young lovers, who win their way to bliss through settings of southern or oriental brilliance or quaintness (a distant harking-back to Greek romances suggests itself). One is a poem, *Floire et Blanche-flor*; the other, *Aucassin et Nicolette*, a *chantefable*, or prose romance mixed with snatches of verse.

Written, if we judge from the language, in the north of France, this tale, one of the purest gems of medieval literature, calls up the landscape of Provence and a fictitious east. A modern reader is startled by a complexity of manner that makes the naïve, youthful story chime in surprisingly with some of the subtlest instincts of our sophisticated minds; an idyllic atmosphere is happily created and sustained, but pierced by gentle traits of sly humour that dispel all risk of excessive sweetness. Shall we not think of Alphonse Daudet when we come upon this quiet ingenuous confession of overstatement: while Aucassin is riding through briar and bush in his quest for his beloved, 'li sans li oissi des braz et des costez et des jambes en cinquante lieus *o en trente*'[1] (italics ours)? An intuition of the value of contrast brings in touches of vivid realism (as the unforgettable portrait of the 'villain' met in the woods). So pleasant is the combination of sentiment and fancy, of loveliness, ardour, chastity, freshness, and wit, that *Aucassin et Nicolette* is not unworthy of a place among the forerunners of Shakespeare's pastoral comedies. The legendary tale knows how to transcend the bounds of locality and broaden out to a dim, dreamy prospect of nowhere:

> 'Aucassins, beaus amis douz,
> En quel terre en irons nos?'

---

[1] The blood spurted from his arms and sides and legs in fifty places, or in thirty.

'Douce amie, que sai jo?
Moi ne chaut ou nos alons,
En forest o en destor,
Mais que je soie avuec vos.'
Passent les vaus et les monz
Et les viles et les bors.
A la mer vindrent al jor,
Si descendent el sablon,
  Lez le rivage.[1]

---

[1] 'Aucassin, sweet friend mine, to what land shall we go?'—'Friend dear, what do I know? Little care I where we are going, through forest or devious ways, if only I be with you.' They cross the vales and the hills, the cities and the townships; the sea-side they reach the same day, so go down to the beach, along the shore.

CHAPTER IV

Lyric Poetry

I. SOUTHERN POETRY

IN this field the claims of the south to separate study cannot be ignored. During the twelfth and early thirteenth centuries there were many 'nests of singing birds' in the regions beyond the Loire. The precociousness which has been mentioned as a general trait of French literature appeared signally in the whole expanse of those sunny provinces. Nowhere else, in what was to be modern Europe, did an intuitive feeling for the musical value of words more early raise language to definite attempts at pleasurable artistry.

Distinguished as the poetry of the 'troubadours'[1] is in many respects, it fell short of its highest promise. No doubt the 'croisade des Albigeois' (beginning of the thirteenth century), led from the north, and which for the sake of religious unity swamped and almost destroyed the civilization of the south, practically put an end to a prosperity and pride that never entirely recovered. But the main cause of the decay was within. The troubadours, flourishing in the circles of the aristocracy, and being themselves often of noble birth, drew their inspiration mostly from artificial sources. Their theme was almost exclusively love, felt and expressed according to a strictly defined code that smacked equally of refinement and convention. In that *courtois* (the meaning of the adjective here keeps close to that of the noun, 'court', with all its associations of dignity, distinction, and culture) relation between the two lovers, the man—a knight if possible, anyhow with a chivalrous soul—must be a humble servant, extolling the perfections of his mistress with religious zeal, and hardly daring to breathe an intimation of his wishes. One can well realize that the effort to elevate and refine love, in circles where delicate women set the tone, and under the influence of an aristo-

[1] This is the objective case, in the *langue d'oc*, of the noun derived from the common verb *trouver* (or make, indite poetry), whose nominative case in the *langue d'oïl* is *trouvère*.

cratic reaction against the coarseness of vulgar manners, resulted in such well-meant straining after a forced, if not an impossible, ideal. Allowance must also be made for the innate tendency to inevitable excess which drives all 'precious' movements, under the stress of their own logic, and failing a principle of self-correction, to an almost absurd pitch. Noble as was the attempt, and fruitful in some of its effects, its literary and social outcomes were not exactly satisfactory. The rigorous pattern resulted in a sameness of subject, and a monotony of manner, against which clever devices of style and tricks of versification put up an elaborate and sometimes brilliant but altogether futile fight.

It would no doubt be unjust to condemn too sweepingly endeavours in which the spirit of poetical intuition and utterance was not seldom alive. Gracefulness, charm, point, and wit are very common; and every now and then the note of a stronger personality rings out, in accents of realism, in satirical verve, in simple directness and delicacy, even in an earnestness that seems the voice of genuine passion. But such poets as were sons of the people, and, having to make a living, went about from court to court reciting their own or others' songs, only too well assimilated the manners of the great.

Before the end of the thirteenth century the decay of the school was patent. Yet in spite of its deep-laid weaknesses the poetry of the troubadours was alive with a creative spark of enthusiasm, and it played a decisive part in stimulating national growths in other countries. It radiated over Spain and Italy; it contributed to awaken Dante's exalted sense of art; 'Petrarchism', in the fourteenth century, was a brilliant and original heir to its tradition; its influence was felt in the north of France; it can even be traced in England. The English, indeed, were directly in contact with it through those provinces of central and south-western France whose fate they so often seemed to have mastered in the confused struggles of the period. After a long eclipse the life of provençal poetry was revived in the nineteenth century, and Mistral is still hailed as the hero who awakened the Sleeping Beauty, now refreshed and gifted with all the depth of the modern soul.

Of medieval southern poetry, all is not condemned to oblivion. Some names are known today in a wider circle than that of the specialists: Guillaume IX d'Aquitaine, for instance, the earliest singer of note; or Jaufré Rudel, whom the theme of the *princesse lointaine* has made immortal; Marcabrun, who revolted from the tyrannical fashion of the *amour courtois* but sought originality in a contorted language; Arnaut Daniel, whom Dante admired, but who had none of the genius of Dante; Bernart de Ventadour, who among all his rivals best succeeded in uttering his emotions sincerely and feelingly; or Bertran de Born, a specialist in political subjects, whose verse is vigorous and bitter. But this preliminary and rather external chapter to the history of French poetry is interesting rather for the light shed on some characteristic trends that were to grow prominent again and again than as one of the greatest ages of French verse. It seems to show that while lyrical inspiration might be more facile in the intellectual and vivacious atmosphere of the south, its deeper creations demanded a concentration of feeling that would rather develop in the more tardy north. The *trobar clus* or esoteric diction, the *trobar ric* or decadent craving for ornament which shared the preferences of most troubadours answered, at that primitive time, to the cults of obscurity and of the precious that were to assert themselves more than once in the future. Artificiality was already the bane of a lyricism that ended, almost as soon as it was born, in such unmeaning triumphs as whole poems made up of stanzas written on a single set of rhymes.

2. THE POETRY OF THE NORTH

No precise date can be mentioned for the first stirrings of the lyrical impulse in the north; under one form or another they must be at least as old as the earliest *chansons de geste*. This spontaneous lyricism may be called popular, its roots being in the ordinary incidents and emotions experienced by all, and its language aiming at easy communication.

The gradual growth of a different fashion of song, influenced by the *courtois* ideal, with more refined and elaborate devices, threw these unsophisticated beginnings into the shade, and very little of the kind has come down to us. We have a few remnants from the twelfth century: *chansons de toile*, sung by women at their spinning-wheels. One example, not lacking in natural artistry, is the anonymous

Gaiete et Oriour. It is a charming, unpretentious masterpiece, with an exquisite sense of the fateful changes in life and a wistful resignation to the inevitable. Its lovely refrain runs:

> Vente l'ore et li raim crollent:
> Qui s'entraiment soef dorment.[1]

A people among whom such things could be born and grow naturally must be granted the innate gift of poetry. The same modest vein was long to remain productive, far from the channels of official literature. It has not yet disappeared; and since the romantic age, in which French consciousness was quickened to the piety of its origins, the *vieilles chansons françaises* have again and again been revived in forms that were later but in a direct line of descent from the medieval songs. They contain much of the essence of the national spirit, and are an ever fresh inspiration to writers and artists.

Meanwhile, in the north the prestige of the southern singers was inciting the poetical impulse to more ingenious and artificial forms of expression. Something was gained in consequence, but it is perhaps not an exaggeration to say that more was lost. Already, by the latter half of the twelfth century, the widespread effects were obvious. Under this stimulus various verse patterns assumed their definite individualities. The chanson, almost exclusively given to the theme of love, was prominent: as in the south, passion is here ardent but respectful, content to grovel in adoration, and appealing to the pity of the loved one for the slightest favour. Such poems were actually sung, and most of the writers composed their own tunes. The 'ballades' dealt with anecdotes or even historical subjects; but as the name suggests (from *baller*, to dance), their connexion with dancing would preclude unduly pathetic strains; so that we have here a clear difference from the wider range of the English 'ballad'. The *sirventes* or *serventois* treated political or satirical themes. The *pastourelles* showed a knight courting a shepherdess, usually to his discomfiture. In the *jeux-partis* two speakers would argue out a case, &c.

In all these types the sense of form, the desire for elegance, wit, metrical and verbal symmetry, were granted a very large share of the poet's creative effort. Such a line of development would lead naturally to an inordinate prominence of the externals of poetry;

---

[1] Let the wind blow, and the boughs sway; to lovers sleep is sweet.

and in a general way, this is the impression we gather from the lyrical output of the three centuries that preceded the Renaissance (thirteenth to fifteenth centuries inclusive). Still, the saving exceptions are everywhere to be found. Not only do these medieval songs afford proof of a remarkable and widely distributed talent for clear and pointed phrasing, of deftness and cleverness in the brilliant handling of verse forms, but every now and then an original personality will break out from the trammels of artifice, or play freely with them and reduce them to their proper value. That the living instinct from which eternal poetry must grow was not deficient in these ages, when rhetorical devices were a binding fashion and an intoxicating pleasure, is attested by the presence of absolute poets; and pre-Renaissance French lyricism gave tokens of the achievements to which, through and chiefly beyond the classical ascendancy, the future was to raise it.

Of the courtly, witty masters of laboured but graceful utterance much need not be said. From the twelfth century one may single out Conon de Béthune, a nobleman who paid his addresses to a great lady, Marie de Champagne, and wrote humorous stanzas which, but for their elaborate rhyme-scheme, might be the ancestors of the *petits vers* of the eighteenth century; and at least in partial contrast, Jean Bodel d'Arras, better known as a dramatist, who put a moving personal note into his occasional songs.

The thirteenth century shows us the same contrasted talents; the majority may be represented by such a highly aristocratic poet as Thibaut de Champagne, with the brilliant ease and elegance of his love ditties, not so impassioned but that an ironical hint will at times be cleverly introduced; and also by a son of the people, that Colin Muset who, plying his *jongleur's* trade in the gatherings of the great, knew so well how to please everybody, drawing his effects from the arch turn of his light self-mockery. Seeds of the future, indeed, are to be found there; one of the main traditions of French poetry will grow from them: all the deft-handed specialists of neat epigrams and charming epistles to ladies will thrive on the undisputed affinity of the French temperament to this kind of poetry. But we are far differently attracted by another lowly born writer, a true literary bohemian, Rutebœuf,[1] whose irony was scathing, and who drew

[1] Second half of the thirteenth century. He tried his hand variously at allegories,

his lyrical impulse from the too real trials of his life. The weaknesses of his style are redeemed by the flavour of his realism and the vigour of his phrasing. His self-pity tries to hide beneath laughter, but the poignancy of distress breathes through this very attempt and stirs our sympathetic response.

The fourteenth century confirmed and hardened the victory of the fixed forms. Guillaume de Machaut[1] did not create, as legend has it, the ballade, the virelai, the chant royal, and the rondeau, but practised them with signal success, and contributed to establish their fortune. Whatever talent and wit must be granted to him, a damaging impression creeps upon his reader that he did not see and feel beyond the scope of his talent. He says a good deal quite agreeably and tellingly, but there is not a spark of poetic suggestiveness in his style. No less famous, and even more of a leader, was Eustache Deschamps,[2] in whose plentiful output there is infallible technical merit and not much else. His best approach to a personal note is a sceptical and ironical sense of relativity which at times—too rarely—deserves the name of humour. It is one of the paradoxes of literary history that Deschamps should have chosen to praise Chaucer, whom he knew and survived, solely for his talent as a translator. But of course the *Canterbury Tales* were beyond his ken.

The fifteenth century from its beginning affords some relief to our craving for the utterance that appeals to feeling if not to the imagination. Two minor but sincere writers meet us first: Christine de Pisan was a dignified poetess who wrote without self-consciousness, at times giving vent to her widowed sadness in otherwise conventional verse. She felt the greatness of Joan of Arc, and had the courage to protest against the traditional carping at women. Alain Chartier was great as a prose-writer in his eloquent indictment of the age, and more than interesting in his poetical work. The consequences of the dreadful tragedy of Agincourt, naturally viewed by Shakespeare through English eyes, are seen in a far other light in

fabliaux, elegies, one drama; wrote against the friars and for the crusades; satirized all the vices of his time. His best pieces are frankly personal laments (*Complainte, Grièche d'hiver*, &c.).

[1] 1300–77; a poet and musician, an innovator in both arts. He wrote *Le Remède de fortune, Le Vrai dit*, &c. A canon of Reims, he was patronized by the kings and their courts.

[2] ?1340–?1410. He wrote an *Art of Poetry* in prose (1392), a long skit against women, *Miroir de mariage*, and a prodigious number of ballades and rondeaux.

Chartier's *Livre des quatre dames*; while the *Belle Dame sans merci*, utterly different in inspiration from Keats's ballad, has genuine emotion and can be forgiven what was to become an imprudent title.

Charles d'Orléans[1] and François Villon stand at exceptional and opposite poles of social origin. The greater miracle is that the prince born in luxury near the throne should have avoided the bane of courtly conventionality. His poems are laboured, but the sincere thought or emotion that has prompted them can bear continual polishing; the result is most often a short, graceful piece—chanson, ballade, rondeau, complainte—in which the charm of the form and of the word-melody does not exceed the delicacy of the feeling. The wistfulness of his theme most often answers the mood of a life which was long under a cloud of misfortune. Later years made some amends, and the inspiration of his verse grew gently smiling, with the indulgent scepticism of kindly old age. It would not be proper to hail in him an augury of the lyrical poetry of the future; he is rather the consummate product of an art that still allowed itself to be ruled by imperious traditions and forms. But there is premonition in such lines as these, whose gift of musical suggestion transcends their actual meaning:

> J'ay fait l'obsèque de ma Dame
> Dedens le moustier amoureux,
> Et le service pour son âme
> A chanté Penser Doloreux. . . .

Villon's[2] life from the first was one of poverty. This, more than his truant years as a student, was the schooling that ripened his mind and heart, and he gathered the bitter fruits of his experiences to the full. For his gift of expression nature and genius were responsible. His poetry truly looks forward to the future: it is spontaneous and fresh, and it coins its own forms, or puts the traditional ones to such uses that their spirit is made new. The volume of his output is small

---

[1] 1394–1465. He was captured at Agincourt (1415), and a prisoner in England till 1441.

[2] François de Montcorbier, born about 1430, perhaps an illegitimate son, was brought up by a cleric who gave him his name. He studied at the University of Paris, got into trouble, killed a priest in a scuffle, was a party to a burglary and theft, served a time in prison, and on at least two occasions narrowly escaped hanging. For a short time he was protected by Charles d'Orléans in his court at Blois. Banished by the Parliament of Paris, he vanished into the unknown in 1463.

but almost all of high quality. His favourite measure is the *huitain*, a brief eight short-line stanza, pregnant and dense, shaped for satire, cynicism, or confession; the ballades and rondeaux that interrupt this pattern in the *Grand Testament* are turned into original expressions of a mood either regretful or more often repentant and melting. The guilt of his life weighs less with us than the admirable humanity and tenderness of his *Ballade de Notre Dame*, a masterpiece which voices the simple faith of his unlettered mother, and which has a delicately sensed appropriateness in its more ample line. The thrill of horror, the recoil at the idea of hell, the deep longing for paradise, elementary but essential emotions of the believing soul, with the vivid realization of death which is the special trait of the fifteenth century, are here caught and sublimated into the most candid and plain effusion; and its absolute sincerity sets it among the great poems of the world, comparable in its universality and inevitability with Hamlet's monologue.

The fearful realism of the *Ballade des Pendus* is not an end in itself, and a glow of faith and hope softens the grim sight of the bones swinging on the gallows. But another ballade, that of the *Dames du Temps Jadis*, gives us the full measure of Villon's astonishing prescience of the modern poetic mind. What we admire here is not only the art which has condensed and stripped the phrasing, giving it point and rhythm, but the intuition of even more subtle values, far beyond the mere object of normal communication: the choice of the haunting refrain, with the lingering sounds that build the main portion of the rhyme scheme and so efficiently call up the sadness of vanishing memories:

> . . . Echo, parlant quand bruyt on maine
> Dessus rivière ou sus estan,
> Qui beaulté ot trop plus qu'humaine:
> Mais où sont les neiges d'antan?

In a century of unshaken religious belief, and when a young civilization could feel afresh, with intact vitality, the crucial experiences of guilt and sorrow, Villon gives us the supreme expression of medieval literature, because he strikes the two major notes of his age. None the less, his genius opens the way to the more complex music of words that will soon begin to play consciously on the twin chords of enunciation and suggestion.

CHAPTER V

Satirical and Allegorical Poetry

I. THE *ROMAN DE RENART* AND THE *ROMAN DE LA ROSE*

No part of medieval French literature is richer than that in which satirical, didactic, and allegorical works can be grouped together. The association will not be deemed arbitrary if due note is taken of the fact that very often all three characteristics appear in the same writings. It is tempting to trace the fortune of these literary forms, as foreign observers have done, to some well-known features of the French mind itself. This has a capacity for clear thinking which enables it to exploit values so effectively that it has little difficulty in providing justification for feelings of disapprobation, from the most personal to the disinterested objections of ethical or artistic judgement. Moreover, a neat and lucid formulation of qualities lends definiteness and point to criticism, while the vivacity of an impatient temper will soon sharpen censure into satire. The *esprit gaulois* and French wit may come in here for their share of responsibility; there is no more alluring field for both than ridicule. As for the popularity of the allegory, it can be linked up with other psychological traits, closely akin to the former: a rationalism of thought, a predominance of the intellectual over the emotional type of imagination. The transference of objects, with their recognizable identity, on to an allegorical plane requires the unerring perception of relations that are not concrete but logical and almost abstract; to follow up the argument on both planes, and discover the attributes of the initial term in the symbolical image, is a joy which early French writers seem indeed to have relished. Such remarks are not unfounded, but should at once be qualified: the trend is more or less to be observed during the medieval period in all Western literatures. Moralizing is then rife, and satire is the necessary preface to the drawing of moral lessons. The main duty of sermons is the castigation of sinners. In the same way, the prevalence of allegory must be connected with a European background, the search for allegorical transpositions being

D

a natural resource in an age when all truth was held to be known, and invention revolved in a narrow circle. Lastly, the *Roman de la Rose*, and chiefly the *Roman de Renart*, are to a large extent spontaneous outpourings of imagination.

Indeed, these aspects of early French literature are primarily reflected in the *Roman de Renart* and the *Roman de la Rose*. Both famous and of wide significance, they are rather cycles of verse than individual poems. The former is the work of a number of authors, some of whom only (Pierre de Saint-Cloud, Jacquemart Gelée, &c.) are known to us by name; the latter was written by two men, who gave a widely different though equally characteristic treatment to a single subject.

The stamp of a collective inspiration is particularly obvious upon the *Renart*. The fecundity of the theme, the number of its separate shoots or 'branches', the many traces of its popularity in the art of the time, the several translations into foreign languages that have come down to us, all tend to show that the central idea answered to a widespread instinct and need of the common man, transcending the limits of provinces and even of nations. The instinct is the love of fun; the need is the sly assertion of independence against the powers that be. These motives, though they overlap, are not exactly contemporary. Two main stages are to be distinguished in the development of the cycle. At first, in the twelfth century, when the vitality of the theme is freshest and its expression most happy, the poems are above all amusing, ironical only with regard to the human characters veiled by transparent animal disguises, masks which have enough substance, are near enough to nature to preserve the necessary measure of interest and probability. This quality, so necessary to all fables, tends to be on the decrease at a later date. In the thirteenth- and early-fourteenth-century branches, such as *Le Couronnement de Renart* and *Renart le Nouvel*, the satire becomes prominent, indeed bitter, and the allegorical value of each incident is more strongly emphasized; the good-natured, fanciful tales of beasts comically like men turn into a fierce indictment of human society.

The hero, Renart, was that eternal favourite of the simple folk, the mischief-making rebel with a thousand tricks, annoying but not radically evil; he would twist the tail of King Lion, get into tight corners, and manage to extricate himself by the skin of his teeth. So popular was he that the French name of the fox, *goupil*, was on his account gradually changed to *renard*. But he becomes the arch traitor, cunning and cruel, in league with all law-breakers, and his insolent triumphs reveal the rottenness of the social frame. This all-too-serious purpose is somewhat toned down by the constant presence, and the pretence, of the 'animal myth'—a symbolical device as old in literary history as the first fables. So ready were medieval readers to enter into the fiction and comply with all its demands that even an awkward number of undeniably human features is not supposed to destroy the actual outline, habits, and reputed character of each animal; Renart the Fox, Ysengrin the Wolf, Tibert the Cat don knight's armour and ride on horseback. . . . The secret purpose of the narrative—to lower the prestige of the feudal order—gets the better of all artistic coherence.

This is an extreme instance. Most of the time the beasts are sufficiently beast-like to remain picturesque, and they appeal to our sense of fun. King Lion's court has of necessity to be the merest sketch; but the setting of most of the stories is distinctly rustic, and their flavour racy of the soil. The world of Chanticleer and his wives is primarily a farm-yard; Renart's castle of Maupertuis is a downright burrow, and you will be stuck in the entrance if you try to rush in; there are labourers at work in the fields, and a fishmonger's cart rumbles along the road. In the first batch of tales the pessimistic picture of Renart's victories is generally spared us, and the craving for compensatory justice that lives in the hearts of the crowd is soothed by the comforting sight of the cheat cheated in his turn. Still, the uninterrupted mockery, lively as it may be, palls on the taste. The atmosphere of many incidents is hard and pitiless, and though the witty narrative is a relief to repressed feelings of wrong, and to a dissatisfaction among whose objects priests and monks have a large share, it is too uniformly dry for a modern reader's full pleasure.

The best parts of the tale move with ease, and the rhymed verse of eight syllables is a fit instrument for light talk, quick descriptions, and humorous hints. There is graphic power in many a passing image, as that of Chanticleer going to sleep with 'one eye open and the other closed, one leg bent and held up, and the other straight'; and genuine art, for example, in the conclusion of this well-known episode:

'Dex,' dist Renart, 'con ore esclaire,
Con ore espurge vostre vois!
Se vos vos gardiez de nois,
Au miels du secle chantirois.
Cantés encor la tierce fois!'
Cil crie a hautime aleine.
Onc ne sot mot, que qu'il se peine.
Qui li pies destres li desserre
Et li fromages ciet à terre
Tot droit devant les piez Renart.[1]

Between the two authors of the *Roman de la Rose*, Guillaume de Lorris and Jehan de Meung, there elapsed a whole generation at least; the former belongs to the first half, the latter to the end of the thirteenth century. But the difference in their mental outlooks is still more pronounced than the interval would imply.

Guillaume de Lorris[2] is a graceful and thoroughly medieval poet. The 4,000 lines he had time to write are strewn very thickly with the allegories which seem to have answered his natural and spontaneous mode of thinking. His design is to represent in a set of figurative episodes the stages through which the course of true love is to pass before the lover can pluck the Rose or win the heart of his lady. So with bold decision Lorris takes his stand at the very core of the poetic imagination of his time. Songs by the thousand are merely commentaries upon this central theme; this is the subject of subjects; in fact, lyrical poetry then had hardly any other. The method, being fresh and sincere, is more acceptable than our sophisticated taste might expect. This is not the dead, wooden, merely verbal allegory of the eighteenth çentury. The symbolism of the poet's imaginings is vividly enough realized by himself and, if we are properly attuned to the manner, by us as well, to avoid much of the cold monotony that one might have dreaded as inevitable. For instance, the figures set up outside the walls of the garden of Déduit (Pleasure) as frightful emblems of the various aspects of a loveless life are genuinely striking

[1] 'Bless my soul!' said Renart, 'how clear, how pure your voice is now! If only you'll abstain from walnuts, your singing will be the best in the world. Do sing once more, a third time!' The other raises his voice, with his deepest breath; sing he must, whatever he may do. His right foot loosens its clutch, and down falls the cheese to the ground, right before Renart's feet.

[2] Very little is known of his life. He was in holy orders, wrote his poem when hardly more than twenty-five, and died young, about 1230, leaving his work unfinished.

in the power of their delineation. There is a springlike fragrance in the picture of the 'carol' (or dance) on the garden lawn, presided over by the god of Love in person, and where the beflowered characters may stand for abstract values but are concrete enough to call up the fancy of some painting by an early Italian master. The fortunes and misfortunes of the Lover in his quest, helped by friendly Symbols, thwarted by malevolent ones, do not reach the desired conclusion; a feudal castle arises by magic, enclosing the beloved, and Danger (a terrifying monster) stands sentry at one of the gates. But we know that if the story had not been cut short all would have ended well.

Besides the persistent and, we must confess when all is said, rather intellectual development of his main purpose, Lorris has a charming lyrical gift, which he indulges now and then. The tale of Narcissus and his reflection in the fountain is a particularly successful example of this. The softly elegiac subject suits the talent of the poet. His imagery is pleasant, his verse flowing, liquid, musical, with a well-marked rhythm. It is only when actual passion should intervene that he is disappointing. The lover's feeling is rationalized and languid and could perhaps hardly avoid being so: to love an allegory is at best a severe handicap.

Jehan de Meung[1] took up the tale again, and added 18,000 lines. He had much to say, and his continuation was a pretext. He preserves the shell of his predecessor's theme, duly labours the plot, and brings it at long last to its logical consummation. Siege is laid to the fortress in which 'Bel-Accueil', the son of Courtoisie, and the Rose are imprisoned together; and after several ups and downs Venus herself spurs the army of love to the final assault. But love here is no longer the intoxicating fever of an eager intellect; it is a law of nature, to be obeyed with no romantic delusion. So a whole philosophy of cool reason is poured into the perfunctory progress of the platonic story. Again and again debates, arguments, long speeches interrupt the narrative. The artistic unity of the work, under the circumstances, falls to pieces. Still, when the worst has been said, Jehan de Meung is not only an interesting thinker, with a vigorous, bold,

[1] Jean Clopinel, de Meung-sur-Loire, near Orleans (1240?–1305), besides the second part of the *Roman de la Rose* (about 1270), translated several Latin works, and wrote a satire, *Le Testament*.

creative personality; he is as well no despicable writer. His thought is animated by a bitter sense of the evils and injustices that stain both the Church and the world. The begging friars—represented by Faux-Semblant, the hypocrite—are a plague; like locusts, they devour everything. Civil society should be reformed with no superstitious fear; governments are man-made, grown out of a kind of 'social contract'. It is wise to marry; but marriage is a ticklish state, subject to many accidents; women, at best, are a necessary evil; a singular anticlimax this, after Lorris's religious devotion to a courtly ideal! In these denunciations and admissions the poet displays a breadth of moral and philosophical doctrine that was not to be equalled in France till the sixteenth century. In his powerful invectives against the parasites of religion he reminds us of Langland, though he has less of the latter's burning fierceness and none of his sombre mysticism. In his thorough reliance upon Nature he anticipates the teaching of Rabelais. His plea against social wrong, his belief in the spiritual equality of men, and his refusal to find nobility in anything but a noble heart mark him out as a pioneer of the modern democratic spirit.

And as he proceeds his expression, somewhat uninspired and prosaic, and his slow movement manage to grow impressive through the sheer impact of dense statements; and this energy of phrasing reaches at times a quality very near great art. He is fond of verse paragraphs running into scores of lines but carried forward by a genuine impulse and not unduly dragging. His rhymes are remarkably sound, and their ease affects us with some of the pleasure of elegance. This robust and sincere writer, compact of rationality and sense, is a major figure in the early development of French thought; through the neatness of his firm, coherent style and the sober force of his line he strikes us as one more token of the instinctive trend towards a classical ideal in literature.

2. THE FABLIAUX

Some 150 of these short narrative poems, dating generally from the thirteenth century, have been preserved. The theory that Oriental and especially Indian stories, carried westward by Arabs and Jews, are at the source of most of them has proved untenable.

More stress is laid nowadays on the cropping-up of similar themes, under roughly equivalent cultural conditions, in many countries.

The 'fableaux' or 'fabliaux' (this Picard form has prevailed) are not exactly of popular inspiration; they appealed to a wide circle, and do not bear the marks of a particular class. In a very general way they may be labelled satirical literature; but their satirical intention is neither precise nor earnest. Their object is simply to raise a laugh, and they succeed by means that are usually fairly broad and may not stop short of coarseness. A good average example among the unexceptionable ones is *Estula*, a tale of rustic farce, based on the rather unlikely circumstance of a dog bearing these three syllables as its name. The mental background in most is that of the *esprit gaulois* —a jollity that turns to ready use the fun of things, and finds more opportunities in the weaknesses of the flesh than in those of the spirit. This vein has never disappeared completely from French life, and mostly runs a modest course on the border of literature properly so called; but its emergences may carry it to a far higher level of art and thought, as in Rabelais and in La Fontaine's *Contes*.

Other aspects of the subject are more varied. The comedy of the fabliaux may deserve the name of humour, as in *Du Vilain qui con-quist paradis par plait*; some of the tales can honestly claim an edifying purpose; in *La Housse Partie*, the conversion of the sinner is brought about naturally and tellingly. With a very different aim, *Le Lai d'Aristote* shrewdly points the moral of the vanity of glib principles. *Le Vilain Mire* deserves the honour which Molière conferred upon the story by taking hints from it. The oldest tale, *Richeut*, redeems a rather crude cynicism with much actual wit.

Written in the eight-syllabled line, which is the common narrative measure, the fabliaux shed a realistic and interesting light upon the manners of the time. Some of the authors are known; Rutebeuf, for instance, wrote several; but the best ones are anonymous. A marked feature of their writers' average intellectual horizon is irreverence—surely a French trait. It shows itself particularly in the abuse of the clergy, and of women, two chapters of existing institutions about which the common man may have felt that his natural and due respect was stiffened to a forced habit by some convention and social pressure—whence the reaction of Gallic independence.

3. DIDACTIC WRITINGS

Realism, a gift of concrete observation, intellectual ingenuity, the shrewd perception of fun are often combined together, and with them a talent of persuasive or forcible exposition. For reasons already touched upon the proportion of didactic works in medieval literature is especially high. Leaving out the merely technical treatises and poems—the poems more numerous than the treatises, as prose develops later than verse and the gnomic value of poetry was then an irresistible attraction—a short list may not be amiss here of writings that possess a measure of literary interest.

That the somewhat hard tone of the *Renart* and the fabliaux did not meet all the needs of the French imagination we are usefully reminded by parallel tales of a very different atmosphere. These are religious or ethical, and fraught with a sincerity of purpose and depth of feeling that lend them a genuine emotional appeal. Such are the many stories in which the Virgin appears as Our Lady of Charity, transcending with her divine pity the laws of earthly retribution. Among them the most justly famous is the *Tombeur de Notre-Dame*, with the true spirit of a parable from the New Testament (in Gautier de Coincy's *Miracles de la Sainte Vierge*, 1220). The inspiration is more allegorical and moralizing in *Le Chevalier au Barisel*, a tale of cruelty and repentance from the Orient, but it has charm and a loosening power on frozen hearts.

Of the many attempts at descriptive study of the natural world—signs of an awakening curiosity from which science will be born, but which is still trammelled in naïvety and an unslaked thirst for prodigies—nothing more need be said here than that the 'bestiaires' and the 'lapidaires' did after all stimulate the imaginations of whole ages.

Among the edifying allegories of man's dual nature, of life as a pilgrimage, and the daily choice between good and evil, one must be mentioned—Guillaume de Diguleville's *Pélerinage de vie humaine* (about 1320). It was a European influence, and has been regarded as a possible source of Bunyan's *Pilgrim's Progress*.

Hélinand's *Vers sur la mort* (last years of the twelfth century) are full of the grim realization of death, with all that pertains to it, upon which the medieval mind dwelt with a kind of fascination, but the theme is raised to a rare vigour of significance by its eloquent and pathetic treatment.

CHAPTER VI

Historians and Chroniclers

THE early historical writings in French literature are closely connected with the progress of the French language itself, and as this evolved prose became the natural instrument of their expression, though verse was not at once abandoned. The first chronicles known to have existed, or that have reached us, were written in Latin; and not a few of those in French are versified stories. A signal example of the latter is the Anglo-Norman poem, *Histoire de Guillaume le Maréchal* (1226), which tells in 19,000 lines the life of William Marshal, first earl of Pembroke.

But the interval was long before the need for truth, and for scrupulous care in recording it, were recognized as paramount among such incentives to the writing of history as a sense of wonder, love of thrilling adventure, and an affectionate clinging of memory to the great figures of a recent past. The Crusades, from the twelfth century, powerfully stimulated the desire to relate experiences that had an exceptional appeal for the imagination. In the crowded list of early chroniclers there are two prominent names, Villehardouin and Joinville, men who actually fought in the Near East. Distinctly later are Froissart, a witness of another momentous struggle, part of the Hundred Years War; and Commines, who watched with sympathy one of the chief builders of modern France, Louis XI, in his dogged though tortuous policy which had decisive results. Together they are responsible for the most remarkable body of French prose before the Renaissance.

One feels warmly towards the transparent honesty of Geoffroi de Villehardouin.[1] His spare relation of stirring events has none the less an epic breadth, while a subdued sense of tragedy and a genuine spirit of Christian chivalry raise the quiet narrative to momentary

---

[1] Born about 1160 of a noble family. He was marshal, or military chief, under the Constable of his native province, Champagne. He played a prominent part in the fourth Crusade shortly after 1200, wrote his *Conquête de Constantinople* in the principality which was cut out for him on Greek soil, and died about 1213.

heights of pathos. His manner no doubt has some of the freedom then inseparable from even the most honest adherence to fact: the historian gives what purports to be the actual words of speakers, not only their general meaning. Again, the descriptions of the broader episodes are loosely constructed, with an effect that is straggling and desultory. But this is the disorder of things seen; practically all the narrator tells us is from memory, and the authority of personal experience clings to every page. Often enough the plain remembrance is instinct with a quiet imaginative thrill when grand sights are called up: the crusaders' fleet sailing in the glory of its thousand banners, all the shields of the knights hung out with their bright crests; or the walls of Constantinople rising into full view, with the city's countless towers and domes, striking wonder and awe into the bravest souls. To us, the impression of archaism in the vocabulary is pronounced and the prose somewhat clumsy; but its graphic power, kept within strict limits, holds the reader fast. And the medieval French, in its manly simplicity, assumes a grace through its very naïvety, not, indeed, childlike, but so fresh and unsophisticated that we breathe in it a gentle essence of candour.

We sympathize with Villehardouin, but Joinville[1] wins our affection. A sweet nature, though not deficient in heroic fibre, he has the charming quality of single-mindedness, being wrapped up in an unselfish emotion, that of hero-worship. As the hero is for once worthy of such a cult, a soul of the truest nobility, the actual or virtual presence of the King diffuses a spiritual atmosphere through the whole book. The full-blooded virility that was fused in Louis with Christian humility is reflected in the natural and frank attitude of the chronicler himself; we have here none of the convention that spoils not a few Lives of the Saints. The good knight does not lack normal humanity when, passing his castle as he leaves for the Crusade, he must look away from the 'beau chatel que je laissais, et mes

---

[1] Jean, sire de Joinville, 1224–1317. He was, like Villehardouin, of noble birth and a native of Champagne, at one time holding the high office of Sénechal under the Comte de Champagne. He took the cross at twenty, and accompanied King Louis IX to Egypt and Syria, sharing with him the hardships of the ill-fated seventh Crusade. He did not take part in the disastrous expedition to Tunis in the course of which Louis died (1270), but thereafter he devoted his life to keeping the saintly king's memory green, and gave evidence at his canonization (1297). He was past eighty when he wrote his *Livre des saintes paroles et des bonnes actions de notre Saint Roi Louis* (1309), in which he incorporated an earlier book of his own Memoirs.

deux enfants'. He is a gifted story-teller, but not a faultless one. Like Villehardouin, he fails to grasp a wide subject and gives a disconnected account, for example, of the battle of Mansurah. But his diction is far clearer, less stiff, than that of his predecessor; and his prose style, slightly invertebrate and rambling, delights by its quaintness and unfailing simplicity. His piety, quite as genuine as the King's, fails to reach the same pitch of self-sacrifice; he naïvely remarks that we should be mad to serve God unless we believed that He could prolong our lives. Courage and high sense of duty are seen in his quiet relation of incidents when his life was in danger, and not less in that of the momentous council where, facing the other barons' wrath, he advised the King to stay in Egypt. Though evocative touches are rare, he can give us realistic glimpses such as the description of the corpses of the French knights carried down by the river whose water the survivors are fain to drink. The seed of the self-criticism and healthy reserve in statement that are the hall-mark of a born historian is alive in his all but last words: what he has seen and heard, let his book vouch for; but 'les autres choses qui y sont écrites ne vous témoigne que soient vraies, pour ce que je ne les ai vues ne ouïes'.

Tone and atmosphere are very different with Jean Froissart.[1] Two centuries separate him from Villehardouin; the age of the Crusades is past, that of the Hundred Years War has come; the feud is no longer between Christians and heathens but between neighbouring Western kingdoms. Although a Churchman, Froissart belongs entirely to this world, and moves through it with insatiable curiosity. While he testifies to the secularization of politics, the horizon of his thought remains essentially medieval. He loves and admires prowess, and makes it his chief theme. Great feats of arms are the crowning honour of individuals and peoples, an end in themselves, and their own justification. We have here no longer the idealistic knighthood of an earlier feudal time, but a somewhat materialized chivalry, dwelling wholly in strength and skill of arms and in the art of fine display. Froissart's narrative is fully conscious of its literary ambition;

[1] 1347–? 1404. Born at Valenciennes of a middle-class family. He took orders, went to England, and was protected by Queen Philippa, Edward III's wife. He travelled in Scotland, France, and Italy; secured new patrons, held an incumbency, returned to England, and died in Hainaut. The four books of his *Chroniques*, written over a period of some fifty years, follow the course of events from 1325 to 1400.

his aim is to please, and he has no moral purpose whatever. He never thinks of asking himself why the rioting peasants, in England or in France, should have been seized with such an inhuman fury. That brute with an athlete's body and a subtle brain, the Comte de Foix, is to him a pattern of the accomplished lord. He is engrossed in the joy of adventure, seeking only the satisfaction of describing impressive deeds and tragic events.

But he does this excellently. Although his language is still tinged with archaism the thought is perspicuous, and closer to us. His long sentences, modelled on Latin oratory, have rhetorical turns of phrase but the rhetoric is not heavy; a genuine animation carries the tale along and we follow ungrudgingly. The writer's zest in his own story is so infectious that even French readers are willing to condone the pro-English bias of the first book. Prowess, the historian pronounces, has been shifting her quarters; her last but one seat was France, but it is England nowadays. The commonplace lesson of it all is that the fate of states, like that of men and women, cannot be foreseen. 'Ainsi aviennent souvent les fortunes en armes et en amours, plus merveilleuses que on ne les pourrait ne oserait penser ne souhaiter.' The tale proceeds with ever new liveliness, and the canvas is crowded with episodes of policy and of fighting; some scenes, like the battles of Crécy and Poitiers, are of ample breadth, and show an instinct of dramatic structure. Our interest is sustained by the skill of a master of narrative style with a gift of vivid, at times realistic presentation. We possess no comparable document of the life and manners of the fourteenth century.

Froissart is a born chronicler; he neither is, nor tries to be, a moralist. Commines[1] is naturally a thinker. Not that he shows himself constantly alive to issues of good and evil, but his fifteenth-century instinct, with the first stirring of the Renaissance, strikes us as shrewd and modern; he is at times not unlike a tamer counterpart

[1] Philippe de la Clyte, sire de Commines, was born in Flanders about 1445 of a rich middle-class family. He was attached first to the Duke of Burgundy, Charles le Téméraire, and then entered the household of Louis XI, whose keen political sense he admired, and served there as a confidential counsellor till the king's death (1483). After an eventful period of transition and severe accidents of fortune, he played a similar part with Louis' successor, Charles VIII, until he fell out of favour, when he retired. He died in 1509. His memoirs, which cover the reigns of both Louis XI and Charles VIII, were first published as *Cronique et histoire faicte et composée par Messire Philippe de Comines*, 1524.

of his contemporary Machiavelli. A cool, reflective mind, he is interested above all in character, in the motives of action, and in the hidden layers of thought and feeling revealed indirectly by the decisions of statesmen. Such penetration is necessarily intuitive; and Commines's masterpiece is his study of Louis XI, a man with whom he naturally sympathized and whom he approached and knew on a footing of intimacy. The French language had contained nothing hitherto equal to this portrait, with the subtle and close truth of its conflicting shades. Psychological analysis, one of the main temptations and strongest points of traditional French literature, was here definitely started on its course. And although ethical considerations are often in abeyance, a moralizing instinct is none the less at work extracting lessons from experience, as in the final remarks passed on Charles le Téméraire, whose life and death were so richly significant.

It matters little that we miss in Commines the brilliance and animated interest of Froissart's pictures; or even that his style is at times heavy and sententious. His prudence and sagacity will not dogmatize, being held in check by a superior sense of the complexity of things and the contradictions in the human heart. The description, for instance, of the desperate attempt made by the citizens of Liége to break through the besiegers' lines, and its failure by the narrowest of margins, is steeped in the full realization of the irony of fate and of the minute accidents that can deflect the logical course of events. There lies the profound wisdom of one of the creators of modern history. At the same time, Commines firmly believes in Providence. For all his quietly pessimistic manner he is not destitute of feeling; a compassionate heart tempers the hard penetration of an experienced student of affairs. So his advice to the great, implicit or explicit, outlines ideas and emotions which later times have stressed more and more: the duties and responsibilities of princes, the unjust lot of the downtrodden, the cruelty of selfishness. The serious burden of the thought often makes the words impressive; and while the narrator has not Froissart's vivacious gift of story-telling, his portrayal of complex circumstance is more adequate. Moreover, he can rise to a note of eloquence, with a measured fullness of sound and rhythm, which is our first intimation of what sacred oratory will grow to be.

CHAPTER VII

Dramatic Literature

IT is safe to assert that the origin of French drama was in the high emotional and imaginative appeal of Christian ritual. At a time when the narratives of Scripture awoke a full response in all hearts and were vividly and literally conjured up by the mind's eye, a longing naturally arose that they might be represented visibly, before the eyes of the flesh. That the desire still persists in France, especially southern France, is evidenced by the Nativities and processions of today. And it is well known that similar origins can be assigned to the dramatic literature of many countries, ancient and modern.

This holds at least of serious French drama, which developed first. The movement was particularly concerned with the major episodes of the Christian year, the Christmas and Easter celebrations. The habit grew of giving allegorical representations, within the church itself, of the events connected with the birth and the passion of the Saviour. At first entrusted only to clerics, the performance was gradually opened to lay actors. The language used was originally Latin; French replaced it by degrees. As the display assumed more importance it became inadvisable to keep it in the nave, so it was shifted to the church porch, whence it passed on to temporary buildings erected outside. Thus arose the dramatic representation of religious subjects, or *Mystères* as they were called from the fourteenth century. The name *jeu*, first given to those primitive plays, was also used for the early comedies, an independent growth that appeared later.

The oldest extant *jeu*, the *Mystère d'Adam*, dates from the later twelfth century, and is a useful reminder of the close intimacy of French and English cultures after the Conquest; its dialect would assign it either to the south of England or to Normandy. It must have been performed in some cloister or relatively free space, as its detailed and interesting stage directions imply more room than even a church porch could afford. Before each of the successive parts a chorus sings in Latin the verses of the Biblical text which refer to it.

So strictly orthodox is the whole that it remains a bare outline, summing up in stark simplicity the story of Eden, and of the Fall and its consequences; the incomplete manuscript stops at the prospect of Redemption. Of art properly so called there can be no shade here, although the Tempter's dialogue with Eve affords some evidence of a sense of character. Nor is any attempt made to tone down the harshness of divine justice. The full force of the idea of the Fall is brought home to the devout spectator with a grim vigour, as efficient as it is naïvely single-minded.

Another kind of *jeu* arose from more restricted aspects of worship. The life-story of some saint with local claims to honour would be staged in the district or city as a token of gratitude or a bid for more favour. In this case again the use of Latin preceded that of French. An outstanding work of the kind is the *Jeu de Saint Nicolas*, by Jean Bodel[1] (late twelfth century). We have in it a remarkable proof that seeds were here dormant which, if they had freely developed, might have given France a drama somewhat akin to the Elizabethan type. Comic and serious elements are united as frankly and naturally as they would be in real life. A zest for sheer fun, for the variety of characters, and the raciness of popular language, makes every scene alive; the theme's opportunities for the introduction of the picturesque, and its quaint humour, are exploited with a sure instinct; edification is not absent, but the whole work breathes a jolly and genial spirit. Everything ends in the triumph of Saint Nicolas, an infallible guardian of earthly treasures, and in the enthusiastic conversion of the Saracens. After this early instance of a *Miracle* (as the plays of this species began to be called), the later and more typical *Miracle de Théophile*, by Rutebeuf (see above, Chapter III) is no more than praiseworthy, with scant originality or dramatic life.

Meanwhile the independent exploitation of comic themes and situations was claiming its birthright outside the sphere of the Church. The critics have come to agree that this was not an offshoot from the main stem of serious drama, although in works of the latter kind appeals to laughter were generally to be found. The comic

[1] A *trouvère*, he belonged to the literary life of Arras, one of the most active centres of culture in the north of France. He wrote poems, including *Le Congé*, a moving piece written on the occasion of his entering a hospital for lepers, where he died in 1210.

episodes that cropped up in any realistic image of life came to be treated apart on their own merits, and a tradition of short, amusing pieces, which afterwards grew in length, was thus created. The thirteenth century offers us two interesting examples, both by the same writer, Adam le Bossu, who takes us back to the seething city of Arras. The first, the *Jeu de la Feuillée* (about 1277) has been termed, not unfitly, the distant ancestor of our modern 'revue'. This work again, in its freedom, realistic verve, and originality, is a not unworthy anticipation of the *Merry Wives* or *Midsummer Night's Dream*. What it lacks most, unfortunately, is Shakespeare's poetry. The touch is somewhat heavy, and the temper of the humour rather Flemish. The fairies do come in, but how weak and material is their spell! On the whole this earliest French comedy stands by itself, pointing to a distant future rich with promises that will not mature for a very long time, and singularly destitute of traits that will soon become representative.

Similar in its fate is our second example, the *Jeu de Robin et Marion*, a *pastourelle* placed in a theatrical setting. It is the earliest French dramatic pastoral, and may also be called the first comic opera. The freshness of the background and atmosphere and some happy turns of genuine rustic simplicity are so pleasant that this slight piece has met with warmer praise in our age than perhaps it deserves. It was a fine effort to weld the idyllic with the realistic; but the touch of the artist here proves far too clumsy. The reader who wishes to enjoy the spirit of the piece, such as it is, and not to crush it under unfair comparisons, had better dismiss *As You Like It* from his mind. Still, the attempt at innovation was all to the good if it could have been followed up.

With the later medieval period (fourteenth and fifteenth centuries), while the *Miracles* remain popular the *Mystères* are the new and growing kind. The former have been practically lost except in an important series of *Miracles de Notre-Dame*, more or less cut on the same pattern: short sketches, revolving round some religious event, drawing no line between matters of faith and of imaginative acceptance. In the familiar, naïve atmosphere the most wonderful happenings are quietly presented. Never was the craving for the supernatural more intense than in the period darkened by the cruel sufferings of the Hundred Years War.

The *Mystères* flourished during the fifteenth century, a development from the liturgical plays of the previous period. Concentrating upon the very core of the drama of faith, they dealt most often with the Passion of Christ. Bodies of trained actors—the Confréries de la Passion—specialized in the performances which were public events, announced months beforehand, and drawing huge crowds to temporary theatres erected near a church. The stage was divided into many mansions, with heaven and hell very conspicuous; the play shifted from one mansion to another. Only men had a share in the acting; the unoccupied players simply sat where they happened to be. Primitive and naïve features thus appear along with a new stress laid on decoration, machines, and staging. The text of the works we have is mostly disappointing, with too much emphasis on the sensational side of the show. Comic scenes, and even low buffoonery, were freely introduced. Other than religious subjects, such as events of national importance, were sometimes presented. The *Mystère du Siège d'Orléans* was performed a few years after the martyrdom of Joan of Arc. The analogy of these features with parallel developments in England, where practically every stage of the progress can be detected, with a slight lag in time, need not be emphasized.

The best-known example is Arnoul Gréban's *Mystère de la Passion*, performed in Paris about 1450, a huge play, running into more than 34,000 lines, and divided into four 'days'. It was so successful that the same subject—a vital one indeed—was treated again and again, often by enlarging parts of the original work. This itself reads well enough; it has a sustained tenor of style, dignity, and an instinct for a balance of qualities; but nothing rises to a high degree of impressiveness. In an adaptation of Gréban's work by Jean Michel d'Angers (1486), with the same title, the comic elements are stressed, but at one point a dialogue between Jesus and Mary strikes us with its power of forceful and pathetic expression; the Virgin pleads with her son against the horror of the fate he is taking upon himself, and he with gentle sternness maintains his firm determination. One can distinguish there some accents worthy of Corneille:

> *Mary.* A mes maternelles demandes
> Ne donnez que responses dures!
> *Jesus.* Accomplir fault les Escriptures!

By the early sixteenth century the *Mystères* were on the decline. The Reformers objected to them on religious grounds, and their public performance was forbidden by decree in 1548.

The comic plays also had their specialized groups of actors, such as the well-known 'Clercs de la Basoche'. The general category includes the *Moralités* (English Moralities), although strains of serious purpose were usually found in them; the *Sotties*, or extravaganzas; the *Sermons joyeux*, or parodies of preaching; and the *Farces*, some 150 of which have reached us from the fifteenth and sixteenth centuries. In this plentiful crop, little tendency is so far to be observed towards comedy worthy of the name, but the abundant roots of comic creation in the intellectual temper of the French are fully revealed. Of poetry there is hardly any trace; the gifts of verve, irony, and fun, genuine if often coarse, are conspicuously displayed, just as in the Miracles and Mysteries a faculty for tragic emotion did emerge here and there. The conditions of a great dramatic development are present, though the growth is still rather stunted.

With the *Farce du Cuvier*, however, and still more that of *Maître Pathelin*, a high level of artistic creation is reached. The latter is a little masterpiece. Nothing is known of the author, or the date—held to be earlier than 1470. The subject is handled with deftness and a sure perception of the peculiar logic hidden in the paradoxes that provoke laughter. The impossible situation is invested with a sufficient degree of acceptability by an obviously symbolical purpose: and tricks are played on each side under the dignified cloak of the law. The sting of the almost continually triumphant cynicism is blunted at the end, when the rascally lawyer is hoist with his own petard. The flabbergasted clothier is a memorable figure in fiction. The form is excellent, pointed and terse, rich in pat phrases that have become proverbs. Here again the instinctive search for a quality that we shall call classical is apparent.

CHAPTER VIII

The Transition

In the fourteenth century the French medieval order, which had given birth to a complete culture in the various fields of action, thought, and art, began to experience the undermining effect of social changes. The growth of the middle classes in numbers, wealth, and influence forced into the body of society unsettled elements for which the feudal system had not provided. The expanding cities claimed municipal independence and won their charters. The power of the kings, with its reliance on administrators and lawyers, upset the foundations of a way of government in which subordination was mostly local and personal. In their long struggle with the feudal lords they received some help from the bourgeois, but the latter were unruly and dangerous allies, as events proved. Other causes may be called accidental. The Hundred Years War shook the foundations of French prosperity and drove the population of whole provinces to a state of despair. The Black Death about 1350 took a fearful toll of the French as of the English. Under these various strains the temper of the age began perceptibly to change. A sense of instability crept into the minds of men; anxiety as to the future became prevalent, and imagination and feeling assumed a darker tone.

The fourteenth and chiefly the fifteenth centuries may thus be regarded as ages of transition. It has often been pointed out that the idea of death then assumed extraordinary sway over the general mental outlook. The fortune of the *danse macabre* theme in the dramatic representations of the age is a case in point. Stress has already been laid on the significance of Villon's poems in this respect. From the end of the thirteenth century Jean de Meung's bold, cynical encyclopaedia of criticism set its mark on the mood of the following age; the influence of the book was widespread and lasting. The persistent satire of some aspects of Church life, and especially of the begging friars, reveals a vein of spiritual dissatisfaction that was to grow ominous in the next age; while the authority of the Papacy was shaken by conflict with emperors and kings, and its own inner schism. After the final failure of the great enthusiastic endeavour of the Crusades a spirit of realism prevailed; and the *Mémoires* of Commines testify to the advent of modern utilitarian politics. There is a diffused sense of rebellion against the artificiality and pretence of the *courtois* ideal; and the revulsion from it can be traced for instance in a quietly satirical novel of the mid-fifteenth century, *Le Petit Jehan de Saintré*, by Antoine de la Salle. This is in many ways an arresting book; the bankruptcy of the high-flown notion of platonic love between a knight and the lady of his thoughts is illustrated in an unexpectedly ironical way by the lady's failure to live up to it; and all the paraphernalia of the feudal pageant at its most glamorous are subtly ridiculed by a formal display of their gorgeous futility.[1] The technique of an exaggeration that assumes the connivance of the reader is handled here with a wittily conscious art. Somewhat coarser in their pleasantry, but equally destructive in their cynicism, are those breviaries of the *gaulois* spirit brought to bear on the misfortunes of husbands and the frailty of women, *Les Quinze joyes de mariage* and *Les Cent nouvelles nouvelles*. In these three works the influence of the Italian *novella*, and of Boccaccio's school, is plainly to be felt.

These various symptoms are not to be overstated. The profound ardour which had raised the cathedrals is not flagging in the fifteenth century, although the 'flamboyant' (decorated) style may signify a falling away from the selfless purity of the greatest Gothic. In Villon's soul despair is still illuminated by faith. The new intellectual birth of the Renaissance will take place in a society whose exuberant vitality had been overcast by a shadow of doubt and a sense of gloom, but not in its deepest roots seriously impaired.

[1] G. Reynier's interpretation, that rules out any such satirical intent, does not seem tenable (*Les Origines du roman réaliste*, chapter iv).

PART II

THE RENAISSANCE

CHAPTER IX

Humanism in France and the Renaissance

THE French Renaissance was later than the Italian, and somewhat earlier than the English. Symptoms of development were apparent in the late fifteenth century. It assumed the size of a movement in the first decades of the sixteenth and grew to full significance during the middle years that followed—roughly from 1530 to 1560. After the latter date its influence, though still felt, was partly checked by political and religious strife. In the history of French thought, life, and art it is the outstanding fact of the age that saw the final emergence of modern France and preceded the coming to a head of all her energies.

The traditional view of the European Renaissance must be revised in the light of more precise notions, both of its medieval roots and of its own inner nature. It is over-simple to assert that the movement sprang from the revelation of the masterpieces of ancient writers, and was thus primarily born and bred in the enthusiasm of literary discovery. The Middle Ages were by no means unacquainted with the substance of the literatures of Greece and Rome, though the Greek texts were mostly known through Latin translations. The fall of Byzantium in 1453, with the scattering of her exiled scholars through Europe, was not the decisive happening so long supposed. It remains to us mainly a symbol of a *rapprochement* of East and West, that had begun in the distant past, during the Crusades. The Renaissance itself was the chief cause of the strong stimulus given to the study of the Greek language and Greek works. In fact, the movement had been astir in Italy before the impact of the Byzantine disaster could be felt. Other definable circumstances, such as the invention of printing about the middle of the fifteenth century, and the great voyages of Columbus and Vasco da Gama in its last decade, with the consequent expansion of the imaginable world, did certainly further the growth of a mental revolution then in progress; but with these we enter a broader field, and pass far beyond the limits of proper literary considerations. In the special case of France the expeditions into Italy that brought about a more intimate intercourse between the two countries from 1494 to 1515 obviously fall into the class of general influences, such as affect the whole course of social history.

Considered from all aspects, and taking into account both its wide diffusion and its inner significance, the Renaissance represents a phase in the development of the Western mind. Periods of marked intellectual growth are natural in the life of a civilization; they have a dynamic character, and witness the germination of seeds which were sown earlier, while the fruit may ripen for later gathering. They are subject to a network of influences, and only occur if the condition of society is favourable or at least not inimical to them. Although the Middle Ages had been far from really static, and had produced something more substantial than hints of what the full flowering of the future could be, they are best regarded as a long period of gestation, ending in the birth of the modern national states. The vigour and accumulated wealth of the now conscious nationalities allowed of departures in all fields, and their vitality sought expression in commerce, industry, government, philosophy, science, and art. The general impression can hardly be resisted that European man was then bursting the shell of the fixed order in which the all but universal sway of the Church had sheltered and confined his immaturity; and in the light of it the inseverable nature of the connexion between the Reformation and the Renaissance becomes clear. Indeed at the very root of the great mental change, underlying even the social expansion that fostered the new birth, a deeper intuition was at work, creating the promise and the sense of another era, and of a further stage opened to the human spirit. The first intimation of it can be traced to the early mystics who had pro-claimed the reign of a purer faith, and the advent of the everlasting gospel. In other ways, at other times, the explorers who multiplied the size of the earth, the scientists who revealed her minute place in an unfathomable world, the scholars who drew from old parchments radiant images of beauty, bore the same witness. In all of them, the mind itself glowed with the sense of a limitless scope offered to hope, knowledge, power, and the fullness of life. The Renaissance spirit properly so called could be described in words similar to those of Wordsworth evoking for eternity a young man's thrill at the dawn of the French Revolution.

The lead taken by France in medieval civilization might seem to have marked her out to start the new movement of the modern mind. But she had identified herself with the achievements of the twelfth and thirteenth centuries, when a Renaissance of a kind had developed, strictly within the frame of the order and discipline of the Church. It was given to Italy, with the disunited but intense life of her principalities, with the initiatives of her bankers, jurists, thinkers, poets, and artists, her nearness to the influences from the East, and the daily sight of the monuments of the classical past, to strike out first, locally and impulsively, for the renovation that was preparing everywhere in the less easily quickened lands beyond the Alps. How the zeal spread northward, and the Italian examples were eagerly followed in one country after another, is a subject that cannot even be adumbrated here.

By the end of the fifteenth century France was recovering from the depression, material and moral, that was the legacy of the Hundred Years War. Her prosperity was increasing, and a heightened consciousness of her legitimate ambitions lent purpose and dignity to the aims and policy of her kings, from Charles VIII to Henri II. All of them, and especially François I, took pride in befriending and helping writers; their courts were intellectual centres. From the time when Louis XII, with his debonair mien and garb, was represented on horseback over the entrance gate of the castle at Blois, to that when Diane de Poitiers' own emblem ceased to appear on the exquisitely carved walls of the Châteaux de la Loire, French architecture and the crafts subservient to it were brilliant expressions of a new idea of life, free from medieval danger and gloom. The latter part of the sixteenth century was to be darkened with the shadows of religious and civil wars; the transition to the relative stability of the classical age was painful, and prolonged by political disturbances. But a period of fervour had begun perceptibly with the auspicious opening years of the century; the atmosphere of the Renaissance could already be sensed, and soon grew intoxicating. It fostered the enthusiasm with which the study of the old texts was on all hands encouraged and pursued; and that study in its turn confirmed and strengthened the intellectual movement.

Scholarship, in such conditions, was endowed with a breadth, an ardour, and a high notion of its vital part in the advance of mind, which made it a close companion to life, and hardly distinguishable from literature. Humanism soon became the fit name for intellectual activities that surveyed the whole condition of man, as depicted with supreme truth in the body of ancient writings. The name by which the Renaissance itself now goes was affixed to it at a somewhat later stage. By the men and women who were its leaders it was seen chiefly as a crusade of the enlightened to dispel the darkness that had befogged, so they thought, the previous ages; and poets, courtiers, and ladies of culture urged one another to wage the good fight against 'ignorance'. A movement of intellectual enthusiasm with an aggressive edge, humanism was thus, down to the middle of the century, and to the constructive work of the Pléiade, the most substantial aspect of the French Renaissance.

Its first task was the elucidation, translation, and commentary of the newly published or revised classics; since all virtue for the formation and improvement of a liberal intelligence, it was very generally held, lay in them. Well before the end of the fifteenth century the great firms of printers had begun their work, in Lyons and in Paris. A name still famous from those heroic days, when printers were also publishers, and even philologists, is that of the Estienne family. When the master of European humanism, Erasmus, visited the French capital in 1495, he found the zeal for Greek studies already alive among the *élite*. The personal influence of Guillaume Budé is at the very centre of the contagion that inspired, within a few decades, a systematic effort, a school, and a tradition for the critical editing and interpretation of texts. That these endeavours clashed with the spirit of conservative circles, especially of the University of Paris, in her own eyes the repository of all orthodoxy, and jealously attentive to the theological bearing of novel ideas, is common history. That her fears were not unwarranted, when an enterprising and vigorous scholar, Jacques Lefèvre d'Etaples, began applying the new methods to the study of Scripture, is no less well known. He was mainly responsible for the growth of a desire to purify the Christian faith from certain undue accretions of time, an effort in which the sympathies of many thinkers and writers, and some of the highest persons at court, were more or less at one. This '*évangélisme*', as it was called, managed to maintain for half a century an honest but dangerous position of compromise between the unexpurgated faith and what speedily became, with Luther, an open attempt at a thorough Reformation. King François I showed a liberal spirit, and even courage, in granting his support to the *évangélistes*; and he gave the humanist movement what proved to be its most active and brilliant focus when he created the Collège Royal de France, the future Collège de France (1530).

After some hesitation, and in a few cases not a little vacillation, almost all the more important writers kept within the fold. But the literary history of the Reformation in France, with its background and accompanying currents of ideas, must be summed up, however briefly, by itself (see below, Chapter XI).

CHAPTER X

Poetry before the Pléiade

THE advent of the Renaissance in France was so gradual that for a whole generation after 1500 the patterns of poetry remained what they had been.

The most reputed poets of that age kept strictly to the late and decadent medieval tradition. Charles d'Orléans and Villon had been isolated instances. The courage and the sincerity of direct, personal utterance were instinctively feared and avoided; the labouring of an artificial form offered a sure path to brilliance for the clever and the uninspired, and the heirs of Machaut and Deschamps were refining further the intricate technique of ballades and rondeaux. *Préciosité* of one kind or another, the chief besetting temptation of over-intellectual poetry in France from the beginning, reigned supreme in the works of writers whose patient addiction to feats of style won for them the well-deserved name of 'Rhétoriqueurs'. Allegory, punning, quibbling, learned obscurity, alliteration, and the most complicated rhyme-schemes were cultivated by them with inexhaustible zeal and stupendous fertility. To their contemporaries they were admirable; to posterity they are ghosts, called to a bloodless life by historians of literature. Jean Marot, Clément's father; Molinet, Meschinot, Crétin have today no other existence, although the bold critic who dips into their works may find that so much ingenuity and subtlety is after all no despicable achievement—if not in the least a poetical one.[1]

In this dearth of authentic accents it is a comfort to meet a writer whose fund of feeling and genuine personality was even superior to his skill. Jean Lemaire de Belges[2] was not proof against the lure of

[1] To some extent, an exception may be made in favour of Pierre Gringore (1475–1538), whom Hugo and Banville were to magnify into a symbol of Bohemianism and popular genius. He was primarily a writer of mysteries and farces. His *Le Jeu du Prince des Sotz* (1511) was a play with a purpose, meant to serve the policy of Louis XII against the Pope.

[2] Born (1473) in Hainaut, a province whose population he held, with historical

rhétorique, and his taste was subject to lapses, but he had a sure instinct and often managed to escape from his discipleship to the Molinet school and his respect for the trite devices of the *Roman de la Rose*. Italy was largely the means of his freedom. Dante was a revelation to him and his sense of rhythm was caught by the grand simplicity and the onward urge of the *terza rima*. He imitated this under the name of *tercet*, thus taking a step that was to be followed occasionally in the sixteenth century, and then forgotten for over 200 years. His attempt at playfulness and grace, in *L'Amant vert*, lacks the deft, light touch of Marot. He is seen to better advantage in the *Temple de Vénus*, which harks back on the one hand to Guillaume de Lorris, by its allegories and touches of fresh scenery, but on the other looks beyond Jean de Meung to Rabelais's realism, satire, and verbal opulence. In this piece Jean Lemaire's gift for metrical initiative is doubly evidenced, the alexandrine being used by the side of the tercet. The worthy 'Belgian's' pride in France, whose enthusiastic citizen he was, breaks out at times in a wild orgy of alliterative 'rhetoric'. Still, he may be termed, according to his light, a good European. In his prose *Concordance des deux langages*, which anticipates Du Bellay's *Deffense*, he calls on Gallic writers to emulate the Italian, French being quite equal to 'Florentine', and wishes that the two countries, then at war, might know no other rivalry than a friendly one. His chief work (prose with occasional verse) is the naïve, impudent, quaint, and charming farrago of legend, invention, and—at times—honest fact, the *Illustrations de Gaule et singularitez de Troye*, where the Trojan descent of the French is expounded to his full contentment. Their ancestor was 'Francus', and who can resist the evidence of such a derivation? But was there at Troy a Francus? The burden of the proof lies with the sceptics; and do we not hear of a natural son of Hector, called Laodamus, who may have borne another name among his friends? As for the city of Paris, is it not clear that its founder was the son of Priam? Ronsard was to take a leaf out of this book. Its smooth, dignified style, in spite of somewhat sprawling sentences, won for the work a signal

pride, to represent Caesar's 'Belgians', he made various stays at princely courts, travelled to Italy, and lived in Lyons. He wrote in verse and prose, his chief work being *Les Illustrations de Gaule et singularitez de Troye* (1509–13). He probably died about 1525.

success; its theme flattered the romantic sense of origins and made a fabulous past convincingly real and familiar. On the strength of his double spiritual allegiance, to his smaller and his larger fatherlands, the adventurous writer goes on to invite the Germans and the French to strike an alliance, and start on one more crusade. The former are only Gauls of the East, as the latter Gauls of the West. 'Or vueille Dieu, que de nostre temps les armes de ces deux très nobles et très puissantes nations se puissent ioindre pacifiquement ensemble, pour recouvrer leur héritage de Troye, lequel possèdent les Turcz. . . .' But history was not to take that course.

Clément Marot

It is easy to be unfair to Marot,[1] for the nineteenth-century revolution in taste has opened a gulf between his manner and our notion of the poetical. Shortly after his own age, the Pléiade eclipsed him—or to us it did, though his prestige kept remarkably high till the romantic era. Nevertheless, history gives him a claim to our attention, and if studied with an open mind his work will justify his permanent place in literary records.

He is a type, not of the whole range, but of one of the central modes of traditional French poetry. A period already conscious of the value of form acknowledged his mastery of the neat, smooth style, and of a terse elegance that could be at will witty, caressing, or sly. He answered the instinctive need for what were to be the classical values; and the turmoil of the Renaissance left him his position, at the head of a line that leads directly to all the writers of *petits vers*— a tribe over which La Fontaine would indolently rule, were there not a Voltaire. One should never forget what he stands for, and the sense of perfection that, after the uncertainties of medieval phrasing, his ease, deftness, and 'finesse' created among his readers.

Like Jean Lemaire, he was a son of the Rhétoriqueurs, and remained faithful to them. His humanist studies seem to have been but slight. The acme of bad taste is reached in the *Eglogue de Madame*

---

[1] Clément Marot, born in 1496 at Cahors, held various posts in noble families, and in the king's household. He was attracted by the *évangéliste* movement, and twice imprisoned. After the *affaire des placards*, he fled to Ferrare, came back, but again had to seek a refuge, first at Geneva, then at Turin, where he died in 1544. He published his early poems (*Adolescence Clémentine*) in 1532; a collected edition of his verse in 1538; and his translation of the *First Fifty Psalms* in 1543.

Loyse de Savoye, with its shameless punning on the names of French cities. But his more genuine personality comes out in several of the *Épîtres*, masterpieces of their kind: *A son ami Lyon, Aux dames de Paris, Au roy pour avoir esté dérobé*, &c.; in many of the *Épigrammes*; in the *Dialogue nouveau*, the *Adieux à la ville de Lyon*, &c. The 'inevitable' word is there, and the direct simplicity that seems but natural, and is indeed, yet somehow is granted only to those with whom nature is the highest art.

Such mainly is the figure time has chiselled; but though true, it is incomplete. Marot has other features, less prominent, but of at least equal interest. Some of his strains are really lyrical as, for instance, the overtones of deep seriousness and emotion of *Le Dieu-gard à la court*; the music and the elegiac sweetness of *Colin et Thénot*; or the realistic and rustic charm of the *Églogue au Roy, sous les noms de Pan et Robin*, a justly famous piece:

> Sur le printemps de ma jeunesse folle,
> Je ressembloys l'arondelle qui vole
> Puis ça, puis là. . . .

Even more, perhaps, one is struck by the subdued pathos, the self-pity broadening into generous indignation, the graphic vigour of *L'Enfer*, whose satirical power recalls Villon. This deep-lying strain links up with the religious earnestness that put Marot in some danger and made his life so restless, though his translation of the *Psalms*, however successful at the time, is a mediocre achievement. The final impression is unavoidable, that in him an unmistakable poet did exist, rarely seen, but plainly visible when the impersonal discipline of his artistic temper was relaxed. This again is significant, for we can thus remark a poetic inspiration, compressed if not repressed, existing side by side with the severely intellectual manner that points so effectively his gentle ironies and witticisms; and the same duality will go far to account for the apparent contradictions of the great French classicists.

Marot's fame and authority contributed more than any other influence to keep the official standards of French poetry unchanged, until the success of Ronsard broke the spell. He was rather the head of a group than the founder of a school. Of his admiring imitators only one may be mentioned here: Mellin de Saint-Gelais (1490–

1558), the very type of the court poet, who wrote rondeaux and ballads by the score; but felt the breath of a fresh inspiration from Italy and, dabbling in Petrarchism, popularized the sonnet.

The *poètes Lyonnais*

These poets stand somewhat apart from the rest, and have some features in common. Three of them directly felt the spell of that active and powerful city, Lyons, and shared its serious spirit. A fourth, Héroet, who was Parisian born and never lived in Lyons, is on the strength of his affinities conveniently studied with the others. They sought instinctively to renew poetry from the inside, through intensity and emotional fervour.

Maurice Scève (1500?–60?), by far the greatest, is an original and solitary genius, who developed according to his own law. Of the man little is known, though he was socially prominent, and for a time recognized as a leader in the literary world, until he was eclipsed by the triumph of Ronsard and his group. These felt with reason, even while hailing him as a precursor, that he had his roots in the past, that he derived from the Rhétoriqueurs, and more distantly from the *trobar clus* of the troubadours (see above, Part I, Chapter IV, 1). But he had turned this technique to quite new uses, aiming at a manner in some respects akin to modern symbolism. His powerful condensation has a force of suggestion that relies upon the echoing virtue of few and carefully chosen words.

If his shorter pieces are omitted his output can be summed up in three poems, slowly matured and published anonymously, and which together testify to the singularly wide range of an audacious mind. *Délie, object de plus haulte vertu* (1544) enshrines in some 450 'dizains', or ten-line stanzas of ten-syllabled verse, with an elaborate rhyming pattern, the reflections and emotions born of a love that never came to fruition, but was the occasion of a painfully won inner victory. Over and above the atmosphere of Petrarchan *préciosité* which characterizes much of the French Renaissance, a properly Platonic idealism raises these dense, often involved, utterances to a higher spiritual level. The poet's ambition is noble, and the partial success of his effort commands our respectful admiration. But too much is demanded, by an uncompromising writer, of himself and his instrument; the thought, while subtle, is imperfectly trained to the lucid analysis of intellectual shades; the language, while boldly adding to its resources in ways that prefigure those of the Pléiade, is not welded into a sufficiently supple medium. Consequently, many of these self-contained stanzas are almost as obscure as they are arresting; and the present-day reader is haunted with the sense of a potential Valéry, born too soon. Every now and then, however, the concentrated heat of a passion that is implied rather than expressed succeeds in melting the mood and the words into weighty, pregnant lines, calling up long mental echoes; and an intuitive perception of the suggestive power of images and sounds enlivens such passages as these:

> 'En la clarté de mes désirs funèbres . . .'
> 'Les sèches fleurs en leur odeur vivront . . .'
> 'Tu me seras la Myrrhe incorruptible
> Contre les vers de ma mortalité.'

Saulsaye, églogue de la vie solitaire (1547) is a lighter, shorter poem and makes relatively easy reading. On the surface it is no more than a pastoral fancy; but the landscape, in its concrete precision, is not of the conventional type; it is loved and described for the sake of its austere, individual charm. Among running or stagnant waters, where quiet lawns and thick copses of willows cover the left bank of the Rhône below its confluence with the Saône, two shepherds, one of whom is obviously the poet, dialogue upon the latter's unfortunate love; and a story is told of how nymphs pursued by fauns were changed into willow-trees. The theme, in the approved classical and mythological fashion, is merely an excuse for what is really weighing on Scève's mind—his thrilled sense of the soul of a place, in a spirit far more romantic than that of Andrew Marvell, a century and a quarter later. A sequestered spot, where solitude reigns undisturbed, both quickens and soothes, not the melancholy of a lamenting swain, but the anguish and the mystery of life; one thinks of Rousseau in his mountain retreat, of Thoreau near his Walden.

> Lieu solitaire, où la Saulsaye épaisse
> Soubs douce horreur est de mort une espèce,
> Où nul (fors toy, et tout désespoir) vient . . .

With a sure instinct of metrical fitness, the poet gives us here, not the rigid stanza of *Délie*, but the continuous movement and flowing rhythm that answer the music of running water:

> Lors je respans mes fleurs dessoubs ma teste,
> En attendant qu'à dormir me convie
> Le son de l'eau murmurant, comme pluye,
> Qui lentement sous les arbres descend:
> Ou comme autour de ces estangs on sent
> Le vent souef parmi les cannes bruire . . .

The last venture is *Microcosme* (1562), a philosophical poem of truly stupendous scope; it compasses the story of creation and the fall of man as far as the death of Abel; then, through the prophetic vision of Adam, the whole progress of civilization, technology, science, and art. That such a canvas should be filled, even in outline, is matter for awe; and it is no surprise that the artistic achievement falls below the standard of the preceding works. A reader is deeply stirred by the grandeur of the subject, and by the broad vistas of thought opened out again and again, often in single lines; but his emotion will be repeatedly checked by the clumsiness or the vagaries of the style. Still, the alexandrine is a happy choice for the ample theme, and among many flashes of rare, illuminating beauty, one may quote this brief touch of repressed pathos when Adam, burying Abel,

> Fossoye un creux en terre, auquel ce corps transi
> Il couche, et l'enterrant son cœur enterre aussi.

Scève's real stature has only recently been acknowledged. No doubt, after long neglect, an excess of reaction is to be avoided; but he should stand high—above Marot in the poetical scale, and on a par with the two leaders of the 'Pléiade'.

Pernette du Guillet (1520–45) was probably Scève's Délie. Her slight figure—she died very young—has other claims to survival. She was the first representative in the French middle-class world of the literary woman—high-born ladies had played the part before— and paid the price in invidious scandal. Her *Rymes* (1545) are partly in the manner of Scève, but some are more personal—chansons, delicately and naïvely impassioned, with a charm of sincerity, and a natural nobility in love.

Louise Labé (?–1565) left a more brilliant name, having been in the intellectual circles of Lyons that admired her and were slightly shocked, a fuller image of what Pernette du Guillet had only adumbrated. Her *Works,* published in 1555 and dedicated to another woman, open with a graceful but outspoken vindication of the feminine right to culture and talent. Her *Elegies,* direct effusions, in language from the heart, contrast vividly with the conventional tone that seems inseparable from even the most genuine love poems of the Renaissance. Her *Sonnets* strike the same note of simple and vivid passion. They do not compare in sustained quality of form with those of Mrs. Browning's series 'from the Portuguese', but they are no less sincere, almost as noble, and even more fervent. The main quality of this poetry is to be quite free from the blight of imitation, all but inevitable in an age when the literary ideal was openly retrospective. Louise Labé's prose *Débat de folie et amour* is a little gem that should secure her a distinguished rank among the writers of her time. Not only is the style perfectly spontaneous and supple, far purer and lighter than that of her more famous contemporaries, but its wit and charm are a transparent veil for serious weighty sense and penetrating intuition of all the complexities of life and feeling. The irony is gentler and finer than that of Erasmus in his *Praise of Folly,* a masterpiece which she must have known, and whose influence she smilingly escapes by ignoring it. As for the doctrine, it is of that high chastity which is not queasy and afraid: it flies in the face of centuries of *amour courtois* and accepts married love as the only complete ideal.

Antoine Héroet's (1492–1568) sole material link with Lyons is that his *Parfaicte Amye* was printed there in 1542. His spiritual kinship with the Lyonnese group, mentioned above, has at its core the same idealistic and moralizing strain in the treatment of love, derived directly from Platonism. Although the point is not explicitly stated, his heroine must be, from the context, a wedded wife; her relation to the loved one, that takes a lifetime to ripen perfectly, only assuming full significance on that supposition. To Héroet's earnest mind, Petrarch and his school dabble in abstractions, weaving a web of far-fetched unrealities, whereas the union of souls and bodies is a most actual experience. In it, indeed, there is a supernatural element, but in order to account for it the poet, who ended his career as a bishop, turns beyond Plato to Christianity. He is a subtle thinker, with a power of moral analysis that seems to point already to the chief preoccupation of French classicism. His close and deep grasp of the richer emotions of a loving heart wins our respect and sympathy; but he underestimates the value of form; his expression is apt to be dragging and prosaic. To some extent we may forgive this deficiency for the sake of occasional merits such as pithy and vigorous expression, occasional flashes of imaginative energy, and a sober but moving appeal to the enthusiasm of ennobling passion.

It is the woman who speaks, and the image of genuine love is drawn in feminine terms. The venture was bold, and the outcome is a creation on a par, in some ways, with the heroines of fiction. She is all devotion and tenderness; selfless, and impervious to jealousy. The man's effort to reciprocate is implied rather than described, but reciprocate he will, for sincere passion is always mutual—an optimistic view, surely. The sublimity of what may be called Platonic mysticism thus raises the heavy progress of the poem to a stirring eloquence. A sense of austere beauty grows upon the reader, and of delicate thoughts aptly worded, as in this, of love:

> Si pénétrant est son feu et subtil,
> Qu'il rend le corps de femme transparent,
> Et se présente au visage apparent
> Je ne say quoi qu'on ne peult exprimer,
> Qui se faict plus que les beaultés aymer.

Marguerite de Navarre (1492–1549)

She was the greatest lady of her time, sister to King François I, and wife successively to the duc d'Alençon and the roi de Navarre. She was also the most cultivated and gifted woman of the French Renaissance, in herself an epitome of its main aspects. She was a patroness and friend to writers and thinkers, and both wrote and took a vivid interest in the philosophical and religious movements of the age.

Her work as a poet is very distinguished, but falls just short of the artistic quality needed to secure outstanding eminence. It is the expression of a singularly active mind, and of a heart that knew to the full the deepest experiences of life. In one talent she was deficient: that of naturally musical and suggestive phrasing. She possessed every other virtue, including those regarded as particularly feminine:

finesse, charm, elegance. The poems published in her lifetime should be classed with the school of Marot, whose epistles she could answer gracefully. Already among these light pieces, however, graver accents could be heard, more spiritual and devout than might have been expected of one in her position.

The volume of the verse credited to her was largely increased at the end of the nineteenth century, and since, by the discovery of much new text (see especially *Dernières poésies*, published by Abel Lefranc, 1896). She now stands revealed as one of the earliest representatives of personal poetry, who laid bare the inmost workings of her meditative mind, and gave intensely sincere expression to her reflections on the disappointments of the world and the peace that is found in God alone. *Le Navire* and chiefly *Les Prisons* are symbolical poems, some passages of which recall the rapt intellectuality of her almost contemporary, Donne. But her concentration, though sustained, is not so powerful, and she lacks the sombre brilliance of his flashes. She wrote exclusively for herself, and was content with a plain, rhythmic statement of thoughts and moods that reaches potential rather than actual sublimity. Her most successful songs, the *Chansons spirituelles*, are shorter, with a more organic structure.

After her death she was chiefly famous as the author of the *Heptaméron*, a collection of seventy-odd stories in prose with occasional verse, corresponding in general plan to the Decameron, and published in 1558. Her indebtedness to Boccaccio is limited to the scheme. A serious purpose can be discovered in these tales, though their declared object is no more than to while away the forced leisure of some fictitious lords and ladies, and the reader's idle hour. A vigorous moral personality, kept in the background, at times gives an edge to narratives purporting to be only the harvest of a sophisticated lady of the court who has heard all the anecdotes and knows much scandal at first hand. To the pure all things are pure; but indeed we are startled at the tone conversation could adopt among refined sixteenth-century circles, and at Marguerite's non-committal tolerance. Her attitude to the miseries of the flesh is not one of coarse amusement but of indulgence slightly tinged with pessimism. A leaning to the *évangéliste* views, if not to those of the Reformers, comes out in not a few passages and underlines this sense of the corruption of human nature. The dissolute ways of monks are much in the foreground. The names of the dozen persons who speak by turns, and who preserve some consistency of character, are thin disguises for historical figures, the author herself being one. She gives us, through episodic scenes and a short description of settings, pleasant sketches of the life and manners of the age. The stories are well told, with a simplicity free from all pedantry, and in spite of the inevitable monotony the theme and atmosphere of each are aptly varied. The subjects are mostly of slight interest; a few rather longer tales, such as the tenth of the first Day, show some promise of the psychological novel of the *Princesse de Clèves* type. But when all is said, the literary merit of the work hardly equals its documentary value; the charm and piquancy are imperfectly served by a language that is not rich, and the style is too consistently fluent not to be a little diffuse.

So, French poetry before the Pléiade is far from negligible. It shows signs of originality and inner significance; what it lacks is the definite artistic purpose that might have stimulated and guided its sense of form. Marot and his group were careful versifiers, but on the pattern of the past. The Pléiade supplied the missing enthusiasm; and while perhaps laying too much stress on the duty of imitation, it opened the way definitely to the high ambitions and achievements of classical literature. Had its triumph been lasting it might have hastened by several hundred years the advent of modern lyricism, whose spiritual and mystical growth springs from seeds already germinating in the sixteenth century.

CHAPTER XI

The Philosophical and Religious Ferment: Calvin, Rabelais

THE sixteenth century is a seminal period, comparable to the eighteenth and contrasting vividly with the relatively static character of the seventeenth. The beginning of the modern era coincided with widespread changes in the definite system of beliefs that had been the foundation of the medieval order. Humanism was the main instrument of a shifting in men's ideas which gradually altered their views on almost all the vital subjects. Not that modern man simply returned to the doctrines possessed by antiquity. But the humanists were eager in their pursuit and diffusion of knowledge; the stigma of ignorance was attached to the mere routine of the mind; and while knowledge was chiefly literary and philological, the spirit with which it was instinct went far beyond the learning of languages and editing of texts. What these activities engendered was the demand for truth, an inquisitive and critical attitude, and a ready willingness to correct time-honoured prejudices. Thus a reassessment of values took place on all hands. Along with the great writers, the thinkers of ancient days were read and studied. They suggested theories of life and conduct different from the reigning orthodoxies, and the impact of their ideas told, consciously or unconsciously, on the very outlook of men and women. So it was that science and intellectual freedom were the daughters of humanism. The Renaissance was the focus of a naturalistic spirit that came to a definite head in certain thinkers and writers. Akin to this were pagan leanings, tingeing literature and art and also the behaviour of not a few of the cultivated circles. A highly idealistic trend, on the contrary, was that of the Platonists, who improved on the diffused Petrarchism of the poets. Such bold assertions of freedom remained exceptional; and the most comprehensive label to apply to the whole field of the philosophy of the Renaissance would be that of rationalism. Taken by and large, the hold of the Christian religion itself was not weakened under this influence, but the temper of belief was widely altered; and the Reformation, concurrent with the Renaissance, had no less far-reaching effects in the spiritual history of Europe.

It would be over-simple to assert that the demands of rationalism were the sole intellectual force by which the French reformers of the sixteenth century were moved. Into their complex of motives there did enter many others—from the human and ethical desire to see abuses and scandals removed, and the craving for a purified mode of worship, to a devout, often half-mystical sense of direct intercourse with God. But according to the present-day interpretation of the reformers' interest it was necessary for belief itself, and dogma, to undergo a sifting process in which the test of acceptance was agreement with the Scriptures; while the test of what constituted agreement, in the final instance, depended on the conscientious judgement, based on reason, of the individual himself. Thus in the eyes of many men and women faith was no longer subject to revelation, as interpreted by the Church, but to a decision, private or made within a dissenting group, of the purport of revelation itself. In spite of Calvin's constant appeal to the authority of the Fathers, the main issue is clear with him. With the *Évangélistes*, who for the most part did not leave the pale of orthodoxy, it is no less plain.

Bonaventure des Périers

Des Périers (1510–44) is a pathetic figure. Reflection having led him early to aggressive unbelief, he expressed his views under the mask of allegory and irony in order to avoid the stake. The book was burnt and not the author, but he had gone too far. His Lyonnese patrons, and even his most generous friend, Marguerite de Navarre, left him to his fate, and he put an end to his life, probably under the stress of poverty. His *Cymbalum mundi* (1537) is the first French example of the anti-Christian satire that was to flourish in the eighteenth century. It is bold, though not equally so in all its parts, and the second Dialogue is the only one of the four that commits itself irreparably. The carefully veiled but transparent argument, under mythological or fanciful apologues, bears the marks of somewhat crude rationalism, and uses weapons that Voltaire will take up again: Jesus is simply an impostor. The author's attitude is by no means entirely negative, and leans to a kind of deism. The gibes at monks and nuns resemble those of the Reformers, but Luther comes in for his share of castigation and the charge of fanatical intolerance is laid at the doors of both parties. Intellectual honesty, some wit, and a good deal of ingenuity have gone into this short work; but it is altogether a youthful fling, and below the level of Lucian or Erasmus. Its undeniable asset is the language, which moves with natural ease and simple elegance.

It is, indeed, the writer's talent that gives Des Périers his lasting claim and makes his premature end a loss to French literature. His translation of Plato's *Lysis* is full of charm. His poems are just good enough to rank among the acceptable imitations of Marot; while his *Nouvelles récréations et joyeux devis* (published after his death, 1558), with matter borrowed from the common store of amusing and somewhat coarse stories, are better told than the tales of the *Heptaméron*, in a style remarkably free from heaviness and lingering archaism. The twelfth, for instance, has been hardly improved upon by La Fontaine in a fable; the thirteenth is a little masterpiece of humour.

Calvin[1]

The most conspicuous figure among the founders of French protestantism is also a great writer, and our concern here is with his literary talent. But there never was a closer association between language and thought. The temper of the man and the doctrine of the teacher are woven with the instincts of the artist into an inseparable unity. All three have contributed powerfully to mould minds not only in France but in Europe and the world.

It was one of Calvin's major tenets that the body of his beliefs was not a personal interpretation of Christianity, but Christianity itself. Without taking sides in a religious controversy, it is possible to point

[1] Jean Cauvin, dit Calvin (Calvinus), born at Noyon (1509), studied the humanities in Paris, and then law and philology. He accepted the beliefs of the *Évangélistes*, was compromised on two successive occasions, and fled twice to various places in France, Switzerland, and Italy. He lived for three years at Strasbourg, where he became acquainted with German reformers. From 1541, as leader of the Reformation at Geneva, he ruled the city, and chastised dissenters rigorously. He published at Basel (1536) his Latin text and at Geneva (1541) his French translation of the *Institution de la religion chrétienne*, developed in subsequent editions. The book was condemned and burnt in France. He wrote much, chiefly in Latin, had wide spiritual influence, and died in 1564.

out that however soundly his ideas may have been based on Scripture and the Fathers, they do none the less bear the stamp of his personality, because the unequal emphasis he distributes over them, and the light he sheds upon his spiritual system as a whole, are so essentially characteristic of the man himself. The gloomy structure erected by a fiercely eager and uncompromising intelligence to give shape and substance to its certainty is and must remain his own work, and time and shifting perspectives have emphasized its weaknesses. At many decisive points the builder followed his own preferences and intuitions, and his construction stands firm only for those who share them. By the faithful at the present day it might be regarded less as a shelter than as a prison.

Man is born of sin in a state of utter corruption. All his natural promptings lead him to evil. No free option is granted him that he may cleanse on his own initiative the ineradicable stain of his being. And yet, the drama of this transient life has a conclusion of eternal glory or endless punishment, and each creature, being from the first destined to one or the other, is deeply responsible for the course he follows. To rebel against the justice of this decree is a gross abuse of our weakly, erring reason and an insult to God. The fall of Adam, which the Creator had foreseen, and our poisoned will, the penalty we all pay for it, are none the less crimes to which His anger and the dreadful severity of His vengeance have been meted out. Such, in its crushing simplicity, would be the scheme of a truly devilish universe but for the tremendous fact of grace. If God the Father is and must be a pitiless judge, an infinite power of mercy lives in God the Son. Christ through His sacrifice has redeemed man and taken his evil upon Himself. So a hope of salvation has been opened to each, and men may be saved, in a proportion of which we are to remain ignorant. It might conceivably be total, since Christ's merits and His love are limitless, but a wise humility, and our experience of the rottenness of the human heart, make us choose to regard it as small. How an individual soul is directed by predestination to one or the other end cannot be safely known even by itself, there being no sure inner sign. The only possible attitude is one of lifelong suspense, our duty being meanwhile summed up in one word, faith. If the absolute surrender of our pride is to be acceptable to God, and Christ's seemingly arbitrary choice has descended upon us, our regenerate self will respond to grace in the act of belief, which is the supreme and all-embracing virtue. Works are not worthless, but they are not indispensable. Some blessed sense of being justified to God may thus dawn amidst all our terrors through the fact of 'communication to Christ'—no mystic rapture, but a rational state based on the perception of actual contact with truth.

Though he does not explicitly claim as much, it is easy to feel that such a state is the foundation of Calvin's moral life and of his vocation. Those who see clearly must act as guides to the purblind; and having no serious doubt that he is gifted with spiritual insight, he writes. The labour of writing brings to him a fuller realization of his own thought, and the intellectual comfort without which there never was an artist in words. That he is one, is true within an austere and limited range. No aesthetic purpose is, of course, present for its own sake. But he aims consciously from the first at a clear, easy, orderly, pure, and pregnant style—he even adds, 'elegant'—without which his mission would not be properly fulfilled.[1] The first version of the French text is closely modelled on the Latin; as edition follows edition, and the writer lets himself go, his manner is given ampler scope, becomes freer, and develops towards its instinctive ideal. This preserves a good deal of the tone and method of juridical argument; the born-and-bred lawyer wants to put his case aptly and to destroy error, as an adversary's fallacy is crushed. As to who is the adversary here, we are left in no doubt: he is, whether at first or second remove, the eternal foe of man. That Calvin has no objection to the tricks of special pleading we realize from the clever management of his dedicatory 'Epistre au Roy', in which the burden of proof is so deftly shifted to the other party. Who are the enemies of order? Not, surely, the Protestants, who, to a conservative mind, might well look like revolutionaries, but those fire-eaters who, in their persecuting zeal, gratuitously charge the Protestants with all heinous outrages, and so upset the peace and quiet of the realm. However radical in most of his religious views, Calvin is very moderate and prudent in his politics: a king is the Lord's anointed;

[1] Calvin's translation of his own Latin work into French is a significant landmark in the history of the gradual rise of the vernacular to literary dignity and common use, even within the field of serious prose. It is interesting to note in this connexion that by the *ordonnance* of Villers-Cotterets (August 1539) the French language became the official medium for judicial debates and state papers.

to threaten property is a fearful crime; the German Anabaptists are abominable; let no law-abiding citizen be mistaken for those monsters!

In the body of the book the argument moves on, impassioned at heart, but self-possessed, lucid, and cogent. It wields that supreme force of demonstration, an absolute unconsciousness of its own postulates. Calvin's idea of an angry and vengeful God, in apparent arbitrariness seeking 'His own pleasure', is that of most minds of the time, but he pushes it to an extreme, in the spirit of the most wrathful prophets, without wincing. When he touches on what he holds to be the weak points in the armour of the Church, his righteous indignation minces no words. He is ever alive to the duty of intolerance. The grossest charges are made, not against the black sheep in the orthodox clergy, but against all clerics. Addressing the King who, though he secretly felt the force of the Reformers' case, was determined to remain strictly within the pale, Calvin calls the Mass, Purgatory, &c., *tel fatras*.

Whatever exception the reader may take to this or that show of violence or unfairness, there grows upon him an irresistible impression of sincerity and eloquence. The dogmatism of it all, the harsh delineation of such a diagram of the spiritual world, are lost upon him as he abandons himself to the sheer pressure of driving logic; and he may even feel himself moved by such a thorough sense of the utter miseries of life. Indeed, a kind of poetry pierces through a style that is not only balanced and soberly musical but appeals to the sensations through the raciness of concrete terms, and at times reveals its imaginative powers by grand Biblical phrases, grown so familiar that they are embedded in the language.

Rabelais

Our first impression of Rabelais[1] is one of sheer jollity and zest.

---

[1] François Rabelais (1483?–1553), born near Chinon, belonged successively to two monastic orders. He frequented humanist circles, studied medicine, perhaps in Paris, taught and practised it at Montpellier and Lyons, published medical texts, travelled four times to Italy with members of the Du Bellay family, again taught and practised medicine, and was given two nominal incumbencies, one of them at Meudon, near Paris. The popular success of a sort of chapbook (*Grandes et inestimables croniques du grant et énorme géant Gargantua*, Lyons 1532) suggested his *Horribles et espouvantables faictz et prouesses du très renommé Pantagruel, fils du grant géant Gargantua*, 1532, which he

We seem to recognize the merry excitement: the heady wine of the Renaissance is working itself off. Humanism has opened vast fields, spurred intellectual hopes. The sense of fresh experience and abounding knowledge wells up all through these extraordinary books. It is less with literary scholarship that Rabelais plies us—though he had read the classics and minor authors extensively—than with the wealth of an erudition that includes the still amorphous mass of science: medicine first, of which he is a master, and its appurtenances; law, civil and canon; government, custom, geography, voyages, the new discoveries; the arts, and the crafts of town and country. And most of all, words—an inexhaustible store of language, learned or popular, national, provincial, dialectal, foreign, with artificial terms thrown in; words, that are to the writer the source of a unique joy. Obviously he cannot resist their spell; the pleasure of an unexpected association repeats itself indefinitely; he is swept off his feet, and the flood pours over whole pages, in endless lists of synonyms and series of epithets.

And yet, we sense him watching every step warily. A cool reason dwells at the core of his eagerness. This typical man of the Renaissance is singularly alive to the errors and excesses that beset his own day, like all past days: dogmatism, fanaticism, pedantry. His favourite attitude is criticism, diffidence; his is the mocking mind. The standard is the golden mean—that tutelary notion upon which the French instinct, and French thought, will fall back again and again; it was Jean de Meung's, and will be Molière's. And so Rabelais, who seems often drunk with words, is a keen satirist of all formulae, tricks of tongue, phrases, jugglery. Scholasticism has been found wanting; but so, equally, have the shibboleths of the present. We are treated to choice samples of the solemn fussiness of lawyers, the brags of statesmen, the empty oracles of the Sorbonists, and even some of the claptrap that clerics pass off for dogma. For all, laughter will be the best remedy—laughter, the privilege of man. Rightminded people best know how to be merry. Through chapter after chapter of *Gargantua* and *Pantagruel* the huge comedy of the world,

followed up with the *Vie inestimable du grant Gargantua, père de Pantagruel*, 1534. Next came *Le Tiers Livre des faictz et dictz héroïques du noble Pantagruel*, 1546; and *Le Quart Livre* (incomplete 1548, complete 1552). A *Cinquiesme et dernier livre*, which came out in two instalments after his death, is held to be not entirely genuine.

and of life, is displayed as a pageant. But if derision is in the meaning it is not in the tone. Appearances are kept, and forms observed, for caution is necessary to a writer in holy orders. The wise will take light hints; they will break the bone, and suck the marrow, finding the joke all the more effective because it is indirect, a matter of half, or apparently serious, statement. Rabelais, indeed, far from being only the god of rollicking mirth, may be called the greatest French humourist, and Sterne was not mistaken who chose him for his master. Local colour is one form of humorous precision; the war of the *fouaces* is framed in the familiar, grotesquely tame setting of a rustic, humdrum, unheroic district on the smiling bank of the Loire. Technical detail is another: the story of the storm which so terrifies Panurge is told as by some old tar—with his tongue in his cheek.

Thus comic invention is everywhere given ample scope. It does not lack variety, but realism is its favourite method; and within the wide possibilities of this some strains crop up so often that the adjective 'Rabelaisian' has become a label for full relish in handling certain aspects of physical life. Coarseness is there, undeniably, and readers to whom nothing can make it acceptable will be nauseated. These would seem to be but few. The miseries of the flesh are faced with no trace of a snicker, and the broad laugh carries with it the cleansing virtue of frankness. Sterne, who is much less shocking, is far less healthy. At bottom, this is not merely the old *esprit gaulois* let loose—the delight in defying taboos and ignoring proprieties; there is a philosophical soul to the cynicism, in itself cheap. There is room for nothing in that full presence of the body but the complete acceptance, which takes the sting from its innocent animality. The mood is not the disgust of the ascetic and the Christian pessimist, but the quiet tolerance of the scientist, the doctor (Rabelais was both), and, to use one term that covers his whole intent, the naturalist.

For nature indeed is the main prop and stay of his ideas. The serious purpose that lies everywhere in the background can best be summed up under this label. It is here that his philosophy is original, improving upon the common tenets of Renaissance humanism. His trust in nature and man sees beyond his age, to a future of progress through reason, in which a distinctly modern ideal is outlined. What religion can be associated with such trends? While the texts by no means support the theory that he had secretly given up Christianity, it must be admitted that his belief is not a little tinged with what will be the deism of the next centuries. His biting satire of monks and clergy would point to Protestant leanings—which he had; but he was repelled by Calvin's intolerance, and his naturalistic faith stands at the opposite pole to that of the Genevan prophet.

His positive teaching has its main focus in the description of the 'Abbaye de Thélème', a humanist, openly aristocratic Utopia, with no room for More's equalitarian dreams. Nor, certainly, are spiritual cravings, properly so called, emphasized in the picture. The stress is laid above all on the easy spontaneity of well-born, naturally refined people; on the sweet amenities of culture, and the legitimate claims of the aesthetic life. Women, in this lay monastery, are admitted as fully equal to men, and the sexes dwell together on unexceptionable terms. 'Pantagruélisme', the most definite formula of Rabelais's ethical code, derives much from the wisdom of Epicurus; it is 'certayne gayeté d'esprit conficte en mépris des choses fortuites'.

His views on education are justly famous. They reflect on the one hand the Renaissance thirst for encyclopaedic knowledge. Boys in colleges are stupefied with merely verbal drill and scholastic routine. A good curriculum should provide for the right use of every hour; let a student learn all day, neglect the chaff of commentaries, and stick to texts. As a result, the programme of Gargantua's studies is formidable. On the other hand a wise cure for bookishness shall be his initiation into the technique of all crafts; and what the training of the body means to health, sanity and mental poise must ever be kept in mind.

There is in Rabelais an artist, great but very unequal. The idea of formal perfection is foreign to him; he works by instinct, and is subject to lapses. His brilliant gift for story-telling finds a felicitous complement in his invention of picturesque characters. The two official heroes, whose early experiences owe their substance largely to actual episodes of the author's youth, develop more or less into his mouthpieces and into symbols of the peace-loving kindliness popularly associated with gigantic size. Far more convincing, and highly keyed up, are the figures of Frère Jean des Entommeures, the burly fighting monk, and Panurge, whose nearest relative in English literature might be Shakespeare's Autolycus—a shifty, shameless, crafty fellow, an amusing rogue, but a pest. Both portraits have the largeness of touch and vigour of tone we admire in Chaucer.

The later books betray some reliance upon artificial development; invention is flagging. The action plods through Pantagruel's wanderings in the fourth part and the more and more allegorical episodes of the fifth, and tedium descends upon the reader. Another sign of strain is the rank bitterness of the open attacks upon all spiritual authorities, no longer castigated with good humour. Altogether, after the first *Pantagruel* in which he tried his hand, Rabelais reached his highest mark in the *Gargantua* and the *Tiers Livre*. There we find the masterpieces of his narrative and ironical art, such as the thirty-third chapter of the former, and also some pages of sustained, grave, and pregnant eloquence, like Gargantua's letter to his son (*Pantagruel*, viii), which should go far to redeem him from the charge of moral levity. A decline then sets in, reaching such a degree finally that the suspicion of another hand cannot be resisted.[1]

[1] Noël du Fail (1520–91), an original figure, should be mentioned here, for his connexion with Rabelais, whom he imitated (not very happily), leaves him, apart from the master, in a secluded chapter of literary history. His *Propos rustiques* (1547), *Baliverneries* (1548), and *Contes et discours* (1586) are charming sketches of peasant life and village manners in a spirit of fresh, sober realism. Their truth was not to be equalled for a long time, even if the scale of the drawing is altogether reduced.

CHAPTER XII

The Pléiade

I. THE GROUP AND ITS CREED

THE Pléiade were actually, for some years, a group of brother poets, perhaps the most coherent in the history of French literature. Possible causes for their rise are not far to seek. Only idealistic motives, and opposition to some privilege, could unite artists who were essentially individualists in such a common purpose. The privilege was the all but official prestige of what may be called, in a loose sense, the school of Marot (who died in 1544). He had left hardly any doctrine, but his example opened a safe path to at least fair success. There was, however, nothing inspiring in an almost exclusively formal art that bordered dangerously upon artifice. It was natural that the dryness, the sterility of a technique of elegance and wit, which only the master could raise to any striking perfection, should be resented. The vitality of the Renaissance was spurring the French genius to high endeavours, and the imitation of the classics, in the manner of the Italians, was obviously the task set for the new generation. This abounding surge of youthful ambition and strength is the real origin of the Pléiade. At other times, the belated legacy of the Rhétoriqueurs and the favour enjoyed by a Mellin de Saint Gelais might have been accepted with indifference. But in the fifth decade of the century their predicament began to rouse protests from eager, generous spirits. Some of them, growing conscious of their affinities, joined forces, and as soon as the magnetism of their combined effort was in the air, more were attracted.

Ronsard was soon to be the chief figure and recognized leader of the group, but at first the impulse came from scholars and teachers, Jacques Peletier, Dorat. The meeting of Du Bellay and Ronsard, in 1545, started a warm friendship, the germ of a league of talent, united by personal sympathy. At the Collège de Coqueret, in Paris, Dorat taught Greek, and the enthusiasm of discovery fired his disciples, Ronsard, Du Bellay, Baïf, and others. Ronsard's first name for the

group—the 'Brigade', a word then freshly taken from the Italian
—simply stressed the bond of a common purpose. From the École
Lyonnaise came Scève's disciple, Pontus de Tyard; from the Collège
de Boncourt, Jodelle, who made a reputation with the first French
regular tragedy, *Cléopâtre* (1553); and Rémy Belleau, who turned
Anacreon—then newly edited by Henri Estienne—into French verse.
When in 1556 Ronsard tentatively used the name 'Pléiade', which
raised some gibes but was eventually accepted, the list was still
somewhat fluid, Dorat being included only at a later date. With the
seven of the final galaxy, some more modest stars, like Peletier, Des
Autels, La Péruse, were allowed at one time or other to mix their rays.

Thomas Sebillet's *Art poétique* (1548) both confirmed and alarmed
the banded faithful. He agreed to the necessity of a poetical change,
but was that dangerous ally, a half-and-half reformer, and showed
far too much leniency to the Marot school. It was then that Du
Bellay, commissioned by his friends, wrote his *Deffence et illustration
de la langue françoise* (1549). The controversy thus started lasted some
years, the outstanding texts on the Pléiade side being Du Bellay's
Preface to the second edition of *L'Olive* (1550), and Ronsard's Preface
to the first series of his *Odes* (1550). The conclusion was a move
towards peace, symbolized by Ronsard's *Ode to Saint-Gelais* (1553);
the new poets had won, but they now knew that in their arrogance
and scorn for their elders they had gone too far.

The *Deffence* is indeed a clarion call, with all the eager eloquence
of young enthusiasm and some of its hasty conclusions. Scholars
have been at pains to trace its theses to Italian works of criticism,
chiefly Sperone Speroni's *Dialogo delle lingue*, or to French books,
like Sebillet's, and as far back as old Quintilian. The harvest is con-
clusive: little remains that is at all original. But the creative force
here lies, as so often, in other than purely intellectual values. An
impassioned feeling, a patriotism, sounds the ringing note of a
declaration that the next two centuries were to make good: it was
now imperative that the French tongue and its literature should rise
to a prominent place in the modern world. If the language seemed
poor the reason was lack of cultivation; due love and care, a full
employment of all resources, including archaic, recent, and technical words, a search for the figurative phrases demanded by poetic
diction must make it equal to its high destiny. In that process the

classical models would, of course, play a part; but not only must the absurd attempt to rival Latin writers in their own tongue be renounced; translation pure and simple from their works must be banned, for it necessarily implied one of two things, slavery or treason. Far different was the wise imitation that would cull a phrase, an image, or a happy flight of fancy, from Horace or Virgil; the modern poet might borrow feathers but his plumage must be none the less his own. To dare was an essential part of his duty, and to attempt nobly. Let him drop the medieval forms whose mould was too narrow for large inspirations, and which had, moreover, been used to satiety. Let French poetry tackle the great genres with which the glory that was Greece and Rome was associated. It was good to practise the epigram, the pastoral, and the satire, but far better to plant the epic, the ode, regular tragedy and comedy, on French soil; and that short ode, the sonnet, which in a limited compass could rise to an ample theme, as the Italians had shown. And most of all, let the poet bear in his heart a fervent, almost a religious sense of the exacting labour to which he must devote all his energy, all his life.

For practical purposes, one may hold these to have been the common precepts followed by the Pléiade. A more cautious, tempered, and adaptable set of similar ideas, put forth a few years afterwards by Jacques Peletier in his *Art Poétique* (1555), stands nearer to the actual practice of the group after experience had toned down early excesses. But the *Deffence* had won in literary history the place of a landmark, which it deserves to keep.

2. DU BELLAY[1]

Ronsard's supremacy was a fact undisputed by his brother poets. Du Bellay acknowledged it with genuine admiration and graceful

[1] Joachim Du Bellay, a member of a noble family, rooted in Anjou, which during his lifetime gave several high dignitaries to Church and State, was born in 1522. An orphan, and early afflicted with deafness, he studied law and then the humanities at the Collège de Coqueret, with Ronsard, Baïf, and others. He published several works separately, e.g. the *Deffence et illustration*, &c., in 1549; a series of love sonnets, *L'Olive* (1549, again 1550); a *Recueil de poésie*; verse translations from Virgil, &c. From 1553 to 1557 he was in Rome, as secretary to his cousin, the ambassador Jean du Bellay. On his return he published *Les Antiquitez de Rome*, *Les Regrets*, *Divers jeux rustiques*, and four books of Latin poems. He lived at court, received an incumbency, wrote a satire, *Le Poète courtisan*, and several *Discours au roi*, and died in 1560.

modesty. And yet, in his own case, the estimate may be revised, for nowadays his intimate and subdued note appeals to us quite as much, or more.

His short career shows a progress towards the kind of poetry best suited to his temperament—personal expression. The sureness of his advance makes him an outstanding harbinger of future romantic developments.

L'Olive is still entangled in Petrarchism and imitation. Its Platonic idealism is a preoccupation of the brain, not an emotion of the heart. But the awareness of suffering which a true poet ever carries within himself—and which, whatever the occasion, has a genuineness of its own, since to him the essence, of melancholy is enclosed in the very flavour of life—stands Du Bellay in good stead. The foundation in fact of his love complaint hardly matters; what counts is its charm and the flowing suggestiveness of its elegiac music. The sonnets, all written in ten-syllabled lines, are not perfectly regular, according to the pattern that was to be settled very shortly after. Such as they are, with their monotony and their too frequent lapses into classical allusions, they ring a truly lyrical note, and deserve to be read, not only for the sake of the justly famous no. 113 but for a number of others no less graceful. The two shorter series, *XIII sonnets de l'honneste amour* and *Les Amours de J. Du Bellay*, have the same musical appeal, with a maturer feeling and a more sober art. Four sonnets of the latter are in alexandrines, and at once justify the departure. by their fuller melody. That the inspiration of *l'Olive* was at least half conventional is plainly confessed in *Contre les Pétrarquistes*, where nature has its fling at a fashion grown hard to bear. But a more moving utterance, welling up from the depths of the poet's repressed self, is the *Complainte du Désespéré*, a singularly naked avowal of the wearing sadness of days, which relies on no art but utter candour.

Du Bellay's best and most typical work is *Les Regrets*. The vein of personal elegy and brooding meditation flows there as decisively as it will, some three centuries later, in Lamartine. Mythological allusion is almost entirely gone. The sonnet, practically regular and written in twelve-syllabled lines, unites a more ample scope with a still easy movement. The singleness of the mood covers a rich variety of themes. The language is direct, and its simplicity does not detract from its vigour. Of these lines, very little but the spelling has aged. We find in them a kind of happy medium between the classical values, the desire for which is already at work, and the pre-romantic ones, to be discerned in the background. Even premonitions of a kind of symbolism are to be met with, as in this passage:

> Las et nous cependant nous consumons notre aage
> Sur le bord incogneu d'un estrange rivage,
> Où le malheur nous fait ces tristes vers chanter,
>
> Comme on voit quelquefois, quand la mort les appelle,
> Arrangez flanc à flanc parmy l'herbe nouvelle,
> Bien loing sur un estang trois cygnes lamenter.

The *Antiquitez de Rome* are a wonderful anticipation of the eighteenth-century poetry of ruins. They have most of the merits of the *Regrets*, but the subject led inevitably to a somewhat more rhetorical treatment.

Du Bellay's gifted personality possessed other features. In the abundance of his occasional verse talent is plentiful, and he is a proof of the fact that a lyrical temper does not preclude, would rather favour, that vivacity of reaction which is the source of realism and satire. A realistic mind may naturally develop into a humorous one, and, indeed, we come across delightful examples of humour and fancy, as the *Musagnœomachie*, or fight of the Muses and Ignorance, or of satirical pieces, like the *Poète courtisan*, as effective as they are graphic. In the *Divers jeux rustiques*, one of the most winning examples of his varied work, the pastoral spirit, whether moulded on some classical precedent or striking out for itself, receives expressions of simple elegance and delicate loveliness. The song *D'un vanneur de blé* deserves its popularity; but many more might be quoted, such as this fragment from the *Chant de l'amour et de l'hiver*:

> Les longs souspirs de ma plaincte,
> Dessus la plaine depeincte,
> S'en volent de toutes parts,
> Et des vents l'haleine forte
> Euanouis les emporte
> Parmy ce grand vague espars.

A vein, rare in French poetry, of familiar sympathy with pet animals enlivens the *Épitaphe d'un petit chien* and *Épitaphe d'un chat*. What is it that gives so much charm to these trifles and makes almost everything that Du Bellay wrote attractive? We must fall back on the spontaneity of a truly poetical genius, a gift which he shared with Ronsard but of which he had, when all is said, an even larger portion. How grand might have been the workings of his creative imagination if his life had not been cut short, one may gather, for instance, from the close of his *Hymne de la Surdité* where, paying his friend Ronsard a generous tribute, he rises in fact above him by a Keats-like fullness of mental realization in which the symbol is naturally invested with concreteness:

> La se void le Silence assis à la main dextre
> Le doigt dessus la lèvre: assise à la senestre
> Est la Melancholie au sourcil enfoncé:
> L'Estude tenant l'œil sur le livre abbaissé
> Se sied un peu plus bas: l'Ame imaginative,
> Les yeux levez au ciel, se tient contemplative
> Debout devant ta face. . . .

3. RONSARD[1]

Ronsard's indebtedness to the classics can hardly be exaggerated. He owed them his high notion of poetry and his ideal of form. Glowing humanist faith was the main inspiration of his art, and his borrowings from Horace, the Anthology, &c., are numberless. At the same time, the very influences that stimulated and nourished him gave his invention, both as to subject and phrasing, a set habit of looking back for time-honoured patterns. His, no doubt, is no purely imitative art. His voice from the first had an individual accent, which strengthened as he grew. But while Nature had made

---

[1] Pierre de Ronsard, born in 1524 at the family manor-house of La Poissonnière, near Vendôme, was a page at court, travelling abroad in that quality, but while still young he practically lost his hearing. He studied Greek with Dorat, took a share in the preparation of Du Bellay's *Deffence*, and published *Odes* (four books 1550, fifth 1552), *Amours* (1552), *Bocage royal* (1554), *Hymnes* (1555), and a collected edition of poems (1560), which established him as the leader of the new poetry. Further editions incorporated minor pieces. In 1573 he published the first four books of an epic poem, the *Franciade*. His grief at the sight of religious and political strife suggested his *Discours des misères de ce temps* (1562–3, &c.). The *Sonnets pour Hélène* (1578) are the outpouring of a belated passion. He spent his last years in retirement, holding small church livings, and revised his poems for new editions (1578, 1584, &c.). He died in 1585.

him a poet, and her gifts marked him out to lead the way into a creative era, he never lost sight of the bounds within which originality had to move. His work, as a result, was more retrospective and allusive than his vigorous genius was cut out for. This, of course, agreed only too well with the limited perspective of his age. His pindaric odes, and his incomplete epic, were hailed by the *élite* with proud delight and awe: did not French literature through him reach the acme of her ambitions? The idea so formed of his supreme merits tended to obscure his more substantial pioneering, and the unjust neglect into which he was soon to fall may largely have arisen from this error. To look upon Ronsard primarily as an echo of the Greek and Latin poets would naturally encourage critics to charge him with having spoken Latin and Greek in French. Whatever the reason, the lesson of his life and achievement was not so plain as it might have been.

To us, his greatness is conspicuous. When Sainte-Beuve and the romantics in the early nineteenth century rediscovered him his fame entered a second cycle that will suffer no eclipse. He holds a place securely among the path-openers of French poetry, and our gratitude goes out to him not only for his anticipation of the classical art he heralded more than the seventeenth century knew, but for the unlimited growth of lyricism that the last 150 years have witnessed, and that now claims him as the most eminent of its early masters.

It would not be fair simply to write off the pindaric odes. Much talent went into the doomed performance, and the energy spent on filling the dead form with life was not entirely wasted. The long poem, *A Michel de l'Hospital*, with really great moments, is a remarkable effort. Still, it is a relief to us, as it was obviously to Ronsard, when the pretence of the 'strophe, antistrophe, epode' is dropped and the poet heads with a sure instinct for the free development of a theme, which in structure and amplitude is subject only to its inner law. This is the very description of the modern lyric, and indeed a fountain of song wells up here that has since played intermittently but never stopped for long. The liberation, we must own, is not complete. A stubborn habit of mythological allusion lingers; commonplaces preserve a hold upon a mind nurtured in the respect of ancient rhetoric, and reminiscent phrasing may clash with the movement of what is thought and felt spontaneously. But as for the language, the fallacious charge that it is pedantically loaded with words foreign to living French and coined on classical precedents has long been exploded. Such cases are relatively rare. The remote flavour of scholarship that is most frequently perceived is a matter not chiefly of expression but of theme, imagery, and atmosphere. In spite of all, could anything be more modern than these stanzas, *A Cupidon* (Book III, Ode xix), which live through music, and music that is subtly suggestive?

> Le jour pousse la nuit,
>   Et la nuit sombre
> Pousse le jour qui luit
>   D'une obscure ombre.
>
> L'automne suit l'esté,
>   Et l'âpre rage
> Des vents n'a point été
>   Après l'orage.
>
> Mais le mal nonobstant
>   D'amour dolente
> Demeure en moi constant
>   Et ne s'alente. . . .

One hesitates to quote such a well-known masterpiece as *De l'élection de son sépulchre*, with its lovely short stanza, conveying so aptly the light dreamy indulgence of a fanciful melancholy; or the stanza, equally short and no less musical, of 'Bel aubespin verdissant . . .'. But a brief passage from the close of the ode *A Monseigneur d'Angoulesme* may be given for the sake of its delicate symbolism:

> Puis comme une voix qui se plaint,
> Au soir, dedans une antre ouie,
> Ou de nuict, comme un songe feint,
> Parmy l'air s'est évanouie. . . .

The love poems are of mixed quality. Whether the heroine be Cassandre, Marie, Hélène, or sundry other names that just flit across a page, enough is known to make good Ronsard's plea that he wrote not from a perfunctory sense of duty to a convention but under the stress of sincere feeling. But the sentiment expressed has little power to move us. Not that the Petrarchism which almost rules over these elegiac strains was merely a fashion of the age. The tradition had grown so binding that the attitude had become natural; and although a vein of sensuousness, warm and thoroughly pagan, crops up here and there in Ronsard's work, the artist's and the man's lives could be pitched in different keys. What leaves us cool is that although love is an individual relation, generalities have so much to do with the emotions expressed that these lose their identity on a plane of commonplace moralizing, enlivened with a touch of self-centred preoccupation. The destructiveness of time is what really stirs the writer—the fading of beauty when passion has not been fulfilled, the shortness of life, and the cheerless comfort of literary fame. So, we have endless variations on *carpe diem*—a theme that would ill suit a disciple of Petrarch, if Petrarch was to be taken quite seriously —and reproachful promises of the immortality a poet can give. But since the world began such elements of universal experience have been transmuted into fine poetry; and it is true that Ronsard very often makes lovely melodies out of these simple notes. Many of his sonnets and odes on themes of love were, in fact, set to be sung by composers of the time, but they have their most genuine music in themselves. 'Mignonne, allons voir si la rose . . .' has a Japanese brevity and perfection of line. *La Mort de Marie* is only mildly pathetic; but 'Comme on voit sur la branche au mois de may la rose . . .' is none the less a gem. The *Sonnets pour Hélène*, written late, express a shade of sentiment graver, and it seems deeper, overshadowed by the reality of an approaching end. And there is logic in the fate that has made 'Quand vous serez bien vieille . . .', where the essence of Ronsard's love poetry is enclosed in fourteen lines, the most popular of his pieces.

After this it is refreshing to come upon particular themes, places, and people in much of the occasional verse, such as 'ecglogues', 'élégies', 'hymnes', &c., in which some of Ronsard's best work is preserved. He loved his 'Vendômois', and gives us pleasing glimpses of a land that is extreme in nothing and has almost every soft attraction. Provincial realism is introduced with a delightful effect in such light pieces as the *Voyage de Tours*; and the appeal to the *Bûcherons de la forest de Gastine* to spare trees that are the haunts of Dryads is not an exercise in classical mythology but an effusion from the heart. *De l'élection de son sépulchre*, again, is the poem of a favourite site. Many adaptations or imitations of ancient texts, especially Horace and Anacreon, are thus stamped with genuineness, and saved from the artificiality that their origin might have implied. Often enough these addresses to friends, fellow poets, statesmen, bring us valuable autobiographical information—as do the *Hymne de l'automne*; *A Rémy Belleau*; *A Jean de la Péruse*; *A Pierre L'Escot*, &c. That the *Hymnes* generally are Ronsard's fullest and most thoughtful utterances, with a breadth and sustained power that makes us think of Victor Hugo, is commonly acknowledged.

To leave the *Franciade* unfinished was the wisest course; but it should never have been begun. The poet vainly tries to galvanize what is hopelessly dead into some sort of life by stressing such concrete episodes as the building of the fleet, and by bathing his story, as often as he can, in the light of nature. His subservience to classical precedent remains strict, and no one would be expected to believe, even imaginatively, in the dim world thus called up, with its faked archaism and strange anticipatory glimmers of a distant era. The choice of the ten-syllabled line, too short a measure, was wrong. Modern poets had yet to realize that equivalents for the ancient epic should be sought, if at all, in radically new fields of literature.

Ronsard was better inspired when, moved by feelings of patriotic anxiety, he poured his indignation and eager entreaties into the *Discours*; in which impassioned eloquence rises at times to grandeur under the stress of his actual fears and hopes. The religious issue is not avoided. In youth he had been shaken by the plea of the Reformers, and in his maturity he sides vehemently with the traditional Church.

When his contribution to the growth of French poetry is assessed, it is seen to have been rich and essential indeed. His name did not long remain associated with advances in which his example was in fact creative. But the bulk of his work, when allowance has been made for his mistakes, belongs now to the record of living verse. His initiatives in the domain of metrical experiment were particularly fecund, and though he made excellent and significant use of light measures and stanzas he stamped himself chiefly on the course of French literature by making the alexandrine (in the *Hymnes*, the *Discours*, &c.), the set form of serious poetry.

4. OTHER POETS

Among friends or sympathizers of the movement one is bound
to respect Ronsard's final choice of the five who, with Du Bellay
and himself, made up the seven stars of the Pléiade. One of these,
Jean Dorat or d'Aurat, owed the honour to other claims than those
of creative poetry; as head of the Collège de Coqueret he played
a decisive part in awaking the zeal of young humanists, teaching
them Greek and revealing to them not only the great classics but
the minor figures of the alexandrine age. In addition, a word on
Peletier, whose death made room for Dorat in the leader's list, will
not be amiss.

Antoine de Baïf (1532–89) had genuine talent of a minor kind.
His love poems (*Amours de Méline*, 1552; *Amours de Francine*, 1555)
have some sweetness and melody, amid a good deal of convention;
the *Météores* (1567) and chiefly the *Mimes, Enseignements et Proverbes*
(1576) aim higher, drawing their inspiration from science, politics,
or ethics with fair success. The pity is that at his best moments Baïf
usually reminds us of somebody else—Jean Lemaire, Ronsard, or Du
Bellay. With a perceptive ear he had an inquisitive and adventurous mind, and he was something of a faddist, declaring for
spelling reform, a phonetic orthography, metrics based on the
length of sounds, like that of the ancients. *Les Etrènes de poézie
fransoêze an vers mezurés* made no mark, but the Académie de Poésie
et de Musique, founded by the king at his suggestion (1570), did
much to associate these two arts more closely in principle as they
were already associated in fact.

Rémy Belleau (1528–77) was probably the most gifted of the five,
as he was altogether the most successful. He turned Anacreon into
French verse (1556), and never was a translation more opportune.
His *Bergerie* (1565) has just enough realism and observation to com-
pensate for a set prettiness that, nevertheless, borders dangerously
on the affected. One piece, *Avril*, has found its way into all anthologies, but he is more than the lucky writer of one good poem. His
most original work is in the *Amours et nouveaux eschanges des pierres
précieuses*, eked out with Biblical paraphrases (1576). The careful
search for delicate analogies that lies confessedly at the heart of
this collection sits pleasantly upon him. He likes gems, and can

polish verse to reflect something of their lustre. A myth will account
wittily for affinities; and the whole makes a handsome compliment
to some noble lady. This is not great poetry; but while the second-
rate, then and at all times, has so much to offer that is merely
commonplace, there is a freshness of invention and wording in lines
like these (from the *Pierre du Coq*):

> Oyseau à la creste pourprée,
> Compagnon de l'Aube dorée,
> Trompette des feux du Soleil,
> Qui te perches à la même heure
> Qu'il plonge en mer sa chevelure
> Pour se rendre alaigre au travail . . .

Étienne Jodelle (1532–73) is of interest chiefly as a playwright,
but his lyric poetry deserves more attention than it usually receives.
Though very different from Rémy Belleau's, it should rank a close
second to it. His collected poems, published soon after his death
(*Œuvres et Meslanges poétiques*, 1574), are amorous, religious, or
satirical. In all a vigour of thought is apparent, a terse phrasing, which
turns not seldom to harshness, but which quite often produces
striking lines. The tercets of *A sa muse* foreshadow the theme of
Vigny's *L'Esprit pur*. The sonnet *L'Amour céleste* expresses a noble
idea worthily. This quatrain from another sonnet may give an idea
of his manner:

> J'aime le verd laurier, dont l'hyver ni la glace
> N'effacent la verdeur, en tout victorieuse,
> Monstrant l'éternité à jamais bien heureuse,
> Que le temps, ny la mort ne change ny efface. . . .

Pontus de Tyard (1521–1605) is an arresting person. He was a
bishop, wrote verse and prose, was keenly interested in science and
philosophy, and even published works in those fields: and he played
a part in politics with dignity and courage. His chief collection of
poems in the manner of Petrarch, *Les Erreurs amoureuses*, filled three
successive books (1549–51–55). He came from the Mâconnais, and
was thus within the circle of Lyonnese influence. His effort to concentrate and refine thought, his treatise on *La Fureur poétique*, his
frequent obscurity, reveal his discipleship to Scève. On the other
hand his connexion with Ronsard's group, whose work he pre-

ceded by a few years, makes him an intermediary between the two schools. He has thus several claims to be remembered, but his poetry is the least valid; it suffers from some artifice and coldness, and only rarely finds sufficient force of expression to redeem these faults.

Jacques Peletier (1517–82) led a wandering life, and was another of those Renaissance scholars who responded very fully to the call of knowledge. His poetic output included *Œuvres poétiques* (1547), *Amour des amours* (1555), *La Savoye* (1572), *Louanges* (1581), but his importance to the literary historian lies mainly in his critical writings (chiefly the *Art poétique*, 1555, of which a word has been said above). His early verse is very much in the manner of Marot, but the *Amour des amours* grafts bolder strains of philosophical imagination upon the current Petrarchism, rising with the flight of the soul to the high heaven of love and poetry. It is a pity that such an original attempt was not matched by beauty and harmony of language.

5. THE HERITAGE OF THE PLÉIADE

The literary heritage of the Pléiade was, to all appearances, not very substantial. The movement had hardly lost its first impetus when religious and civil strife broke out, and for nearly thirty years purely artistic issues were obscured. When the wise rule of Henri IV pacified the country, the diffused longing for peace and order came to a head in the desire—itself a pointer to a discipline of ideas and forms—for a clear and coherent hierarchy of values. At the deepest level of intention the Pléiade had worked for no other ideal, but on the surface its very zeal and enthusiasm, its ambitious poetical attempts, and some excesses in the imitation of the classics stamped it with the characteristics of a revolutionary and erratic endeavour. The idea began to spread that Ronsard and his friends had done violence to the genius of the national tongue. When Malherbe in his turn reformed French poetry, he rose against an unsettled condition of the language and an uncertainty of taste in which the responsibility of the Pléiade was apparently involved, and he censured Ronsard pitilessly.

But while he condemned, he imitated him; and a saner view of the course of literature must acknowledge the lasting effect of the idealism and talent which had gone into the effort of the Pléiade.

Malherbe started from a conception of poetry, of its exalted nature, quality, and dignity, that had been expressed, and illustrated, by Ronsard and his friends with a clarity and a determination unknown before. This high purpose and the sense of aesthetic and moral duty were the legacy of the group to the future, silently integrated in the background of assumptions that supported the creative activity of the classical century, and in time becoming a permanent part of literary tradition. How Ronsard became a vital and individual influence again at a far later date belongs to the history of the Romantic movement.

CHAPTER XIII

Learning, Politics, History

WHILE the ardour of the French Renaissance was not extinguished, it was sobered in the many anxieties that beset the latter half of the century. The new learning had permeated daily life and was thus more perceptibly in touch with the problems of a modern nation that felt herself coming of age. Serious disturbances were undermining the increasingly ambitious authority of the kings, while the established Church was threatened with disruption. The chapter of the Italian wars had closed, but France remained uneasily aware of the formidable power of Spain, and the steady growth of Elizabethan England was changing the balance in the north, creating a solid centre for the hopes of the Reformed groups. The editing, study, and commentary of old texts were still the chosen task of scholars; but controversies of all kinds kept arising—civil, moral, and political issues which tended to eclipse humanism. It was now that the French people awoke to a clearer consciousness of their long past and an interest in their national origins. It is thus permissible in a survey of the literature of the time to associate learning with political thought and history.

Amyot[1]

Amyot's work is in some ways a transition between the earlier and the later aspects of the Renaissance; there lingers in it some of the naïve idealism of the first flush. His claim to figure among the great humanists should not be based on the depth of his erudition but on the natural ease with which he turned the lessons of the past into spiritual food for the present. The graceful paganism of the Greek novels was deemed innocuous by the future bishop, but in Plutarch

[1] Jacques Amyot (1513–93), born at Melun of humble parents, taught at the University of Bourges, became tutor to the children of the royal family, *grand aumônier de France*, and bishop of Auxerre. He translated Greek novels (*Daphnis et Chloé*, 1559) and Plutarch (*Vies des hommes illustres*, 1559; *Œuvres morales*, 1572). His old age was darkened by the hostility of the fanatical Ligueurs in his diocese.

he found less specious incitements to Christian virtue. The age was ready for such doctrine; the cult of heroism suited the temper of a time when the spirit of chivalry was becoming transformed into a sense of exalted duty to the fatherland. In France especially the *Vies des hommes illustres* were to be for several centuries a source of patriotic inspiration and, at revolutionary moments, of republican fervour. There had already been partial translations of Plutarch. At the request of François Iᵉʳ Amyot accomplished the whole task, to the delight of innumerable readers. The pleasure we still have in his company has its roots in a fortunate and genuine, because spontaneous, harmony. The French author's *bonhomie* corresponds to the moralizing good nature of the Greek writer; the simplicity of his style and the looseness of sixteenth-century syntax are well adapted to the supple, easy-going manner. Never did narratives seem more faithfully to follow the course of events. Amyot's long, invertebrate periods are obviously not the outcome of a thought-out construction; they grow leisurely by the addition of one circumstance to another, as in the natural unwinding of memory. A perfect rendering of the original is not always to be taken for granted, and modern criticism has picked flaws in the scholarship; but the achievement is of the order of creative literature, and Plutarch's translator is justly given a place among the pioneers of French prose. Even the language of modern thought is his debtor for a number of words, coined on the pattern of a vocabulary that treasured up the wealth of ancient culture.

Henri Estienne

One of a famous dynasty of printers, publishers, and scholars, Henri Estienne (1531–98) united learning and literary talent no less brilliantly than Amyot. The union, however, in his case as well, did not prove entirely successful; while the writer always commands our respect, the scholar's fancy sometimes indulges in vagaries that take a pundit's breath away. But as a freelance of philology and a polemist, his gifts of intuition, wit, and style stand him in very good stead. He was chiefly stirred to combat by his susceptible linguistic nationalism. Although thoroughly steeped in Latin and familiar with the Italian tongue, he was a vigorous champion of his native language at a time when 'latinismes' were a constant tempta-

tion, and 'italianisme' a dangerous mode, encouraged by a Florentine queen. Estienne's *Précellence du langage françois* (1579) professes
to be only the first sketch of a promised work, which Henri III
urged him not to delay; but the scope of the book could hardly
be fuller, or perhaps we should say more ambitious. The cause is
good, and there was room for a spirited defence, since even cultivated French circles seemed hardly aware of the loyalty due from
conscious citizens to the common means of expression. Still, we
blush today at the evidences of a partiality which will be fatal to
the sanity of judgement. The grounds upon which French is pronounced superior to Italian are at times singularly weak or even
disingenuous, though several observations passed upon the genius
and facilities of the former are penetrating and highly suggestive.
The *Deux dialogues du nouveau langage françois italianizé* (1578) are
lighter and more entirely pleasant reading; the courteous debate
between Philausone and Celtophile raises many issues, some beyond
the pale of philology, and handles them with sense and graceful
ease. We have here an early example of a manner that was to become
characteristic of a whole province in modern French literature. These
treatises keep the fame of Henri Estienne green. His more specifically
learned works, like the *Thesaurus linguae graecae* (1572) and his bold
attempt at a satirical survey of the more external elements in Roman
Catholic worship (the *Apologie pour Hérodote*, 1566), have much
historical interest, but not the same appeal for the common reader.

Étienne Pasquier

Étienne Pasquier (1529?–1615) was another who united learning
and literature. An eminent representative of the higher middle class,
which was claiming, and securing, a larger share of public affairs
and of culture, he stands, like the noble-minded 'Chancelier',
Michel de l'Hospital, an advocate of tolerance at the darkest core of
a fanatical age. His *Exhortation aux princes* (1561) is a forceful plea
for freedom of conscience. In his controversy with the Jesuits, and
chiefly in his *Catéchisme des Jésuites* (1602), he uses the ironical method
of damaging, involuntary self-exposure which Pascal was to make
famous in the *Provinciales*. His *Recherches de la France*, published over
a long period from 1560, and the outcome of his impassioned interest in the national past, are his sentimental apology for the Gauls,

whose few obscure records he investigates with loving care and acumen, though not always in a sufficiently cool spirit. Not that he is lacking in critical faculty, but he tries to reconcile caution and feeling, as he candidly confesses. From the institutions and manners of earliest France he proceeds in due course to a survey of French poetry and the French language, and in his tentative way approaches many subjects more or less for the first time. Indeed, when all is said, Pasquier's robust and rich personality is predominantly that of a writer; he lives through the attraction of his style no less than the penetration of his mind; and his delightful letters deserve more than the occasional attention of the historian.

Claude Fauchet

The approximation to the modern idea of scholarship is clearest with Claude Fauchet (1530–1602). His attitude is definitely critical. More guarded than Pasquier's, his intuition does not grant itself the same free play; he makes fewer lucky guesses, commits fewer errors, and lays down safer foundations for the truth. His style has the relative heaviness of scrupulous statement, but is not destitute of graphic power. While he follows the tradition of the ancients, and purports to give the actual speeches of historical characters, he knows how to resist the spell of a legend: no Trojan Francus or Francion for him, no ampulla divinely brought to Reims, no preaching of the Apostles themselves in Gaul. A lawyer, with a sense of the respective rights of sovereign and subject, a sound Catholic, but of the 'gallican' way of thinking, he shares in the widespread love of language and poetry. Even more than his *Antiquitez gauloises et françoises* (published from 1579 to 1602), his *Recueil de l'origine de la langue et poésie françoise* (1581) retains its value as sound pioneer work, and is still a useful record of very early French writers.

Meanwhile, in the unsettled condition of affairs, controversies of all kinds were rife. Religious and political differences called forth numberless treatises or libels. Of the voices that rang out on this or that side, some have won a definite place in literary annals but only a few can be mentioned here. No contemporary orator was more famous than Michel de l'Hospital (1505–73), whose grave eloquence is weighted with a noble feeling of respect for all sincere belief.

Étienne de la Boétie (1530–63), Montaigne's friend, poured a youthful republicanism, which had no doubt been nurtured on the memories and masterpieces of Greek and Roman liberty, into a *Discours sur la servitude volontaire*, or *Contr'un*. When published after his premature death, in 1576, it encouraged the spirit of opposition to the progress of a practically unlimited monarchy. The Latin works of François Hotman (*Franco-Gallia*, 1573, translated the next year), and Duplessis-Mornay (*Vindiciae contra Tyrannos*, 1578), gave vent to the fierce reaction roused among the Protestants by the Massacre of Saint Bartholomew, and which attacked the root of the monarchical principle itself. Jean Bodin (1520–96) is a quieter figure, with the authority of a disinterested and almost impartial thinker. His lucid analysis of the conditions of government is instinct with the wisdom of an experienced and widely read observer. He is the mouthpiece of the sanity, ingrained in the upper middle class, which was to check the worst excesses of absolutism and, without the help of any effective constitution, keep the French monarchy alive for two centuries. His awareness of the fundamental dissimilarities of races, temperaments, and classes makes him a forerunner of Montesquieu. In his *Response de Jean Bodin aux paradoxes de Malestroit*, he feels his way to an analysis of the interplay of social forces that anticipates the point of view of political economy. His main work, *Les Six Livres de la république* (1576), tries to steer a wise and middle course between the dangers of tyranny and anarchy— two rocks, of which he confesses he deems the latter worse. He has the good sense to write in French, in order, he says, to reach a wider audience; but his massive chapters frighten the modern reader away, and he hardly reaps the benefit of a clear, simple, healthy style, occasionally enlivened by eloquence and vigour.

The *Satire Ménippée* (1594) has a background of national thought and temper that owes very little to the Renaissance. It is the joint work of several middle-class writers, all sympathizing, in the differences of the time, with the moderate party of the 'Politiques'. In it the common sense of a people quick to perceive weak points in any armour, gifted for the criticism of unreason, and impatient of all excess, ridicules the antics of the 'Ligue'—a loose organization of monastic and lay zealots who had been parading the streets, rousing popular passion to fury, and driving the king away for shelter. The success of the skit was immense; it did much to clear the air, bringing to a head the deep-laid longing for order that helped Henri IV to pacify and reconstruct the realm. The writers instinctively hit upon the method that Pasquier was to use shortly after in his *Catéchisme des Jésuites*: the chief 'Ligueurs' are made to speak and, with pompous cynicism, give away their brazen charlatanry and sinister intrigues. Very slight exaggeration or distortion is enough to turn their essential lack of sanity into grotesqueness. The trick is handled successfully though not always with the light touch required by the game. The fun is only now and then masterly, equal to that of Rabelais or Molière; the readiness of public feeling had much to do with the enthusiastic reception. The whole satire is anonymous, but we know the names of its authors and to some extent their respective shares. A cleric, Jean Leroy, is credited with the general plan. The best work in the ironical manner is that of Nicolas Rapin. Jean Passerat penned most of the clever humorous verse. At the end the pretence of indirectness gives way, and Pierre Pithou (1539–96), impersonating d'Aubray, the head of the Politiques, voices the views of the 'tiers état' or middle classes—the harm done to the suffering nation by the selfish rivalries of the great, and the fanatical abuse of religion—in a long speech of bitter, nervous eloquence. 'C'est assez vescu en anarchie et désordre', he asserts decisively. 'Il n'y a paix si inique qui ne vaille mieux qu'une très juste guerre. . . .'

Pulsing as it was with activity in all fields, the French sixteenth century could yet indulge the retrospective mood; and the study of the past, the scope of which was being widened by Pasquier and Fauchet, made decisive progress towards its modern method in the work of Jacques-Auguste de Thou (1553–1617). A magistrate, he applied the lawyer's scrupulous mind to the sifting and relating of events, and he shows the penetrating judgement of a close observer of public affairs. But in the conflict between Latin and French as the language of scholarship, he made the wrong choice (*Historiae sui temporis libri*, &c., 1604–20; not translated till the eighteenth century). His Memoirs, turned into French earlier, reveal a singularly attractive personality.

Monluc,[1] a memorialist rather than a historian, is out to tell us

[1] Blaise de Monluc (1502?–77), born in Gascony, was for fifty years, off and on,

exclusively what he has seen and done. His manly figure must not be idealized, for he had, with a good deal of pride, some vanity, and named his book purposely after Caesar's. He could be both humane and, in self-defence, cruel upon occasion; and some suspicion still lingers as to the origin of his fortune. But within his narrow field he is a reliable witness. To the facts he vouches for, and that make up his personal epic, no doubt can attach: his exceptional bravery, his miraculous escapes, his fine sense of companionship in arms, thrill and win us. Though he knows his limits, and does not attempt a broad canvas, he throws a welcome light upon the inner working of an army, and adds precious detail to our understanding of what took place on the battlefield. His manner, spontaneous in spite of the polishing, is often involved and sometimes clumsy, but its transparent sincerity, and his racy wording, hold us fast. Not the least of his good points are his rare and shrewd flashes of humour. Contrary to everybody's expectation, the English who were besieged at Boulogne evinced some propensity to show their backs in very good time. Are these the stubborn warriors, a French officer asked, who used to terrify our ancestors? 'Non, Monsieur', luy dis-je, 'croyez que les Anglois qui ont battu anciennement les François estoient demy Gascons, car ils se marioient en Gascogne, et ainsi faisoient de bons soldats.'

Brantôme,[1] an altogether different man, is in many respects another Froissart, with a more sophisticated mind. His curiosity is about life on the surface, which he describes with gusto in a series of anecdotes. He is satirical and rather cynical when dealing with the women of the period, garrulous but graphic in his account of captains and kings. His themes called for no construction, and he gives us none. The biographical sketches are superficial; but of acts,

engaged in most of the wars, fighting his way from the lowest to the highest rank in the army. When charged with maladministration he wrote the story of his campaigns to justify himself, and between then (about 1593) and his death he revised his manuscript. The *Commentaires, où sont décrits tous les Combats, Rencontres, Escarmouches, Batailles, Sièges, Assauts*, &c. (the publisher's title), appeared in 1592.

[1] Pierre de Bourdeille, abbé et seigneur de Brantôme (1540?–1614), a pushing and adventurous churchman, travelled much, and saw something of the wars and of life at court. After a fall from his horse (1584) he retired and wrote. His *Vies des hommes illustres et grands capitaines français, Vies des grands capitaines étrangers, Vies des dames illustres*, &c., were circulated in manuscript and published during the latter part of the seventeenth century.

gestures, and memorable sayings, he is a diligent though uncritical chronicler. He enjoys gossip and scandal, has heard much, and tells it all indiscriminately and just well enough to reward the general reader. The historian has some use for his picture of contemporary manners.

CHAPTER XIV

Dramatic Literature

THE French dramatic instinct was not in abeyance during the earlier phases of the revival of learning. Till about the middle of the sixteenth century the medieval forms, though perceptibly decaying, were still favoured by the many. The stimulus towards decisive change came from other quarters, with the determination of the humanists, shared by cultivated circles generally, that the national literature should be enriched by plays of a new type, founded upon the tragedy and the comedy of the ancients. This was the major contribution of the Renaissance to the progress of the stage in France, and the force behind a series of experiments out of which French classical drama finally evolved.

Something of the enthusiasm of the learned percolated to the man in the street; and once the experiments were begun, the strain necessary for the working out and implanting of an imitative aesthetic was borne, on the whole, passively or willingly, by the broader mass of the public. The readiness of the French mind to accept values that met its needs of clearness, regularity and order had much to do with a choice that settled the fate of dramatic art in France for more than two centuries. It was a basic fact of temperament, and accounts for the difference between the average tastes of audiences in the Paris of Henri III and in Elizabethan London. But it is also true, as we know from manifold evidence, that a desire for easier satisfactions and for a pleasant relaxation of all strains was ingrained in the main body of French playgoers. Again and again throughout the process of development we meet with plays that demanded no effort and brought cheaper pleasure to the crowd. As the period advanced, regular tragedy and comedy seemed at times to be threatened by popular or hybrid genres—farces, tragi-comedies, the irregular tragedies of Hardy, the Italian Commedia dell' arte. But as soon as the significant masterpieces are contrasted the difference is again clearly evident. English drama found its supreme expression in Shakespeare, not in Ben Jonson; and the deepest forces of the French genius came to a head in Corneille and Racine, not in Alexandre Hardy.

The colleges were naturally among the most active centres of humanist zeal and took a leading part in the initial stages of the new drama. Not only were ancient plays studied, they were also performed under the guidance of teachers, in Latin first (Greek being still a restricted privilege), and then in French translations or adaptations. The favourite texts were those of Seneca for tragedy and Terence for comedy. In due course, Greek plays began to be read, discussed, and digested. The technique and appurtenances of ancient drama received a good deal of attention, on the basis of the scanty knowledge then available; and the specialists were set to work to probe such recondite matters as the use of the chorus, the wearing of masks, and staging. Dramatic criticism was nurtured on Aristotle and on the work of his modern Italian commentators. In such an atmosphere of mutual encouragement, spreading over all the literary circles, the Pléiade being naturally prominent, the great ambition was at last fulfilled and original plays were written in French on the exact pattern, as was thought, of antiquity. Writing naturally led to performance, and scholastic audiences were prepared to welcome the newborn wonder with the proper degree of enthusiasm. The king and great persons of state might be present, or performances might even take place at court. To reach the general public was another matter; and down to the end of this more or less artificial period, during which classical French drama suffered its scholarly growing-pains, it should be borne in mind that many plays were composed, printed, read, and so perhaps had an influence, without being put to the final test of actual production.

Among these early efforts, whether tragic or comic, no very great works are to be found. The period of preparation and trial was to be sufficiently long to fashion the instrument the masters were to wield; and, in addition, the perceptions of the public had to be sharpened and guided. But if genius proved rather slow in awakening to the possibilities of the newly evolved forms, a measure of responsibility should be charged to the very excesses of humanist zeal. Imitation was recommended, taught, and exacted with such unanimity that the spirit of initiative was of necessity awed and discouraged. Docile subservience to the matter and manner of ancient plays was pretty universal; only by degrees could the notion of discipleship be relaxed and the creative impulse given a freer scope. Lastly, experience of actual production was too infrequent among the authors; their tendency would naturally be to write in order to be read—a condition unfavourable to the progress of dramatic art as such.

Tragedy

To Étienne Jodelle (see above, Part II, Chapter X) is traditionally granted the honour of having written the first regular French tragedy (*Cléopâtre captive*) and the first comedy (*La Rencontre*), performed in the winter of 1552–3. But like many other beginnings, this date is somewhat symbolical, for Théodore de Bèze (1519–1605), a leading Protestant humanist, had written his tragedy of *Abraham sacrifiant* at Lausanne in 1550.

Cléopâtre, a slight and naïvely inexpert piece, follows Plutarch closely, adding to the story of the queen's death but one character, 'l'ombre d'Antoine', and filling five thin acts with monologues and moralizing choruses. Although the handling of verse is capricious, the poetical quality of some passages is the only merit of the play. But it has historical interest in prefiguring what were to be the features of French pre-classical tragedy for the better part of a century. The new authors will show little sense of what action and dramatic suspense may be; they will set hardly any store by the study of character; their effort will aim chiefly at creating not properly tragic emotion but lyrical and pathetic effects; they will deal in long speeches, and their chorus proceed to utter moral commonplaces. Seneca with his rhetoric, and a superficial interpretation of Greek tragedy, were the main sources of these errors. Upon the background of such general traits, however, a few writers were able to stamp their personalities in an arresting fashion.

The *César* (1561) of Jacques Grévin (1538–70), for instance, is distinctly better than Jodelle's play. It has some indications of action in the conflict of characters. Written in alternate masculine and feminine rhymes, it has energy, and not a few striking lines. Defending his chorus, composed of Caesar's veteran soldiers—a departure from ancient models—Grévin wrote these wise words: 'il nous est permis d'oser quelque chose . . . diverses nations requièrent diverses manières de faire'; sane maxims, too rarely acted upon. Jean de la Taille (1540–1608), whose *Saül* is rather disappointing, does better as a critic, and has interesting glimpses of the true light (*L'Art de la tragédie*, 1572). He may have been, in a general way, indebted to Scaliger and Castelvetro, but he draws directly from Aristotle, emphasizing pleasure as the genuine object of art and thus discarding Horace's ethical utilitarianism. He lays due stress upon action, and the spectator's emotion, in which tragedy lives and has its being. His main views, however, agree with those fast becoming the body of the doctrine, and upon which classical orthodoxy was to be built. He adopts Scaliger's insistence upon the unities, thus contributing to the success of a dogma that was for a long time to remain central in French drama. He gives a more pointed form to the theory, no less essential, of the difference between tragedy and comedy—the former treating a great and moving theme in noble language, and culminating in disaster; the latter painting life, with its ups and downs, in familiar style, and ending happily. But the two outstanding names are Robert Garnier and Antoine de Montchrestien.

Garnier[1] began with the usual imitation of Seneca, and there is only some promise in his first plays. *Marc-Antoine* gives us the long monologues, the rhetoric, and the moralizing of the chorus. But at times an inner fire keeps the wording alive, and poetry steals into the declamation. After six tragedies on pagan subjects he was better inspired in treating a Biblical theme—an initiative to which parallels can be found during this tentative period. *Les Juifves* is the best and most typical example of the identification of the lyrical with the tragic, in which are to be seen both the weakness and the originality of those pre-classical plays. Critics have good reason to deplore the obvious *confusion des genres*, but what alleviates the sin is that lyricism here borrows from the situation a deeply moving power and becomes the explicit rendering of emotions which pure tragedy has preferred to imply with a few pregnant words and in the silent eloquence of events. Another excuse for Garnier is that he has caught the spirit of his laments from the Bible, and the close resemblance

---

[1] Robert Garnier (1544?–90), born in the west of France, studied law and filled judicial posts. He wrote poems, then tragedies, from *Porcie* (1567) and *Marc-Antoine* (1578) to *Les Juifves* (1583); one tragicomedy, *Bradamante* (1582).

strikes easily vibrating chords in the spectators. There is some action in the play, some uncertainty until the end; and the characters— especially that of the Queen Mother to the Jewish King, Amital— are rather more than sketches. Much use is made of what recent critics call from the Greek stichomythia, or dialogues in single lines that clash like swords, a device frequent in Euripides and Seneca. Altogether, the style, with its eloquence aiming at sublimity, antici- pates Corneille, while the rich Biblical colouring points to the Racine of *Esther* and *Athalie*. These are high claims for a play written in 1583, of whose performance at that time nothing is known. It must be admitted that many discords break the intuitively sought harmony, for the writer's art is still far from perfect.

Montchrestien[1] was endowed with even greater originality. The vigour of his temper is reflected in his adventurous life. He relied far less on the imitation of ancient models, and stood largely upon his own feet. The conception of regular tragedy, at that later date, already taking shape, could be instinctively followed, and the trend to classicism was growing more and more perceptible. At the same time Montchrestien is first and foremost a poet; what he stresses is not action, and pathetic lyricism, not mere eloquence, is his single-minded aim. His own feelings, often melancholy, set the tone of his choruses, which are mostly real odes, reading much like Malherbe. In fact, he owed something to Malherbe's criticism; and the easy rhythm of another popular poet of the age, Desportes, seems to have influenced his manner. On the whole his style is more firm, natural, and simple than Garnier's, but the inner ardour radiates out no less. In his best play, *L'Escossoise*, inspired by the death of Mary Queen of Scots, he shows his Protestant leanings in his care to avoid blackening the figure of the English queen, while his lyric fervour is so strong that Mary's monologue after learning her fate breaks into short, equal paragraphs which might be called 'stances'. There are many fine snatches of a poetry that is indeed by no means inferior to Garnier's, with a peculiar sweetness of rhythm. Four lines

[1] Antoine de Montchrestien (1575?–1621), born in Normandy, published his tragedy of *Sophonisbe* (1596); four more tragedies, among them *L'Escossoise*, and also poems (1601); and a last tragedy, *Hector*, in 1604. He killed his adversary in a duel, then spent some years in England. On returning to France he tried his luck in industry. He published a *Traité de l'économie politique* (1615), and perished in trying to stir up a Protestant rebellion in Normandy.

from a chorus, with their emphatic repetition of words merged in a musical flow, may be instanced:

> Possesseurs éternels des grâces éternelles,
> Viuez paisiblement en la maison de paix:
> Le temps rendra tousiours vos liesses nouuelles,
> La fleur de vos plaisirs ne flestrira iamais.

Yet here again the artist is gifted, the art often charming, but not supreme. Errors of taste, conceits, faults of proportion, and an intensity that will not suffer restraint, remind us that this period of literature is not classical but baroque.

Comedy

The comedy of this age is on the whole poorer than the tragedy. The imitation of Terence, whose polish French humanists, contrary to the English taste, preferred to the comic strength of Plautus, was not very fruitful; comedy feeds largely on concrete life and manners, and the background was now very distant from that of the Latin writers. The difference might have been minimized by exploiting the fundamental similarity of individuals in all ages, but was more than the mediocre playwrights could accomplish. So they fell back on the stock-in-trade of the old 'moralities' and farces, all the more ready to hand as they had not ceased to be performed. Farces, with the newly imported ballets and 'mascarades' from Italy, were indeed quite fashionable, the latter especially in court and aristocratic circles. Pleasure was thus sought not from the sources of laughter tinged with reflection but from cheap contrasts, absurdities, and gross fun, or from the spectacular appeal of shows similar to the English masques.

In the field of comedy we meet again with Jodelle, Grévin, and Jean de la Taille; even Garnier's name may be mentioned, as his tragi-comedy, *Bradamante*, founded on Ariosto, was not only very successful but in its handling of comic themes managed to preserve some artistic dignity. Jodelle's *Rencontre*, the earliest French regular comedy (1553), is lost. His *Eugène* (1574) is a weak attempt, relying on worn devices and with coarse jokes conveyed, singularly enough, in verse of a facile quality. Grévin's *La Trésorière* (1558) and *Les Esbahis* (1560), again in verse of the pedestrian kind, make rather a better figure. The development of the commonplace, realistic, plots is, on the whole, satisfactory, and at times their rough verve has some of the fresh naturalness that saves Molière's broadest farces from vulgarity. *Les Esbahis* in particular has a distinctly national flavour and reads like the forbear of a long series of bourgeois comedies, or of 'vaudevilles'. Jean de la Taille's *Les Corrivaux* (1574) claims to avoid the easy successes of 'farces and moralities', and to take a leaf out of the book of the ancients. It is indeed nearest to what a true imitation of Terence might be. The prose dialogue is familiar without being low, and some of the characters are both amusing and lifelike. The author's instinct for comic situations and scenes is true, and we only wish he had shown it to the end, which is rather artificial.

Odet de Turnèbe, who died at twenty-eight in 1581, left one play, *Les Contens*, printed in 1584. This is quite a literary creation, the work of a gifted young man who has read Terence and much else and can embroider cleverly on traditional plots, adapting them for the French stage. He writes well, with a turn for graceful banter. The occasional looseness is redeemed by sincere feeling. Rodomont the bragging captain is a good replica of a well-known type, and Françoise the procuress (perhaps modelled on the Spanish Celestine) is first-rate. The comedy lacks the promise of original growth, but it is the best of its period.

Pierre de Larivey (1540?–1612), the son of an Italian, drawing freely from Tuscan plays, which he imitated or adapted, published six comedies in 1579 and three more in 1611. Although no actual performances can be traced, they were widely read, and Molière among others was to take suggestions from them. Larivey's dialogue has remarkable ease and vivacity. A good example of his manner is *Le Fidelle* (1611), a play of such length that it must have been cut drastically if it was ever staged. But it makes pleasant reading, and the freedom of tone is excused by liveliness and verve. Whatever may have been the author's indebtedness, he has entered into the spirit of the theme—a vindication of the truth of women—with genuine gusto. Some scenes are quite brilliantly handled; and the mixture of eloquence, feeling, and fun seems an augury of the sentimental comedy of the eighteenth century. The prodigious pedantry of 'Monsieur Josse'—a Molière name—will have echoes in *Les Femmes savantes*. In spite of grievous faults—among them a strange infusion of coarse realism with genuine nobleness—Larivey is a born writer and playwright.

CHAPTER XV

Late Sixteenth-century Poetry

THE teaching of the Pléiade was all of endurance and high ambition; it was a call to a collective effort in order to win the highest prestige for the poetry of France. By the time Ronsard died it seemed almost as if circumstances had doomed this crusade to failure. Religious and civil struggles were destroying the unity of the people, and cutting short all thoughts beyond the issues of the moment. Even the most fashionable poet of the new generation, Desportes, appeared to be relaxing of set purpose into a light, careless mood, content with shallow inspiration. He might be regarded as an anticlimax to Ronsard.

But too much should not be made of such symptoms. The influence of the Pléiade had sunk deep, and remained the chief factor in the development of French poetry. The religious strife, which could itself be a stimulus, was reflected in an intense desire for earnest expression, harmonizing with the more genuine spirit of the Pléiade. Ronsard's own *Hymnes* and *Discours*, the poems of Du Bartas and d'Aubigné, are notable cases in point. These latter voiced the feelings of the Protestant party, but against them might be set the parallel endeavours of Catholic poets. The stress laid by the Pléiade upon form was producing wide though various and apparently contradictory effects. Some writers polished their lines with artistic care, others were content to charge them with impassioned eloquence and imaginative beauty. One way or another, the serious and dignified alexandrine decidedly became the favourite instrument of French poets; the elaborate pattern of the sonnet remained in fashion, while the four-line stanza or 'stance' was replacing the various forms of the ode.

The tendencies at work were thus far from simple. The age was one of conflict, as the craving for pre-classical order and measure clashed with the fire, the irregular energy, and the 'precious' taste of baroque inspiration. It was to be Malherbe's task to smooth out these differences and give them a coherent unity.

Du Bartas

To a believing mind, no subject could be greater than that which du Bartas[1] had the audacity to treat in his *Sepmaine*: the Creation, the Fall, and the Scriptural story of man, reaching through all its past stages to the future as far as Doomsday. So it is nothing less than the whole scheme of spiritual destiny, in the setting of the universe. The most devout readers would find in it a vindication of poetry, since it could be exalted to such uses. Even more than the French, the English public were thrilled, particularly when Sylvester's translation made the poem one of the most cherished possessions of the Jacobean age; and Milton was encouraged to begin his religious epic by the lasting success of a somewhat similar effort.

In France the fame of Du Bartas declined very rapidly. His faults were fatal to him as soon as classicism was in the ascendant, and he was not granted even a passing mention by Boileau. The verdict has been accepted silently ever since, but must be revised if a poet is to be judged on his merits first, and only next upon the errors of his art.

It took Milton's humanism and his exquisite taste to temper grandeur with simplicity. His French predecessor had not the same culture and delicate perception. Carried away by the enthusiasm of his theme, he pitched his style in an over-intense key; his eloquence shades off into bombast. Letting himself go wholeheartedly, he did not pause to sift the promptings of his invention, and the trivial or the childish crops up with the sublime. Relying naïvely on the tenets of the Pléiade, he coined too many compound adjectives that soon looked alien to the genius of the language. He did not even hesitate to repeat the first syllables of adjectives—an unfortunate trick of emphasis, for such horrors as *pé-pétillant* and *bou-bouillonnant* would have killed any poem. But the number of those grievous accidents has been exaggerated, and the writer's vigorous imagination, the genuine virtues of his style, its energy, graphic power, and very often its musical harmony, must not be forgotten. Du Bartas was a born poet who wrote naturally in words that sang; and his ear,

---

[1] Guillaume de Saluste, seigneur du Bartas, born in 1544, fought for the Protestants, and was sent by Henri IV on missions to England and Scotland. He died in 1590. He published religious poems, among which *La Sepmaine*, 1578, is outstanding; *La Seconde Sepmaine*, unfinished, appeared in 1584. Translated by Joshua Sylvester, its greatest success was in England.

when all is said, was remarkably sound. He may have caught the easy movement, the regular breaks, and the sweetness of his verse from Desportes; but no mere imitation, apart from a gift of Nature, would account for the typical rhythm of his alexandrines. Let a short quotation, taken almost at random, speak for itself:

> Ainsi l'âme du monde inspirant dans nostre âme
> Les éternels effects d'une éternelle flamme;
> Puis l'âme comme forme inspirant dans le corps
> Et ses nombres sans nombre, et ses divins accords;
> Eust paré sa beauté d'une beauté suprême,
> Et l'eust rendu non moins immortel, qu'elle mesme.

Desportes

As to du Bartas, though not for the same reasons, it is tempting to be unfair to Desportes.[1] The man wrongs the poet. He managed his social career so cleverly that his careful art seems only a piece of his calculating policy. Moreover, poetry with him did renounce some of her higher aims, and his translation of the *Psalms* came all too opportunely not to look like a prudent compensation for his light verse. But all that is more or less irrelevant. What matters is that Desportes often wrote charmingly. No doubt he followed his Italian or Spanish models far too closely. Doubtless, again, he has little to say that is deeply felt, and his thought is mostly of the precious or far-fetched kind. But among poets of this type he should rank high. His wit, elegance, and clever conceits make him a precursor to the Voiture, Benserade, and Mainard school. His intuition of the music of words was not really creative, but some intuition he did possess; his sweetness and harmony, the regular cadence of his lines, his apt phrasing, make him the eldest of the French *petits maîtres*. The 'Icare' sonnet, always quoted, is certainly fine; and this tercet of another sonnet reminds us of Daniel or Drayton at their best:

> C'est pourquoi je craindrais de mourir en aimant,
> Non pour fuir la mort, mais de peur seulement
> De perdre mes douleurs, si je perdois la vie.

[1] Philippe Desportes (or des Portes), born in 1546, was tonsured but did not take orders. He frequented fashionable circles in Paris and published his poems *Premières Œuvres*, 1573, *Derniers amours*, 1583. He was a favourite of Henri III and on friendly terms with Henri IV. He received several incumbencies, translated the Psalms (1587–1603), and died in 1606.

D'Aubigné[1]

The genius of poetry lived in d'Aubigné; but never was proof more plain that genius, self-criticism, and taste are different things. He lacked the discipline of classicism—a deficiency all the more glaring as he was a cultivated humanist and as, owing to a natural gift, his instinctive expression shows several of the qualities that the next century was to emphasize: point, for instance, a marked and balanced rhythm and a terse vigour. Although he sins repeatedly against artistic propriety, some of his short verse reads like Malherbe, and many of his detached lines have Corneille's energy and ring. At the same time, he does not only point to the near future. His fervid, intense vision, bold flights of imagery, and inspired lyricism are essentially romantic. His work thus stands as a rich synthesis of promises and realizations from which one very clear lesson emerges —the necessity for the severe pruning that poetry was next to undergo. The impetuous rush of his impassioned utterance carries along much dross and many prosaic lapses, together with great beauties of idea and form. The fire of his religious zeal lights up grand vistas of burning denunciation, exaltation, and prophecy, but it cannot dispel the occasional mists of obscurity, soften the excesses of a violent, crude realism, or alleviate the dragging, awkward flatness of too many passages.

From the beginning of *Les Tragiques*, a poem in seven books (Misères, Princes, La Chambre dorée, Les Feux, Les Fers, Vengeances, Jugement), the reader is struck with the strength of feeling and imagination that creates an impressive manner, so sincere that its emotional force throws into the shade whatever may be due to art—an art present and active, but singularly erratic and fitful. The style tends naturally to antithetical construction, and abounds in conceits, some quite brilliant, others shockingly strained. The whole is above all uneven; the ardour that makes it eloquent, often sublime, is indistinguishable at times from rash impatience; after smooth,

---

[1] Théodore-Agrippa d'Aubigné, born in 1552 of a noble and cultured Huguenot family, studied the humanities and many branches of knowledge. From early youth he fought for the Protestant cause and was several times wounded: latterly he was in favour with Henri IV, but after the king's death he fled to Geneva and spent his last ten years there. His *Tragiques*, written from 1577 to 1579, were first published in 1616, the *Histoire universelle* in 1619–20. His religious pamphlets were published, the *Geneste* in 1617 and the *Sancy* posthumously. He died in 1630.

musical moments come rough, jolting lines; the best phrases are rarely polished and rounded to perfection. Still, one is left with an admiring sense of strong originality and of a near approach to a masterpiece. The flaws can be forgotten, the tedious, drawn-out descriptions vanish from our memory. Even the fierce hatred, the scathing indictment of the poet's chief enemies—the sinister Italian queen, Catherine de Médicis, the effeminate king, Henri III; the corrupt prelates, the cruel judges who revel in blood and tears—are eclipsed by the tenderness that cherishes the martyrs, the enthusiasm of a visionary faith, and the beauty of the lyric stanzas, the songs which interrupt the still too sedate run of the argumentative couplets. Examples of these are the appeals to God at the end of Book I and Book III, or the final pages, with the hymn of the blessed and the rapt prospect of the heavenly world.

Far more than ancient writers, the Bible is the source of what is most living and pregnant in the imagery. The theology has all the uncompromisingness of the age. No attempt is made to divest the idea of God of very human attributes of anger, resentment, and revenge; and the theme of eternal punishment is gloated upon. Milton's divinity by the side of d'Aubigné's is modern and rational. The bitter tale of persecution and wrong is too much repeated not to defeat its own ends. When we turn certain pages, we have supped full with horrors. Still, the citizen is not lost in the partisan: Book I has a fine address to France; Books III and IV pay a tribute of admiration to England,

> . . . où les vertus estranges
> La font nommer pais, non d'Angles, mais des Anges,

and to Queen Elizabeth, whose rule is supremely just.

Towards the end the poem rises to a more equal level of passionate and oratorical but firm and restrained eloquence; and we have philosophical poetry of a high order. The occasional lapses do not impair a collected and continuous quality that leaves us with a sense of genuine power. When all allowances have been made, *Les Tragiques* is one of the great French poems.

CHAPTER XVI

Montaigne[1]

NOT only are the *Essais* fragmentary, with no pretence of any structural plan, but as they proceed, changes are apparent in the mental attitude they reflect. The changes have been carefully studied and justly emphasized; they cannot properly be dealt with here. A brief account must fasten on the salient features of the work, those that best convey its general spirit and characterize by far its greater bulk. Let it be said only that at the beginning Montaigne is keeping what amounts to a commonplace book in which, between quotations from his favourite authors, he airs his remarks on the vagaries of mankind. Farther on he quotes no less, and still gives us a series of disquisitions on disconnected themes; but a central subject has gradually won the first place, and stamps the broken development with an implicit unity: what the author is out to give us is a full portrait of one man—himself.

This was the capital innovation. No such thing had yet been attempted in literature or was to be repeated for a long time. The various 'confessions', whether of Saint Augustine or Rousseau, the many memoirs and autobiographies, are no exact parallels; they

[1] Michel de Montaigne was born in 1533 at the manor-house of Montaigne (Périgord) of a merchant family with the surname Eyquem, that had won wealth and bought an estate; he was steeped in Latin from his childhood, attended the Collège de Guyenne, Bordeaux, under Buchanan, studied law, and after a few years at Périgueux was appointed conseiller au Parlement de Bordeaux. Later he became mayor of Bordeaux (1581). His friendship with La Boétie was ended by the latter's death in 1563. He retired to his country estate in 1571, after translating and publishing a Latin treatise of theology written by a fifteenth-century divine, Raymond de Sebonde. The composition and the publication of his *Essais* were spread over a number of years (first chapters written 1572–3; two books published 1580; third book written, 1586–7 published with the others and much new matter, 1588). The relation of his journey (1580–1) through central Europe and Italy, written by himself and a secretary, was discovered and published a century later (1774). He died in 1592. A posthumous edition of the *Essais* (1595) was prepared from a copy of the 1588 text, with the author's corrections and additions. This copy is kept at Bordeaux and has been the basis of recent re-editing.

serve some edifying, polemical, or justificatory purpose. The essential difference is that Montaigne's stocktaking, while deliberate and open, has no aim beyond itself. It tries unaffectedly to be truthful and, roughly speaking, it is. The preoccupation with one's self that is natural but may so easily be naïve, and which it is difficult to dissociate from a modicum of egotism, has nothing childish, unpleasant or narrowly personal here. The whole thing possesses the interest and value of a monograph on a human being, without the methodical display of a modern scientific study but showing the penetration and respect for fact of a psychological investigation. Such as they are, the *Essais* prefigure the course which the classical century was to take in France, with the stress laid on the study of the soul, and the literary artist, for choice, finding his most definite task in a collaboration with the moralist.

Montaigne was too lucid not to be aware of the almost inevitable objection. No one individual enjoys hearing about others, and by tacit agreement the ordeal is to be avoided by making the subject of self taboo. The foreword, 'Au Lecteur' (1580), meets the expected reproach half way: 'C'est moy que je peins. . . . Je suis moy-mesme la matière de mon livre; ce n'est pas raison que tu employes ton loisir en un subject si frivole et si vain.' This with a half-smile, we fancy. Indeed, the writer's compunction is subtly ironical. What if the reader should belie all the rules of etiquette by finding pleasure in such a grossly ill-behaved book? To begin with, it is no easy matter to probe one's consciousness to the depths; there may be some attraction in the difficulty of the feat: 'C'est une espineuse entreprinse, et plus qu'il ne semble, de suyvre une alleure si vagabonde que celle de nostre esprit; de pénétrer les profondeurs opaques de ses replis internes; de choisir et arrester tant de menus airs de ses agitations. . . .' But this is not the main point. When once a thoughtless reaction has been overcome, self-love discovers a satisfaction in the study of another self. The exploration of one consciousness, if penetrating enough, reaches the common background of human nature; and what fascinates us is the bearing of the analysis on the mysterious world which we all carry within ourselves. 'Thou fool, that believest I am not thou!' These famous words are Hugo's, but the substance of the thought is diffused throughout Montaigne's book.

Whims, fads, slight tricks of gesture are thrown upon the canvas, just like the more significant habits of the body and the mind. No idealization is perceptible; a good-natured, ingenuous candour presides over the leisurely painting. Although Montaigne had some experience of war, nothing can be less heroic in tone than the whole image. There was a stoic ring in some of the first essays, with Cato as a pattern, but this tension soon eases and Socrates becomes the hero. The best wisdom is to follow nature, which means renouncing all pretension and strain. Why should we be ashamed to own that the pursuit of honest pleasure is our object? Life is short; it becomes man to make the most of it, observing the rule of moderation, and satisfying the needs of the head and heart no less than those of the senses. This eclectic epicureanism is once expressed in words that anticipate Pater's: 'Principallement à cette heure que j'aperçoy la mienne [vie] si briefve en temps, je la veux estendre en pois; je veus arrester la promptitude de sa fuite par la promptitude de ma sesie; . . . à mesure que la possession du vivre est plus courte, il me la faut rendre plus profonde et plus pleine.' When the plague broke out in Bordeaux, Montaigne, then mayor, did not return to the city—as no one, in fact, thought it his duty to do. He claims no taste for martyrdom: 'Je suivray le bon party jusques au feu, mais exclusivement si je puy.'

This reliance on nature will be Molière's inheritance; the addiction to the wisdom of Epicurus will be La Fontaine's. In Montaigne one of the deeper veins of French thought comes to the surface and will be a prominent feature in the classical make-up; in many ways he is the counterpart of Pascal and Descartes: his *doute provisoire* is no preliminary stage but a soft pillow for a sensible head to rest upon. In spite of the famous medal he caused to be struck, and his motto *Que sais-je?*, it would not be quite accurate to regard Pyrrhonism, which he certainly accepted for a time, as his definitive attitude. Nevertheless, he found the essence of his conclusions upon life in the relativity of all things human. Man is 'merveilleusement vain, divers, et ondoyant . . .'. 'Nous ne voulons rien librement, rien absoluement, rien constamment.' Reason is no unvarying and sure test of truth; to trust it absolutely is to build on sand—though Montaigne in his last essays is a little less critical of it. When all is said, there is nothing permanent but God.

The idea of God may seem out of place in such a thoroughly earthly atmosphere. But Montaigne's religion, while by no means mystical, is a solid element of his personality. His half-scepticism is at the very root of it. The 'Apologie de Raimond de Sebonde' (Book II) is a central piece in the *Essais*. Far from being vindicated, the fifteenth-century theologian's argument comes out radically ruined. Our faith cannot be founded upon reason. Reason, the weak instrument of our much-vaunted knowledge, is powerless to establish the vital certainties that we need, and fails to grasp the perpetually shifting substance of things. So the right-minded believer—and man cannot do without belief—must put up with a humble submission to the divine teaching that has again and again proved its value. On this foundation Montaigne bases his adhesion to orthodox catholicism, and he stands decidedly on the conservative side in the religious struggles of his time. Rome, in fact, did not object to his book, which was only censured far later.

Such an outline fails to account satisfactorily for the sympathetic response Montaigne has awakened in successive generations of readers. A dry summary excludes the generous and warm humanity that dwells at the core of his thinking. Not only does his *livre de bonne foy* set a high and rare example of sincerity; his clear-sighted survey of the world within works out, as it needs must, to the deepest humility. La Rochefoucauld will be his disciple, and modern psychoanalysis should count him as a precursor. 'Que chacun se sonde au dedans, il trouvera que nos souhaits intérieurs pour la plus part naissent et se nourrissent aux despens d'autruy.' His conservative bent has no other origin: experience has taught him that new-fangled theories take but slight account of human nature, and reforms most often prove worse than traditional evils. But his preference for letting things and people alone is not selfish and cynical; it is steeped in a genuine, a kindly acceptance that is very much like love. The instinct of tolerance is strongly rooted in Montaigne, and he feels only horror for the fanaticism and the cruelty then almost universal. A magistrate, he knew what the torturing of prisoners meant, and condemns it unreservedly. He is not merely passive, he refuses to be driven into acquiescence when his heart rebels. That he had a heart, who can doubt? 'Toute autre science est dommageable à celuy qui n'a la science de la bonté.' And his maxims are very far from those of a thorough sceptic when the supreme test, that of conduct, arises. In the thousand uncertainties of life, 'se rejetter au parti où il y a plus d'honnesteté et de justice'. The man who experienced such glowing friendship as that which bound him to La Boétie, and could refer to it in such admirable words, had in him the soul of nobleness.

His empirical mind mistrusted the adventurous flights of reason but adhered to a respect for facts that is the truest spirit of science. The play of his thought is inspired by a dislike of what is abstract, an intuitive sense of the indispensable value of the concrete. No chapter of his book is more rife with golden wisdom than that which explains his views on education. Pedantry of all kinds he finds distasteful; for book lore he has but little regard. Children are overworked, and stuffed with stupefying knowledge. Let their teachers have 'plutost la teste bien faicte que bien pleine'; let judgement be cultivated more than memory; the proper atmosphere of the school is joy, as that of life is serenity and 'une esjouissance constante'. Brought up a humanist, Montaigne knew that far too much store was set by the sayings of the ancients. A Latin scholar, he would have eased the burden that made so many boys miserable. 'C'est un bel et grand agencement . . . que le Grec et Latin, mais on l'achepte trop cher. . . .'

Montaigne has that excellent virtue of simplicity, a spontaneity of expression that is beyond art because the words well up from a rich inner fullness of experience. His style is original and conscious, but in no wise laboured; his phrases are fresh and juicy because his language has its roots in the vivid sense of things. 'Le parler que j'ayme, c'est un parler simple et naïf, tel sur le papier qu'à la bouche; un parler succulent et nerveux, court et serré.' This directness and his perfect freedom from affectation are already heading for the classical ideal, but in the *Essais* we enjoy a more supple and racy quality of speech than will be compatible, as a rule, with the more self-conscious correctness of the next century. His catholic taste does not shy at dialect: 'Que le Gascon y arrive, si le Français n'y peut aller. . . .' No doubt quotations come so naturally to his pen that an index of the authors he refers to runs into sixty close pages. But he wishes to use no other French words than those commonly heard in the marketplace of Paris. How far we are from the excess that Rabelais ridiculed in the *écolier limousin*!

He created the essay, a literary form for which such a brilliant future lay in store, and was great because he dared be himself, a proof of moral and intellectual courage which so far few had shown. Although alive to the claims of rhetoric he let his thoughts flow in a rambling order, which is nevertheless not disorder, as the impulse of a living mind fuses them into an organic whole. Readers the world over have enjoyed the charm of his free and easy gait, and the lesson has not been lost on a legion of followers. His influence can be detected in Shakespeare, and it has remained an active force in English and European literature. The English have sometimes objected to his scepticism, but more often they have relished his truth to nature and the occasional streaks of humour in his concrete imagination and quiet style. His conversational manner contributed to shape the instrument for that unpretending exchange of remarks between cultivated men and women which the next ages were to turn into a social art. On the other hand, the serious, even earnest language of some of his more weighty chapters, especially among the last *Essais*, set a pattern of sober, moving eloquence which at times comes near to the rhythm of prose poetry.

He stands decidedly apart from the main current of rationalism, destined thenceforth to spread wide over France; and perhaps only Montesquieu, like him a native of the south-west, struck a similar dissenting note in the 'philosophical' eighteenth century. His intuitive and experimental thinking makes him a harbinger of the distant future, nearer to our own day than to the intervening periods. His language has aged less than that of Rabelais, and his permanent place among the masters of French literature is no less securely held.

PART III

PRE-CLASSICISM (1590–1660)

CHAPTER XVII

General Remarks

THE literature of the seventeenth century—or, more precisely, of its latter half—was hailed by contemporary opinion not only in France but abroad as the supreme flowering of the French genius. The epithet 'classical', to which it did not itself lay claim, but which was gradually associated with it, has remained in common use, though with something less than its original value. There was even a time, during the height of the romantic upheaval, when its significance, within some circles at least, took on a decidedly pejorative shade. That bitter fight has long given place to a more temperate feeling. Nevertheless, a problem exists upon which even the shortest history of French literature must dwell before attempting to assess the present-day appeal of works still invested with the halo of prestige.

Of the outstanding merit and significance of the 'classical' age there should be no doubt. The stages through which the mind of France had passed before that time had already very far advanced the process of maturation: the energies of thought and feeling that grew with the national consciousness were fully developed; they had learnt how to express themselves; and the language itself had been moulded into an efficient instrument, in need only of some further polishing. The social forces behind all artistic expansion were converging to bring about an intellectual climax; and the strongly personal reign of Louis XIV soon assumed the characteristic features of one of those periods when abounding strength in the body of the State is matched by the radiating power of its culture. These are matters of sheer fact on which all judges will agree. But rather different views may at bottom be entertained of the light in which the works of this period are to be considered. Should they be regarded as a unique achievement, in which the original mind of France once and for all brought forth its most genuine fruit, so that every crop, before and since, is to be appreciated by that standard? Such was the belief long held, and many French readers still cherish it obscurely, in spite of changes in taste. To offset such an estimate, it may be pointed out that the genius of French literature cannot be enclosed in one formula; its polyvalent quality, so to speak, has been repeatedly established by the lesson of experience. New aspects of this genius have been revealed, and others might still appear. Moreover, a time comes when the life of an art can only be refreshed through the renovation of both spirit and form; and even the specific and so far seemingly indispensable element of nationality can only avoid being an obstruction to renewal if it proves supple enough to grow and change with the nation itself. So, the literature of the classical age no longer awes us as a final and complete pattern that exhausted the best possibilities of the French instinct. On the contrary, the process of analysis has destroyed the illusion that it stood in its massive simplicity as the unalloyed product of one doctrine and one temper. In the light of careful study it appears to us far more complex than it did one generation ago. The romantic tendencies perceptible in the sixteenth century, together with the trend towards classicism, can still be seen embedded in its very substance. They were more or less in the foreground all through the unsettled period that preceded the decisive advent of the classical age. During that age itself, after 1660, they were hidden but still active; and since, from the most distant ages of French thought, the life in them had never been completely extinct, their re-emergence into the declining classicism of the eighteenth century is less surprising.

A practical consequence of these remarks is that the seventeenth century can be treated without hesitation as falling naturally into two main periods. The earlier, pre-classical period lasted till about 1660, when the *grand roi* began to preside over a rich display of genius and beauty. The second, the classical era, lasted from 1660 till about 1715. The former, with which we are concerned in the present section, was a long period of transition in which the characteristic aspect of the baroque still predominated. In its literature we are clearly aware of the interplay of various promptings of independence on the one hand, and, on the other, of a unifying desire for the victory of rule. It seems appropriate to examine first one set of tendencies and then the other, aided by principles of analysis and classification which have their roots in aesthetics, not in history. But in both cases the tendencies were favoured by social influences which require a brief mention.

From his abjuration of the Protestant faith in 1584 the firm, wise rule of Henri IV alleviated most of the evils that had their roots in the anarchy and feuds of the civil wars. But after his murder in 1610 the relapse was dramatic and grievous; the Queen Regent, Marie de Médicis, failed to hold in check the disruptive influences of political disorder, financial folly, and strife. A strong minister of State, Cardinal Richelieu, from 1624, and especially from 1630 when his hold became more secure, curbed the rebellious spirit of the nobles and imprinted a vigorous stamp of unity and order upon all aspects of society. His action, persistent in the teeth of constant opposition, ceased only with his death (1642), one year before that of King Louis XIII, whose chief claim to our gratitude is that he permitted Richelieu's rule. Again a queen was Regent, until young Louis XIV came of age; and Anne d'Autriche was clear-sighted enough to support the clever Italian-born prelate, Cardinal Mazarin, whom Richelieu had chosen for his successor. Victories in the Thirty Years War soothed the pride of France and added several provinces to the State; but errors of government caused the turmoil of the 'Fronde', a civil war in miniature, which for five years shook and impoverished the realm, letting loose social and moral excesses of all kinds. Mazarin weathered the storm, managed to seize the reins again, set the nation's house in order, and brought the struggle with Spain to a successful issue. His death in 1661 practically coincided with the king's majority. Thereafter, a widespread desire for stability and dignity, disgust with the lawlessness of the Fronde, served the turn of a self-willed monarch, who fully intended that France should be great and that he himself should be the supreme symbol of her greatness. The more tranquil phases of these vicissitudes were of a nature to encourage the idea of literary discipline, while the agitated ones were an effective stimulus to the free impulses of writers.

CHAPTER XVIII

The Promptings of Independence

IN so far as the discipline of literature is concerned, the French Renaissance had acted in two complementary ways, of which the effects became increasingly manifest during the first years of the seventeenth century—the transition period. It had quickened the sense of beauty and the desire for expression on the one hand, thus making writers aware of the dictates of the individual temperament. On the other, it had discovered virtues, which it stressed as superior, in the ancient models, and conceived the notion of an impersonal body of rules, the first of a privileged experience which all men would profit by observing. Awareness of the individual temperament fostered a spirit of independence which showed itself in resistance to the growing and in the long run irresistible ascendancy of rule. Other sources of resistance lay in the after-effects of the previous period, during which the unity of faith had been disrupted and the civil power shaken, and the partisan mood had kept widely active.

I. THOUGHT

The Reformation had asserted the right of the modern mind to a reinterpretation of Scripture. But it was only in the most extreme sects that individual opinion was given an entirely free scope, and a rigorous limit was in fact set to beliefs that revolved strictly within the orbit of Christianity. The half-Pyrrhonism of Montaigne, meanwhile, had opened to human reason other paths, leading quietly away from the mere affirmations of faith, though he had not himself followed them to the end. His example is plainly apparent in his disciple and friend, Pierre Charron (1541–1603), whose book, *De la Sagesse* (1601) was reissued in a revised edition (1604) just after his death.

Nothing can be more sensible than Charron's doctrine of wisdom. It starts from what is at bottom the elementary psychology of the self. The tabulated description of man, his faults or weaknesses, his mental powers, is entirely objective. The facts of our nature, condition, and life in society are surveyed dispassionately, and on that plain basis the art of good conduct is built. The name of God is not omitted, and due homage is paid to Revelation. But at a time when behaviour was inseparable from dogma it was a bold departure to erect a system of self-sufficient ethics on purely rational and experimental foundations. In spite of his moderation of argument, Charron was denounced by the vigilant guardians of orthodoxy. The 'deists' of the eighteenth century hailed in him one of their first precursors. He writes good French, fresh and full of meat, less suggestive and original than Montaigne's but more uniformly transparent.

It is not so much the mellow humanism of Montaigne as the more aggressive attitude of Des Periers that reappears in the *libertins*—a word much used then in two meanings that shaded off into each other. The idea was that taking liberties with the common Christian faith and making free with sexual morals were narrowly connected excesses, deriving one from the other. As is well known, the second sense was gradually to supersede the first. But their association is on the whole justified by the men who, during the early seventeenth century, made the word familiar to a wide circle.

Literature, properly so called, has little to glean from their works. Most of their writings are in Latin—a lingering tradition of scholarship, and perhaps a measure of prudence. Such is the case with Gassendi (1592–1655; *Opera omnia*, 1658), the most influential thinker among them. He began by throwing out hints and making inferences that went far to endanger religious philosophy, especially the Christian theory of the physical universe. Next, welding his views into an interpretation and defence of the doctrine of Epicurus, he took every precaution not to clash with orthodoxy. In the thought of his time his empirical bent made him the chief representative of tendencies opposed to those of Descartes, the great champion of methodical rationalism.

All the shades of freedom, from the believer's critical attitude towards the externals of faith to sheer atheism, were represented among the libertines. They may, however, be grouped roughly in two categories: the men of the world—nobles, courtiers, soldiers, poets—who obeyed and spread a fashion of loose or blasphemous satires, epigrams, or songs, which were circulated anonymously and thus created scandal, though rarely endangering their persons; and the *libertins érudits*, the scholars and responsible writers who ran more serious risks and had to be careful with what was intended for publication. In spite of genuine merit, the *Dialogues d'Orasius Tubero* by La Mothe le Vayer (1588–1672), *Mascurat* by Gabriel Naudé (1600–53), the *Lettres* of Guy Patin (1601–72), and other works of this school, are of far greater interest to the historian of ideas than to the general reader.

The outward conduct of these men changed significantly during the third decade of the century. In private intercourse they hardly abated the audacity of their talk, and the atmosphere of gatherings within the higher circles remained often free or even licentious, but the reaction of the spiritual and civil powers against such irregularities made itself increasingly felt. The burning of an Italian atheist, Vanini (1619), and the public prosecution of Théophile (see next section), who narrowly escaped the stake (1623), were dramatic warnings that did not pass unnoticed. Yet it was only after the middle of the century that the fashion turned, and cynicism became a sin against propriety. Thenceforth the butt of the satirists was hypocrisy.

2. POETRY

By the very first years of the seventeenth century the issue was already plain, between the two ideals of laboured art and spontaneous poetry. Hardly had Malherbe (see next chapter) risen to a position of authority as an unofficial laureate, and sharply criticized Desportes in the name of correctness, when the latter's nephew, the young Régnier,[1] stood up in defence of his uncle, and of free inspiration.

Something of Villon's spirit descended upon Régnier. He was a cleric, moving in well-bred circles, and keeping within the law. His cynicism is tame beside that of Villon, and bitter experience did not stir him to the depths of anguish and pathos. But he is at bottom a

---

[1] Mathurin Régnier was born in 1578; his mother was Desportes's sister. He took orders, spent some time in Rome as secretary to Cardinal de Joyeuse, then lived in Paris, and was appointed canon of Chartres cathedral in 1609. He published successively thirteen *Satires* from 1608 to his premature death in 1613. Four more, and sundry pieces, were printed posthumously.

rebel who derides the superstition of honour and indulges with an easy conscience the desires of the natural man. In art, as in life, he is all for freedom, and instinct. The poet's duty is to 'laisser aller la plume où la verve l'emporte'; and pruning, polishing, and sweating over words are the makeshifts of a dull brain and the illusions of a pedant. He followed his own precepts, and wrote with a facility that is the source both of his virtues and faults. There is a freshness, an ease, and a lilt in his lines, and a remarkable vigour of phrasing; but the construction is apt to be faulty, the grammar and the propriety of terms are not unexceptionable. His language is to us more archaic, being more racy and popular, than that of his contemporary Malherbe. Satire, which he was not quite the first to write in France, is for him but a pretext for making free use of his graphic pen; of genuine moral ardour he shows very little. In their evocative force and imaginative realism his best passages, such as the skit on the *fascheux* (Satire VIII), remind us of Donne's satirical pieces, though inferior and with less acid intensity. Of the rhetorical manner of most Latin satirists, and their harping on commonplaces, he usually has too much. For special praise we should single out the portrait of the hypocritical procuress (*Macette*, Satire XIII), and, best of all, the humour and Flemish gusto of *Le Mauvais Gîte* (XI), or the sustained, sensible argument of *Le Critique outré* (IX), with the immortal sketch of genuine, unpainted beauty:

> Rien que le naturel sa grâce n'accompagne;
> Son front, lavé d'eau claire, éclate d'un beau teint. . . .

But one remembers with most sympathy the gentle humility of *Régnier apologiste de soy-mesme* (XII):

> Car, quoy qu'on puisse faire, estant homme, on ne peut
> Ny vivre comme on doit ny vivre comme on veut. . . .

Racan's[1] early connexion with Malherbe, and the general course of his career, would seem to betoken anything but a literary freelance. Yet he was no orthodox follower of the new poetic doctrine, with

---

[1] Honoré de Bueil, sire de Racan (1589–1670), born in the west of France, was a page to Henri IV, then to the comte de Bellegarde, and knew Malherbe. After some years in the army he settled not far from Tours, and led the quiet life of a country gentleman. His pastoral play, *Les Bergeries*, performed in 1618, was published in 1625. He published some occasional verses and also wrote in prose. His last work was a free rendering or verse paraphrase of the Psalms.

its severe insistence on correctness. In his practice, and even in his declared principles, he always advocated more elasticity and freedom. He could well afford to scorn the labour of a painstaking writer: numbers came to him without effort; and by a rare dispensation, facility did not deprive his language of a faultless elegance. But sweetness of metre is not sufficient; and his *Bergeries*, very successful at the time, are to us incurably artificial and cold, in spite of some fresh touches of nature and although his smoothly flowing lines are not always devoid of firmness and vigour. His best work is to be found in the unpretending verse of the *Ode to Balzac* or the *stances* to 'Thirsis'; and in not a few short pieces, which are very near the purity of classical art without paying too dearly for it with loss of natural charm. Moreover, much will be forgiven him, because of his independent judgement in his *Lettre à M. L'Abbé Ménage*, where he points out that a play which conforms to the rules is not necessarily beautiful. He even contends that the perfect observance of the rules in a plot is hardly compatible with the free impulses of impassioned characters. This shows no prescience of the coming of Racine; but with how much second-rate drama does it not tally!

It is difficult when dealing with Théophile[1] not to dwell sadly on the might-have-been. His gifts entitled him to a place among the great French poets of all ages. The work of his short, imprudent, dramatic life still counts as the best of his generation. But he died before he had quite found himself, or resolved his inner conflicts. He remained sane despite all his excesses; and truth, for his type of genius, lay naturally in intuitive perceptions. Far too much ridicule has punished the exuberant conceits of his *Pyramus*, a lyrical play with beauties of the first order and with an imaginative intensity in the expression of love which recalls some Elizabethan dramatists. Just after he had committed himself to these wild freaks of fancy

[1] Théophile de Viau, born in 1590 near Agen of a Protestant family, studied in the south-west, joined a set of wandering players, registered at Leyden University, mixed in Paris with dissolute sets of *libertins*, and at one time had to take refuge in England (1619). He published *Poems* (1621), and won a great success with his tragedy of *Pyrame et Thisbé* (1621). He was compromised in a scandalous publication, and, though recently converted, was sentenced to be burnt (1623). He was given shelter by the duc de Montmorency at Chantilly, tried to escape abroad, was arrested, and after long confinement in Paris was banished the kingdom (1625). He was again protected by Montmorency, but died the next year from the effects of hardship and excess. His collected *Œuvres* were published in 1626.

we find him writing with golden sense of the significant simplicity that should characterize a good style. His critical ideas were bold but healthy. He admired, but was not prepared to copy, Malherbe; each writer should be faithful to himself, and *he* refuses to drudge: 'Jamais un bon esprit ne fait rien qu'aisément.' Similarly, he considers it wrong of the moderns to imitate the ancients (*Fragments d'une histoire comique*). That he possessed the secret of the stripped purity which is the sure note of classicism no one will doubt who has read his *Élégie à une dame*, his letters, or the verse passages in his translation of the *Phaedo*: he was instinctively attuned to the Attic compound of direct-ness and grace. But his art is rich and synthetic; and while he an-nounces the next age, his more striking originality comes out in a remarkable sensitiveness of feeling and perception that is more proper to the romantic and post-romantic eras. His love of nature blends sensibility, subtlety, and music in lines that thrill a twentieth-century reader. He could evoke the spirit of the fruitful land of his childhood, the banks of the Garonne, with a precision in lusciousness that the nineteenth century thought it had discovered (*Plainte à un sien amy, Lettre à son frère*). He could summon up a humorous medley of hap-hazard associations in lines that one might describe as 'surrealist' ('Un corbeau devant moy croasse'). In spite of inequalities and signs of negligence, the best-known odes, like *Le Matin*, *La Solitude*, are enchanting. And what poet's or artist's eye, until the impressionists came, and painted their water-lilies, ever took in with such loving accuracy the interplay of light and shadow in the water?

> Les rayons du jour, esgarez
> Parmy des ombres incertaines,
> Esparpillent leurs feux dorez
> Dessus l'azur de ces fontaines;
> Son or, dedans l'eau confondu,
> Avecques ce cristal fondu
> Mesle son teint et sa nature,
> Et sème son esclat mouvant,
> Comme la branche, au gré du vent,
> Efface et marque sa peinture.

In several ways Tristan l'Hermite[1] is a brother poet to Théophile—

---

[1] François l'Hermite, sieur du Solier, who wrote as 'Tristan', was born in 1601 (?). He was a page at Court but ran away, spent some time in the army, then led a life of

a younger brother, with a comparable charm, and a somewhat less decisive originality. Together they do much to establish the thesis that the triumph of classical rule deflected the natural development of French lyrical poetry for a century and a half. But lyricism is not everything, and the French creative genius gained much from the ascendancy of order that it could ill have afforded to lose.

Tristan has his mannerisms, his faults of preciosity, at times irritating, often venial and charming. He was, like many others, under the influence of the *Adone*, a poem by the 'Cavalier Marin' (Marini, 1569–1625), that took France by storm. He wrote sonnets, elegantly turned, with an amorous and dying fall; pretty love poems that make no pretence of being addressed to one lady alone (*L'Amant secret*, *La Louange du vert*, &c.). In his *Orphée* we find a gracefully pagan feeling and a talent for reanimating ancient themes which foreshadow the manner of André Chénier. But, like Théophile's, his most happy inspiration is a fresh, delicate sympathy with nature. One of his earliest poems, *La Mer*, depicts in graphic language, as precise and ingenuous as the brush of a primitive painter, the changing features of the sea, under varying lights; no one had yet regarded the ocean so discerningly. In the *Promenoir des deux amants* the dreamy silence of a shady walk, and the fascination of water, are fondly dwelt upon, and expressed with the suggestiveness of modern symbolism:

> L'ombre de cette fleur vermeille,
> Et celle de ces joncs pendants
> Paraissent être là-dedans
> Les songes de l'eau qui sommeille. . . .

Tristan's art is unequal; he has no perfect piece; blemishes of taste and prosaic flaws spoil good passages. He took risks deliberately, on principle, and has the faults of his virtues. Of his plays—especially the *Mariamne* and the *Mort de Sénèque*—a word will be said later. His significance, on the whole, is twofold: he reveals the seeds of romanticism deeply latent in the French imagination and, at the same

pleasure in Paris; took service with the duc de Guise, and was disappointed in his expectations. He died of consumption in 1655. He had written much for the stage, mostly with success (tragedies: *Mariamne*, 1636; *La Mort de Sénèque*, 1644, &c.; several comedies). His collections of poems were *Les Plaintes d'Acante*, 1633; *Les Amours*, 1638; *La Lyre*, 1641; *Vers héroïques*, 1648.

time, the magnetism that was attracting literature, even among the rebel poets, towards a classical purity of form.

Among the poets of the pre-classical age, the nineteenth-century romantics singled out Saint-Amant[1] especially for their precursor. His irreverent gaiety appealed to them no less than his feeling for nature. He is indeed a curious personality, with features richly varied and picturesque. No writer of his generation was more thoroughly independent. To the end, he laughed and rhymed as he pleased. Many of his light, fanciful pieces are called 'caprices', that pedants might not gauge them by solemn standards. His line of descent is not from the ancients, through the Pléiade, but from the most native tradition of the *esprit gaulois*, through Rabelais and Régnier. But this boon companion, alive to all the fun and flavour of material life, had in him a fine gift of soft, subtle music and an exquisite sense of the inexpressible. In *Le Contemplateur* he penned these often quoted yet still wonderful lines, so prophetic of the symbolist future:

> Tantost, délivré du tourment
> De ces illusions nocturnes,
> Je considère au firmament
> L'aspect des flambeaux taciturnes;
> Et, voyant qu'en ces doux déserts
> Les orgueilleux tyrans des airs
> Ont appaisé leur insolence,
> J'escoute, à demy transporté,
> Le bruit des ailes du Silence
> Qui vole dans l'obscurité.

Description of landscape was already common, but *La Solitude* added novel touches in which the next century was to revel—the thrill of a ruined castle with a ghost, and the wild charm of a marsh, 'tout bordé d'aliziers, D'aulnes, de saules et d'osiers'. Another prophetic piece, *Le Printemps des environs de Paris*, shows a discriminating eye for more subtle shades than the age had yet learnt to distinguish. Thereafter, this lovely poet of moods lets loose upon us an irresistible

---

[1] Antoine Girard, who claimed to be sieur de Saint-Amant, was born of a Protestant family, near Rouen, in 1594. He turned Catholic, travelled; fought in the wars, visited several capitals in the suite of an ambassador, and led a gay life in Paris and Rouen. He published several collections of poems (*Œuvres*, 1629, 1643, 1649, &c.); also an 'Idylle héroïque', *Moyse sauvé*, 1653. He died in 1661.

deluge of wit, epigrams, and drollery. The realist and the satirist give place to the burlesque writer (see Section 3).

Another unexpected side of Saint-Amant's performance is his *Moyse sauvé*—almost the only epic of his time that still bears reading. Wisely, he labelled it *idylle héroïque*, hinting that its tone would be mostly familiar, which it is. Among snatches of genuine poetry and many fine lines intermixed with anticlimaxes of all kinds, it tells the Biblical story in a spirit of popular, almost naïve home-liness—not ridiculous, as Boileau in a hidebound moment would have it, but sweet after so many other bards' strained attempts at sublimity.

3. REALISM AND THE BURLESQUE

Realism is a very old but not the first form of literature. The earliest, most instinctive need for expression springs necessarily from a direct feeling, whether of love, wonder, hatred, or fear; and the desire to show things more truly as they are is always a reaction of some sort against the error of having shown them as they were not. There had been streaks of the realistic intent in the variegated tissue of medieval moods, and the sixteenth century had stimulated the wish for truth in all fields. But the worship of ancient writers, as privileged depositories of perennial truth, was itself a cult, in which the acceptance of imaginative, if not imaginary, values played more or less the part of dogma; and the spirit of Petrarchism, which so largely pervaded Renaissance thought and art, was essentially ideal-istic. The sentimental novel, shortly after 1600, began with *Astrée*, creating a fictitious world in which thousands of d'Urfé's readers were willing to live. So the realistic literature of the transition period is an assertion of independence, a protest against the authority of traditional conventions and imposed attitudes. Since it was a para-mount convention to regard all Greek and Latin works as incom-parable models, the rebellious instinct found relief in handling them irreverently. The psychological background from which they sprang was the same as that of realism, and the two strains, from that point of view, are intimately connected.

It has been rightly pointed out, first, that the vogue of the bur-lesque in France had its rise with Scarron, in the atmosphere and

under the influence of the 'Fronde'; and that there had been precedents and models in a number of Italian writers from the fifteenth
to the seventeenth centuries. This holds good chiefly for the term in
its wider sense, for the Italian *burlesco* covers the whole field of the
facetious. In its more restricted usage, which gradually predominated,
to denote the belittling of great themes, epic or tragic ones in particular, by familiar treatment so as to create a contrast, the French
mode of the burlesque, like the English, persisted throughout the
classical and post-classical periods. It may to some extent have been
due to a craving for release from the pressure of a somewhat conventional scale of values, and could thus be a parallel symptom to the
revolt of the 'moderns' against the ancients.

Charles Sorel's (1602–74) realistic impulse is definitely a reaction.
His *Francion* (1623) is animated by the hatred of a very young man
for the stupid pedantry of schoolmasters and the prudish hypocrisy
of society. Another motive, derision of *Astrée*, and of sentimental
pastorals, is only occasionally to be detected in this work, but is
clearly evident later in the *Berger extravagant* (1627) which owes
something to the powerful lesson of *Don Quixote*. Even the cloven
hoof of the *libertin* is plainly seen, though this feature was toned
down in subsequent editions. *Francion* is a picaresque autobiography
in which the coarseness of the picture is a good deal spiced with
humorous exaggeration; but it has freshness, and the flavour of
sincerity; and the narrative, although desultory, is taking. There is fun
in the satire of the jealousies of men of letters; but the main interest
lies in observing the birth of a theme that was to assume such importance in the modern novel—the history of a character, and the
struggle of the individual with his environment.

Brief mention should be made of Tristan's graceful, gently ironical
prose tale, *Le Page disgracié* (1642)—part of which is enacted in
England—as a link between Sorel and Scarron. But meanwhile
Saint-Amant had passed from the lyricism of his youth to a decidedly
burlesque inspiration. He is a master of invective, and his indictment
of the Roman scene (*Rome ridicule*) is scathingly cynical. An English
reader who was tolerant of Gallic insolence and rashness might do
worse than try the huge humour of *Albion, Caprice héroï-comique*.
The majesty of Olympus is treated disrespectfully in *Le Melon*. In
these and more poems of the same kind much is to be condoned;

but our enjoyment of their verve, lilt, and humour and of the rich, vivid language overwhelms every objection.

Scarron[1] had the perhaps unenviable privilege of identifying his name with this minor genre. Political satire cannot reach a higher pitch of scurrilous bitterness or a ranker flavour than in the *Mazarinade*, a verse pamphlet that gives no quarter and that the victim never forgave. The *Virgile travesti* was very successful, and public opinion at a time of stiffening orthodoxy did not resent the glaring breach of literary etiquette. A little of it can be amusing, but the inverted values and the easy transposition of the epic into vulgar familiarity are tricks which soon pall. There is not very much comic invention, but such as it is the short, tripping line carries it along very well. *Le Roman comique* is more enjoyable; it is intended as another 'travesty', this time of the heroic novel, and does not try to conceal the fact. Far better than the ten volumes of the *Cyrus* (see below, Chapter XIX), we are told, are the Spanish short stories. Indeed, the incidents that crop up at each stage in the path of an itinerant company of players through the fat, pleasure-loving cities of western France, are described with animation, although too many adventitious tales interrupt the narrative and some episodes are cheap in their brutality. The good humour of the story-teller, and his genial reliance on our tolerance when his conventional tricks lie bare, are pleasant. The picaresque seasoning, and the picture of provincial life about the middle of the seventeenth century, awake the same sort of interest as do the parallel and later scenes in Fielding and Smollett. But this unfinished work is not by any means the great book it might have been. The realism is heavy, and the spicing of romance or sentiment does not quite make amends.

Once divested of the false glamour of Rostand's play, Cyrano de Bergerac[2] is an original figure, and singularly taking. Among the

---

[1] Paul Scarron (1610–60), after a merry youth, was gradually crippled by disease, and found his solace in writing parodies, skits, epigrams, and burlesques. His chief works are, in verse, *Typhon ou la Gigantomachie*, 1644; *Le Virgile travesti*, 1648–59; in prose, *Le Roman comique*, 1651–7.

[2] Savinien Cyrano (1619–55) called himself 'de Bergerac', from the name of an estate near Paris. He joined the army, was twice wounded, lived a free and often penurious life, studied under Gassendi, and wrote plays (*Le Pédant joué*, printed 1654, *La Mort d'Agrippine*). His main work, though ready long before, was published after his death, as *Histoire comique des états et empires de la lune*, 1657; the complete text appeared first in 1921 (*L'Autre Monde*).

'irregulars', who in straggling order preceded the marshalled ranks of the classics, none had more intellectual fertility, if not actual coherence. His short life, clouded by ill luck, imprudence, and misfortune, only allowed him to scatter the seeds of his teeming invention. A later posterity was to acknowledge its value; and Fontenelle, Swift, Voltaire, and several other writers of *voyages imaginaires* found ideas in him and improved upon them. But his daring evocation of fictitious worlds stirred in his own day an uneasy sense of aggressive heterodoxy which, though partly unjustified, often turned to hostility. Indeed, most of the traditional customs of our civilization are openly flouted by his satire, even if religious faith is not directly attacked. The working of his mind is not by any means methodical, and his sketches—more often serious than comic—of the wonders of the moon and the sun are a mixture of wild fancies and astonishing intuitions. The whole is, one must confess, somewhat disturbing to the demands of orderly thought, and appeals rather to the free imagination of the artist and dreamer than to the staid judgement of the scientist. Cyrano honours Descartes while contradicting him. He takes the main outline of his cosmology from Copernicus and the epicurean system; but a high philosophical irony and a genuine humanity, comparable to those of Sir Thomas More, are the soul of his Utopias. He writes with an elegant ease, a blending of wit, poetry, and cogency, and except that a few of his words and phrases have aged, his style already reads as smoothly as some eighteenth-century philosophical romance.

4. DRAMA

From the point of view of construction it might have seemed, by the end of the sixteenth century, that French drama was within close reach of its goal of regularity, for which it had clearly been making. The tragedies of Grévin and Garnier, for instance, the comedies of Jean de la Taille and Turnèbe, were recognizable sketches of the classical type, in spite of such elements as the strong admixture of lyricism in the former. On the whole, the transition period of 1590–1660 did not fulfil this expectation. Development towards regular pattern was repeatedly broken and freedom of construction and manner again and again prevailed, while the continuing popularity of tragicomedy in itself pointed to heterodox tastes and preferences. Delay may also have been due, to some extent, to the instability of a period of political and intellectual unrest. But when everything is taken into consideration the main factor lies obviously in the resistance of a very important section of French audiences to the severity and austerity of a perfectly regular dramatic art. In the France of Henri IV and Louis XIII there were seeds of a popular culture very much like those that flourished in Elizabethan and Jacobean England; and it would be incorrect to regard the tragedy of Racine as the inevitable fruit of the temper of a whole people.

Alexandre Hardy (1570?–1631) is a case in point. His fertile, vigorous talent threw off plays with extraordinary ease and fecundity. He claimed to have written some 600, of which he printed only thirty-four (tragedies, tragicomedies, and pastorals; all the comedies are lost), in five volumes. Thus, given an entirely free range, and heedless of ancient models, his creative instinct developed a dramatic technique which in many ways resembled that of the average Elizabethan playwright. He stakes everything on action and movement; his drama shifts freely through space and time; his violent plots awaken powerful thrills of emotion and horror; murders take place upon the stage, and rapes are just screened off. *Scedase, ou l'hospitalité violée*, has the sombre intensity of *Arden of Feversham*. Another play, *Panthée*, of a heroic character, reminds us not unworthily of Corneille. These are tragedies; but such a tragicomedy as *Procris* has moving scenes. Even the study of character is not neglected, inner conflicts being simply but strongly delineated. Lastly, the style is lit by flashes of vivid imagination, and some passages rise to actual beauty. With all these gifts the paradox is that Hardy's name, famous in his own age, should have been practically forgotten in the next. One may trace this fate to the very source of his power—an energy that never gives itself time to cool. His art is too rapid not to be negligent; the abundant flow of language is spoilt by turgidity, and by queer word-formations due to mistaken imitation of the Pléiade, while the verse has vitality but is not regular. Hardy said he admired Malherbe in the ode, but that his rules would be pedantic and cramping to a dramatist; so he let himself go too fully, and paid for it when the character of literature was changed. Still, he deserves better treatment than our neglect.

Jean de Schelandre (1585?–1635) is no less interesting to the historian. He was born of a Protestant family, like several writers of the period. From his early youth he wrote poems in the spirit of a rebel against Malherbe's discipline. His chosen masters were Ronsard and du Bartas and he laughed at the polishers of verse, who prune away the beautiful to make room for the pretty. His temperament preserved much of the vigour and the romantic tendencies of the late sixteenth century—strength of imagination, a feeling for nature, a love of far-fetched conceits. Our curiosity is roused by the fact that he spent some time in England about 1608, when he probably saw some of Shakespeare's plays. As, moreover, English players had come to Paris several times during the preceding age, the last recorded visit being in 1604, his acquaintance with English drama may be postulated; but any assumption of influence, however natural, must rest on conjectural grounds. He first cast his play *Tyr et Sidon* (1608), dedicated to the English King, James I, in a roughly regular mould. He mixed comic with tragic elements to some extent, but laid more stress on character than had been done previously. His *Cassandre* is a study of feminine love drawn with a directness and realistic vigour that anticipate Racine's *Phèdre*. The unities are in principle respected; long speeches are frequent, and most incidents are recounted. In its lyrical colouring and musical eloquence the play follows the pattern of Garnier and Montchrestien. After this classical beginning, Jean de Schelandre in 1628 recast his work into a tragicomedy that spreads its ten acts over two *journées*. This second *Tyr et Sidon* might be the older play by fifty years, not the younger by twenty. It admits a strong element of farce, cuts down long speeches, puts events actually under the spectators' eyes; the choruses are dropped and the unities entirely ignored. It is so striking an example of the 'irregular' stage that a French critic, Jusserand, has found its technique practically identical with that of Shakespeare. A preface, by François Ogier, underlined the author's intent in words that have a prophetic ring, raising the flag of modern independence, censuring passive imitation, and pointing out that in dramatic art, as in life, tears and laughter could be intermixed.

Two very successful plays, by the two best lyrical poets of the period, contributed to maintain the prestige of the irregular stage. Théophile's youthful tragedy, *Pyrame et Thisbé* (1621; see above,

Section 2), became a byword for two centuries thanks to Boileau's ridicule. Whether our modern taste has grown more liberal, or we are more tolerant of the precious because we are again infected by it, it is difficult to say; but while half a dozen passages are really in very bad taste, the bulk of the play passes muster with us far more easily. It belongs decidedly to the order of baroque romanticism and indulges to the full a fondness for extremes of feeling, and an impassioned energy of language which was not to be seen or heard again on the French stage before Victor Hugo. In spite of some rant, and egregious conceits, the lyricism at times reaches genuine sublimity and true pathos in the expression of despairing love. Tristan's *Mariamne* (1636), though performed only a few months before Corneille's *Cid*, was not eclipsed by the latter's brilliant success. The author disclaims any intention to deal in conceits; and although he is not quite so good as his word, his general manner is sober and his dramatic style firm. Still, it is an exaggeration to see in it, as has been done, an anticipation of Racine. The main features of the play are rather lyrical; Herod's ravings at the end belong to the order of romantic display; and the poet's art, for all his fine intuitions, is essentially uneven. His *Mort de Sénèque* (1644) was rather better, with a free construction and intense beauties which have won for it from some critics the label 'Shakespearian'. One can object to the epithet without being unfair to a really tragical rendering of a great subject, not unworthy of Tacitus's masterly outline.

Rotrou[1] was not insensitive to the influence of Corneille, whom he admired and praised generously. But though to some extent he followed the change in public taste that resulted in the gradual disappearance of tragicomedies, he was a romantic by temperament and remained faithful to his instinctive preferences. For his plots he went chiefly to the Spanish playwrights; his natural bent was to mix the comic with the tragic, and he never gave up tragicomedy altogether. *Saint-Genest* has been somewhat overpraised; it has fine moments, especially towards the end, and beautiful lines, and well

---

[1] Jean Rotrou, born at Dreux in 1609, began writing for the theatre at eighteen, and produced or adapted a number of plays, mostly tragicomedies, often taken from the Spanish drama and preserving its loose structure. He studied law, retiring to his native city as a magistrate in 1639. His later plays included *Saint-Genest* (1645) and *Venceslas* (1647). He refused to leave Dreux during the plague, and himself succumbed to the disease (1650).

supports the inevitable comparison with the spiritual sublimity of Corneille's _Polyeucte_, performed a few years earlier. But the subject involves frequent shifts of action from the plane of human psychology to that of the supernatural, and drama is then replaced by wonder and edification. The main fault, however, is the strange failure of a style distinguished by eloquence, original imagery, and both ease and nervous strength, but which fails to command clarity, elegance, and correctness of phrasing. _Venceslas_ is a better play, with scenes in which the sustained force of argument reminds one of _Cinna_ and _Horace_. The tragic emotion, as with Corneille, often lies in our painful and exalted sympathy with heroic self-sacrifice and the nobleness of great characters. Maxims, and sentiments crystallized into lines of great purity, often raise the style to a high pitch, but it drops again continually to low levels of clumsy and strained expression. Facility was Rotrou's evil genius, and his two best tragedies just fall short of being undoubted masterpieces.

CHAPTER XIX

The Victory of Rule

THE object of the preceding chapter has been to study groups of writers of the pre-classical period whose works reveal the persistence of literary trends not reducible to the quest for order. Such symptoms of independence are numerous and important. Yet the fact remains that the ideal of regularity did eventually triumph, and that upon its final success the structure of French classicism was erected.

What can account for the victory? It seems advisable not to trace its causes exclusively either to social factors or to intellectual needs, though both were concerned in the process. On the one hand, political France was longing for a firm and stable government—a desire fulfilled when Louis XIV took the reins of administration into his own hands; and though absolute monarchy was soon enough to reveal its dangers, for a period it proved a relief. Circumstances generally now combined to bring about an age of authority, hierarchy, and rule; and once this trend of social evolution was recognized, acceptance of a clear-cut scale of aesthetic values followed almost as a matter of course. On the other hand, and over and above this, classical art was welcomed instinctively on its proper merits, and owed much to the imponderables of the French intellectual temper. The romantic tendencies, weakened by prolonged exercise, were defeated; they gave way and were repressed, driven to a hidden life, finding only a partial and indirect outlet in the very works of their adversaries. Readers whose taste had been shaped by the experience, which they obscurely and vicariously shared, of several generations, felt that the time had come when logic and order—or what looked reassuringly like them—must have their way; the clear, equable light of reason could now, at last, spread freely over creative effort and critical appreciation alike. The leading critics took charge, and voiced the common decisions, with which they were concerned, and owed their prestige mainly to their concurrence. The era of classicism was bound to come as its coming was demanded by the inner rhythm of the French mind; it was to be not necessarily the supreme consummation but at least a central period in French development.

I. THOUGHT

Stability through faith

During the first years of the seventeenth century a sense of disruption and danger to the religion of the French people was in the air. Although the victory of the Reformation in France was clearly becoming unlikely, and though the Edict of Nantes had put an end to the fight for freedom of worship, the wounds left by the long struggle were not healed, and the progress of the *libertin* movement seemed to jeopardize the future of dissent as much as that of orthodoxy. The powerful effect of the Counter-Reformation, felt all through western Europe in the later sixteenth century, had been till then more perceptible within the Church than in the world without; from 1600 to 1660 it assumed its full force, and decidedly reversed the direction of the main intellectual current. The monarchy of the *Roi très chrétien*, Louis XIV, thus benefited from one of the most important causes of its undisputed establishment; a majority of the nation was consciously rallying round traditional positions that had been apparently shaken; and it was generally felt that obedience to the will of the king, as well as to the teachings of the Church, were two inseparable duties of right-minded citizens. This change in manners about the middle of the century is reflected in the fact that the public expression of the views of the *libertins* was for a period discouraged and censured, when not rigorously punished, with full general approval.

Several men by their writings and discourses had already, before Louis XIV ascended the throne, helped to bring about this steadying and refreshing of faith. Only two can be mentioned here: Cardinal Pierre de Bérulle (1575–1629), of the Oratoire, the author of *Discours de l'estat et des grandeurs de Jésus*, 1623, and more important as a thinker and divine than as a writer, and Jean-Pierre Camus (1583–1652), bishop of Bellay, who taught, with signal and popular success, through the indirect channel of Christian novels.

The Church has canonized François de Sales,[1] and his personality

[1] François de Sales, born in Savoy (1567), studied in Paris and Padua, entered the

had more than any other single agency to do with the revival of French piety. His most influential work, the *Introduction à la vie dévote*, grew out of letters of spiritual advice addressed to a lady; and so this survey of the ways and means that can lead to holy living, though it aims at universality, is pitched in a feminine key. This does not entail any undue softening of the doctrine; François de Sales is singularly clear-sighted, well aware of the thousand tricks the natural being will employ in order to slip through the network of prohibitions that surrounds him. Some of his remarks, indeed, are not only shrewd but blunt. His quiet sanity and sense of order provide a rational basis for that warm zeal in the fulfilment of religious duties which he calls devoutness; and his temper has the full lucidity of the classical mood. At the same time, far from being dry and cold, his rationalism is suffused with an almost mystical spirit, and he lays stress mainly on the self-abandonment of the creature to the love of God, the beginning and the end of true piety. His unfailing appeal, the reason for the spell which he cast over a whole generation and of the many 'conversions' he effected, lies in the winning charm of a transparently sincere and humane character. His style has been compared with Fénelon's, but its vocabulary is far more simple, and its smoothness owes nothing to literary care, being only the uninterrupted flow of inexhaustible charity. It has aged in nothing but a few words and phrases, now obsolete. To suit his unconventional approach François de Sales uses familiar similes from everyday experience; but this domestic imagery verges at times upon something more objectionable, curiously resembling the fanciful euphuism of John Lyly: 'car, comme les boucs touchant de la langue les amandiers doux, les font devenir amers . . .'. Surely this reads like *Euphues*. On the whole, the secret of the immense popularity and the lasting effectiveness of this treatise must be sought in the tenderness, humility, and modesty of the teacher; in his glowing picture of the happiness that blossoms naturally and inevitably upon the stem of holy living, whether at the very heart of the world or at the bottom of a monk's cell, François de Sales sounded the right note, for which his age was athirst; he humanized the temper of French Christianity at a time

---

Church, and became bishop of Geneva, labouring in his see as spiritual director, administrator, and preacher, and with an influence that radiated over the whole of France. He wrote *Introduction à la vie dévote*, 1608, *Traité de l'amour de Dieu*, 1616, &c.

when both the Catholic and the Protestant faiths had been hardened by their bitter struggle.

There is a marked difference of tone, but no real opposition, between this spiritual suavity and the more austere spirit of 'Port-Royal'. The first reformers of the convent of nuns were in touch with François de Sales; the core of their doctrine was and remained the love of God. From 1635 the commanding personality of their confessor, the Abbé de Saint-Cyran (1581–1643), was the centre from which radiated the influence of the Louvain professor, Cornelius Jansen, afterwards bishop of Ypres. Stress was now laid on the degeneracy of modern worship from that of the primitive Church; on the greatness of God no less than on his charity; on the presence of original sin in the corrupt heart of man; and on the necessity for salvation, of the mysterious gift of grace. Orthodoxy was to be purified by the meditation of the doctrine of Saint Augustine, whose teaching Jansen's book, the *Augustinus* (1640), purported to sum up. From Port-Royal 'Jansénisme', as the new Catholic doctrine was called, spread to wider circles of sympathizers. The monastery, with its nuns, their spiritual directors, and the *solitaires* or recluses who, in close association with them, led lives of asceticism and study, often teaching school in the so-called *petites écoles*, was one of the main sources of the moral strength that lay deep beneath the surface of the classical period; and the profound inspiration it provided is Port-Royal's most genuine claim to inclusion in a survey of French literature. The men who wrote there on themes of divinity or scholarship tended naturally to scorn aesthetic aims; and they had, moreover, to think of self-defence. The prestige of their seminary was obnoxious to many, and even roused political fears. Controversy, court factions, and cliques made for an interrupted existence: the convent was finally, in the next period, to be closed up and its inmates dispersed (1710). Such books as *La Fréquente Communion* (1643) by Antoine Arnauld (1612–94) and the *Essais de morale* (1671, &c.) by Pierre Nicole (1625–95), the most widely read, are now the concern of the specialist alone. Of more general interest to us are the facts that Racine was a pupil at the 'little school' and that the spiritual destiny of Pascal—whose outstanding importance demands separate study—was largely moulded by these men. The ideal of the *honnête homme*, by way of contrast, belongs not to the field of religion, but to that of social ethics. It was not properly a rule of life but a code of manners; and one may see a sign of the increasing sophistication of the age in the gradual assimilation of the latter to the former. Correct behaviour was now becoming the test of virtuous conduct. This use of *honnête* gained currency from about the year 1630, when Nicolas Faret's *L'Honnête Homme ou l'art de plaire à la Cour*) made it a recognized label. It was reserved for Antoine Gombaud, chevalier de Méré (1607–84), to set the seal on its popularity (*Conversations*, 1668; *Discours*, 1671–7). The inevitable comparison with the English idea of the gentleman tends to show that the French concept is more intellectual and less properly ethical. Culture as well as manners make the *honnête homme*; and noble birth, the badge of the medieval and Renaissance *gentilhomme*, now recedes into the background. The evolution that will democratize the English gentleman in the nineteenth to twentieth centuries takes place earlier in France, to the benefit not of the lower classes but of the bourgeoisie. The *honnête homme*, whatever his origin, exists in his relation to social life and may not, in his inmost self, possess that streak of altruism, almost of Christian charity, thanks to which the gentleman, according to a famous description, will take care not to inflict the slightest unnecessary pain upon any one. The *honnête homme* wishes primarily to please, which is not quite the same thing, and in his efforts to please he shows the supreme gift of discretion and tact. As La Rochefoucauld was to put it, 'il ne se pique de rien'; and he is thus a more evolved type than the sixteenth-century courtier, whose self-expression was far less reserved. At bottom, the new French ideal arose from the refined intellectualization of social life. It stressed the duty of sparing all surface susceptibilities, and made full allowance for the many-sided interests of polished men and women, at the same time excluding the pedantry of all technical display. This open-mindedness and the supple sense of measure fit in with the universality of a rational age and with the exquisite balance that is one of the aims of classicism.

Descartes[1]

Descartes is usually considered the very exemplar of French

[1] René Descartes, born in Touraine (1596), studied at a Jesuit school, saw active service in Holland and Germany, travelled extensively, spent some years in Paris,

rationalism and the view may be accepted, with two modifications. In the first place his reliance on reason did not cramp his spirit of development; he had, after all, his night of revelation and visionary enthusiasm, like Pascal. Again, his audacious attempt to build up a coherent system of the whole universe had its counterpart in the strictest spirit of intellectual caution; he dwelt with ideas but kept a firm hold of the concrete; he was the prophet of experimental science, as of modern philosophy. Others, like Galileo or Newton, had made or were to make more startling discoveries in physics, but none quite equalled the breadth of his mental horizon, his clear view of the immense tasks confronting modern man, and of the method of attacking them. His inventions, even if relatively narrow in immediate scope, were unlimited in significance; to his French mind, logical, systematic, but realistic and sane, it was given to lay down principles, map out the great unknown, and indicate paths that pioneers would follow. Moreover, one can sense the humanitarian inspiration behind his sedately and lucidly planned but not selfish endeavour; he dreams of a new medicine that can cure disease; of such progress in knowledge that man may become the master of Nature. In his awareness, his sense of relativity, he is an heir to Montaigne. Carefully and cleverly avoiding all conflict with the Church, he is no *libertin* but a sincere Christian who obeyed Cardinal de Bérulle's suggestion that he should devote his rare powers to establishing solidly the existence of God and of the soul. Considered with all his parts he represents the union of a steadfast faith with a modern eagerness of spirit that could for a time reconcile the forces of tradition and reason. Various encounters and sympathies, with persons and of the mind, such as his concurrence with Corneille's exaltation of the will and theory of generosity, would in themselves have placed him in the forefront of the coming classical age, but it was to this attitude of moderation and synthesis, which tempered without

mixing with scientists and divines, then stayed for some twenty years in the Low Countries, busy with meditation and experiments. His views having been attacked, he returned to France and accepted Queen Christina's invitation to Sweden (1649), where, weakened by hardship and cold, he died in 1650. He had published the *Discours de la méthode*, in French, as a preface to three short treatises (1637); the *Méditations*, in Latin (1641), translated and republished by a friend, with the objections of scholars and the author's answers, in 1647; the *Principes de la philosophie* (1664), in Latin, translated and republished the same year; and the *Passions de l'âme*, 1649.

abating the full demands of man's rational being, that he owed his position as the greatest intellectual ally of its constructive effort.

His doctrine remains to us a monument, still imposing though superannuated and partly fallen into decay. He was right in thinking that the study of Nature should be tirelessly pursued, and that the intuitions of a philosophical mind must be constantly subjected to experience. But his almost single-handed labours brought him only to the entrance of the vast worlds that his successors have been endlessly exploring for three centuries. His theories as to general physics and physiology have only an historical interest. The wonder is that so many of his views should yet be valid, or at least resemble the gropings of genius after dimly divined truths.

His main theses are familiar. At the outset the confused mass of ancient and medieval learning crumbles before the philosopher's critical gaze. The discovery of truth must follow four carefully worded maxims, the first of which is that no value is to be accepted 'unless it has been clearly seized and approved by the intelligence', as a notion clear and distinct to the understanding. So, the *doute provisoire* works its full havoc. But one certainty emerges: he who doubts, thinks; and to think is to be. This does not mean that existence and thought are linked by any kind of metaphysical necessity: their inevitable association is perceived intuitively. And it is on this firm basis that he erects a solid structure of affirmations; man's experience is in contact with the world of thought, which is soul, and with the world of matter, which is extension. The idea of an infinite and perfect being, present in our minds, implies the reality of that being; and God in his turn vouches for the truth of our perceptions. The movements of the material universe are circular, as Nature has no void, and one thing moves only by propelling another, eventually returning to its former place. The changes in our bodies are connected with the circulation of the blood, from which there emanate very small and subtle particles, the *esprits animaux*, that produce impressions on the sentient organ, the *glande pinéale* in the brain. The actions of the body are answered by the passions of the soul, which are not evil in themselves but must be moderated by the will and transformed into the staid composure that is a condition of virtue. A wise man will submit to Providence, take things as they are, and try to change himself rather than the world.

Metaphysics, physics, physiology, psychology, and ethics are thus welded into one system, the lasting worth of which is the fruit of the rigour and honesty that went into its structure. The weaker links in the chain have long been destroyed, but some of Descartes's analogies and connexions are still valid. He established, for instance, the correspondence between the emotions and the blood, the passions and the body, in a manner which the physiological psychology of the last half-century has revived. The unity he tentatively propounded between algebra and geometry has become part of the current theory of mathematics. The method of analysis has been extended to all the fields of science.

Descartes's chief importance as a writer lies in the fact that he deliberately chose to compose his *Discours de la méthode* in French, so as to be intelligible to the average man. The merit of his style has been somewhat overrated: the *Discours* was written under the influence of Latin construction; many sentences are overloaded and far too long; and the manner contrasts painfully with the ease and elegance of his contemporary Balzac. But he had a powerful source of clarity in the strength of his mind; and he expressed himself with a sober precision and moderation illumined by rare glints of intellectual humour; his treatise on the *Passions de l'âme* is better and far more simple.

2. POETRY

Malherbe[1]

Boileau's sigh of relief ('Enfin, Malherbe vint . . .') has ceased to be passively condoned. The implied judgement is grossly unjust to what preceded and what accompanied the champion of correctness and the rules. But while no longer seating him in solitary eminence on a higher throne than any poet except the greatest, a candid critic must acknowledge his solid merit. His taste was not unimpeachable

---

[1] François de Malherbe, born in Normandy (1555) of a Protestant father, joined the Catholic Church, stayed for a time in Provence, then from 1605 in Paris, where the favours of Henri IV, and later of the Queen Regent, gave him the standing of an unofficial Laureate, writing mainly for the Court and, though he still lived modestly, with the authority of a literary lawgiver. His earliest important piece was the *Larmes de Saint Pierre* (1587); his other poems (odes, consolations, *stances*, sonnets, *Paraphrases des Psaumes*, &c.) were first collected in 1630. He wrote prose translations of Latin authors, and died in 1628.

from the beginning. His adaptation from the Italian of Tansillo's *Larmes de Saint Pierre* has many fine passages but abounds in glaring conceits. From openly baroque art he rose to classical purity through an inner process of experience and reflection. By 1610 his doctrine was complete and sufficiently well known to be summed up in Deimier's *Académie de l'art poétique*. Substantially, Malherbe's doctrine embodied the time-honoured theory of perfection, but with the stress laid almost exclusively on formal faultlessness. A good artisan will do honest work, shirk no difficulty, and throw no dust into the eyes: this is exactly Malherbe's code of duty. Poetry is no longer divinely inspired, but the forcible expression of sustained thought; it may be moved and moving, but should by all means preserve its clear balance. Let the poet labour and prune untiringly: it is a craft to write lines, as to play ninepins. If the words are aptly selected and combined, beauty will arise, whether the thought be original or not. A good writer must avoid dialect or vulgarisms, and use terms only in their purest sense; the laws of grammar must never be allowed to suffer for the sake of poetic measure; rhyme must satisfy the ear as well as the eye; the clash of vowels between two words is to be severely proscribed; none but the end-stopped type of verse is quite correct, and the pause must be in the proper place. As for similes, they must be confined cautiously within the actual possibilities of Nature.

This negative code came to be the all-in-all of the ageing Malherbe, who sharply criticized his predecessors, or the younger poets, for every falling-off. But when we turn to his own work we find it much better than his somewhat tame doctrine would lead us to expect. He has little free gift of inspiration and nearly always has some train of thought to follow. In what he has to say he uses mostly the type of rhetorical commonplace dear to orators. But to the development of his theories he does nevertheless bring an instructive discretion and a gift of fit and felicitous phrasing, while his lines move with an unforced rhythm. Behind these estimable virtues there is more—a genuine sense of the stately march of grand stanzas, an intuitive perception of musical and evocative values, noble imagery, and at all times the creative gift not of a versifier but of a true poet. His longer odes hark back to Ronsard, with more elaboration but no less vigour. His personal lyrics have a dignified candour that happily diversifies the austerity of his talent. If the badge of classicism is the survival of a form that never loses its appeal, the best of Malherbe belongs indeed to the treasury of classic French poetry.

Hard to please as Malherbe was he did not disapprove of his contemporary Jean Bertaut (1552–1611), and he approved of two younger poets, François Mainard (1582–1646) and Racan (see above, Chapter XVIII, Section 2). Bertaut owed this favour to a natural elegance and to the wisdom he showed in taking a leaf out of Malherbe's book. As a result he is remarkably regular, but his smoothness often flows from real warmth of feeling, and he has flashes of actual poetry. Such a simple strain as this possesses the genuine quality of some popular refrain:

> Félicité passée,
> Qui ne peut revenir,
> Tourment de ma pensée,
> Que n'ai-je en te perdant perdu le souvenir!

Mainard has been unjustly neglected by posterity. His compact manner and laboured but felicitous perfection are not unworthy of his master. He has more sensuousness and grace, and 'anthology' pieces are easy to find among his odes, sonnets, and 'stances'. He handles equally well the rounded and majestic alexandrine or the eight-syllabled verse, a measure fit at will for a lyric or an epigram. As for Racan, his discipleship to Malherbe left his independence untouched, and he has already figured among the freelances.

The poets of wit

The importance of Voiture[1] is that he added a shade to the self-realization of intellectual France. The art of conversation in circles where cultivated women set the tone had for long been a prominent feature of social life, but it was he more than any other member of the select company that met at Madame de Rambouillet's who brought it to an acknowledged perfection. His special contribution was the exercise of a gift that for many foreign observers has always

---

[1] Vincent Voiture, born at Amiens (1597), was for some time attached to the Duke of Orléans, and he also travelled in Spain and as far as northern Africa. From 1636 he was an *habitué* of the Hôtel de Rambouillet (see below, Section 4), a successful wit and critic. His letters and poems were collected after his death in 1648.

been a characteristic aspect of the French mind—finesse, the sharp perception and just rendering of delicate values in the analysis of thought, feeling, or art. Since the conversationalist leaves no record, it is in his prose and verse writings that we must find grounds for Voiture's reputation. That he should have been immune from the fashionable vice of *préciosité* is not to be expected; but he succumbs to it with an apologetic half-smile, and prizes such baubles at their proper worth. On the whole his taste is naturally pure, as his style is free from affectation. The manner of Balzac still showed a tinge of self-consciousness and oratory; that of Voiture is more simple. At the same time, he can without pedantry convey a serious meaning and noble sentiment, or combine dignity and weight with sublimity or playfulness; and he invariably shows exquisite tact in his choice of words. Among his most famous letters, the one he wrote on hearing the news of the recapture of Corbie (24 November 1636) may be cited as an example of his best manner. Very few of his attempts (*Lettre de la Carpe au brochet*, &c.), are overdone. His love-letters, equally clever and charming, are on a lower plane, for passion has no part in them. He handles verse as easily as prose, and his many rondeaux revive a form that suited his talent for gentle impertinence. His best verse, however, is to be found among the *Épîtres* and *lettres en vers*, where the eight-syllabled line moves nimbly and gracefully, throwing off countless kind or ironical innuendos with the utmost skill as it moves. This, again, is a foretaste of the future; a century and a half of French literature will turn out thousands of these light, brilliant pieces; Voltaire's will be more incisive but no better.

Isaac de Benserade (1612–91) enjoyed a high reputation in his own time; the critics placed him on a par with Voiture as a drawing-room poet. Two sets of highly cultivated men and women quarrelled over the comparative merit of his 'Job' sonnet and Voiture's 'Uranie'. The 'Job' has a fine conclusion; but that is about the best one can say of Benserade's whole output. Hardly a spark that even resembles genuine emotion can be detected in his epigrams, epitaphs, ballads, paraphrases, or feats of translation (Ovid in rondeaux, Aesop in quatrains, &c.). Wit, elegance, a light touch are on the surface, but there is at bottom a rather heavy insistence and some scurrility. The less pleasant aspect of the worldly manners of the time—the years before the young Louis XIV had sown his wild oats—is here revived.

The case is different with Jean-François Sarasin (1614–54), whose finesse is more delicate and of more sterling quality. The spirit alive in him is one of purest classicism, of which, indeed, he was a precursor, for he died on the eve of the great age. He succeeds easily in the reconciliation that was to be an achievement of the period—the fusion of naturalness and simplicity with the tension of an acute analytical mind. His prose writings (*Histoire du siège de Dunkerque*, *La Conspiration de Valstein*, and the *Dialogue, s'il faut qu'un jeune homme soit amoureux*) are models of clear, firm, sober narrative and of witty, charming debate; *La Pompe funèbre de Voiture* is a delightful *jeu d'esprit*, with a spice of not ungentle raillery. Part of his verse is only second-rate and no more; some, like *La Seine parlant à la Fontaine de Forges*, equals the best *badinages* of Voiture. That the soul of poetry did breathe in him, through all his liveliness and wit, we may feel, for example, in this stanza of the *Ode sur la bataille de Lens*:

> C'est assez, Vesper s'avance,
> Il faut quitter nos chansons;
> Le vent qui rompt le silence
> Murmure dans ces buissons;
> Le soleil tombe sous l'onde,
> La nuit va couvrir le Monde,
> Et sur la terre, et les flots,
> Le sommeil ouvrant ses ailes
> Espand les moissons nouvelles
> De ses humides pavots.

His deliberate adhesion to the doctrine of classicism asserts itself in his *Discours de la tragédie*, which overpraises Scudéry's *Amour tyrannique* but supports the cause of dramatic regularity with telling vigour.

In later years attention has justly been called to the full stream of religious poetry that flowed uninterruptedly through the central decades of the sixteenth century. It was written by a group who fall into the class of orthodox writers, for they did not rebel against canons of expression or belief, and their spirit contrasts strongly with the loose, iconoclastic spirit of most independent poets.

Still, many freelances eventually became orthodox as age and experience sobered them; Tristan l'Hermite, Racan, and Saint-Amant, for instance, are among the singers of edifying themes. On the Protestant as well as the Catholic side collections of hymns, meditations, and paraphrases in verse were published, with something of the expected characteristics of the two creeds. Mention can only be made here of Bishop Antoine Godeau (1605–72; *Poésies chrétiennes et morales*); or of Georges de Brébeuf (1616?–60; *Entretiens solitaires*), poems of solid merit, genuine inwardness, and firm, sustained quality of phrasing; or, chiefly, of the great dramatist Pierre Corneille (see below, Chapter XX), whose rendering of the *Imitation de Jésus-Christ* does honour to the force of his genius as well as to the fervour of his faith. In a general way, such works testify variously to the profound desire for a reflective, meditative, and composed strain of poetry, a tributary, as it were, to the broad stream of incipient classicism.

3. REFORMERS OF LANGUAGE AND ART

The conflict between the writer's independence and his subjection to rules was fought out mainly, as will be seen at the end of this chapter, on the field of the drama. But more widely, in the whole domain of literature, the issue came to a head during the earlier half of the century; and by gradual consensus of opinion the victory lay with the doctrine of regularity and order. One cannot resist the inference that in arriving at this decision, and in spite of all contrary tendencies, the collective judgement of the French people was guided by a definite preference which, growing more or less subconsciously in the minds of thousands of readers, by degrees shaped the course of the national literature, and so led to the emergence of the classical age proper. To try and elucidate the problem on the psychological plane by survey of a sufficiently large number of individual test cases is out of the question here; we can do no more than hazard an explanation of causes from the final result. But before the full-grown classicists are studied some brief attention is due to lesser writers who made a name for themselves in pointing out and discussing this or that aspect of the general issue.

One outstanding fact of French history—not only literary, but social—is to be recalled first of all—the creation by Cardinal de

Richelieu, about 1635 (the stages of the foundation spread over several years), of the Académie Française. Some writers had been meeting weekly to thrash out problems of their craft; the great minister saw his opportunity, and by developing this nucleus into a recognized body, with regulations, a set number of *académiciens*, and formal gatherings, made it a powerful agency to serve purposes of government no less than of art. The new institution, at the beginning, was meant to watch over the progress of the French language, and by means of its official decrees and publications, to preserve the purity of speech and style at a time when correct usage was still imperfectly established. It attracted most of the successful writers, and its authority grew fast enough to give it, before long, the standing of a public adviser in matters of criticism and taste. Needless to say, all its influence was exerted in favour of what may be called thenceforward the orthodox manner of writing.

Claude Favre, sieur de Vaugelas (1585–1650), is at the head of a typically French lineage: the series of modern grammarians and critics, who, combining scholarship with an appeal to a wider public, have catered for readers keenly interested in the proper use of language. Problems of diction and style are dear in France to the cultivated classes, whether provincial or Parisian; and he who competently lays down the law is sure of a pleased and grateful audience. Vaugelas was neither the first, nor the only one in his own lifetime to devote himself to this fascinating subject; the ladies and the wits of the 'Hôtel de Rambouillet' had been sifting and testing the vocabulary of *honnêtes gens*; the foundation of the Académie française—to which Vaugelas belonged from the first—showed the same desire at work in learned circles. But when the *Remarques sur la langue française*, part of which had been circulated for some time, were published in 1647, the book met with a particularly warm reception, and its success was lasting. The worthy author deserved success by the size, the objectivity, and the modesty of his inquiry; he makes no claim to personal judgement in such awful matters; no single person, he declares, has a right to pronounce upon words, the sacred instruments of human intercourse; what an observer can do is to collect and present the facts of usage 'que chacun reconnoist pour le Maistre et le Souverain des Langues Vivantes'. The sovereign, no doubt, is capricious; but the madness is not without method:

'Il n'y a rien de si bizarre; si est-ce qu'il ne laisse pas de faire beaucoup de choses avec raison.' When this background of reason is apparent, Vaugelas draws attention to it; in other cases he will more often bow, and invite us to bow; he rarely allows himself to hint that on special points the rulings of usage might be corrected. His remarks are proffered without any perceptible underlying plan to link them. Each problem is sufficient unto itself, and interest is born again at every step. The only principles to be gathered from the instinctive decrees of use and wont would be those of clearness and euphony; but these are not formulated in so many words; the need to avoid ambiguity, or clashing sounds, is simply mentioned. Such was the survey, which generations of French readers perused with delight. It bears witness to the respect and love they felt for their language; and to the sense and tact of Vaugelas, tempered with a shade, perhaps, of over-timidity. He was a modest contributor to the rise of classicism. His action, added to other, similar, forces, may have tended to cut off the French tongue from its living roots in the habitual speech of the whole people—of the lower classes especially, by which language is constantly refreshed and invigorated. But if in so doing he made French a less proper tool for the flights of lyricism, he did much in compensation to fit it admirably for intellectual conversation, and for the varied scope of a rational literature.

The aim of Vaugelas was to weed out the uncertainties, discrepancies, and vulgarisms that could still cloy the pen and lower the pitch of the artist. Balzac[1] was himself that artist; his proficiency as a faultless writer of prose was hailed with admiration and patriotic pride by men and women who could think of no higher achievement. He is not a mere stringer of words and polisher of phrases; the surprise when reading him is to find that little or no straining after effect is perceptible; he has point, wit, rhythm, and elegance, but he shows golden sense also, and discretion. Montaigne had stamped French prose with his personal, supple, leisurely, and yet

---

[1] Jean Louis Guez, sire de Balzac (1597–1654), born in Angoumois, was sent on various missions, and then tried unsuccessfully to obtain a position at Court. Finally he gave up, retired to live on his small estate, and to correspond with friends in literary or aristocratic circles. He published a very successful collection of his *Lettres* (1624); *Le Prince*, 1631; *Le Socrate chrétien*, 1652. *Aristippe, ou de la cour*, came out after his death. He is, of course, to be kept distinct from his namesake, Honoré de Balzac, the nineteenth-century novelist.

penetrating manner; but his was not a style one could imitate. Balzac, among others, but better than any, on the eve of the classical period evolved a pattern of writing so well adapted to the central genius of the language, that it offered a model to all. One might follow it without equalling the master, but one was at least sure to do fairly well. After him writers had to cease complaining, as they had done so long, that their instrument was ill suited to their efforts; French had become a medium which in clarity, finesse, and range of delicate shading showed the attic quality of the best Greek. There still lingers in Balzac some tinge of the rhetoric that was the legacy of the Renaissance interpretation of Latin eloquence; a further degree of lightness and directness was still desirable, and was to be reached after him; but he served the turn of classical prose-writers to perfection, with their staid gravity and dignity. The instinctive craving of the French mind for balance, order, and neatness has in it also a sense of artistic finish. Balzac satisfied this fully. His sobriety is elegance, and his rhythmic measure deftly soothes a subconscious need for poetry. It is tantalizing to find that in the opinion of a contemporary this paragon talked even better than he wrote. A good example of his writing is the opening of *Le Prince*, with its fine harmony of tone, season, and the mood evoked. In such passages we find the vague and continually varied symbolism of real art, and a strain of the music that is the only true echo of feeling. The 'discours' on *Le Romain* is more simple and stripped, condensed into briefer sentences, and seems to point the way towards the analytical style of the eighteenth century. As for Balzac's letters, none is more graceful, brilliant, telling, yet tactfully phrased, than that in which he defends Corneille's *Cid* against its arch-enemy, Scudéry.

Chapelain,[1] whose significance as a critic has only lately been recognized, is the central character in the whole process that brought about the final ascendancy of *les règles*. He was widely read, and a

---

[1] Jean Chapelain (1595–1674), born in Paris, was reputed for his learning and talent, and played the part of a literary adviser to Richelieu. He drew up the first regulations of the Académie française, and wrote *Les Sentiments de l'Académie sur le Cid*. By his letters and treatises (*Lettre sur les 24 heures*, 1630; *De la poésie représentative*, 1635?), he exerted an important influence on the development of literature. Word of an epic poem he had begun, *La Pucelle*, roused great expectations, which were disappointed when the first twelve books appeared (1656). The last twelve remained in manuscript, and were published in 1882.

resolute admirer of the ancients, though not impervious to the possibility of new attempts on the basis of old practice. He showed initiative in one direction particularly, by holding that the *merveilleux chrétien* had its legitimate place in literature. The assurance and solidity of his doctrine gave special authority to his spoken or written word. To his clear, dogmatic and slightly pedantic mind, the artist's duty was all included in his obedience to traditional obligations; by departing from them, a writer would inevitably go astray, but by respecting them he would, no less inevitably, create beauty. As for the deeper origin of the rules, Chapelain saw it, not in Aristotle, but in reason: the three dramatic unities were solidly founded upon logic and verisimilitude. On these grounds he objected to *Le Cid*: the play, he asserted, violated probability, the unity of place, and moral decorum. His verdict, in other respects, was not without moderation and good judgement. The failure of his *Pucelle* saddened the end of his life. It is pathetic to see the old poet, in his Preface to the last (then unpublished) books, point out desperately that having applied all the rules, he *must* have written a fine epic. In fact, Boileau's pitiless ridicule has unduly prejudiced posterity against a poem that no one reads, on the comfortable assurance that it is not readable. Though frequently strained and tedious, *La Pucelle* has interesting merits. It displays a warm and vigorous, if somewhat hectic imagination, and abounds in passages of descriptive and evocative force. Its verse is technically competent and sonorous. Only the reader is too plainly aware that the author's notion of grandeur implies grandiloquence; and that he thinks it an absolute duty to introduce all the devices of ancient epics—full-dress comparisons, chiefly, at regular intervals. Still, many modern poems based on the same theme, the most tragic and moving in French history, are almost all more indecorous, and no better, than Chapelain's conscientious and unequal effort.

Among many critics whose treatises, prefaces, letters, &c., helped to give coherence to the principles of the literature of the classical age, mention may be made of Pillet de la Mesnardière (1610–63), the author of a *Poétique* (first and only part, 1639), full of Aristotle, as interpreted by the Italians; and of the Abbé d'Aubignac (1604–76), whose *Pratique du théâtre* (1657) professes to be indispensable for all playwrights. This significant work is a guide to contemporary opinions and preferences, without which the more second-rate French classical dramatists would hardly be intelligible. Criticism, d'Aubignac points out, actually adds to the enjoyment of books, since it explains their beauties: 'Car on goûte avec plus de satisfaction les belles choses, quand on peut découvrir les raisons qui les rendent agréables.' On the stage, verisimilitude is all. 'La vraysemblance est ... l'essence du Poème Dramatique, et sans laquelle il ne se peut rien faire ny rien dire de raisonnable sur la scène'; which of course cuts at the root of all possible appeal to the spectator's 'willing suspension of disbelief'. No wonder, then, that the writing of plays should be very largely a matter of cleverness, ingenuity and labour: 'combien de méditations, de veilles et de réflexions' they have cost their authors! This goes some little way, but not far, to explain Racine and Molière; and the worthy Abbé, in his very elaborate and full treatise, has not made sufficient allowance for incalculable factors.

4. SENTIMENT AND REFINEMENT

The thought and the trend of the classical age were mostly intellectual; a rational aesthetic was almost bound to have its germ in the cult and the practice of reason. Malherbe, Descartes, Balzac, were effective thinkers and writers; but a great period of literature must be fed from all sources to bear rich human fruit, it must have its roots in complete humanity; and a good deal of sentiment did enter into the psychological preparation for the half-century in which the heroic grandeur of Corneille, the half mystical visions of Pascal, the passion of Racine, variously probed the depths of the human soul. A word has already been said of the religious revival—whether orthodox or Jansenist—that preceded this transitional period. Attention must also be paid to the broad vein of feeling that cropped up in the sentimental and heroic novel, and to the refining action of the *précieux* movement. These elements do not strictly belong together, but as testimonies to the increasing influence of women they possess a more than superficial unity. The lasting success of *Astrée*, the welcome given to the romances of Mademoiselle de Scudéry, the prestige of the Hôtel de Rambouillet, were so many indications of the rising tide of femininity which brought with it a renewal of idealistic love, the worship of heroism, and a determination to purify and

exalt language as well as life. It also did much to counteract the disruptive tendencies so clearly apparent in, for instance, the *libertin*
movement, and in the persistent, though now repressed and hidden
progress of scepticism. Threatened with disintegration under the
stress of destructive reason, French culture sought instinctively for
the balance that is ever one of its chief objects; and a determined
stiffening of the will and of moral courage, a readiness to allow room
for healthy sentiment, were evident preparations to meet the immi-
nent spiritual strain. Thus were secured the mental sanity of the
classical age, and the relative equilibrium of its art.

Astrée, written by a man, is a book in which woman's spiritual
influence is paramount. It harks back, far beyond Montemayor's
Diana—that widely popular Spanish romance—beyond Petrarchism
itself, to the tradition of *l'amour courtois* and to Christian chivalry,
which had died historically, but which lived ever in the human
heart. D'Urfé[1] is a devout believer, and if the scene of his pastoral
story is still an officially pagan Gaul, this is only due to his scrupulous
reverence; his work is steeped in a purity and tenderness that obviously derive from Christianity. The huge and sprawling novel,
which took some twenty years to write, appeals unreservedly to the
taste for romance; fresh, and frequently improbable, incidents continually revive the reader's sentimental interest in two perfect
lovers: she, Astrée, a pattern of delicate feminine honour; he, Céladon, a miracle of self-sacrificing loyalty. The course of true love is
repeatedly crossed; villains, rivals, and jealous women make trouble,
and the situation is several times desperate, before things work out
finally to a happy ending. Any value the book possesses nowadays is
obviously not in such a plot. A modern, sick with the now obsolete
convention, will swallow this grumblingly, but if he can keep an
open mind he will find merit in the tangled variety of the incidents,
and the differentiation of the characters. The charm of *Astrée*

[1] Honoré d'Urfé (1567–1625) was born at Marseille, of noble parents, but his
family belonged to the Forez, where he was brought up. He fought with the Ligue,
then retired to the domains of the Duc de Savoie, his relative. Marriage in 1600 with
his sister-in-law, whose union with his elder brother had been annulled, rewarded a
long-felt passion. He was fighting against Spain when he died, and had published
religious poems, a pastoral, some *épîtres morales*, and a novel, *Astrée* (first part 1607;
second 1610; third 1619; fourth, posthumous, 1627, with a fifth written by another
hand).

lies chiefly in the freshness of a sensibility that has remained young, and revels in the picture of an innocent Arcadia, where idealized shepherds—d'Urfé frankly confesses to it—lead lives of leisure, speak a refined language, and feel the passion without the fever of love, wrapped up as they are in soothing, quiet scenery: that of d'Urfé's own Forez. But there is force as well in the grip of the writer's imagination upon the sufferings and heroisms of the heart. Something of Richardson's bitterness in *Clarissa* already lives here in the determination, not Puritan but didactic, that inflicts upon poor Céladon tortures he bears with unfailing, meek fortitude. The Cornelian grandeur of allegiance to an almost superhuman duty exalts these scenes, and goes far to explain the hold so long maintained by *Astrée* in spite of Sorel's ridicule, upon numberless French or European readers. It was accepted into the conscience of the age as a lesson in noble living, and through it French literature recovered some of the moralizing influence of the *chansons de geste* and medieval romances. Naïve sincerity keeps its sentiment sweet, with very little of the mawkishness of the eighteenth century. D'Urfé's style, again, while opening the way for such precious vagaries as the *Carte de Tendre*, shows few objectionable conceits, and flows on in unassuming simplicity.

After *Astrée*, romances flourished for a long generation, inclining more and more to the heroic strain, and laying stress on a highly fictitious background of history. Such names as those of Gomberville (1600–74; *Polexandre*, 1637) and La Calprenède (1614–53; *Cassandre*, 1642–5; *Cléopâtre*, 1646–57), appear often enough in the Memoirs and letters of the period, to show proof of their widespread popularity.

With Madeleine de Scudéry[1] the gap is practically bridged between the heroic novel and the refining effort of *préciosité*. As a novelist, she claims to have no masters except 'l'immortel Héliodore, et le grand Urfé'. Her personal bent is decidedly towards the study

---

[1] Madeleine de Scudéry (1607–1701) was for a time an *habituée* of the Hôtel de Rambouillet, and from about 1650 opened a *salon* of her own, to less aristocratic but still distinguished visitors; her 'Saturdays' were crowded and brilliant. Under the name of her brother George (1601–67, himself no negligible writer), she published romances: *Ibrahim*, 1641; *Artamène ou le Grand Cyrus*, 1648–53; *Clélie, histoire romaine*, 1654–61; and at a later period of her long life, ethical disquisitions (several series of *Conversations*).

of character; conflicts of feeling are noted in a precise and somewhat primitive manner: 'Il y avait des moments où Artamène', her hero, felt thus; 'il y en avait d'autres aussi . . .' when he felt differently, and the division of moods is repeatedly made clear, as an important aspect of the truth, not to be passed over. Her psychology, like that of Corneille, is markedly intellectualist, and makes insufficient allowance for undefined, inexplicable states. The emotions she deals with —and especially that of ardent but respectful love—are pitched in the same intense key as those of *Astrée*; the noble-souled heroes and heroines reach the same height of selflessness; and there is the same vast profusion of pseudo-historical incidents. The 'three-decker' of Victorian days is indeed a small pinnace in the wake of these ten-volume Leviathans. Yet the endless story, winding to and fro amid side-issues and parenthetical tales, still wins our interest; not by the piquancy of contemporary allusion, which has vanished, or the portraits of living persons, whose originals are now hard to discover, but because we share the liking for unashamed romance which is a foible of young and old. It is only fair to add that though her imagination is fired with the past, the authoress steers clear of pedantry; she has a natural gift, and writes easily and gracefully. With her, *préciosité* is an essence, diffused rather than concentrated in conceits. She is one of those lucky writers whose obvious defects are, in the end, entertaining.

Molière's amusing comedy (1659) justly made fun of the fringe of ridiculous and affected hangers-on who inevitably vulgarized the refinement of the genuine *précieuses*. This name gained currency about 1654, and at once acquired a pejorative connotation. It denoted a kind of fastidious pride, a holding one's self precious, and putting too high a price on one's pretended distinction, at the expense of the common run of women. There certainly was some sinning of that sort; but beneath the hostility it provoked there was also a remnant of the prejudice which had always met woman's first attempts to overcome the inferiority of her culture. In a general way, the tendency to an esoteric, even if somewhat involved mode of expression, is as old as French literature itself. The land of clarity was no less the land of artistic refinement, and refining upon language had been a temptation dear to French writers from the earliest schools of medieval poetry. The desire assumed a slightly different form during the long period of transition that followed the Renaissance, when the instruments and conditions of the literary art, and language itself, were repeatedly tested. Women then stepped forward, and took the lead; to serve their turn, the materials of the writer's craft had to be freed from dross, in the shape of uncertainties of taste, and provincial or popular contamination. The problem now was to generalize propriety, and to establish a definite scale of aesthetic values. It shaded off into questions of tone, manner, composition, and rules; and passed beyond these to the definition of good behaviour, and even of good conduct. Such treatises as Castiglione's *Courtier*, in the sixteenth century, had already testified to the natural links between these topics. Delicate subjects such as the relation between men and women, love, courtship, and marriage, were inevitably drawn into the field of debate; and, once admitted, they assumed a privileged place.

The famous *salon* of Catherine de Vivonne, Marquise de Rambouillet (1588–1665), in her mansion near the Louvre, was for almost half a century (approximately 1610–50) the focus of this social, literary, and ethical movement. Most of the distinguished men and women of the Court, the Town, and literary and philosophical circles were frequent or occasional visitors. A kind of democracy of the talents prevailed within the fairly wide barriers of caste thus maintained, although Voiture, with his outstanding prestige, often played the part of arbiter. Regular meetings were held, themes set, new writers or books discussed, and issues of philosophy or ethics tackled with intrepidity. Wit was in great demand, and a gift for conversation a sure 'measure of entry'. But although dangerous ground was thus constantly skirted, a wrong impression should not be formed of these gatherings, which were by no means a school for scandal, amorous intrigue, or pedantry. The sense and fine perception of the hostess, the genuine worth of the characters and minds that came into contact, to their mutual satisfaction and benefit, kept the atmosphere free from licentiousness, pretension, or snobbery. The Hôtel de Rambouillet made a definite contribution to the final formation of a language fit for the analytical expression of ideas and feelings, clear and exact, stamped with dignity and simplicity, and also to the polish of manners, and a notion of the unassuming intellectual intercourse of the sexes that inaugurated the tradition of the

French literary *salons*. Lastly, at a time when the Court was still not entirely free from grossness, it gave an example of true delicacy in speech and conduct.

When the great Marquise de Rambouillet died, her ascendancy was inherited by Madeleine de Scudéry, whose more moralizing temper stamps an even more strongly marked refinement of spirit upon *préciosité*. She still, of necessity, made love her chief subject, but she sublimated it to an almost unnatural degree. Its main element, she never wearies in saying, is or should be 'tenderness', a feeling that her heroine, Clélie, thus defines:

> C'est une certaine sensibilité du cœur, qui ne se trouve presque iamais souverainement qu'en des personnes qui ont l'âme noble, les inclinations vertueuses, et l'esprit bien tourné; et qui fait que lorsqu'elles ont de l'amitié elles l'ont sincère, et ardente; et qu'elles sentent si vivement toutes les douleurs, et toutes les ioyes de ceux qu'elles aiment, qu'elles ne sentent pas tant les leurs propres.

A generous description indeed, which raises human nature to its most exalted level. But on this strongly spiritual plane the actual union of the sexes is an idea that feminine susceptibility tends to dismiss; and this provides some ground for the satirical features in the characters of Molière's *Femmes savantes*. None the less, the high ideal of *préciosité*, in its more genuine essence, enriched French literature with a range of feelings that widened and ennobled its scope. Not exactly Racine, but Marivaux, and later Rousseau, are foreshadowed in Aronce's remark (*Clélie*) that tenderness is 'une qualité encore plus nécessaire à l'amour, qu'à l'amitié', so that those who are destitute of it 'ne connaissent point une certaine mélancolie douce qui naist de la tendresse d'un cœur amoureux; et qui l'occupe quelquefois plus doucement, que la ioye ne le pourrait faire'. We have here the actual enlargement of sensibility, of which the *Carte de Tendre*, drawn and printed in the novel, with its detailed figuration, is only a fanciful and allegorical presentment.

Thus *préciosité* entered into the very substance of classicism, as both a stimulant and an irritant. In so far as it was a ferment of purer thought, expression, and language, it strengthened the purpose and added to the effectiveness of the classical endeavour. To the extent that it broke the golden rule of measure, tended to prize some elements of art too highly, to the undue benefit of formal refinement, it roused the instinctive dislike and protest of the more lucid classicists themselves. So, during the heyday of the school, it was one of those bosom enemies that we denounce the more willingly because they are close relations, and might be mistaken for one of ourselves.

5. REGULAR DRAMA

The decade 1630–40 saw the decisive swing in the history of the French stage toward regular patterns. The spirit of the age favoured this development, and lent to the defenders of the rules the persuasive force that ideas generally owe to their coincidence with the needs of the public mind. Before La Mesnardière's *Poétique*, and long before d'Aubignac's *Pratique du théâtre* (see above, Section 3), it was Chapelain whose voice rang out first and clearest. His *Letter* to Godeau (1630) explained the 'point of view of the learned', and exerted immediate influence upon Jean Mairet (1604–86), the playwright whose career most signally reveals the trend of the time.

His first plays took after the free model then in fashion; his *Sylvie, tragi-comédie pastorale* (1626) owed much to Racan's *Bergeries*, as to Théophile's *Pyrame et Thisbé*. It appealed to romantic sentiment, and treated themes of love poetically, with occasional touches of realistic humour. The most successful scene showed a combat of wit between a shepherd and a shepherdess, who very neatly reduced him to silence. Only a few years had elapsed, when Mairet revised d'Urfé's *Silvanire* (1630) so as to make it conform to the unities; then, in a preface to the published play (1631), he gave the first full explanation of the classical dramatic doctrine, laying stress especially on the unity of time. His practice, in his immediately following output, was somewhat mixed; but the success of his *Sophonisbe* (1634) put an end to whatever hesitation he may have felt.

This is an arresting play and, much more than Tristan l'Hermite's *Mariamne* (1636), may win for Mairet the honour of being called a 'precursor of Racine'. It is not faultless, and just falls short of being a masterpiece. Its perfect regularity is of great historical importance, but has little intrinsic value for us, except that in so far as obedience to the rules means artistic concentration, it lends impressiveness to the plot, which is no less simple than that of *Bérénice*. A powerful imagination is at work in the evocation of an African world, tragic in its ardours and sensualities, but the chief interest is decidedly psychological. The choruses have been cut out; friends and 'confidants' allow the main characters a full explanation of their feelings, which are often delicately or subtly shaded; and a fine discretion is at work in the choice of what is shown on the stage. The whole drama is in verse whose equal, rhythmic movement, together with the firm precision and sober force of the language, answers very fully to the ideas associated with the epithet 'classical'.

Mairet's contemporaries felt at once that a landmark had been reached, and that the secret expectation of many minds was fulfilled. Thenceforward the rules had won, and with ups and downs, inequalities and relapses, their period of ascendancy had begun. How settled their authority was we can gather from the history of Corneille's pathetic efforts, to correct his own impulses, and to make his plays conform to the proper standard of regularity.

CHAPTER XX

Corneille

THE very list of Corneille's[1] plays tells its own tale. His work is more varied and abundant than that of the general run of the great classical writers, whose genius has tended to concentrate on a moderate crop of carefully ripened fruit. Stress can only be laid here on his essential achievement, the great tragedies.

To the generation of 1660 he stands as a precursor, with the light of the morning still upon his face. By his vigour and the native independence of his spirit, he does not yet belong to the period of full discipline, when the idea of rules was bred in the bone of each new artist. He learnt about the rules, and accepted them; in his touching modesty—the modesty of a proud man—he did his best to conform, and apply them thoroughly. But he never felt entirely at ease in the strait jacket, and it never sat absolutely well upon him, argue as he might in his sharp, interesting 'Examinations' and 'Prefaces'. His early comedies were free; a strictly orthodox period (*Horace* to *Polyeucte*) followed; and hereafter he again began to take liberties. This aspect of his career, though of secondary importance, is not negligible, since he gave the matter so much of his genuine concern.

Is *Le Cid* a tragicomedy? He called it so at first to forestall objections; and we may leave it at that. Indeed the ending is 'happy'. But

[1] Pierre Corneille was born of upper middle-class parents at Rouen (1606), and for a time practised at the Bar. He wrote comedies and tragicomedies, from *Mélite*, 1630, to *L'Illusion comique*, 1636, and a tragedy, *Médée*, 1635. The triumph of his tragicomedy, *Le Cid*, 1637, roused the jealousy of rivals and the censure of critics (*Sentiments de l'Académie sur le Cid*, 1637). This discouraged him for a while, but he won fresh triumphs with the tragedies: *Horace*, *Cinna*, and *Polyeucte*, 1640 to 1642. *La Mort de Pompée*, *Rodogune*, *Théodore*, *Héraclius*, *Andromède*, *Nicomède*, 1643 to 1651, tragedies, and the comedies: *Le Menteur*, *La Suite du Menteur*, 1643–4, *Don Sanche d'Aragon*, 1649, were less uniformly successful; the failure of *Pertharite*, 1652, kept him away from the stage for seven years. He made new attempts, mostly successful, with *Œdipe*, 1659, *Sertorius*, *Sophonisbe*, *Othon*, *Agésilas*, *Attila*, *Tite et Bérénice*, *Pulchérie*, *Suréna*, 1662 to 1674. He collaborated with Molière and Quinault in *Psyché*, 1671, and between 1651 and 1656 he had translated the *Imitation* into verse. He died in 1684. His critical writings, in which he mainly discusses and justifies his own work, are of general value.

who will look for actual elements of comedy in this stirring, exultant, chivalrous play, of which every French boy knows passages by heart? Chapelain's strictures have lost their point altogether. What if the plot cannot be entirely reconciled with the unities of place and time? What if the proprieties are technically violated, because Chimène receives Rodrigue in her own apartment, and allows him to hope that she may eventually marry the man who, to avenge his own father, has killed hers in fair fight? To us the two lovers seem worthy of each other and we give them our blessing. What counts more with us is that within Corneille's clear and logical sense of drama there does burn a fire, which has sometimes, and not unjustly, been called romantic. The youthful spirit of defiance with which *Le Cid* is instinct, the *romancero* atmosphere borrowed from the Spanish play of Guilhem de Castro (1621), harmonize with an imaginative intensity that finds a natural outlet in phrases and images more exuberant than are warranted by the composure of a purely classical style. Lyricism is present and active beneath the tension, and the 'stances' of *Le Cid*, as those of *Polyeucte*, are dictated by a need for full musical expression that was too strong to be resisted. The same energy of conception and writing lends its original character, for instance, to that impressive tragedy, *Rodogune*. But if Corneille's genius is composite, it is only the richer in its appeal.

Yet these features, marked as they are, do not form part of his deepest personality. In it we find a profound sense of human nature, with its supreme conflicts and the tragic alternatives to which they lead, and which, at moments of great crisis, take on exceptional significance. A strongly ethical element is conspicuous in all these problems; they concern the moral conscience primarily; the victory at stake is the full mastery of the will over circumstance, and over the sources of weakness that we carry within ourselves. Corneille is mainly interested in the clashes between passion and duty. Here his art asserts its thoroughly and genuinely classical nature; everything is subordinated to a pure and dominating issue, that works itself out in terms of the decisions of the soul. However complicated the incidents, this psychological study is stripped and reduced to a finely simple scheme, which realizes the very essence of French classicism. Such is especially the case with the three tragedies immediately following *Le Cid*, and in which Corneille's invention, reacting against the freedom of his earlier plays, confined his plots to the narrowest limits: *Horace*, or the conflict between love and patriotic obligation; *Cinna*, or the choice of a lower or a higher conception of political expediency; *Polyeucte*, or the war between attachment to a creature and the exclusive claim of Heaven. These alternatives are presented with an incisive neatness which leaves no room for equivocation. Though seldom over-emphasizing the didactic intent, they liberate in us whatever idealistic urge there may be, and stimulate us to live nobly.

The very atmosphere of Corneille's plays breathes heroic grandeur. Self-mastery, which thus appears as the epitome of virtue, includes duty under all its forms: subservience to a high ideal, whether honour, loyalty, or faith; to 'glory', or to feminine pride in chastity; and even to revenge, which is, Corneille insists, 'une passion noble et mâle'—when it moves, we may suppose, beyond personal grievances, into the wider field of family or national allegiance.

These struggles are shown against the dignified background of mainly historical settings, which Corneille often borrows from the annals of Rome, as if he felt that the majesty of Roman memories suited the pitch of his own genius. He likes to depict issues of government, war, or clashing ambitions, and to debate them with the power of a mind well trained in legal argument. Love has its ample share among the motives of great actions and plays its part in every tragedy; but love here is much less a passion, a fatality that carries blinded beings to their fate, than an exaltation of virtue, a quickening of the sense of 'esteem' in the subject, founded on a just appreciation of 'merit' in the object. It is not a weakness, but the noble acknowledgement of high worth; it is akin to spiritual fervour, and inseparable from heroism. As such it can be conquered only by duty; and of this Corneille's work is rich in examples. Chimène's prosecution of Rodrigue, whatever may be said, is a case in point, and Polyeucte's behaviour to Pauline is another. Though generally subordinated to a master motive of sentiment or pride, the characters are not unduly simplified, and several, especially among the women, are finely shaded studies, like Chimène herself. But their conflicting moods can be forecast with sharp accuracy, and the translation of mood into action presents small difficulty; so that the psychology of those dramas is evident. It is not superficial, for the poet's intellectual perception is visibly sure of its hold on the inner world; and as that world to him is almost free from the tangled mysteries of morbid feelings, the assurance cannot be pronounced deceptive. The emotion he most often rouses in us is admiration; and irony, mixed with haughtiness, is one of the moods he most successfully conveys.

Corneille's verse has life and vigour, in spite of the frequent temptation of long arguments. He does not, on the whole, make excessive use of monologues, a form inevitably favoured by the analytical spirit of classical drama, and he knows how to force into dialogue the driving, animated energy of conflicting wills. His characters express themselves with a spontaneous eloquence communicated by his own robust temper. To call it rhetorical would be most unfair, for the sentiment is as lofty as the phrasing is highly pitched. His diction shows admirable qualities, a nervous strength, a fitness, and a precision that match the intricacies of all political or moral themes; his clear mind compresses thought into maxims and sentences, many of which have become proverbs; while his inmost ardour spreads a colouring of imagination and poetry over his style. Still, in spite of careful revisions, he never brought his manner to the perfection of elegance that Racine, for example, was to achieve. Voltaire, and many others, have been at pains to point out the signs of haste, the awkward turns, the archaisms, that mar several passages, especially at moments of flagging inspiration; but such fault-finding usually brings its own punishment, and almost all these critics have fallen into gross injustice and obvious pedantry.

Corneille remains a living presence in the inmost shrine of French literature. Indeed he has expressed some of the lasting elements in the moral personality of his race, and at times of national disaster Frenchmen return to him as to one of the fountains of their strength. Modern scholars have emphasized the variety of his work; his thirty-odd plays compare in number with the output of Shakespeare, but they are spread over a far longer period, and their quality is far less even: at least half of them are today read only by the specialist; with two-thirds, performance is out of the question. Still, few, if any, are without some features of power or beauty. His comedies add something to his strength as a dramatist; he does not possess Molière's abundant comic vein, but he has wit, invention, ingenuity, and even charm. *L'Illusion comique*, *La Galerie du Palais*, *Le Menteur*,

play upon amusing features of characters and manners with a freshness of fancy and a delicacy of touch hardly to be expected from his
austere genius; in some respects he has been compared with Marivaux.

Realism of an original kind is often to be found in the comedies,
whereas in the tragedies we are given a highly selective and thus incomplete image of life. But it is in these masterpieces that he has
explored regions of the mind and heart that remain his own. For
many of us, doubtless, they lie outside the bounds of experience, but
they are invariably convincing, and part and parcel of a noble conception of human nature. The sublime was his chosen sphere, and
gives his work a character which is very different from the mere
grandiloquence of fine writing. Similarly, his touches of romance
are free from the declamation that is the besetting sin of many
romantic plays. He enjoyed the rare privilege of being able to fuse
grandeur with substance; and he deserved it, because his own soul
was great.

CHAPTER XXI

Pascal

DURING the last three centuries Pascal[1] has won the admiration and respect of each new generation of Frenchmen. An even warmer note of sympathetic love has sometimes been added, but not always, for his powerful personality demands, to be fully accepted and identified with one's own ideal, a spiritual enthusiasm that will not be repelled by a somewhat inhuman austerity. He is in fact, that most admirable and untoward of creatures, the uncompromising Christian. He was a saint, not *évangélique* (in the French sense), but *Janséniste*. The image we have of him from one of his sisters is not to be trusted in every particular; still, it strikes us as that of an essentially pure and supremely unselfish character, in no way sparing himself, but animated with a zeal that sometimes outran charity, if not discretion. The turn his temper took after his second and decisive 'conversion' led him away from the world, where he had mixed for a while; thenceforth he knew only the ardour and rigour of his faith, and could no longer, he tells us, endure with a light heart that men should be content to remain uncertain about their future state. Meanwhile, the blade-like penetration of his mind made him the greatest unclerical apostle of his time, more profound in his approach to religion than the most famous preachers and divines. Of course,

[1] Blaise Pascal, born at Clermont in 1623, the son of a high official, was taught by his father and showed extraordinary precociousness, especially in the sciences. He followed his father to Paris and Rouen; published a treatise on *Les Coniques*; invented a calculating machine; and was converted to the stricter faith of the 'Jansénistes'. He still moved in worldly circles for a time, published several scientific treatises, and may at this period have written a *Discours sur les passions de l'amour* (discovered in the nineteenth century). After a spiritual crisis in 1654 he adopted an ascetic mode of life. To support his Jansenist friends against the Jesuits he wrote short pamphlets, the eighteen *Lettres Provinciales* (1656–7), which were very successful. He had planned a Defence of the Christian religion, but his health failed him, and he could only jot down on scraps of paper the notes which were the fruit of intense meditation. After his death (1662) these were collected and published by his friends under the title of *Pensées* (1669). Modern editors have followed various plans in reorganizing the text of this work.

however, while duly humble and submissive in his belief, he was too independently creative to be wholly orthodox.

His astonishing genius was not only one of the most precocious on record; it took in the whole range of thought, from severely rational processes to the most poetical and intuitive ones. His scientific work, which inspired several technical treatises, remains a landmark in the modern study of physical nature, for besides his actual inventions, he opened new paths and started trains of calculation or research. In this field he was methodical, guarding against error at every consecutive step. A problem was a torment, but each flash of illumination was subjected to most careful test and experiment, before the result could be tentatively proposed as knowledge. He devoted his youth to interests and activities of this nature, then he turned from the material to the spiritual universe.

An incident in the life of his family brought him into contact with the wave of Jansenist influence and settled the course of his short literary career. Won over to the cause of Port-Royal, and after the mystical episodes of his second conversion giving up every other purpose, he wrote for the general public in order to defend the group of scholars who were being assailed by the powerful Société de Jésus, and threatened with prosecution. Was Arnauld guilty of harbouring and expressing the condemned tenets of Bishop Jansen? The discussion of this point was the occasion for one of the most brilliant series of pamphlets in the French language. The eighteen *Provinciales* are letters supposedly written by a Jesuit father in Paris to a friendly 'provincial' or head of a country branch of the order. The method is that of irony and indirect satire; the fictitious writer naïvely drifts into damning admissions, and repeatedly gives away his whole case. Pascal handles the savagely efficient technique, which was of course not new, with supreme ease. At the root of his dexterous, elegant, and murderous art, one can feel the repressed violence of long pent-up indignation. From the theme of grace, the subject broadens out to a full indictment of the Jesuitical doctrine, or at least of its worst excesses. Taking the offensive, Pascal exposes the thesis that allowed the faithful to follow as probable almost any opinion put forth by a competent doctor; or, again, which excused ill-doing if one could conveniently plead good intentions; or which made silent quibbling upon the sense of a word a sure device for conveying untruth without actually uttering a lie. When thus laid bare, these glaring abuses of what had been tolerated as *casuistique*, to be used with judgement on special occasions, could but shock lay opinion, and the *petites lettres* were immensely popular. That some momentary unfairness entered into the conduct of the case, historians more or less agree; but as regards the essential justice of the argument, there are few dissentient voices. Carried away by his animus, Pascal had trespassed on unsafe theological ground, and his *Lettres* were eventually to be condemned by Rome. Still, their pointed energy, supple art, and variety of tone, from irresistible humour to burning eloquence, had made them a monument of French prose.

Far different in their unfinished, disconnected state, the *Pensées* are none the less Pascal's masterpiece and a far greater book. Study of this text must never be allowed to obscure its history. Two main parts may be distinguished in the rough order which has gradually been evolved. The first, a general survey of man's natural condition, is of outstanding value; the second, where the defence of the Christian religion is directly tackled, though certainly no less important, is of less interest as soon as the reader abstracts himself from its special point of view. What strikes one throughout, but chiefly in the first part, is the spare, condensed meaning of each word; we have here the pure essence of thought. The direct, terse, impatient language, that says things once, and once only, in the briefest manner, though it does not best serve the end of artistic pleasure, is ideally suited to a thinker's purpose and makes all other books seem diffuse and long-winded.

As the preliminary stage in his apologetics, Pascal probes deep into the tribulations by which man is beset, and which inexorably determine the course of his existence. His findings, expressed with the vigour of a naturally strong imagination, in dramatic terms, but without the slightest shade of rhetoric, vividly convey the misery of our lot. This is not exactly pessimism, but rather the fearless acceptance of reality in a mind sustained by a constant sense of the supernatural, upon which it can fall back at will; an acceptance shorn of all the illusions, conventions, and timidities man has fostered in secret as a shelter for his shivering state. No other writer has more eloquently taken stock of the ills that flesh is heir to; and these pages anticipate the 'anguish' that our satiated modern age draws from the bitterness of life. Pascal's intention is that this despair should be fully recognized, so that from it may spring an irresistible desire for any supernatural help religion can afford.

The rest of the book establishes the claim of the Christian faith to proffer such help with the validity of a divine message. The broken fragments of these sections, now stripped to a few words, now expanding to full paragraphs, are burningly alive with conviction; the plea throughout is the emotional utterance of a great mind, supported by the intimate knowledge of Scripture, but deriving its main strength from its hold on the deeper life of conscience. But cogent as the argument is, it fails to act unreservedly on all of us. When he passes from the philosophy and tragedy of human fate to historical and theological matters Pascal loses some of his incontrovertible authority: a more profound acquaintance with Christian origins, and the comparative study of religions, have undermined part of the ground upon which he took his stand, as he thought, securely. The famous *pari*, his symbol for man's policy of common-sense calculation, based on reason, towards the mystery of this universe, grates upon many susceptibilities, as being more utilitarian than spiritual. Moreover, in his better-advised moments, did he not point out that belief is no matter of argument, but grows from the inner disposition of the soul? 'Tu ne me chercherais pas, si tu ne m'avais trouvé.' What remains as admirable as ever is the pregnancy of his style, and his use of elliptic images to open up grand vistas of thought.

So, time has not entirely spared his work. But in most respects Pascal stands outside his century; not a purely classical genius, but a member of the perennial family of French thinkers. His style, whether in the *Provinciales* or the *Pensées*, cannot age, because it is of the very quintessence of the French language. Seen in his total significance, he does not belong to the rationalist school of his period; he is, rather, a counterpart to Descartes, whose greatness he acknowledged, but with whose general trend he sharply disagreed. One of his major contributions to thought is the distinction between the *esprit de géométrie* and the *esprit de finesse*. He was a thorough master of the former, but the latter appealed to his deeper instincts and more genuine nature. He should be reckoned as the chief precursor of the intuitive philosophy that has increasingly asserted itself since his day against the tradition of medieval scholasticism, and independently of the doctrine of reason; and thus in some ways he has his touch of romanticism. But every label is unfair; his was an all-round mind, fearless and complete; poised on the conflicting, sensitively strung forces of the intellect, but neither a thinker nor an artist of the properly rational type: his supreme care was for truth, not for measure or balance; and truth was primarily, he said, to be known by the heart.

PART IV

THE CLASSICAL AGE (1660–1715)

CHAPTER XXII

Molière

THERE had been several attempts at the higher comedy before classical literature came of age, but none, except those of Corneille had made any lasting mark. Molière[1] raised this expression of the French genius to the supreme level of the best in any other kind.

His relation to classicism is both somewhat superficial and very intimate. Although he went through the usual course of studies, he was not steeped in the traditional culture of the learned circles; his training was largely independent, modern, one might even say national and popular. Like Shakespeare, he acted before he wrote plays; and the wide experience of an itinerant player gave him the full technique of the stage in its most practical aspects. Ancient

[1] Jean-Baptiste Pocquelin, born in Paris, 1622, the son of a prosperous upholsterer, studied the humanities in Paris, and probably law at Orléans. He founded the 'Illustre-Théâtre', 1643–5, with a group of players, and took the name of Molière. For twelve years, with a new cast, he toured the provinces, chiefly in the south, performing all kinds of drama, writing sketches of his own, then comedies: *L'Étourdi*, 1655; *Le Dépit amoureux*, 1656. He returned to Paris in 1658, and produced *Les Précieuses ridicules*, 1659; *Sganarelle*, 1660, both successful. He settled in the Palais Royal playhouse and married a young actress of his company, 1662. He again had great success with *L'École des maris*, 1661, and *L'École des femmes*, 1662, which he defended against critics in *La Critique de l'École des femmes* and *L'Impromptu de Versailles*, 1663. *Tartuffe*, 1664, roused fierce opposition, was banned, amended, and won complete success in 1669. *Dom Juan* followed in 1665. After the cool reception of *Le Misanthrope*, 1666, the public showed more favour to *Le Médecin malgré lui*, 1666; *Amphitryon, George Dandin, L'Avare*, 1668; *Monsieur de Pourceaugnac*, 1669; *Le Bourgeois Gentilhomme*, 1670; *Les Fourberies de Scapin*, 1671; *Les Femmes savantes*, 1672; and *Le Malade imaginaire*, 1673. During the performance of this Molière was taken ill and died a few hours later. His complete works include more sketches, farces, *divertissements* of various kinds, and ballets, one of which, *Psyché*, was written in collaboration with La Fontaine, Corneille, and others.

models he knew, and used to some extent; but with him instinct, and a miraculously strong creative impulse, were law.

On the other hand, Molière is a classic in the truest sense of the word, because the spirit of classicism was inherent in his nature. His artistic temperament was naturally balanced, and he had an absolutely sure instinct for what was sane and reasonable.

Though as an actor he was equally happy in tragedy and farce, his chosen field as a writer was from the first the comic, which he so mastered in all its ranges that modern philosophers have gone to his works to study the causal elements of laughter. He shows no fastidiousness; he can take a leaf out of the book of the Italian players, who had been attracting French audiences; and while he criticizes mere *turlupinades*, and draws the line at a pun, he does not disdain some of the tricks that were the stock in trade of street performers. Stage business and facile effects of every description, Scapin beating his master, grotesque errors, malapropisms, contradictions and conrasts, all come in for their share. The crudest fun is somehow endowed with an ease and good humour that save it from vulgarity. By degrees his comic genius rises above the domain of repetition—the easy, unexacting, almost mechanical repetition of stock situations and characters—and attains the level of the psychological; and at once, the vast ranges of human absurdity lie revealed, the unbending stupidity, crooked impulses, perverse habits, fads, whims, pedantry, or bigotry which can turn ordinary human beings into puppets. No writer has shown more freshly or more subtly how infinitely ridiculous men and women can appear to the philosopher's eye, simply by remaining obstinately true to type.

For the most part his varied comic figures are drawn with the nicety of touch and the sense of the implicit which characterize genuine art. They border upon authentic humour, but with Molière we do not usually get the sentiment that is supposed to be an ingredient of this. His laughter often leaves a dry taste in the mouth, and his comedy does smack of the social castigation that Bergson has emphasized. Still, it would be wrong to deny his plays the flavour of humanity; from the gallery of his sketches and studies, as a whole, there does not emanate the bitterness of a pessimist; a more generous glow warms even his most realistic satires, and he does not make man despicable to man.

Carelessness or creative

In the construction and development of his plots he shows conspicuous gifts of invention and also of imitation. It has been abundantly proved that he did not scruple to take hints right and left, from the ancients and the moderns. Critics also agree that he is apt to wind up his plays as best he can, often enough with some indifference to the deep-laid logic befitting the conclusion of ideal drama, and in this his technique has the breadth and the relative carelessness of the great creative artists. Nor was he very particular about the precise distinction of kinds. Tragedy can be sensed, with an implicit tension, in the background of many of his works: *L'École des femmes*, *Tartuffe*, *Dom Juan*, *L'Avare*, are cases in point; but his pregnant sense of actuality and life passed lightly over such formal discrepancies, which he felt himself fully entitled to ignore. Nature approves of the contamination, and to be natural is the highest requisite of art. With their frequent appeal to our sympathies and even our emotions, his plays have an indestructible unity of spirit which they share with Aristophanes, Plautus, and the Shakespeare of the comedies.

Thus it pays to read him for amusement alone, though, of course, he has other and more precious rewards in store. Comedy with him performs much of the task which in modern times was to fall mainly to the share of the novel. The picture of life and manners is part of his object which, he repeats, is to study man in general; he is not out to whet our curiosity by drawing the portraits of individuals; and he consistently rejects any identification of his characters. But man in general means, he confesses, chiefly the man of his time; and his work is a broad canvas on which we watch mid-seventeenth century society in being. He had observed it under all its aspects, in the provinces, in Paris; standing close to the show, but apart from it, with the keen, reflective expression we like to fancy on his face; making many friends, and more enemies, he could rely sufficiently on the support of the Court and the king to bear the brunt of the jealousies, the anger, and the spite he provoked. The main body of the middle classes, the 'bourgeois', with their oddities, mediocrities, whims, and their essential honesty—as he saw them—give the picture its background; the lower ranks are represented by artisans, a few peasants, and mostly the servants, male and female, among whom are several of his most lively creations—Sganarelle, Sosie, Martine, Dorine—cheeky, resourceful men, impudent, vivacious,

impulsivity — fresh ideas

witty maids; all more or less endowed with the gift of the gab, and adding a wealth of picturesqueness to types that were already traditional. Inseparable from these are their masters and mistresses, the lovers, whose fortunes they will serve, and who, without being conventional, are generally not very convincing. The more prominent groups are those of the aristocracy—not the great, but the minor nobles, 'chevaliers' and 'marquis'—and the professionals of all kinds. We are given unforgettable glimpses of the pushing crowd at the entrance to a *levée*; of Mascarille skipping in his beribboned breeches; of the beaux and snobs, the *Précieuses* and their ecstasies, Vadius and Trissotin caressing and quarrelling; of the teachers who strut and glower at each other round Monsieur Jourdain's Turkish garb, of Monsieur Loyal, the bailiff's man, and his sinister meekness. Doctors are Molière's pet target; he lets fly at them savagely, and whatever unfairness he may show to the profession as a whole, it will generally be conceded that the onslaught was then largely justified. Allusions, of course, to particular events or incidents, may be read into this or that play; the doings of the 'Confrérie du Saint-Sacrement' in *Tartuffe*, for instance, or the latest amour of Louis XIV in *Amphitryon*; but this is not the aspect of history upon which Molière's works, with their wealth of living scenes, throw the most welcome light.

The richest source of our interest lies deeper, in the ethical valuations with which his study of social man is pregnant. There would be no point in the mere affixing of labels. What matters is to re-create, with all their complexities, actual examples of virtue and vice, and it is here that his genius is perhaps most remarkably successful. The need for bold, intensive characterization to overcome the limitations of stage production is fully met, and though normal verisimilitude is, of course, extended in the process the portrayal of individuals as individuals is none the less lifelike. That Harpagon is miserliness incarnate, that Alceste has turned into the very type of a noble absurd dreamer, desperately straining after an impossible rectitude; that Tartuffe has become the pattern of rank religious hypocrisy, does not endanger their amazing convincingness as persons, and the ethical effectiveness of the portraits is in proportion to their truth. Molière's spiritual children may be a far less teeming progeny, but his best-known triumphs are comparable to those of Shakespeare.

Instincts and Reason?

What is less concentrated is the suggestion of a personal philosophy diffused by the whole wide, penetrating survey of the behaviour of men and women. Some of the tenets are patent enough. Molière puts his trust in nature, like Rabelais and Montaigne. A considered, moderate optimism colours the views of this thinker, who was keenly aware of the thousand shades of evil, and whose life was a constant fight against enmity and disease. Such a faith in the essential worth of human instincts implies a generous spirit, in which the heartlessness of satire has no place. Reason is a natural guide, and its prime lesson is the error that besets all excesses; safety as well as wisdom lies in the golden mean. Molière's conception of upright womanhood is in touch with this ideal: the simple reasonableness of Henriette, even the naïvety and sheer obedience to instinct of Agnès, are better than the distortions or crabbed artificialities of the *Précieuses* and Bélise. There is no disputing the fact that the author means Philinte to be not only a more sensible person than Alceste, but a better citizen, friend, and lover. This realistic, rational, and classical ideal apparently leaves little room for values of romance, poetry, or mysticism; and it must be owned that we are here at the core of one of the main traditional types of the French temperament and of French thought, but one only. In the fundamental issue of religion, again, it is not safe to pronounce on what Molière really believed. Too much must not be made of *Tartuffe*, as the author takes every precaution to avoid the charge that his indictment confounds true devotion with the false. Yet one can understand the fury of the zealots, and they had some ground for their plea that it is not possible, on the stage, to dissociate two attitudes whose expressions are often identical, since their actual distinction is all a matter of the inner will. The unsolved riddle of Molière's work, however, is *Dom Juan*. The first part of the play appears to support the conjecture of a rationalist and deistic attack on established Christianity, an anticipation, as it were, of the assaults of the eighteenth-century sceptics; but the latter part shows us the hero in damaging and belittling attitudes, and seems really to concur with the general scheme of the popular legend. Perhaps the least unwise conclusion would be that Molière did not resolve the conflict in his own mind; or that having hinted as much as he thought he could, he felt obliged not to disappoint the crowd, who expected thunder and lightning.

One of the most admirable qualities of Molière's plays is the ease and naturalness of his dialogue. Even when they work up to a comic climax, to one of those *mots* that sum up a person or clench the paradox of a situation, the repartees follow and provoke one another as in life itself. Only a complete hold on the vital logic that dictates what men do and say 'in character', can reach such perfection. This means possession of his creation by the playwright, or of the playwright by his creation; Shakespeare, here again, is the inevitable parallel.

Molière is a great writer in every way. Whilst his prose from the beginning was admirably racy and vigorous, his verse for a time was not altogether free from constraint, which shows in awkward constructions and obscure phrases. These difficulties were soon surmounted, and ease and grace at their happiest are to be found in, for instance, *Amphitryon*, whose *vers libre* compares with the best of La Fontaine. In prose nothing can improve upon the directness, force, and nervous simplicity of *Dom Juan*. Indeed, both in prose and verse the gift of language belongs to Molière by a sort of native right; he has full command of the French of his age, and handles it with such perfect mastery, that it is indeed the French of all time.

CHAPTER XXIII

La Fontaine

ONE part of La Fontaine's[1] work overshadows all the rest. In the *Contes*, where much talent is wasted on loose themes, with a sort of ingenuousness that is an alleviation, though no excuse; in the sundry pieces of the most various kinds, from the elegy to the didactic poem and the opera, our curiosity is almost always repaid; they possess that elusive quality, charm, that the kind-hearted voluptuary received from an indulgent fate. It would be unfair to omit any mention of the delightful *jeu d'esprit*, *Clymène*, or the tale, *Les Amours de Psyché et de Cupidon*, the prose and the poetry of which are of equal loveliness; or of the heartfelt lines *Aux nymphes de Vaux* and that wistful noble confession, *Discours à Madame de la Sablière*. But the chief interest of these, and many others, is to reveal the personality of the writer. This expressed itself fully in the *Fables*, to which La Fontaine owes his perennial fame, and on which attention may be focused.

The doubtful privilege, still clinging to them, of being a textbook for schools, has tended to obscure the significance of their chronological order. In their sequence a development can be traced, and two main aspects of the writer's temper, not contrasted but complementary, appear.

The sophisticated realist is more conspicuous in the first books. He takes his subjects from Aesop or Phaedrus, and treats them with a brevity second only to their own. The economy of phrasing is

---

[1] Jean de La Fontaine, born at Château-Thierry, 1621, studied the humanities, thought of taking orders, but married and bought his father's office (maître des eaux et forêts). He drifted away from his wife and son, settled in Paris, and devoted himself to poetry. He enjoyed the hospitality of a succession of patrons, especially Madame de la Sablière, and was a popular guest and friend, half in the literary world, half in retirement. Shortly before his death (1695) he turned from his rather free mode of life to piety. He published a variety of works which included *Clymène*, 1671; *Adonis*, 1658 and 1669; *Le Quinquina*, 1682; *Les Contes*, 1665–91, mostly from Boccaccio; *Les Amours de Psyché*, 1689, in prose and verse; and the *Fables*. The first six books of these appeared in 1668; five more in 1678–9; the twelfth and last in 1685–94.

intensified by the light ease of the 'free verse', the verse-lines of unequal lengths which serve excellently to underline the hints of a slightly cynical wisdom. The lessons conveyed are those of prudence; no out-of-place sentiment is wasted, and the world is taken as it is—a hard school for the weak, the improvident, and the dull. Animal and human characters are intermixed in a number of short serio-comic episodes, very much on the lines of the stories which have passed current from the flood, and in which each beast has acquired a character of its own, made up of partly individual, partly conventional traits. The narrative style is lively, and the wit satirical. The easily memorized apologues, with a quiet argument and a surprise twist at the end, are not beyond the grasp of clever children, who love to follow the details of a plot, and whose sense of justice demands only that the trickster should be eventually tricked. The familiar touches, the picturesque figures of the actors, the impartial observation of manners, endow these sketches with a concreteness that appeals to young minds. In a slight degree, the animal saga thus gradually unfolded may afford them some of the amusement and pleasure they derive nowadays from animal stories. But here the appeal to the imagination is very limited; a sensitive temper may even resent the harshness of the picture; and not a few writers, among them Rousseau and Lamartine, have denounced the shaping of children's sensibilities by such texts, which indeed would seem better fitted for sophisticated adult tastes.

The other La Fontaine peeps out from the beginning, and taking courage so to speak, asserts himself as he proceeds, probably reaching the high-water mark in Books VII and VIII. Modern readers will prefer this more ample expression of an author who is nothing if not genuinely human. This aspect of the *Fables* seems to offer us a compensation for moods we cannot help missing in all the dignity and sustained impersonality of classical literature. Here we have a writer who makes little or no effort to appear other than he is; he confesses his faults, and finds relief in sincerity. The promptings of the heart are his most cherished rule, and he sighs with regret because worldly prudence cannot be ignored. He is indolent, and likes to follow his fancy in the choice of subject, or to digress at will. He is keenly susceptible to nature, and calls up a wood, a pellucid stream, the joys of solitude, in pregnant, unforgettable words. To beast and bird and peasant, the chosen heroes of his allegorical comedy, he is uniformly kind; his sharp wit is stirred to satire only when the Court, the great, the fuss of official pomp, thrust themselves upon his moral seclusion. Lyricism, if by that word we mean the free expression of the self, is almost absent from the central period of the seventeenth century; here is one of the welcome exceptions.

This complex personality, however, is by no means divided. The two La Fontaine are one, and shade off into each other. For better or for worse, the author of the *Fables* was too uninhibited to be a psychoanalytical case. The ironic pessimist lets us see tremors of feeling; the man of sentiment is ever ready for some delightfully sly allusion. Altogether the fascination these short tales have for us lies in their varied tone, their spontaneous manner, and changing humour. The philosopher, in whom both tempers are reconciled, is often present. He takes risks, and not only tilts at what he dislikes—women, marriage, boys—but commits himself to a criticism of horoscopes, denies the determinism of things; praises but contradicts Descartes; insists that beasts are not machines, but sentient beings. He can handle ideas with a supple audacity which resembles that of a fox, feeling the pricks of an empty stomach.

Fables are as old as the hills, but taking them for all in all no other fables are similar to these. La Fontaine's art is highly original, and its power is increased by the absolute candour that refuses to heighten any effect above its natural pitch. The subjects of his vast comedy *aux cent actes divers* are practically always borrowed; invention does not reside in the matter, a classical view. But each theme is renewed by being immersed in the actuality of a shrewd sense of life. The writer has observed animals and knows enough to give his sketches acceptable features and some relation to the real. Still, what his amused or gently saddened glance has mostly fed upon, is the wealth of individual characters, and of social attitudes, affectations, dress, habits, in the world of man. A student of zoology will reap very little from his work; an historian of manners and a moralist may gain more. Clothing human ways in animal garb is an ancient trick, which he performs with a more fresh, flexible and piquant dexterity than any writer before him, or since. His surest source of triumph is that in his cleverness he retains a measure of innocent *naïveté*, and can re-create the direct perception of the primitive hunter or the rustic; and it is only this faculty of reducing psychology to the level of elementary experience that may, to some extent, be said to put him in immediate contact with the child's mind.

With a few telling strokes of the pen each plot is provided at the outset with a background of scenery and manners. This is as it were the basis of his art. As soon as the tale is under way, and chiefly when the conclusion is in sight, all pretence is dropped, and the apologue winds up in maxims, so pithy and so aptly worded, that most of them have become proverbs. Every cultivated Frenchman's memory swarms with them.

La Fontaine keeps his vocabulary within a relatively limited range, with no straining for romantic brilliance. He confesses to a fondness for some old words, and every now and then takes in a dialectal or technical term. But substantially he writes in the clearest, most genuine vein of the *honnête homme*'s expression, with a perfect ease of style due to his unfeigned, natural simplicity—a simplicity that can be vigorous, and is ever elegant. Academic commentators have found occasional fault with his phrasing; but even when they are pedantically justified, the writer's negligence is to us one more charm. As for his verse, the secret of his smooth, flowing measure lies not only in his instinctive gift, but in a craftsmanship so finished as to efface all trace of itself. The metre of classical French poetry, with the all-but universal predominance of the majestic alexandrine, was at all times threatened with monotony and stiffness—a danger that only the greatest artists were able to avoid. It was genius that inspired La Fontaine, as it did Molière, to secure the variety and graceful suppleness of *vers libre*. The manner in which the length and rhythm of the lines follow the meanderings of the thought is an absorbing and fruitful study.

CHAPTER XXIV

Racine

RACINE'S[1] work is one of the supreme achievements of tragedy. No doubt other types before and since have answered other tastes, fulfilled the wishes of different intellectual groups; and the theory is no longer held that the finest essence of the dramatic art can be represented by one form, and one alone. But it seems possible to say, first, that the creative instinct of the French genius during the classical age was best embodied in the Racinian pattern of drama; and secondly, that no modern parallel to the Greek archetype has more closely approached its intrinsic purity of manner.

Racine indeed felt no doubt as to the model he should adopt. He was steeped in the humanist tradition, and his study of Sophocles and Euripides gave him an intimate acquaintance with their technique. At the same time, it is impossible to over-emphasize the originality he brought to his imitation. In one essential, particularly, the novelty of his art is conspicuous: the passions he explored were those of human souls grown infinitely more conscious of themselves with the course of ages. Beside his full portrayals those of his ancient predecessors are sublime and pregnant sketches.

After a short apprenticeship, he fastened on his object; and his

[1] Jean Racine, born in Champagne, 1639, early orphaned, and brought up by a Jansenist grandmother, studied at Port-Royal and in Paris. He was intended for the Church, but wrote poetry, mixed with men of letters, among whom were La Fontaine, Molière, Boileau, and found his promise encouraged by the Court. After sundry attempts, he made a mark with his tragedies, *La Thébaïde*, 1664; *Alexandre*, 1665. Then, breaking away from his masters, he satirized Port-Royal in a published letter, 1666. His next dramatic successes were *Andromaque*, 1667; *Les Plaideurs,* a comedy, 1668; *Britannicus*, 1669; *Bérénice*, 1670; *Bajazet*, 1672; *Mithridate*, 1673; *Iphigénie*, 1674; *Phèdre*, 1677. Meanwhile critics and rivals were embittering his life (Pradon's *Phèdre et Hippolyte*, 1677). He married, was reconciled with Port-Royal, 1677, and lived piously in half retirement. He was, with Boileau, appointed historiographer to the king; and at Madame de Maintenon's request he wrote for the boarders at the Saint-Cyr school for officers' daughters two religious dramas, *Esther*, 1689, and *Athalie*, 1691. *Athalie* had small success when published. He died in 1699. His complete works include lyrics, translations, epigrams, prefaces, orations delivered before the Académie française, and letters.

first great play, *Andromaque*, is perhaps his masterpiece. The concentration of his technique is unrivalled. He strips his matter of every appendage that goes to make up the infinite richness of life. He ignores the obscure forces of character, since his lucid analysis tries to explain everything by the light of reason: did he not describe his wonderful study of Phèdre's diseased heart as 'ce que j'ai peut-être mis de plus raisonnable sur le théâtre'? This effort to see dark things clearly is far from making them superficial; modern psychology is even anticipated at times, as when he analyses the causes of Nero's love for Junie. But nature, social circumstance, the pageant of happenings, the poetry and the music of fresh experience, all that Shakespeare includes in his grasp as he goes, Racine neglects on principle, at least as his direct aim; the inner world alone rivets his interest, with the parasitic growth of passion and its tangled consequences. Yet it is unfair to charge his drama, as has often been done, with the impoverished purity of a strained, crystallized substance. In fact, he presents or suggests the environment of the action by means of a thousand brief and telling strokes. He prefers an actual foundation for his plot from history or from dignified and accepted legend. *Britannicus* is steeped in Tacitus, and the condition of the Roman state at the critical time when Nero revealed himself is the background of the play. *Athalie* is a splendid evocation of Biblical fervour, heroism, and violence. It has been rightly pointed out that, while Corneille's heroes are disembodied spirits, those of Racine are living creatures, who breathe and ache and shiver and burn.

Character is his object, but character in its reaction to the most powerful of stresses, passion. Here, again, one must guard against hasty negatives; it is not true that he has neglected every strong emotion except love. Ambition, hatred, revenge, pride, the various shades of motherly affection, friendship even, and other motives, all have a share in his studies; but they are not the centre of the perspective, and Racinian tragedy is undoubtedly focused on love. This passion, in Racine, has nothing to do with the soft idealized emotion upon which literature had endlessly thriven. It is an intoxication of the mind, that deprives it of its freedom and balance, a blind urge, fatal in its birth, normally destructive, often cruel; the madness of Phèdre, Nero's desire for Junie, are only extreme examples of such mental derangements. On the grim vigour of the picture, under the smooth elegant surface of Racine's art, all will agree. To its truth one may object that it is somewhat one-sided, laying stress, in fact, on possessive sensual love, and making scant allowance for more spiritual attachments; a trend the more surprising, as the poet was justly reputed to be a master of tenderness, and his Andromaque, for instance, or his Bérénice, had drawn tears from innumerable fair eyes. Nineteenth-century critics have tried to lessen the paradox by insisting on Racine's temperamental irritability and, for all that it was subdued, fierceness. Again, it is also true that his realistic image of passionate love is just what would cling to the mind of a young man, brought up by the austere and pessimistic teachers of Port-Royal. Whatever ultimate value one may attach to this aspect of his work, it is without doubt one of the contributions literature has made to psychology.

Moreover, by his study of passion he was opening a new path for art, away from the reticence and discretion in which his old masters would have confined him. They disliked his audacious candour, and he retaliated with damaging irony. But the seeds of piety had been sown too deep in him, and they awoke in the crisis of his moral life, after the bitterness of the cabal against *Phèdre*. He kept silence for many years, and when he wrote again for the stage, it was to compose *Esther* and *Athalie*. Besides, he had never yielded fully to the temptation of a downright realism that, if well advised, Christian apologists could have exploited as well as denounced. In *Bérénice*, Titus wins a Cornelian victory over his love. In *Britannicus*, Burrhus has words that point unambiguously to the responsibility of the will in passion: 'On n'aime point, Seigneur, si l'on ne veut aimer. . . .' The general note of his character-drawing is thoroughly classical in its fine shading and avoidance of crudeness. His Nero is an incipient monster, with a touch of sadism, but not a romantic bugbear. The men and women he has invented or re-created have the spark of genuine life, and leave a lasting image upon our memory.

The impression he makes, of dealing with the actual stuff of human reality, is in nowise destroyed by the plain conventions of his drama. Critics have objected strongly to the obvious fact that his art rests on a measure of artifice. A modern reader with a reasonably open mind should be ready to disregard this. The device of 'confidants', universal in the tragedy of the classical and post-classical periods, is imperiously demanded by a technique that relies much on self-analysis and self-expression; it is after all a substitute for the monologue; and we may as well tolerate it, feeling that the hero, in talking to the confidant, is talking to himself, and to us. Such tricks are part and parcel of all dramatic craft, and Shakespeare has his share of them. Long speeches have been another standing grievance with Anglo-Saxon readers; they do not occur in Racine so very frequently, and even the *récit de Théramène* is necessary, since the event itself can neither be omitted nor directly shown. At the root of the whole difficulty lies the very notion of an 'explicit' psychology, the idea that the inner tendencies of beings are more accurately perceived by us, if they receive a formulated expression. This is perhaps where Racine is sometimes positively at fault; he does not make enough allowance for the groping uncertainties of our self-knowledge, and will even show a character frankly confessing to himself secrets of his consciousness which he would not like to face, much less to put into words. These are merely blemishes upon a presentment of human nature that is penetrating, though by no means unduly severe, and bathed in the serenity of great art.

Art is the outstanding word in any appreciation of Racine. His native genius must have been of the strongest, to stand up with impunity to such a degree of labour and skill, and not to sink under such a weight of intention. The perfection of his form suits the clarity of his purpose, the precision of his psychology, the immediacy of his dramatic effects. All is suffused with a light that is not cold for being equable and calm. The chief element of this Elysian atmosphere is the style, so sure and smooth that the most tragic horrors it has to convey leave its surface unruffled. Refining has not weakened the fibre, and the tissue remains firm and compact. Elegance and choice here are gifts of nature, and the resources of the language, its expressive power, fluidity, and harmony, are used to the full with no apparent effort. How surely a truly classical instinct gives each quality of phrase its correct value, and preserves the highest quality of all, simplicity, we shall realize, for example, if we study the well-known words of Joad to Abner (*Athalie*, I. i): 'Celui qui met un frein à la fureur des flots . . .', &c. Never was sublimity more even. Or again, if we take the measure of Andromaque's dignity and tact in her trying interviews with Pyrrhus.

It must be owned that some traces of *préciosité* linger in Racine's style; and he did not discard the traditional vocabulary of love, with its well-worn metaphors (*feu, flamme, allumer, brûler,* &c). But against that weakness, one may set the strength and effectiveness of many arguments, of maxims and compressed phrases that admirably convey the pith of a situation. Indeed the dialogue can be Cornelian in its thrust and parry. No less remarkable are the frequent touches of something very near imagery, born of an imagination nurtured on ancient poetry, and on the grand similes of the Bible; never unduly developed, but fused with the body of the words. The music of Racine's verse, again, has a beauty that might have cloyed the hearer, but does not, because it is relieved by the variety of the breaks, and the diversity of a smooth but supple and changeful tenor of natural utterance. Ample periods and single sinewy lines are intermixed. The evocative names of mythology, the sonorous syllables that echo an inner song or call up vistas of legend, are handled with a keen sense of their suggestive power. It is impossible to refrain from quoting: 'La fille de Minos et de Pasiphaé . . . .'

Bajazet, Mithridate, Iphigénie, all have features of their own, but bear the stamp of the same playwright. *Les Plaideurs* is a very amusing comedy from Aristophanes, cleverly dressed in a provincial French garb. *Esther* and *Athalie* hold a place apart in Racine's work. Here love is not a main motive of action; two subjects from the Bible are treated in a spirit which it is not perhaps disrespectful to call that of sacred opera—a genre then entering upon its successful career. Both, and especially *Athalie,* are powerful appeals to the poetic imagination. Their inner structure is much like that of Greek drama, with choruses filling the intervals between the scenes. The intervention of Providence leads to conclusions which have been foreseen, our emotions are roused, but not our tragic suspense. The magnificent lyricism of the choruses, the wealth of Oriental imagery, transform these pieces into dramatic poems of rare beauty and superb grandeur.

Racine's prestige is as certain of survival as French classicism itself, in which it is rooted. Romantic cavilling has had its day; foreign lack of appreciation has largely yielded to a more receptive and intelligent sympathy; and new aspects of his work which have been discovered and emphasized by the passing centuries have only added to the fundamental reasons for his greatness. While this was happening, French drama was gradually forsaking the Racinian model in favour of a bolder technique, more elastic, and more fully adapted to modern needs; yet it has perhaps never reached an equivalent purity in the consummate adaptation of artistic means to high ends.

CONTEMPORARY PLAYWRIGHTS

Racine had poetic rivals, some of whom were thought by his own age to shine equally with himself. Two who may be singled out are: Pierre's younger brother, Thomas Corneille (1625–1709), who cleverly managed not to be crushed by his surname, and Philippe Quinault (1635–88). The former wrote brilliantly and much, trying his hand at several dramatic kinds; the worst that can be said against him is that he generally resembles someone else, not excluding his illustrious elder brother. One of his tragicomedies, *Timocrate*, 1656, was extraordinarily successful; and two of his tragedies, *Laodice*, 1668, and *Ariane*, 1672, should also be remembered. Quinault's survival is safe, because in a secondary field, opera, he was a leader. After writing comedies, tragi-comedies, tragedies (*Astrate*, 1663; *Pausanias*, 1666), in which love has a prominent place, and stress is laid complacently on shades of feeling, while the flowing, graceful style seems to call for a musical accompaniment, he had the happy idea of setting up in partnership with a composer, Lulli, of Italian origin, whose melodious inspiration had won first place in the favour of the Court and the people. Quinault supplied the plots and libretti, Lulli the scores, and the staging received its full share of attention. From *Cadmus et Hermione*, 1673, to *Armide*, 1686, the joint work of the two men triumphed repeatedly and opera was started decisively on its modern career. It had some influence in shifting the centre of dramatic interest from the strictly psychological plane of the greater classics to more external happenings, a change in keeping with the eighteenth-century craving for renovation.

CHAPTER XXV

Religious Thought and Oratory

THE full greatness of Bossuet[1] appeared only gradually to succeeding generations; and the scale of values attached to his work has altered with time's changing perspective. The historian, the polemist, the author of didactic or controversial writings, have receded into the background; their information is of course incomplete, and their zeal is one-sided. Nowadays they are read only for pleasure—a somewhat austere gratification one must confess. The tendency is now to lay chief stress on the writer and the orator; and the poet present in Bossuet's *words* has been increasingly recognized. So, the man who at first stood pre-eminently as the champion of impersonal authority and the exponent of faith through the language of reason, appeals to us now as an original artist, in whom the repressed fire of impassioned imagination rouses intellectual energy to almost romantic ardour.

Our knowledge of the *Sermons* is incomplete; the texts we have are drafts and are not wholly trustworthy, for Bossuet's habit was to write a first outline with incredible ease and then to make substantial alterations, improving much, and at times striking out passages that we cannot but admire. Every sign points to his caring only for the impression his addresses actually made on the minds and hearts

[1] Jacques-Bénigne Bossuet, born at Dijon, 1627, the son of a magistrate, studied at Dijon and Paris, took orders, and at Metz, where he was a priest, engaged actively in parochial duties, controversy, and patristic reading. Off and on he preached in Paris with great success, sometimes before the Court. He was made a bishop in 1669, and next appointed tutor to the Dauphin, 1670–81, writing treatises for his charge which were published at once (*Discours sur l'Histoire Universelle*, 1681), or after his death (*De la connaissance de Dieu et de soi-même*, 1722; *Politique tirée de l'Écriture Sainte*, 1709). His *Sermons*, much altered in the delivery, were not published by himself; the *Oraisons funèbres*, for a score of years from 1669, associated him with the official occasions of mourning. He was appointed to the see of Meaux, 1682, and devoted much energy to polemics in defence of orthodox faith or morals: *Histoire des variations des Églises protestantes*, 1688; *Maximes et réflexions sur la comédie*, 1694; *Relation sur le quiétisme*, 1698; *Défense de la tradition et des Saints Pères*, written 1692–3, published 1753. He died in 1704, leaving a number of treatises, occasional writings, letters, &c., in addition to the works already mentioned.

of his hearers. In our view his best *Sermons* are those of the first period, when the preacher abandoned himself more fully to his eager temperament, and was not yet subdued by the sense of his exceptional responsibilities. That on *La Brièveté de la vie*, reshaped later as a homily *Sur la mort* (1662), is a fair example of his moving eloquence, sinewy, terse, rich with brief implicit images:

Je ne crains point d'avouer que c'est du sein de la mort et de ses ombres épaisses, que sort une lumière immortelle pour éclairer nos esprits touchant l'état de notre nature. Accourez donc, ô mortels, et voyez dans le tombeau de Lazare ce que c'est que l'humanité; venez voir dans un même objet la fin de nos desseins, et le commencement de nos espérances; . . . venez voir le triomphe de la vie dans la victoire de la mort.

But, conversely, the *Sermon sur la mort* has been a model for the construction and main heads of the *Oraison funèbre d'Henriette d'Angleterre*; and indeed the characteristics of the Sermons reappear on a larger scale in the Funeral Orations, which are more deliberate expressions of what is at bottom a mood akin to the lyrical.

The drawbacks inseparable from these latter compositions were many and serious; Bossuet felt the burden to the full, and disliked the genre, which he turned none the less to unsurpassed artistic uses. His masterpieces—such as the oration on Henriette d'Angleterre—are triumphs of imaginative grandeur and genuine pathos. The conventions besetting the subject are all mastered, and the stings taken out of them. The awe attaching to the persons of the fallen queen or warrior is duly recognized, and dismissed; and the accent of Donne's 'Death, be not proud' rings out in magnificent prose. The violent contrasts to which the lights and shadows of our human lot lend themselves are underlined by no timorous hand, while the eternal commonplaces of the nothingness of our dust, and the infinite possibilities of our spirit, are powerfully etched in black and white. No language ever reconciled more directness and simplicity with such force and evocative gift. The natural rhythm of Bossuet's style is one of its most remarkable traits; a quality due no less to a sensitive ear, half consciously at work, than to a keen instinct for logical interrelation and balance:

Car encore que notre esprit soit de nature à vivre toujours, il abandonne à la mort tout ce qu'il consacre aux choses mortelles: de sorte que nos pensées qui devoient être incorruptibles du côté de leur principe, deviennent périssables du côté de leur objet.

It is this Bossuet who keeps his place among the masters of the classical age. One can sympathize with the fastidiousness that refuses to find his best in his most popular work, and seeks it rather in the more spontaneous *Sermons*, or in the unpretending *Méditations sur l'Évangile* and *Élévations sur les mystères*; but this will remain a pundit's view. The vast extent of his output may well increase our admiration; still, only one part of it belongs at present to living literature. As for the man, nothing can deprive him of his impressive single-mindedness. Flaws have been detected in his personality, and it may be conceded that his defence of orthodoxy was at times more vigorous than Christian: he was harshly unfair to Fénelon, to Molière, and also to Richard Simon, whose crime was that his exegesis moved ahead of the times. But his onslaught upon comedy, for instance, was psychologically justified, if art must at all costs avoid the risk of hurting susceptible minds—a thesis, it is true, that few will accept. The more searching light thrown upon his character has left it thoroughly human, and noble in its heroic, selfless devotion to spiritual duty.

To us, looking back on an age when religious eloquence flourished more than ever before, or since, Bossuet stands obviously far above other contemporary preachers. Yet the audiences of the time gave an even warmer recognition to Bourdaloue (1632–1704) In him, a Jesuit, we have a keen student of the world, who conveyed his knowledge of human nature in clear cogent disquisitions that answered the prevailing taste for moral analysis. Where Bossuet carried the argument to emotional heights, Bourdaloue riveted it on a more rational plane. Not that sinners were let off easily: his ethical standard is firm and exacting. The *Sermon sur l'ambition* probes the intricate recesses of social pride, at a time when precedence and rank were everything. That on *La Pensée de la mort* makes determined use of the distressing image of a corpse. All is logical, convincing—and cold. Another preacher, Bishop Fléchier (1632–1710), has a more winning manner; he possessed charm, and severe critics have charged him with making conscious use of it in his writings. The reproach has rarely any foundation, and his smooth, elegant style is usually free from anything like meretricious ornament. His most successful efforts were funeral orations, which, though far below those of Bossuet, handle their subjects with dignity and sustained power. That on Marshal Turenne (1676) is justly regarded as his masterpiece. We have another bishop in Massillon (1663-1742), who carries the tradition into another century, and with him the change of time and manners is plainly apparent. Religious oratory now sheds its special allegiance to scripture and dogma, shifting its ground towards an almost purely human basis, and approximating closely to a lay discourse, which mixes common sense with appeals to the heart. A philosophical age may have overpraised this enlightened mode of preaching, but we can understand, and share, Voltaire's very high appreciation of the *Petit carême* (1718) for other merits than the faultless style. There is genuine courage for instance in the pitiless description of the flowery path down which the great naturally descend to corruption (*Sur les tentations des grands*), and the accent of an awakening social conscience is heard in the Sermon on *L'Humanité des grands envers le peuple*.

Malebranche's[1] intense and persistent meditation, starting from the main conclusions of Descartes, erected upon them an original body of thought. The quiet audacity and the high spirituality of his doctrine bear witness to the properly metaphysical needs of the French mind, which had by no means fallen into abeyance in the rational atmosphere of the age. The wits and the sceptics had their fling at his *vision en Dieu*; but his chief works were repeatedly reprinted, and his influence is confirmed by numberless testimonies from contemporary thinkers and writers.

The great difficulty of the Cartesian system was the relation between extension and thought, body and mind; how could they act upon each other? Malebranche is driven by the demands of his intrepid logic to the assertion that appearances are deceptive: there is no such interaction, but an endless series of concomitant phenomena held together by God's omnipresent action. We do not actually see objects, but the Divine will has decreed that, for instance, the

[1] Nicolas Malebranche, born in Paris, 1638, studied theology, took orders as a priest of the Oratoire, and led a contemplative existence. His works included: *De la recherche de la vérité*, 1674-5; *Traité de la nature et de la grâce*, 1680; *Méditations chrétiennes*, 1683; *Entretiens sur la métaphysique et la religion*, 1688; *Traité de l'amour de Dieu*, 1697. He died in 1715.

impact of rays of light upon our eyes should be accompanied by, though it would not in itself cause, our perception of the ideas in the Creator's mind that correspond to objects. It is not a man's mental force that raises his arm, but the divinely appointed laws by means of which our conscious wishes are inseparable from muscular motions associated with them. Whatever the category of being, a creature cannot be the cause, it can only be the occasion of all that takes place.

Thus it follows that our life is intimately and thoroughly interfered with by eternal preferences which are not our own; and here no less than with Spinoza, an intoxicating sense of the divine may be said to underlie the whole interpretation of experience. But Malebranche's system is not pantheistic; just as God is distinct from matter, what we 'see' in Him not being the objects themselves, but the ideas corresponding to them in His mind, so those centres of our moral responsibility, our persons, are no illusions: God has left us free to suspend occasionally our perceptions of associations which He has created, with a view to permit, and not to destroy, our spiritual autonomy.

The *Recherche de la vérité* is not written with artistic care; its relaxed and somewhat diffuse style had to be corrected and improved in subsequent editions. But the persuasive honesty and vigorous independence of the mind that expresses itself in this great work make it an outstanding book. In close contact with the science of his time, Malebranche advanced still further the integration of philosophy and research that owed its inception to Descartes, imprinting on it a more strongly religious character; and he permanently enriched psychology, as well as ethics, with the fruits of his penetrating investigation.

CHAPTER XXVI

Worldly Writers

THE *Mémoires* of Cardinal de Retz[1] are one of the most entertaining examples of many works of this type composed during the later seventeenth or the early eighteenth century. They were the fruit of the leisure of retired men of action, of writers, or ladies of fashion, and were mostly published posthumously. The arrogant and unedifying personality of the cynical Churchman who had a genius for making enemies, but who did also win the staunch affection of friends, has somewhat obscured his deeper qualities of mind, and the more sympathetic traits of his character. He could be generous, and not always from motives of self-interest. He described frankly the inner workings of a conclave, but defended the good name of the institution, and he ended his life in piety. He left remarkable sketches of his contemporaries, and the uncanny penetration with which he puts his finger on what were or may have been their weak spots was, of course, guided by anything but charity; yet, when he finds the virtues he reverences, courage being first on the list, he acknowledges them. Courage indeed he possessed himself to a remarkable degree; the account of his escape from Nantes, and of his sufferings on the long, heart-breaking journey to safety, is as sober as it is vividly dramatic.

So we cannot find it in us to despise or hate the man. Some will even confess to a sympathy, not unmixed with respect. Two further reasons for our esteem are the rich harvest of wisdom that he managed to gather from his adventurous career, and his genuine honesty. There is not the slightest shade of humbug about the Cardinal de Retz. He is too keenly intelligent not to see through others,

[1] The forebears of Paul de Gondi were Italians from Florence. Born in 1613, he took orders, was deeply concerned in the plots and parties of the Fronde, and experienced various changes of fortune. He was appointed a cardinal, and archbishop of Paris; imprisoned by Mazarin, he escaped abroad, and was pardoned, resigning his see in return for a compensation. His *Mémoires*, written in retirement, and published only in 1717, cover the whole period of the civil broils. He died in 1679.

but he sees through himself just as clearly, and admits to his faults—generally errors of judgement—with unaffected candour. He loved intrigue, but he handled it with great skill; and what matters more, his long experience was material for a suggestive philosophy of the politician's difficult calling, its ways and means, triumphs and failures, based on a searching knowledge of the prime element in all politics, human nature. The remarks and maxims scattered through his *Mémoires* make up a body of disillusioned, but not exactly pessimistic lore, that statesmen might do worse than study: its core is a lively, concrete perception of the thousand and one reasons why a politician should expect little, and should ever be supremely modest, cautious, though not weak, and ready for all the chances of incalculable fortune.

The book has thus a psychological and moral substance that adds greatly to its value as an historical document. This has certain obvious limits, but if serious doubts can be entertained as to the author's impartiality and objectivity, he does nevertheless throw useful light on the public and private life of the French, Spaniards, and Italians during the mid-seventeenth century. Yet his *Mémoires* owe their survival chiefly to their literary merit. Here, again, faults are patent: loose construction, too many digressions, a lack of proportion, and a style more capricious than correct, often awkward, bearing the marks of the uncertain age that preceded the establishment of the classical pattern. Few readers mind these blemishes: the book holds us fast, the story itself is often as good as a thriller; but the author's irony, graphic descriptive powers, biting characterization, and humour are worth even more.

La Rochefoucauld,[1] though not among the greatest, is one of the most typical writers of his age. What made him a quintessential classicist was not culture, for his knowledge of the ancients was slight. But with unerring intuition, he fastened upon the most humanistic of subjects: human nature. He presented his experience

---

[1] François de Marcillac, born in 1613, the heir of an illustrious family, distinguished himself in the army, joined the opposition to Richelieu, and then to Mazarin, fought in the Fronde and was severely wounded. On succeeding his father as duc de la Rochefoucauld he was pardoned, after which he lived in half retirement, a familiar guest successively of the *salons* of Madame de Sablé and Madame de La Fayette. His *Mémoires* were published abroad in 1662. His *Réflexions ou sentences et maximes morales*, 1665, went through several editions, corrected and enlarged, down to 1678. He died in 1680.

of it impersonally, in the approved manner of the time; and for his means of expression he selected the highly condensed form of 'maxims', i.e. pointed remarks worded as briefly as possible. The choice was not original. The writing of pregnant 'sentences' and of 'characters' or portraits, had long been a fashion: La Rochefoucauld handled the same tool with outstanding success, and it remains stamped with his name. His fastidious, sparing style, again, is a matter of temperament and instinct. Traces of *préciosité*, no doubt, linger in it; he loves antithesis, and sometimes indulges a conceit. Yet his taste is of the purest, and he has the gift of direct, simple, precise statement. When at an earlier date he wrote under stress of feeling, in the *Apologie de Monsieur le Prince de Marcillac*, he turned out such faultless, naturally elegant periods, that they have been said to mark a stage between Guez de Balzac and Pascal's *Provinciales*.

He owes his fame to one book, the *Maximes*. Among his other works, the *Mémoires* are sober but cold, far less taking than those of Retz, while the few portraits, including one of himself, the letters, and the *Réflexions diverses*, on various topics, are uniformly distinguished, but of unequal interest. Some only of the last show the keen observer and moralist at his best. The some five hundred *Maximes* of the 1678 edition, to which should be added the rejected and the posthumous ones, are what matters.

They have at bottom one object: an indictment of the cheap self-satisfaction of the unthinking person. The mood that begets them is not misanthropy, or pessimism. The writer owns to melancholy, but claims to keep an open mind. His point of view is the philosopher's, and what he seeks to establish is the truth of our moral state. If anything further is to be descried behind this purpose, it is the Christian notion of unregenerate nature. Some passages stress the point: the creature studied is man as the fall has left him, though the privilege of grace may raise a few to another condition.

He supports his main thesis with various assertions. Our so-called virtues, he says, are deeply contaminated with *amour propre*, which is universal. Interested impulses lurk under the masks of practically all feelings and acts, even those that are apparently conducive to sacrifice. No heroism, no love but can reveal these secret impulses of self-seeking. The demonstration is relentlessly pursued through a survey of individual and social behaviour; and it is round this axis

that most, but not all, of the 'maxims' rotate. Quite a few are irrelevant, loosely connected, or related to the centre by nothing stronger
than a negative attitude to current values. The classicism of La
Rochefoucauld is not one of structural form; he hates pedants, to the
extent of feeling comfortable in disorder. No attempt is made to
correlate each critical remark explicitly with the underlying principle, of which indeed his occasional formulation seems to be purely
haphazard; or to suggest a further proposition, more deeply hidden,
though at times half revealed: the belief that the primacy of self is
rooted in natural laws, that there is an organic background to character, so that our temperaments, our *humeurs*, rule us through the
demands of our self-interested personalities; a psychological point
of view that owes much to Descartes, but substitutes irony for the
philosopher's composure.

La Rochefoucauld, in fact, discovers nothing new. What he said
was all, or should have been, familiar before. The shock, and the
scandal, to which the sentimental women of his acquaintance confessed, was due to the fact that the complacent optimism of their
conventional attitude to life had received a jolt. The analysis of the
motives of human conduct in the *Maximes* is mostly truth—what
one may call by that name. But it is wrong to conclude that our
nature is thereby hopelessly tainted. Things remain very much as
they were, and there are still many 'good' human beings who are
charitable and virtuous because it gives them pleasure to be so—a
very harmless form of selfishness. On the contrary, it is La Rochefoucauld's sense that he is boldly upsetting false values that is slightly
naïve; and no serious thinker would let his judgement be governed
by such errors. This deceptive illusion of having torn the mask from
the face of mankind adds to the pathetic appeal of a writer whose
melancholy was genuine and who lived a truly noble, idealistic life.
One only regrets that, having justly traced a preoccupation with
small cares to littleness of mind, he should himself have suffered such
great distress because his wife was at first refused the right to sit
down in the king's presence.

Maxims are an artificial kind of literature, with a merit that lies
mostly, perhaps, in their epigrammatic piquancy. Even when the
order of the words is inverted the sense will remain quite or almost
as true. Those of La Rochefoucauld are not all good, some being too

obvious, others mere repetitions, or sheer paradoxes. His psychological perception, though fine, is of too intellectual a cast, and admits but rarely of a frankly concrete approach. But a large number of his sentences are solid gold, and convey fresh, penetrating thought in the best possible words. A book of such stimulating wisdom, much of which attains the perfection of form, will not be allowed to die.

The product of a time when the conditions of life encouraged letter-writing as a leisurely, often a consciously artistic mode of self-expression, Madame de Sévigné's[1] correspondence ranks easily first among several brilliant examples. Other letters can be, and have been, even more sparkling, or may convey a more moving sense of personal drama, or they may bear more widely on the course of events, whether political or social. These of Madame de Sévigné show a lively wit, but can be serious; they tell an anecdote or sketch a portrait delightfully, but make no parade of descriptive talent; they often have an emotional theme, the passion of a mother's heart, torn by the parting from a beloved and poorly responsive daughter, but this grief is sentimental, intemperate, confessed to with apologies, shamed by its own excess; they reflect the incidents that stirred the public mind during the climax of a great reign, but do not attempt to outline the full historical panorama, or to inquire deeply into underlying causes. So they are supreme in none of these respects, but can claim distinction in all; and the unique quality of their appeal is due to their absolute spontaneity and to the lovely, unselfish, and vivacious personality they reveal.

Madame de Sévigné's proverbial fondness as a mother did not exhaust the generosity of her heart; she was the best of friends, and the group which comes to life before our eyes in the letters includes some of the most distinguished figures of the time. The exciting and anxious atmosphere of decades during which war was the actual or threatened background of the national life, breathes through these

---

[1] Marie de Rabutin-Chantal, born in Paris (1626), early an orphan, married the marquis de Sévigné (1644), who was killed in a duel (1652) leaving her with a beloved daughter and a son only less beloved. She did not leave the world of society, but devoted herself to family affections and friendly intercourse. Her daughter's marriage (1669) and the ensuing separation, were the beginning of a correspondence that lasted with few breaks till her death in 1696. Her Letters, for the most part preserved, have been published in gradually expanding collections during the last two centuries.

pages, in the ebb and flow of shared emotions, the overflowing sympathy with the mourning of some, the glory of others. The fortunes and misfortunes of soldiers and statesmen, the news and the gossip, the triumphs of preachers and writers, the shocks and scandals of town and Court, are recorded faithfully, but freely, by a witness who claims the full right of amused, often humorous, comment. Not only the throbbing pulse of the great world is thus reanimated, but the quieter life of country places, as seen from the shady retreats of Livry or Les Rochers, and although the picture is fragmentary, we are given indeed the very form and pressure of the time. In its documentary value this correspondence, whatever its limitations, is second to none.

But we return invariably to the person of the writer. Being immune from pretension of any kind, Madame de Sévigné has every feminine grace, and not the slightest shade of coquetry; she is out to please her daughter, or her friends, by sharing with them the pleasures and interests, the joy or sadness of the day, and she obeys no other impulse. Her manner reflects this complete absence of self-consciousness, and its winning simplicity and sincerity wield a spell far more potent than laboured correctness. She expresses herself with sober piquancy, in sentences that are clear, easy, at times headlong; and the miracle of her style is that its distinction and artistic quality owe nothing to art; seldom, even, does a note sustained, an effect developed, imply some measure of artifice. She is a born writer, with a gift of felicitous improvisation and the further advantage of belonging to a civilization still in its early maturity. The freshness of the French tongue before the levelling and pruning process of the mid-seventeenth century is felt when she coins, as Mademoiselle de Scudéry puts it in the fictitious portrait of 'la princesse Clarinte', 'certaines expressions naïves et spirituelles qui plaisent infiniment'.

She is very much the child of her age. No snob, she yet believes in the absolute value of noble birth; though broadly humane, she relates the burning of La Brinvilliers with surprising equanimity. She has culture and taste, a fine literary perception. She considers La Fontaine's fables 'divine'; but she admires Bourdaloue more than Bossuet. She is perhaps most original in her love of solitude, fields and woods, and her inborn sense of harmony between mood and landscape. Still, there is nothing romantic about her; religious, sensible, and steady, as well as a vivacious and charming woman of the world, she shares to the full the healthy robust spirit of her classical time. In the trials of life she shows courage, and an almost heroic fibre, for instance, when she praises, at the height of Racine's success, the higher, manly beauties of 'notre vieux Corneille'.

The fame of Madame de la Fayette,[1] like that of her friend La Rochefoucauld, rests on a single book; and no less than the *Maximes*, *La Princesse de Clèves* illustrates the tendency in French literature of the period towards the deliberate study of the inner man. Her few other writings are of less interest, with perhaps the exception of the *Comtesse de Tende*, a very short story of remarkable power, that reads like the outline of some tragic novel of the modern realist school.

In the *Princesse de Clèves* she obeyed her instinct, and told at length a tale of passion held in check by honour, and unfulfilled. Precedents can be found for the various strands interwoven. In the heroine's moral courage the spirit of Corneille is alive: *Astrée* and Mademoiselle de Scudéry's novels had treated love as an incitement to spiritual nobleness; Racine had explored the twisted emotions of a woman ravaged by jealousy, and the renunciation of lovers had given *Bérénice* a pathetic grandeur. Madame de la Fayette contributes the more detailed scrutiny of moods that falls within the province of the properly psychological novel. Thus, with all her classical restraint, she points the way to a fertile territory of modern literature that writers of fiction have not yet ceased to explore.

Doubts have been raised as to how far her own theme and method were original, and the claims of possible collaborators have been advanced, with no definite conclusion. She may have borrowed the idea of her boldest episode, the confession Madame de Clèves makes to her husband of the guilty love threatening to master her will; but her moving treatment of it is all her own. No less significant is the stress laid on the complexities of human emotions and motives. At

---

[1] Marie-Madeleine Pioche de la Vergne, born in Paris (1634), married the comte de la Fayette (1655), lived in touch with the Court and literary circles, and was a close friend of Madame de Sévigné. Her friendship with La Rochefoucauld ended only with his death, and influenced both his writings and her own. She was widowed in 1683 and died in 1693. None of the three works, *La Princesse de Montpensier*, 1662; *Zayde*, 1669–71; *La Princesse de Clèves*, 1678, was published over her name. *L'Histoire de Madame Henriette d'Angleterre* and *La Comtesse de Tende* appeared after her death.

the heart of a professedly rational age, Madame de Clèves, after anxiously debating with herself, is represented as having acted, in a momentous issue, half-consciously, almost against her will: 'Elle trouvait qu'elle s'y etait engagée sans en avoir presque eu le dessein.' When, after her husband's death, she refuses to marry her lover, the reasons for her action are left in some ambiguity; she puts forward successively an obligation to the memory of her husband, who has died of a broken heart, and her fear of the transitoriness of passion. The author probably considers that both reasons are genuine, though either would be sufficient.

Madame de la Fayette is no perfect artist; the construction of her novel might be improved, and in her plot she shows excessive indifference to verisimilitude. Her style is not without awkwardness. But her French has native elegance, and what one must call aristocratic distinction. In the supreme scenes, her refined understatement makes her language impressively forceful.

Antoine Furetière, 1619–88, was no frequenter of aristocratic circles; but he catered for their amusement by drawing a satirical picture of the middle classes. *Le Roman Bourgeois* (1666) is a somewhat disconnected series of scenes and sketches that constitute a lively survey of French manners about the middle of the seventeenth century. It is realistic without coarseness, and at least in some parts successfully humorous. The author is not without sympathy with his subject: his heroes, he says, will be 'de ces bonnes gens de médiocre condition, qui vont tout doucement leur grand chemin, dont les uns seront beaux et les autres laids, les uns sages et les autres sots . . .'.

CHAPTER XXVII

Boileau

BOILEAU'S[1] significance today is not what it was for earlier centuries. He is not to us the actual leader of the classical age, but a highly representative writer, whose work is the best illustration of a literary doctrine which he did not originate, and which was not the practice of his time. His *Art poétique* was a guide and gospel not to the generation of La Fontaine and Racine, but to their successors. Its influence, in the long run, strengthened at the very core the resistance offered by a surviving literary ideal to the forces of change; the romantics were not mistaken in singling out Boileau for their arch-enemy. But in identifying him simply with the conservative and formal spirit in poetry, they made no allowance for his own personal temperament, and for the need to appreciate him on his merits.

Neither is it true that he did yeoman service by purifying taste, and ridding the world of writers who might dangerously monopolize public attention. The taste of the period was already experiencing a gradual and collective reaction, and shaking off the spells of *préciosité* and *pointes*, when Boileau began to write. As for his onslaughts on Grub Street, we watch them with mixed feelings. They showed undeniable courage and were useful in pricking a few bubbles, but they hurt men who did not deserve such vicious lashing. Chapelain and Quinault are cases in point; but there might well be a good deal to say for others; in any case the over-production of books had been finding its corrective in the sifting process of time. Boileau had a gift for sudden repartee and surprise attack; and he indulged it to the

---

[1] Nicolas Boileau-Despréaux, born in Paris (1636), studied the humanities and law, was called to the bar, but devoted himself to poetry. He made friends—among them men of high birth, and men of genius—and also enemies with his biting *Satires* (six published in 1666; the number rose to twelve). Protected by the king, and appointed his historiographer, he wrote *Épîtres* (twelve in all), a burlesque poem, *Le Lutrin* (1674–83), an *Art poétique* (1674), a translation of Longinus, and sundry minor pieces and epigrams. He died in 1711.

full, encouraged by the example of Latin satirists, and secure in the
sense that a charge which could be so pointedly phrased must be
well founded, and was at any rate amusing. That he honestly believed in his mission, no one will deny; and in fact his perception
was generally sound. But what was the result of his sallies? He
affixed an unmerited stigma on many names, and contributed little
to raise the standard of literary judgement. Most of all, however, he
heightened his reputation as a master of ferocious epigram. During
the second part of his career he took pains to appease the rancour of
some of his victims.

Apart from such attacks, which were so characteristic that they
occur, besides the *Satires*, in practically all his work, the claim long
put forward in favour of the *législateur du Parnasse* rests, finally, upon
the *Art poétique*. This very unequal and largely disappointing sketch
of a literary aesthetic has no structure or organic development; it
consists of disconnected remarks and precepts, often negative, and
concerned variously with general advice to writers, the salient
features of genres, and surveys of ancient or modern poetry. Though
clear and cogent in argument, particularly on themes of law or
divinity, Boileau was no philosopher. What may be called his
central theses are not singled out for argument. They agree closely
with the common doctrine that the Renaissance had extracted from
the ancient critics. Nature is to be the pattern of art, and reason the
poet's preceptress in interpreting nature. Beauty and truth are thus
very intimately related; there is no stricter obligation than to obey
the demands of one's subject-matter, and to be honestly one's self.
Simplicity is the hall-mark of good art; conceits and meretricious
ornament, no less than coarse allusions, must be strictly avoided.
Lucidity is indispensable, and it will be reflected in the ease of expression. Endless care should be given to the elegant correctness of
phrasing and style; to write well requires long, exacting labour.
Lastly, the various features of faultless verse are reviewed explicitly.

All this is sound advice. If it will not make a good poet, it may
perhaps help him to avoid some faults. It is needless to dwell on the
definitions of poetical forms that were already becoming more or
less antiquated. The free lyricism that has since come to be regarded
as the all-in-all of poetry is represented indirectly by the ode and the
elegy, and of these only traditional types are considered. How to

concoct a full-dress epic is described in respectful detail; as if the genre had not been plainly dying. The vogue of the burlesque is censured, at the very moment when Boileau himself was writing the *Lutrin*. Any appeal to the grandeur of Christian subjects on the stage is prohibited, in spite of *Polyeucte*. It would be unfair to expect Boileau's perspective to differ from that of his age; still, the remark must be made that he never sought to widen it. His historical account' of poetry in Greece, Rome, and the modern era is marred by gross errors of proportion, such as the drastic undervaluation of Ronsard and his school.

Nevertheless, whatever fault may be found with his critical theories and judgements, his practice is the vigorous example of an art that commands our respect. The achievement of his *Art poétique* was that it formulated with precision, at least in matters of detail, a code the classical period could recognize as a lucid explanation and fit illustration of its cherished ideal. His other works are no less successful within their cautiously limited scope. He is a master, not exactly of poetry, but of a terse and telling prose, smoothly elegant, forcible, pointed by excellent phrasing and the rhythm of carefully constructed verse. One should not compare him with Dryden, who had more fire, but his achievement is not unlike that of his great admirer, Pope.

Nothing is further from Boileau's art than a preoccupation with form for its own sake. His scrupulously polished manner is meant to set off a matter of genuine value. Not only does common sense—an infrequent virtue after all as we know—give value to his psychological and ethical remarks: though no creative moralist, he is a shrewd observer, and his studies of character and life are no less lively than they are persuasive. This is what sets a pleasantly fresh stamp on the reflections and anecdotes of the main body of the *Satires* and *Épîtres*; and they are relieved from the risk of insipidity by the vein of realism which spreading through the whole, gives it piquancy, raciness, and colour. Such a full, concrete perception of the flavour of things betokens a certain kind of imagination; if poetry, properly so called, is anywhere to be found, it is in the rich power of suggestion, often physical, at times almost brutal, that strikes an original note in what otherwise remains a strictly impersonal art, founded on reason. The instances of this are innumerable; and French readers are continually surprised to find that lines from Boileau learnt at school remain obstinately fixed in their minds, because they so vividly evoke little absurdities of everyday life, common to all experience. Realism associated with a sober, self-possessed treatment of the absurd is the main fountain-head of humour; and that Boileau has a good claim to be considered one of the best French humorists of his age is abundantly evident in the pretence of high solemnity that throws the excellent fun of the *Lutrin* into relief, a pretence sturdily maintained, though every now and then he slyly invites us to see through it.

Herein lies the solid core of a value that has withstood the test of long time and of changing taste. Dethroned, Boileau has won and will keep a fair province in his own right. His saturnine, somewhat cramped and bitter wisdom, the hardest expression of which is surely the *Tenth Satire*, on, or shall we say against, women throws light upon a strong personality, something akin to that of Dr. Johnson, and no longer concealed from us by his smooth style. A large number of his sayings have entered the permanent treasury of French literature, because they are golden sense clearly conceived and aptly worded.

CHAPTER XXVIII

Transition

I. CHANGING THOUGHT

THE temper of the seventeenth century altered noticeably during its last period. The reign of Louis XIV was to continue till 1715, but with a declining prestige. Political events, and the defeats of France in her struggle with the united powers her ascendancy had alarmed, were external signs of change. But apart from these, and to a large extent independently of them, inner forces were at work, silently shifting the balance of intellectual tendencies. The classical doctrine still ruled the world of letters; more firmly, indeed, than ever; but it was already classicism with a difference, and the basis of its power was being gradually undermined. Well before a new age of literature could definitely be said to have begun, the transition was taking clear shape, though this is more perceptible to us now than it was at the time. To describe it by itself seems advisable.

Something must be allowed for the view that the course of intellectual life in each nation, and even in such wider collective units as cultural groups of peoples, is subject to cyclic changes. During the middle years of the century the processes of the mind had been more strongly subjected to the discipline of reason, and stricter limits had been set to the vocabulary suitable for their expression. The relative freedom that was the legacy of the Renaissance had been curbed under the ascendancy of rule, and since feelings are the unruly element in our consciousness it was natural that the relaxation of philosophical and artistic orthodoxy should in its turn be associated with the reassertion of sensibility. The break-up, which was also the occasion for seeds that had long been dormant to begin to stir, began in the late decades of the century. Its signs are written large over works of the period and its various aspects can thus be very briefly surveyed together.

It has been suggested already that the triumph of classicism had repressed but not destroyed the erratic impulses of fancy, independent thinking, and sentiment. In the same way, the reviving vitality of these impulses did not destroy the sway of classical principles. Reason and nature were still the approved watchwords, but they gradually acquired a different meaning. Nature can be seen, if regarded in the clarifying, generalizing light of intelligence, as a system, a set of habits, and this was what it suited the classicists to find, or nature may appear to concrete observation as a mass of irreducible phenomena and conflicting forces. The thinkers of the new age took more and more into account the multitude of accidents and circumstances; the individual, long neglected, became the eagerly sought object of all inquiries. While traditional reason was, or purported to be, common to all men, and eternal laws had been laid down in its name for the poet or the philosopher, it tended now to be an ever fresh urge to know and to understand, a refusal to be content with general abstractions. The quest for the variety of the world was resumed with new zeal, and the awakening scientific spirit, in France no less than in England, appears as a characteristic feature of a period when the Académie des Sciences was founded (1666), a symbolical parallel to the Académie française.

Meanwhile the narratives of explorers and travellers stirred the imagination with tales of exotic climes and strange customs. They also inspired a number of 'Voyages Imaginaires' which made disingenuous use of the wonders of the universe to insinuate subversive views about philosophy, religion, and morals. Christian dogma was rarely assailed outright, but the tradition of the *libertins* remained alive, and in a bolder spirit the deists put forth their plea for a reasonable faith. The method Descartes had propounded and illustrated began to show even more plainly potentialities that his prudence had managed to veil; its professed followers kept within the pale, but the spirit of general inquiry it had let loose threatened the main positions of accepted belief. The shape of the eighteenth century, and especially its first part, the age of enlightenment, was already discernible at the end of the seventeenth, in trends of thought which the champion of faith, Bossuet, watched with undisguised misgiving. A force to be noted among those making for change was the intellectual influence from Great Britain. The literature, manners, and fashions of France had left a deep mark on those of Restoration England and cultural contact was to continue despite the reaction during the reigns of

William and of Anne. Even before, though chiefly after the Revolution, English philosophy and science were making their influence felt across the Channel, so that the names of Newton and Locke became familiar to cultivated Frenchmen.

One last main aspect of the transition was the controversy between the *anciens* and the *modernes*. Were the masterpieces of antiquity to be considered in perpetuity as models that could be imitated but not equalled? This was the tradition bequeathed by the Renaissance, but dissentient voices were now heard, and the widespread feeling came to a head most pointedly in the *Parallèles des anciens et des modernes* (1688–97) by Charles Perrault (1628–1703), the charming teller of tales that are among the treasured possessions of all French children (collected in his *Contes de ma mère Loye*, 1697). Fontenelle, Saint-Evremond (see further), and others, supported him, whilst Boileau headed the conservative party. The battle continued for several years, with ups and downs, subsided for a time, then flickered up again after 1700 in the episode of Madame Dacier's translation of Homer. The issue of course could not be decided in principle, but it was enough that the all-round supremacy of the ancients should have been openly challenged; it was now shaken, and the bold initiatives of modern thought were the freer for the changed atmosphere.

2. THE SCEPTICS: SAINT-ÉVREMOND, BAYLE, FONTENELLE

Both Saint-Évremond and Bayle spent a great part of their lives abroad, though the independence of mind that drove the one to England and the other to Holland remained the decisive factor in their growth. Both are good examples of the change in thought, and the cosmopolitan vein which now becomes apparent in French literature is well illustrated in their works.

The interesting personality of Saint-Évremond[1] owes its most original characteristics to the fate which decided he should be steeped, for all the more creative part of his life, in English influences. Nature

[1] Charles de Saint-Denis, sieur de Saint-Évremond, born in Normandy (1616) was a man of the world, whose biting wit and political independence led him to seek shelter in England (1661). Later he was offered a pardon but refused to leave the land that had welcomed him, and died there (1703). His tomb is in Westminster Abbey. Besides many lighter works, he wrote serious treatises, among them the *Réflexions sur les divers génies du peuple romain*.

had endowed him with the sharp perceptions and ironical wit of a polished Frenchman; his exile tempered these somewhat negative gifts with a more sober and reflective sense of values. His earlier works, like the *Comédie des Académistes*, 1643, and the *Lettre sur le traité des Pyrénées*, 1659, marked him out as a satirist, the latter more brilliantly than the former, and with more severe consequences to himself. The *Conversation du maréchal d'Hocquincourt avec le père Canaye*, 1656, had already shown something much more than facile humour, and reads today with some of the effect of Anatole France. The discovery of England intensified this more sober spirit: *Sur les tragédies*, 1677, and *De la comédie anglaise*, 1677, show an awakening receptivity to the merits as well as the faults of a provokingly foreign genius, and are interesting attempts in what was to be a new field, the comparative study of literature. 'Les plus honnêtes gens du monde, ce sont les Français qui pensent, et les Anglais qui parlent. . . .' The *Réflexions sur les divers génies du peuple romain* call up anticipatory gleams of Montesquieu. But it is of Pascal that we think on reading the essay on *Religion*, that longs for a time when faith will shift 'de la curiosité de nos esprits à la tendresse de nos cœurs', and ,'rebutée de la folle présomption de nos lumières', will fall back on 'les doux mouvements de notre amour'.

Bayle,[1] an equally keen critic, is more rigorously intellectual, and more single-minded. His letters none the less have a charm of genuine kindliness, and reveal a lovable personality. The popularity of his *Pensées sur la comète* and *Nouvelles de la République des Lettres*, even with the women of the time, was due to his remarkable gift for the clear and animated presentation of matters of philosophical or literary controversy. His *Dictionnaire* is not exactly the work of an unbelieving scoffer, but Voltaire had some ground for calling him 'le premier des dialecticiens et des philosophes sceptiques'. These volumes, full of a scholarship that is no doubt incomplete and fallible, but which rests upon prodigious reading, are the arsenal from which

[1] Pierre Bayle was born in 1647 near Foix of a Protestant family. He studied at Toulouse, was converted to Catholicism, but returned to his former faith (1670) and thereafter had to live abroad, at Geneva and Sedan, and then at Rotterdam, where he taught philosophy and history. He published a periodical, *Nouvelles de la République des Lettres*, 1684–7, also *Pensées sur la comète*, 1682, several times revised, &c.; but his main work was the *Dictionnaire historique et critique*, 1697, corrected and expanded in 1702 and 1704–6. He died in 1706.

many eighteenth-century free-thinkers drew their light weapons for use against orthodoxy. The method is one of cautious, indirect warfare. In due order, the notable figures of classical and sacred history or legend are enumerated, the text stating what is known of each, with references, and the 'remarks', or notes, often longer than the text, quietly commenting with apparent respect on the odd, absurd, or unseemly aspects of the tradition. The ironical intent is plain, but it is allowed only to flicker over the whole learned discussion. The lesson conveyed is not entirely one of doubt, but also of diffidence, criticism, and reserved judgement. The present is called in to throw light on the inconsistencies of the past. The innumerable ways in which sheer fiction mixes with fact, or replaces it, in the body of accepted belief, are at bottom the subject of the work. This prodigious survey of the accumulated dross of ages has some of the quaint touches that enliven Burton's *Anatomy*; it is, however, more rational, and instinct with the ambition to sweep away mountains of fallacies, to make room for the sounder structure of knowledge. As a writer, Bayle has a light, deft touch, resembling Voltaire's. In his outstanding contribution to thought, the *Pensées sur la comète*, he considers, in fact, the possibility of erecting a system of aesthetics independent of dogmatic faith.

More discreet and more fortunate than Saint-Évremond and Bayle in the management of his worldly interests, Fontenelle[1] reconciled a measure of independence with every kind of literary and social success. He is the first of many popularizers who have made a special task of diffusing scientific knowledge. He was excellently gifted for the work, for though without originality as a philosopher, he had a sure grasp of problems and a clear, agreeable literary style. In the *Pluralité des mondes* he undertakes to bring the new astronomy within the grasp of the female intelligence and to lay no greater strain on the attention in so doing than would be needed to read the *Princesse de Clèves*. He fulfils his pledge, with much elegance and

---

[1] Bernard le Bovier, sieur de Fontenelle, Corneille's nephew, born at Rouen (1657), tried his hand at poetry and drama, with indifferent results. He then wrote *Dialogues des morts*, 1683; *Entretiens sur la pluralité des mondes*, 1686; *Histoire des oracles*, 1687; *Digression sur les anciens et les modernes*, 1688, &c., all highly successful. His long life—he died a centenarian in 1757—allowed him to win membership of most learned bodies, French or foreign, including the Académie française and the Académie des Sciences, with the latter of which he associated himself more particularly.

talent; advancing conjectures, such as the presence of living beings on other planets, but guarding against unfounded assertions. The *Histoire des oracles* treads very gingerly on more dangerous ground. Translating and freely recasting a Dutch treatise in Latin by Van Dale, Fontenelle solidly establishes the thesis that contrary to the accepted notion, the oracles of ancient times are not to be fathered on demons, and did not cease at the coming of Christ. He takes every precaution to spare the susceptibilities of the orthodox, and his tone is so even, his candour so prepossessing, that no sense of danger to cherished beliefs need be felt. Nevertheless, the whole argument is bound to undermine the very idea of the supernatural, and to cast a doubt upon the reality of miracles. The book remains an example of the methodical but unpedantic discussion of historical matters. The *Dialogue des morts*, Fontenelle's first work of note, still deserves reading, so lucid and wisely realistic is its fine perception of the relativity and imperfection inseparable from human values.

3. LA BRUYÈRE, FÉNELON

La Bruyère[1] aptly epitomizes and concludes the psychological inquiry consistently pursued by the classical age. In the title of his book, imitated from Theophrastus, he stresses its reference to the manners of the age. But his real aim, he declares again and again, is to study man in himself. This wider purpose is indeed apparent in the work. 'Characters', or pen-portraits, had been in vogue all through the century; in the ones we are considering the likeness sought was to a category, a type, or class, and only exceptionally to an individual. Profiting by chance resemblances with this or that contemporary, a number of 'keys' to La Bruyère's *Caractères* were published at once, causing no little annoyance to the unfortunate author. His repeated protests may be accepted, although he cannot always have been unaware of the likeness, and on occasion must have courted it. On the other hand a few humorous exaggerations, like the portrait of Ménalque, the absent-minded man, are pushed

---

[1] Jean de la Bruyère, born at Dourdan in 1645, entered the household of the Prince de Condé as tutor to his grandson, and was pensioned by him or by his heir to the end of his own life. He published a translation of Theophrastus and, as a modern addition to it, *Les Caractères ou les mœurs de ce siècle*, 1687. Several enlarged editions of this had appeared before his death in 1696.

with obvious bravura beyond all likelihood. Taken as a whole, the work presents us with a picture of the behaviour of men and women in the aggregate, seen through the eye of a shrewd observer. What Montaigne had done on the basis of a single self fully analysed, is accomplished here, with not altogether different results, from a directly opposite point of view, the variety of mankind matching the diversity of one man.

If one leaves out the 'symbolic' portraits, of a chiefly poetical value, La Bruyère shows himself a close and acutely penetrating painter; either assembling his experience into pregnant sketches of typical figures, or distilling it into remarks that convey an essence of reflection in a few words. The latter are often genuine 'maxims' of the La Rochefoucauld pattern; expressed like his in epigrammatic, antithetical style; equally thought-provoking, but conveying a wisdom that, less systematic, keeps on the whole more closely to the truth.

The psychologist here, free and bold as he is, remains subservient to the moralist, and we are once more faced with the contradiction that few students of human nature are logical enough to escape. La Bruyère is a realist and a pessimist; he has probed our weaknesses to the dim excesses in which the psycho-analyst, more than two centuries later, will find his chosen ground; there is hardly an impulse of our secret, repressed self of which he is not somehow aware. His indictment is severe. Men, he asserts, have not improved since the world began; they are incurable; and yet he writes, he points out, in the fond hope of curing them. The craving for expression will out, with or without encouragement. The middle classes are censured sharply for their selfishness and greed, and what will later be called their snobbishness. The great, when their turn comes, are still more vigorously punished. Women are not spared, and the morals of the late century, a period when devoutness was officially in the ascendant, are painted without indulgence. Special emphasis is laid on the jealousies of writers. Altogether, La Bruyère is a saturnine critic, discontented with the present. Yet he remains a man of his age: he praises the *Roi Soleil* more warmly than was necessary; and he is a staunch Christian who derides the *libertins* and has earnest chapters on the proofs of orthodoxy. In some respects only do his sentiments and beliefs foreshadow the future; he bitterly resents injustice and oppression and his social conscience is awake to the sufferings of the poor peasants: 'On voit certains animaux farouches . . . .' In the inevitable clash, which he already foresees, he, a member of the privileged class, takes his stand with the people: 'Je veux être peuple. . . .'

He is a classicist to the core; his art and style are instinct with an exacting sense of the just balance, the perfect phrase. Literature indeed, he thinks, can only be renewed through attention to form: 'Tout est dit, et l'on vient trop tard. . . .' Immune from the pedantry of a perfunctory cult, he still worships at the shrine of the ancients, and refuses, in the quarrel, to throw in his lot with the moderns. In his dissatisfaction with the increasing artificiality of life and thought one senses that his mind, in spite of all, is hearkening to the tremors of the coming age; and in his longing for nature, the fields, and the freshness of simplicity, he has accents that foretell Rousseau.

The artist in him, with his gift of careful, sober writing, and his tendency to understatement, smacks far less of the 'precious', as has sometimes been said, than of the somewhat impoverished language of an over-fastidious period. But his classical smoothness is free from the lingering tradition of oratory; his short sentences, spare, light, with a fondness for varied constructions, anticipate the quick, flashing style of Voltaire. For such a degree of deftness he is still too dignified, but his intuition points this way. And in spite of his robust sense of moral order, he has let go the substance, if not the principle of composition; his book is made up of chapters, each chapter of disconnected paragraphs, and he vainly pleads that from one to the other some sort of progression can be found.

Fénelon[1] belongs even more markedly to the transition. Born in the middle of the seventeenth century, he lived well into the next, witnessing the sad end of the great reign and dying in the same year as Louis XIV. Religious doubt has nothing to do with his awareness

---

[1] François de Salignac de la Mothe-Fénelon, born in Périgord (1651), of a very old family, entered the Church, and was appointed tutor to the duc de Bourgogne, the son of Bossuet's pupil, who showed excellent promise but died prematurely. He was created archbishop of Cambrai, was attacked by Bossuet, and condemned by Rome because he shared the 'quietist' views of Madame Guyon. He retired to his see, where he died still under a cloud (1715). His works, mostly written for his charge, include *De l'éducation des filles* (1687), composed in the circle and perhaps at the request of Madame de Maintenon; *Les Aventures de Télémaque* (1699); *Dialogues des morts* (1712); prose *Fables* (1716); *Lettre à l'Académie* (1716), &c.

of change, for he was a Churchman and a devout believer. He held fast to the main tenets of tradition; but he had a supple, eager, and resolutely open mind, which made him a pioneer in several directions. An unforgettable sketch of his winning personality has been drawn by Saint-Simon, the memorialist who never sinned through over-indulgence. Its most striking feature is the union of charm and strength. A thorough aristocrat, he showed the most genial simplicity of manner. He allowed his Christian feeling to be tinged, under the influence of Madame Guyon's half-mysticism, with that *quiétisme* which was mainly a self-abandonment to the love of God, but his whole life shows that his energy was in no wise relaxed by the doctrine. When censured by the Church he submitted to reproof, but in his spiritual advice preserved a note of suavity that distinguishes his letters of religious guidance.

A penetrating, fluid sweetness marred by no hint of negligence or mawkishness is likewise the character of his style. He joins force with elegance, and his political treatises have a vigorous, moving eloquence. Writing was to him a gift, which he never abused.

The popularity of his works, and chiefly of *Télémaque*, a favourite textbook for many generations, made them a persistent influence. The appeal of their manner is less important to us than the ideas they suggest. The *Éducation des filles* is still restricted in its outlook by a traditional notion of woman's part in life; but on the upbringing of children in general Fénelon writes with a concrete and liberal sense of the true process of education. The *Dialogues des morts* and the prose or verse *Fables* are graceful tutorial exercises, written for the instruction of a pupil, but well worth reading with no aim but enjoyment. In *Télémaque* we find that the stress has shifted from old to new values. The tale of adventure is very pleasantly told, and imaginative; but it reveals too much of its didactic inspiration. The edifying fiction has been grafted on to the grand naturalism of Homer to serve purposes that jar slightly on our notion of what is fitting. What interests us more is the whole background of thought and sentiment that it expresses. The ideal, well-ruled state of the picture is, of course, a golden Utopia; still, there is much wisdom and courage in the criticism freely levelled at the uses and abuses of the absolute monarchy then in power. The theme of war and peace is handled in the most reasonable and humane spirit. Still more significant than the political and social outlook is the writer's heartfelt longing to escape convention, whether of daily life or of sentiment. Some episodes in *Télémaque* recall *L'Astrée* and testify to the persistence of an idyllic dream, made all the stronger by the growing artificiality of the modern world; others seem to anticipate Rousseau.

The *Lettre à l'Académie* is no less worthy of note. Fénelon here shows himself far more alive than Boileau to the real issues of literary aesthetics. His freely intuitive judgement can lead him to a rather paradoxical notion of verse and poetry, but it often asserts itself fruitfully, as he proposes that taste should replace dogma as the all-sufficient guiding principle in the art of writing. He is sincerely regretful that the repeated exertions of the classical age should have resulted in excessive pruning of the French language. The whole formal treatise keeps strictly within the bounds of a Churchman's nice reserve, but such hints as these, and others both positive and tentative, endow it with an all but audacious originality.

PART V

THE ENLIGHTENMENT (1715–60)

━━━━━━━━━━━━━━━━━━━◦)(◦━━━━━━━━━━━━━━━━━━━

CHAPTER XXIX

The Need for Light

DURING the first half of the eighteenth century, the features of the transition sketched in the last chapter were strengthened and developed. The new period bears the distinctive mark of a rational tendency, so outstanding that few ages of literature can be so safely classified under one label. With most writers of the time beauty was not the primary object; it became as it were the by-product of an energy that spent itself in the eager pursuit of truth. The language, by now a relatively perfect instrument for the expression and discussion of ideas, dropped the last traces of the oratorical and synthetic spirit that still lent fervour to classical prose. It was content to be supple and clear, somewhat impoverished indeed, but offering unlimited scope to analysis and debate. Reason being in charge of the search for truth, its method was criticism and argument, and this was successful in proportion as it worked out to knowledge and clarity of understanding, to a sense of intellectual illumination. Thus the idea of light (*les lumières*) assumed a central place in the phrasing and mental perspective of the French eighteenth century; a fortune paralleled by that of the German watchword, *Aufklärung*; while the corresponding English term, 'Enlightenment', was to be used in this historical sense only at a later date, and often with a slightly pejorative shade of meaning.

The French Renaissance had experienced the thirst for light; but it was then a richer and broader impulse, guided by an ideal of humanism in which beauty and all the higher values had a place by the side of truth, and which a religious or a political strain often impregnated but did not essentially alter. By degrees, as the discipline of the classical age forced itself upon the ardour of the humanist revival, the monarchy and the orthodoxy narrowed down the limits within which critical inquiries could be safely conducted. So, when the authority of the king and the Church suffered a weakening process at the end of the era of classicism, the new intellectual urge, a distinct after-effect of the Renaissance, assumed a far more aggressive turn. The fight for light was no longer waged, as in the sixteenth century, against what was held to have been the benighted ignorance of the Middle Ages; it was aimed at a nearer, more tangible darkness, that was felt to be willed deliberately by arbitrary systems of faith and government. After the death of Louis XIV, an awe-inspiring personality in spite of his weaknesses and the disasters of his last years, the inferior prestige of the Regent and of Louis XV could no longer repress the increasing restiveness of French citizens, though the administrative yoke remained as stiff as ever; and the example of orderly freedom set by the English began to sow seeds of invidious comparisons in a nation heading thenceforward for its Revolution. The indulgence quietly shown in England to the profession of deism, and the toleration of religious sects, were no less suggestive object-lessons; and English influence became inextricably woven in with the fabric of eighteenth-century French thought. The *libertins*, who had been for some time silent or reticent, spoke and wrote with renewed boldness; the confession of incredulity among men of letters, or in aristocratic circles, was no longer a defiance of the law; and a tacit consensus of opinion seemed to open the way for a collective endeavour to eradicate the abuses of the past, with which the present was still all trammelled.

Since these critical activities were inseparable from the thrashing out of concrete issues, the writers in an overpowering majority took sides with the reformers, and made up groups that more or less coalesced into a party—that of the *philosophes*, a label denoting readiness to make the solution of all problems dependent solely upon reason. The grand scheme of an *Encyclopédie*, or general inventory of extant knowledge, compiled in a purely objective and scientific spirit—an enterprise in which most of the eminent minds of the mid-century met—gave the philosophical age its climax and fit symbol.

Lingering darkness was to be expelled by the light of reason. But through an apparent paradox, the temper of the century had barely found its stable unity in a mood of rationalism, when sporadic symptoms of dissonance and contradiction became clearly perceptible. Strains of sentiment had already cropped up among the writers of the Transition (see Part IV, Chapter XXVIII) after 1715. They grew more abundant and stronger. Deeper than the effect of social and political changes was the inner rhythm of the mind itself, and the cyclical law that presides over the development of European thought. After a prolonged period of predominant intellectualism, the emotions were called upon to reassert themselves; and the eighteenth century became eventually the age of sentimentalism, no less than that of rationality. The opposition of the two currents remained hidden for some time beneath a partial and superficial analogy; for, just as the intelligence was attacking the obsolete, the absurd, and the false, so the emotions were rebelling against a cool or dry tone of life: there was rebellion in both; and a typical aspect of the century was a kind of humanitarian and logical eagerness, in which the demands of the head and the heart were curiously blended. But there was a lag between the tides of rationalism and of sensibility; the former was at its height when the latter was still only rising. About 1760 there was a distinct turn, and when once sentiment was in full motion the clash with rationalism became clearly unavoidable. Despite overlapping, the age of Rousseau was different from that of Voltaire. There was some superficial agreement on practical points, but the two leaders stood at opposite poles of thought; and the sentimental movement introduced new intellectual and artistic growths which have provided rich nourishment for French literature ever since.

CHAPTER XXX

Montesquieu

MONTESQUIEU'S[1] contribution to French literature can be summed up for our purposes in three works. His other writings are by no means negligible and should be included in any complete survey.

The *Lettres persanes* delight a reader by their display of witty, brilliant satire and accomplished writing. There is not much originality in the subject; exoticism had been in the air; the coming of an ambassador from Persia to the French king had struck the popular imagination; the trick of making a visitor from abroad voice the reaction of nature and common sense to a sophisticated civilization had been tried more than once. Montesquieu pointed the devices and heightened the irony. The piquant descriptions of French manners are interlarded, in other letters from home, with duly spiced accounts of what took place among the traveller's wives during his absence. The whole thing is very clever and amusing, but might seem just a little cheap, were it not for the masterly economy and sober polish of the style. Weight is added, as well, to the irresponsibility of a merely satirical purpose, by not a few thrusts that reach the core of absurdity hidden beneath the paradoxes of French life. The philosopher is at work, and his aim is not only laughter, but light. Political and religious abuses are attacked, no longer covertly as by Bayle, but clearly and aggressively, thus revealing the temper of the age. One may even detect some seeds of sentiment, embedded in what is altogether a shining example of the execution that can be wielded by reason, using the weapon of intellectual ridicule.

[1] Charles Louis de Secondat, born at La Brède near Bordeaux in 1689, and early a member of the Parlement de Guyenne, inherited an estate and the title of baron de Montesquieu (1716). He tried his hand at several subjects, mainly scientific; published the very successful *Lettres persanes*, 1721; spent part of his time in Paris, moving in literary and social circles. He travelled extensively in Europe, spending two years in England (1729–31) before settling in his native castle of La Brède and publishing *Considérations sur les causes de la grandeur des Romains et de leur décadence*, 1734; *L'Esprit des lois*, 1748, the latter a work of wide international influence. He became half blind and wrote only minor pieces till his death in 1755.

His-*Considérations sur les causes de la grandeur des Romains*, &c., show another aspect of Montesquieu's genius; they are entirely serious and thoughtful. Even the style is very different, pithy, pregnant, compressed into brief paragraphs in which every word is calculated. The book sets out to unravel the network of causes that first favoured the growth of Rome, and then brought down her empire, through a process of inner decay that preceded the attacks from without. The nature of the inquiry is thus historical, but its method and manner are those of philosophy. Facts are conveyed by allusion or implication; stress is laid on influences, mainly political and social, though at one end of the scale the physical conditions within which the Roman power had to develop are given proper attention, while at the other end moral and psychological trends in the mind of the people itself are no less carefully emphasized.

Such excursions into philosophical history may, and here do, strongly appeal to our sense of the interrelation of things, and cast an exciting light upon a great drama. On the other hand it goes without saying that the undertaking is fraught with dangers. Modern historians will tolerate it grudgingly, and will insist that such a godlike faculty of illumination cannot be acquired without infinitely patient labour. Was Montesquieu sufficiently possessed of the facts —all the accessible facts—to read with such assurance the complex of causes that brought about a national catastrophe? Of course he was not; and who could be? The *Considérations* are not a history, but a psychological and moral essay. Modern research has added much, altered much; still, his study of the available documents was penetrating; the main outline of his construction, chiefly founded on traits of the character, temperament, and life of the Romans, yet stands. Particularly valuable is his analysis of the policy, hard, driving, tireless, by means of which the Republic wore out, divided, and conquered all her rivals; and of the corruption that set in when civic virtue could no longer rely on the constant stimulus of danger.

This is a great book, full of the best substance of a reflective mind, setting a high standard for the suggestive interpretation of the past. It is written with a strength and a dignity of statement that suggest some quieter, less dramatic and romantic Tacitus.

To the cultivated opinion of the time, the claim of *L'Esprit des lois* to be regarded as Montesquieu's masterpiece was overwhelming and he derived most of his international fame and influence from this work. Today we are impressed by the majesty of the fragments into which the vast edifice has irreparably crumbled. But it is not what it purported to be—a synthesis of the innumerable derivations through which the central fact of law is reflected on the metaphysical, the cosmic, and the human planes, the last being in its turn subdivided into the political, social, economic, religious, and ethical systems, that have gradually built our modern civilization. The scope is indeed all but universal, taking in the past as well as the present, and one must admire the bold magnitude of the task. But it was hopeless from the first. At bottom Montesquieu's attempt is to do for the history of mankind what he had achieved with very fair success, in his *Considérations*, for the growth and fall of Rome. But the matter here is so immense and elusive that it baffles even his vigorous grasp, and the sketchy, tentative character of many parts is only too plain. The author, moreover, falls a victim to a verbal fallacy. One and the same name covers both abstract laws, the *lois* which he defines as 'les rapports nécessaires qui dérivent de la nature des choses', and the human conventions of all kinds, concrete and definite, that regulate the working of society. He tries to invest the latter with some of the cosmic inevitability of the former; but they are by no means 'necessary' and are obeyed only if they are accepted. In the transition from metaphysics to jurisprudence, the thread of continuity breaks up again and again.

Still, if these ill-advised ambitions are dismissed, the bulk of the work is rife with views of momentous importance, that have been integrated in the common doctrine of statecraft. Montesquieu is deeply aware of the connexions, open or secret, that make the body politic of each nation a complex organic whole; his remarks, pitched in an objective, realistic key, are an antidote to a rash impatience of reform. He was not the first to point out the outstanding influence of physical conditions, the soil, the climate; but he stressed these factors with unforgettable force. He made his mark particularly with his examination of the motives that enter into the proper functioning of each form of government. That a monarchy rests on honour, a despotism on fear, and a republic on virtue, is a simplified scheme, which none the less sets a useful lesson for democracies to ponder; but Book XI ('Des lois qui forment la liberté politique dans son rapport avec la constitution'), and especially Chapter VI, 'De la constitution d'Angleterre', are epoch-making; the distinction of the three powers: 'législatif, exécutif, et judiciaire', the emphatic warning that they must be kept separate, and the analysis of the means by which English wisdom has solved the problem, have left a lasting stamp upon most modern political endeavours, from the American and the French revolutions to contemporary changes.

As a work of literature, *L'Esprit des lois* is too unwieldy and unequal to be popular. Written in the sententious style of the *Considérations*, but without all their even compactness, it is more often consulted than read. Yet, when all is said, it remains a commanding monument, with battered wings and proud towers, an honour to its author's comprehensive intelligence, his shrewd and intuitive perception.

CHAPTER XXXI

Voltaire

VOLTAIRE'S[1] many-sided personality appears in all the literary chapters, and almost over the whole course, of the eighteenth century. But by right he belongs to its former half. His eager inquisitive mind, his critical bent, link him up with the rationalist age; he is identified with the advocacy of intellectual light. On the other hand, and not only because his life was long, he shared in the temper of the later decades. Between 1760, the symbolic limit of the Age of Enlightenment, and his death (1778), the 'patriarch of Ferney', though by no means giving up his fight against 'obscurantism', let his mellowed mood take on a more distinct colouring of philanthropy. He defended individual victims of oppression even more

---

[1] François-Marie Arouet, born in Paris, 1694, of modest middle-class parents, studied the humanities at a Jesuit school, turned early to literature, had a tragedy, *Œdipe*, performed with success and published under the *nom de plume* of Voltaire, 1719. He wrote an epic poem, the *Henriade*, 1728. When his independent spirit brought him into various clashes with the authorities, he was imprisoned for a while at the Bastille, cudgelled by a nobleman's servants, and had to take refuge in England, 1726–9. There he gathered the materials for the *Lettres philosophiques*, 1734, and finished the *Histoire de Charles XII*, 1731. Further plays: *Brutus*, 1730; *Zaïre*, 1732; *Alzire*, 1736; *Mahomet*, 1741; *Mérope,* 1748, achieved his fame. His advanced views again aroused suspicion and he spent some years with Madame du Châtelet at Cirey in Lorraine. After the poetical essays of his youth, mostly of the lighter kind, he wrote longer philosophical poems, including *Le Mondain*, 1736; the *Discours sur l'homme*, 1735, *La Loi naturelle* and *Le Désastre de Lisbonne*, 1756; also prose novels, *Zadig*; 1747, *Micromégas*, 1752. At the invitation of Frederick II, king of Prussia, he resided at Potsdam from the summer of 1750 to the spring of 1753, finished one historical work, *Le Siècle de Louis XIV*, 1751, and prepared another, the *Essai sur les mœurs*, 1756. Disappointed with kings as well as governments, he tried Switzerland, 1754, clashed with the Consistoire of Geneva, and settled in France, very near the Swiss border, at Ferney, from 1760; whence his unceasing output, and his correspondence, allowed him to preserve the ascendancy of a European leader of thought. Philosophical novels, *Candide*, 1759; *L'Ingénu*, 1767, and late plays, *Tancrède*, 1760, &c., with many occasional pieces of prose or verse, kept him before the public. In a *Letter* to the French Academy, he strongly opposed the growing cult of Shakespeare, 1776, and in open controversies he defended the victims of legal or religious persecutions. Returning to Paris, he was welcomed with general enthusiasm, and died soon afterwards, 1778. His *Letters* form a large part of his complete works.

warmly than he attacked authority, religious or civil, and along with the concrete, there crept a touch more of sensibility into his crusades. The ironical adversary of Rousseau, he was yet not very far, in his comfortable hermitage, from taking a leaf out of the book of 'life according to nature'. Nevertheless, the significance of Voltaire should still be studied together with the intellectual movement that culminated in the *Encyclopédie*.

To his own time Voltaire was pre-eminently a poet and playwright. The pendulum swung heavily against him during the nineteenth century, and probably too far. We can read with pleasure many of the short pieces of verse penned through his youth and maturity, provided we bear in mind that they are prose—terse, witty, elegant, cut into metric lines that run with ease and have at times even a musical value in the instinctive adaptation of sound to sense. Satires of this kind, epigrams, elegies, apologues, dedications, epistles, had been from the time of Marot the staple of 'lighter' French verse; they now filled scores of the small volumes which in dainty though dusty leather still make a show on the classical shelves of libraries. Among the graceful versifiers of his age Voltaire cuts a good figure. The neatness of his phrasing, his nimble wit, his dexterous touch, are remarkable; and he can surprise us with a free pattern of interlocked rhymes, or a genuine effusion of feeling—as in *Aux mânes de Monsieur de Génouville*. Knowing his limitations, he never attempted the ode. His only approach to one is in the epistle *A Madame du Châtelet, sur la philosophie de Newton*, 1736, where the wonders of astronomy rouse him to Miltonian enthusiasm:

> Confidents du Très-Haut, substances éternelles,
> Qui brûlez de ses feux, qui couvrez de vos ailes
> Le trône où votre maître est assis parmi vous,
> Parlez: du grand Newton n'étiez-vous point jaloux?

But Voltaire nursed epic hopes, and built high expectations upon the *Henriade*.[1] It is usual with critics to give this poem no quarter. That an ineradicable artificiality dwells at the heart of it, and corrupts everything, must be conceded; still, there hardly ever was a venture more nearly saved from disaster by sheer cleverness. The subject is impossible, and deft handling will not make epic poetry of it; but

[1] Of his most grievous error, the mock-heroic *Pucelle*, the less said the better.

a reader with an open mind may like a few passages and be interested in more. Among the latter should be placed the glowing picture of English liberty, at the end of Canto I; with the former, Potier's speech (Canto VI), a good piece of political oratory. Altogether the odd mixture of a pagan background with modern history, of a classical hell and heaven with the rational views of a deist, and— strangest of all—with Christian miracles, like those performed by Saint Louis; the contrast, finally, between episodes and images savouring of the stalest tradition, and the free unconventional treat- ment of the general theme, produce a monster, that the writer's infinite talent has licked into some sort of decent shape.

Cleverness again is the inevitable keyword in an appreciation of Voltaire's tragedies. He imitates the plays of Corneille and chiefly of Racine, their situations, characters, turns of style, so well that he goes beyond mere imitation, and creates acceptable works of art, on a traditional pattern that he has truly made his own. His instinct is fine enough to master the genuine spirit of classical simplicity— a virtue he rightly admires in the Greeks, and no less in Racine. The language and the manner of his *Mérope*, for instance, as would happen with such a theme, are bathed in a discreet light of soberness and reserve that wins our warm esteem; in its sustained power such a scene as IV. ii is truly fine. But this purity of inspiration is with him a lucky accident, and soon flags. We gather the same chequered impression of his power of rousing tragic suspense. He has some deeply moving scenes, and *Zaïre* is in this respect his best achieve- ment. On the other hand, he does not always succeed in steering clear of melodrama, the less so, as his experience of the English stage, during the fruitful years of his voluntary exile, gave him a sense of the energy with which emotional climaxes could be used in tragedy. In this respect his instinct was always a little unsure; after discover- ing and admiring Shakespeare, or at least some features of his genius, and contributing to popularizing him in France, he took up a far more critical attitude, and tried to exorcize the demon he had let loose on the French stage. But when Orosmane (*Zaïre*, v. vii) thinks he hears, in the stillness of night, *un bruit affreux*; when he kills himself, with words that remind one of Othello's last speech; or when Séide on the point of murdering Zopire seems to see 'Ces traits de sang, ce spectre, et ces errantes ombres' (*Mahomet*, IV. iv), one feels that Voltaire was not proof against the magnetism of the English example.

Such traces of influence do not perfectly coalesce with a dramatic ideal that remains orthodox, and alien to effects of physical or imaginative violence. It is indeed in their composite quality that the inner weakness of these estimable plays chiefly lies. Political propaganda by a polemist with an axe to grind, things spoken *at* the public, whether attacking tyrannical kings or fanatical priests, too often mar the dramatic illusion. Or, on the contrary, emotions are exploited that Voltaire would have shown more consistency in ignoring. We admire Corneille's *Polyeucte*, but what shall we say to imitations of Christian sublimity in *Zaïre*?

It is probably as an historian that Voltaire's claim to be an innovator in literature stands safest. The relatively new field allowed his gift of intellectual initiative to make itself felt more easily than did older domains under the paralysing burden of long tradition. The *Histoire de Charles XII* rests on a solid foundation of knowledge; it is in spirit truly modern and objective. Not that the writer has no moral to draw, but the *Remarques sur l'Histoire* and the *Nouvelles Considérations* breathe the sanest assurance as to the tasks that matter most, and the way to tackle them. Not only is the underlying philosophy good; these pages also contain a premonition of the 'sociological' point of view that the future was so decisively to stress. Let changes in manners and laws be the historian's main object: 'On saurait ainsi l'histoire des hommes, au lieu de savoir une faible partie de l'histoire des rois et des cours.' The life of the Swedish king is in fact told very intelligently, in clear, orderly fashion, with point and elegant brevity; the narrative sets graphic details in vivid relief, stressing the personality of the hero against a background of circumstance, like a good historical novel.

A bulkier work, *le Siècle de Louis XIV*, is of richer substance. Its aim is stated in terms that adumbrate the purposes of twentieth-century historians: 'On veut peindre, non les actions d'un seul homme, mais l'esprit des hommes dans le siècle le plus éclairé qui fût jamais.' It is thus the collective picture of the mind of a period. To some extent, however, Voltaire is still bound by contemporary prejudices; a 'century' for him approaches 'perfection', more or less, as it achieves a well-rounded evenness of standard; and the French reader is not surprised to find that the *Siècle de Louis XIV* drew nearer to this ideal than the ages of Pericles, Augustus, or the Medici. Still, the book does not lack candour and impartiality. Blame is laid, when it is due, on the *Roi Soleil*'s ambition and errors; the king's arch-enemy, William of England, is praised for his civic and manly virtues; and the story is told from a European, rather than a French, point of view. The sincere liberalism and the humanity of a thinker rising to a great theme are really inspiring, while the writer's talent is admirable. It is only where the Church or the Middle Ages are concerned that a niggardly spirit of hostility and narrowness creeps in and the serene ideal succumbs to a partisan mood. The second part brings us the long-expected account of the social and moral life of France; and at once it becomes clear that Voltaire, right as he is in his new valuation of factors, still clings to the traditional yard-measure. The study of the economic and administrative basis upon which the France of Louis XIV was built is of the slightest. The writer stands on more familiar ground, and gives us fuller satis-faction, when describing what one might call the public manners of the time; the fine arts—literature, science, and religious quarrels. The progress of the language, and the ways through which 'dans l'éloquence, dans la poésie, dans la littérature, dans les livres de morale et d'agrément, les Français furent les législateurs de l'Europe', are justly summed up. And so, in spite of all its uncertainties and deficiencies, the book is not only pleasant reading but an important landmark in the development of history.

With the *Essai sur les mœurs* we fall to a lower level of art. The general aim is no less clearly grasped but the execution is less care-fully worked out. The book was meant as a cyclopedia of *tenden-cieux* knowledge, for the particular use of Madame du Châtelet, a lady with a finely 'philosophical' mind. It attempts to trace the growth of civilization, including those early Oriental societies so long unknown to the West, or ignored by it. A mass of half-ascertained facts is thus industriously accumulated, and displayed with relative order, in a clear and animated style. The generous soul of the drama is man's faith in his painful rise from humble beginnings to a great future; but along with the hope, a good deal of the impatience ʹof progress is stressed; the tone is often polemical. Legends are demolished in the name of truth, and truth—or what might pass for it—put forward instead. From the time of the establishment of the Christian Church, her influence is tested, and often condemned. The work's chief interest today lies in the vivid light thrown upon the author's sources of information and his practical, ethical tenets.

Voltaire's novels remain the most living part of his literary output. They are the best repository of his philosophical ideas, a means of liberation from the burden of reflections he owed to experience; and they are, moreover, written with all his wit and sprightly talent.

Zadig, ou la destinée, is a pure gem of ironical fancy, shrewd wisdom, and lively style. In its general intention it anticipates the fuller argument of *Candide*. The background of Oriental manners is handled with much skill, but is largely borrowed from the *Lettres persanes,* and few of the episodes are original. Still, the touch of the magician refreshes and renews everything. The odd incidents that keep crossing Zadig's path are the symbolical price to pay for the waywardness of an inscrutable Providence; things will settle down roughly in the end, and our lot probably be acceptable, but never in the way we had hoped or wished for. If we are, or try to be, wise our wisdom will win us bitter enemies—Voltaire here is probably voicing his resentment against the unmerited hardships of his life. Some conventional elements linger in the plot, as the hero's impassioned love for Queen Astarte—a feeling the author depicts with his tongue in his cheek—or the episodes in which the paraphernalia of chivalry and tourneys reappear. But none the less the book is radically sophisticated and modern; in its terse persistence of bitter satire it is not unworthy of mention in the same breath as Swift's *Gulliver*, a more powerful and a cruder work, and known to Voltaire.

The influence of *Gulliver* in *Micromégas* is far plainer and Cyrano de Bergerac's older 'imaginary journeys' have a share as well. The lack of originality is compensated by the unfailing liveliness and the wit. Of special significance, as an expression of Voltaire's philosophical views, is the ridiculous figure cut by the disciples of the various European doctrines, ancient or modern, with the sole exception of the English followers of Locke.

Candide is a great book, but not one to treasure on a favourite shelf or read more than once. Its indictment of the natural course of

things is of unparalleled bitterness, but when its vitriol-etched scenes
have branded themselves on the mind they have no further wealth
of wisdom to reward familiarity and meditation. Swift is not more
savage; Johnson's *Rasselas*, published a few weeks later, and not
indebted to it, is thoroughly different in spirit, despite some similarity of outline. Grieved and sore from his German experiences,
shocked by the Lisbon disaster (1755), Voltaire let himself go and
poured out all his accumulated rancour against life. So there is here
no attempt at objectivity or fairness; nothing can be farther from
reality than this purely fanciful apologue, conducted by the sheer
will of a desperate pessimism, revelling in the rank joy of the sordid,
the cruel, the indecent, and the absurd, and moving through a bewildering series of impossibly ironical chances. Since the work
possesses the force of one of the major interpretations of common
experience, it stands supreme in its own field, and could not be
spared from the list of sinister masterpieces. The inner violence is all
of the spirit; the tone, the mood, the manner remain in perfect
keeping with the cool composure of post-classical writing. In that
driest atmosphere we come across one unexpected gleam of feeling:
meeting again his wildly beloved Cunégonde, now hideous and a
frump, the hero quietly remarks: 'Je suis honnête homme, et mon
devoir est de l'aimer toujours.' One wonders whether Voltaire
wrote this seriously, or with the smile that mocks, all through the
story, the stubborn foolishness of the sentimentalist and the optimist,
pitilessly buffeted and bruised by the strokes of the real. *Candide* is
hardly a novel, but a tract against the 'all's well' illusion of Leibniz
and some English deists; the characters are mere sketches, and the
dialogue is stripped to the simplicity of linear utterance. With a
somewhat similar intent, Flaubert's *Éducation sentimentale* will stand,
one century later, at the opposite pole of a rigid realism.

From that uncompromising height of destructive derision *L'Ingénu*
takes us down to a more indulgent irony. The fashionable theme of
the 'noble savage' in contact with our insincerities yields a rather
thin crop of reflection and humour. While fun is poked at Rousseau's
fiction of man in a natural state, the tone of the tale shows a relaxing
of fibre, and some approximation to Rousseau's sensibility. It is
permissible to find that the hero, though he does not, it seems, lack
wit, is mightily long in learning anything from his European

experiences. The most valuable part of the story is the last, with its outspoken denunciation of social lies, and championship of the down-trodden, also its deliberate choice of the sad, tragical conclusion necessitated by the firm issues of the book.

Candide's final cure for the ills that flesh is heir to: 'Il faut cultiver son jardin', may be honoured with the name of practical wisdom; to the label of 'philosophy' it should lay claim only in the wider and looser sense. Indeed Voltaire's repeated attempts to justify fully, in so far as he was concerned, the common pretension and title of most writers of the time are all of this nature. Philosophical thought of a potential kind is diffused through the bulk of his writings; even if there is promise of a more concentrated essence, the reader is usually disappointed. The *Traité de métaphysique*, for instance, is very largely devoted to questions that now belong to psychology—a science then not yet recognized. When he most definitely commits himself, Voltaire deems that the existence of God is more likely than His non-existence; that the whole origin of good and evil lies in social utility; as to the soul, 'Je n'assure point que j'aie des démon-strations contre la spiritualité et l'immortalité de l'âme; mais toutes les vraisemblances sont contre elles.'

The *Lettres philosophiques* placed Voltaire in the forefront of the bold and aggressive writers who professed unorthodox views. It is not possible to do justice to the wealth of their ideas; one can only say that they were to France the first full revelation of the intellectual originality of England. They are written at the start in an exquisitely amusing manner, with a perfect intuition of the method of humour. Then with cogent force and nervous eloquence they lay stress on typical aspects of English freedom in religion and politics then being discovered by the French in a mood of wonder and awe. We must admire the quick intelligence of an observer who could penetrate the significance of alien customs, manners, institutions, and ways of thinking. The English had horrified Europe, two generations earlier, making a name for themselves as the beheaders of kings; the French, then relatively more sedate, were to follow suit, and to be held up in execration by the British; during the interval, the freshly won discipline of public life beyond the Channel is here duly extolled, and set up as an example. Locke and Newton figure as the conquerors of Descartes, and his exploded *tourbillons*. The last seven letters are a very suggestive survey of the literature and the writers of contemporary Britain; with the Abbé Prévost's account (see further, Chapter XXXII), published at practically the same time, and of almost equal interest, but less widely read, they are a landmark in the story of the mutual discovery of the two countries.

The poet and the philosopher are at one in the *Discours en vers sur l'homme*; and though neither rises to supreme eminence, their union is to the profit of both. The ideas expressed, which are by no means commonplace, but maxims of ripe reflection, gain emphasis from their poetical garb, while the lines, with their firm and full rhythm, are the more memorable for their thoughtful content. The *Poème sur la loi naturelle*, in its four parts, has inferior moments but advocates mutual tolerance with sincere, eloquent charity. Resignation appears as the last word of human wisdom; and the final prayer to God is not unworthy of being compared with Pope's.

The *Poème sur le désastre de Lisbonne* voices the moral shock which was to reverberate deeply in *Candide*. It sets a powerful emphasis upon the tragic fate which threatens man on every side. Voltaire has written better lines, but nothing in verse that is more moving. The sage's attempt to preserve his rational serenity breaks down openly, and the cry of suffering and doubting mankind rings out.

The *Dictionnaire philosophique*, on the contrary, is an arsenal of engines to batter this or that article of historical Christianity. It is obviously an imitation of Bayle, and more openly aggressive. Most of the entries are brought in for the sake of anti-ecclesiastical gibes. What saves the writer's tactics from the charge of monotonous partisanship is the style, as ever clear, nimble and biting.

No study, however short, of Voltaire's work can pass over his *Correspondance générale,* a prodigiously sustained outpouring of his daily thoughts, cares, activities, and feelings and one of the most plentiful wells of 'French undefiled'. Volume after volume is filled with letters jotted down with wonderful ease and yet, in their rapidity, touching no subject without leaving their mark upon it; and constituting, as a whole, a fascinating survey of the incidents, events, and characters of more than half a century. The writer gains very much more than he may lose from a form of self-expression that approximates to a roughly sincere confession and reveals a man with a very fair share of weaknesses but rich in genuine humanity.

CHAPTER XXXII

Poetry

APART from Voltaire, the poetry of the Enlightenment lacks very distinguished names. Since the age was bent upon the spreading of intellectual light, it had not much to do with the communication through suggestion that is the proper method of genuine poetry. The writing of verse was certainly a fashionable exercise, but prose might have served equally well for the matter expressed—wit, didacticism, *galanterie*, the sifting and weighing of values. Argument of one kind or another was supreme. Still, a fair number of writers possessed enough emotional or imaginative ardour to strike off thoughts and phrases pregnant with the sense of beauty. They are of their time, but to some extent transcend it, and stand in relation to it more or less as exceptions.

Among them Jean-Baptiste Rousseau[1] was long held to be the most eminent. He had more vigour than any of his contemporaries; they felt it, and admired him, even beyond his deserts. With all his energy, he can be rhetorical, and loves a good commonplace only too well. Still, among his general, second-rate odes, some rise to actual grandeur of accent—an achievement served by a proper use of Biblical style and a gift of terse, neat phrasing; while the handling of the verse, in its relative freedom, can have merit. Such are Odes X of Book I, IX (*A Monsieur le Marquis de la Fare*) and X (*Sur la mort de Monseigneur le Prince de Conty*) of Book II. In the *Épîtres*, several remind one, not of Malherbe; but of Boileau (*Aux Muses*); and one of the Allegories (*La Volière*) is charmingly like Marot. Altogether Rousseau's unequal inspiration stands him at times in good stead. His art is always careful, and his language restrained.

The case of Louis Racine (1692–1763), the son of the dramatist,

[1] Jean-Baptiste Rousseau, 1671–1741, born in Paris, of a modest family, was known early for his verse. He made some friends, but his proud, harsh independence made him more enemies. He was banished, it would seem unjustly, by the Parlement, and spent most of his life abroad, in Switzerland, Belgium, and England, where his collected *Poems* appeared in 1723.

is different; he had talent, but was modest and over-conscientious, and spoke deprecatingly of his verse. The world was only too ready to take him at his own valuation; the more so, as his two poems, *La Grâce*, 1720, and *La Religion*, 1748, have only a very austere appeal. But an austere, didactic theme is not necessarily fatal to poetry; and to read Louis Racine is a pleasant surprise, for he is better than his persistent reputation of dullness. *La Grâce* is a feat of subtle argument and clear expression, but hopelessly prosaic and cold. *La Religion* gradually reaches a measure of intellectual anima-tion and nervous eloquence, not unworthy of the masters to whom it humbly refers its severe doctrine: Pascal and Bossuet. The theme —no less than a full apology for a believer's faith in Christianity— is courageously pursued through six cantos, culminating in a final choice between the half-hearted compromise of deism, and the total imprudence of faith. We find here again some of the calm sublimity of Jean Racine's *Athalie*, allied to a sharp vigour not unlike that of English metaphysical poetry; as, for instance, in these lines, on the love of God:

> Ses temples sont nos cœurs. 'Quel terme, direz-vous,
> Doit avoir cet amour qu'il exige de nous?'
> Si vous le demandez, vous n'aimez point encore.
> Tout rempli de l'objet dont l'ardeur le dévore,
> Quel autre objet un cœur pourrait-il recevoir?
> Le terme de l'amour est de n'en point avoir.

Or these, on the necessary humility of reason:

> Je ne dispute point contre un maître suprême.
> Qui m'instruira de Dieu, si ce n'est Dieu lui-même?
> Dans un sombre nuage il veut s'envelopper;
> Mais il est un rayon qu'il en laisse échapper.
> Que me faut-il de plus? Je marche avec courage,
> Et content du rayon, j'adore le nuage.

The sustained, quietly impressive quality of many such passages ought to rank the poem with the fair successes of French philo-sophical poetry. But what justice could an author expect, who struck his breast in his Preface as sincerely as Louis Racine does?

J'avoue qu'en renonçant aux beautés brillantes de la fiction, il faut peut-être renoncer aussi au titre de poète, et se contenter du rang de versificateur;

mais comme l'utilité des hommes doit être le principal objet d'un écrivain sage, je serais assez récompensé de mon travail, si ma versification contribuait à imprimer plus facilement, dans la mémoire, des vérités qui intéressent tous les hommes.

One is tempted to break another lance in defence of Le Franc de Pompignan, 1709–84, whose chief enemy was not himself, but one even more dangerous, Voltaire. Two or three murderous epigrams have destroyed him apparently for ever. And yet his valuable achievement is more than the justly famous and much-quoted ode on the death of Jean-Baptiste Rousseau. The *Poésies sacrées*, 1751, are an interesting attempt to overcome the basic defects of post-classical lyricism: its fund of exhausted themes, and its worn-out poetic diction. His method was to draw more fully than had ever been done in France from the rich store of Scripture—not only the psalms, but the hymns and prophecies—by means of translations and adaptations. This return to fresh, however old, sources of inspiration and imagery is akin to what was later to be the central endeavour of Romanticism. In order to capture more safely the promptings of Semitic imagination, Pompignan often founded his poems, not on the Latin, but on the Hebrew Bible. His intentions are excellent. He deplores, with good grounds, the inroads of the newfangled 'Philosophie' upon the traditional emotions.

C'est aujourd'hui le siècle de la Philosophie; tout est à présent Philosophie; expliquons-nous, tout prétend l'être. Notre Prose et nos Vers retentissent de ces grands mots, Philosophie, Sagesse, Vérité, Vertu. On dissipe nos Préjugés; on éclaire nos Esprits. Quelle lumière affreuse, ou plutôt quelles ténèbres! Pour allumer le flambeau de la Philosophie, on éteint celui de la Foi.

To come out with such forcible statements, at the peak of Voltaire's age, was for a bishop to speak in character, but for a poet to court disaster with the critics. Pompignan suggests that Biblical poems in French might be written to fit the admirable *motets* of La Lande. 'Je désirerais de plus que le sentiment en fût l'âme, et qu'il perçât toujours par quelque endroit jusque dans les sujets qui paraîtraient moins l'exiger.' This obviously points to the coming sentimental reaction. With such aims in view, he frankly, even crudely, rendered the primitive violence of the Hebrew text; and so doing, he far exceeded the tolerance of his readers' sophisticated tastes. The result, to us, is none the less remarkable, as in the *Cantique de Moyse avant sa mort* (Book II); or in these few lines from *La Prophétie de Joël* (Book III):

> La vapeur dans l'Air allumée,
> Le feu, le sang et la fumée
> Couvriront l'Univers tremblant;
> Et dans un cercle de ténèbres
> La Lune en ces momens funèbres
> Roulera son globe sanglant.

However, even in Book IV (*Hymnes*), where the pattern of the stanzas is more free and varied, what is lacking is the bold harmony of great art. It is instructive in this respect to compare, for instance, the sing-song of the *Hymne pour le jour de la Nativité du Seigneur* with Milton's admirable metrical achievement in his ode on the same subject.

A few more poets deserve a passing mention, in this age of prose. The *Ode sur le temps* (1762) of A. L. Thomas (1732–85) is one of those solitary masterpieces that sometimes break the tenor of a mediocre writer's career; its grand theme, firm thought, and forceful expression deserve the honour Lamartine was to do it when he used two of its half-lines in *Le Lac*. It shows a sense of the majesty an occasional short line can add to a series of alexandrines.

> Invisible torrent des siècles et des jours,
> Tandis que ton pouvoir m'entraîne dans la tombe,
>   J'ose, avant que j'y tombe,
> M'arrêter un moment pour contempler ton cours.

Gresset's (1709–77) *Vert-Vert* (1734) is only a *jeu d'esprit*, a witty 'badinage', gracefully told, and worthy of the drawing-room reputation that clung to it; far emptier, and less brilliant in fact, than Pope's *Rape of the Lock*. A more substantial token of his talent is his verse comedy, *Le Méchant* (1747), full of Molière, but built on a new psychological intuition, that of the modern *amour du mal*, or delectation in evil, a sketch of the morbidity that the marquis de Sade was soon to make his own theme. This disease of the soul is, of course, contrasted with dear Sensibility: 'Le véritable esprit marche avec la bonté.'

Alexis Piron (1689–1773) made a name with his sharp wit, that dared to engage Voltaire in public battle and was not always defeated. As a talker he has left but the ghost of a remembrance; his written epigrams are no better than hundreds from contemporary collections. His poetical comedy, *La Métromanie* (1738), was praised in his day, but disappoints us now.

CHAPTER XXXIII

Drama

DRAMA during the post-classical period shows the gradual drying up of the sources from which the works of the great masters had drawn their vitality. Both tragedy and comedy can now only tap secondary veins of character and passion, the leavings of the richer materials that had supported creation in the preceding age. So a natural necessity drives them to abandon the more obvious fields for the sake of particular aspects of the inner world. But a surer intuition leads them also to seek for a lasting renovation in a spiritual change now defining itself more and more clearly as the longed-for rebirth of the soul of man. Before the middle of the century was reached, sentiment had begun to permeate both literature and life; it found its way at once into drama; and under its influence the traditional types of tragic and comic plays approximated to one another in *comédie larmoyante* and *drame bourgeois*, equally bent on giving a truer and more direct vent to the complex actuality of feeling.

I. TRAGEDY

In this chapter again, Voltaire (see above, Chapter XXXI) stands not only as the universal man of letters, but as the most conspicuous playwright. Although new tragedies were now being written by the score, only two names should be mentioned by the side of his.

Crébillon[1] staked everything on a sombre violence of situation and deed, eked out by a style that aims at forcefulness, and reaches it at the cost of some occasional rant. His best moments occur when his concentrated energy strikes out lines packed with meaning, urged forward by a powerful impulse. The spirit of his predecessors is active in him, and his tragic utterance is not unlike that of Corneille.

[1] Prosper Jolyot, sieur de Crais-Billon, dit Crébillon, 1674–1762, born at Dijon, lived in Paris on a modest judicial charge, and wrote tragedies which were performed with success: *Idoménée*, 1705; *Atrée et Thyeste*, 1707; *Électre*, 1708; *Rhadamiste et Zénobie*, 1711. In spite of a long eclipse, he remained a leader of critical opinion. His last triumph was *Catilina*, 1748.

One wishes his language could equally well have mastered the supple unfailing elegance of Racine, for it is too often marred by strained or contorted phrases. *Rhadamiste et Zénobie*, when due allowance has been made for these faults, is a fine play, full of the impending sense of fate, fitly compact in construction; it may be ranked not far below the great tragedies of the seventeenth century. In *Atrée et Thyeste* Crébillon's failings are more apparent; still, it is a vigorous 'revenge tragedy', destitute of the poetry of the Elizabethan type, but painting an unforgettable picture of morbid hatred. The thrills of horror to which the Fifth Act works up did in fact, we are told, rouse some protest among the audience.

Houdar de la Motte's chief importance lies in the field of critical doctrine as such and he will be studied below (see Chapter XXXIV). But there is an unpredictable strain in his shrewd, paradoxical mind, and this arch-enemy of traditional poetry allowed himself the distinction of writing one of the finest verse tragedies of the period. *Inès de Castro* (1723) was very successful in its day, and still today preserves its appeal. The intellectuality that is usually a feature of La Motte, and no doubt freezes many of his shorter poems, is here a source of strength, in the firmness of thought that clenches a number of lines into formulas or maxims; while the play is saved from coldness by the intuition that has made the heroine a moving study in feminine nobleness. There is no touch of romanticism in her, but the self-possession of a truly heroic soul. The only hint of a changing aesthetic is the appearance on the stage of her young children—a departure from classical tastes censured by the learned, but found deeply pathetic by most spectators. The scene in the Fourth Act (IV. iii) when the Spanish grandees sit in Council, and the speeches for and against the prisoner, have the nervous eloquence of Corneille. Indeed, La Motte seems to have clearly realized the possibilities of his plot; and for once intelligence was as efficient as instinct.

2. COMEDY

The comic plays that have survived from the beginning of the period are openly dependent on the tradition of Molière. Dancourt (1661–1725) scored with his *Chevalier à la mode* (1687) because he staged a problem that was already growing prominent: the conflict between aristocratic exclusiveness and the pushing ambition of a wealthy *bourgeoisie*. His method was to mock lightly at the cynical manners of the declining *grand siècle* rather than to satirize them; and amusing as it is, the piece hardly holds out the hope of any dramatic regeneration.

Nor is there much promise in Regnard.[1] He could make an audience laugh, and turned his gift to good account. But in his devices to create mirth hardly anything is original. *Le Joueur*, reputed his best play, rises little above the level of farce. Gambling is a bitter and dangerous vice, but all sting is here taken out of it. There is one happily inspired scene in which Valère, every penny lost, has Seneca read aloud to him for the comfort of his philosophy. Hector, his humorous valet, is second cousin to Molière's footmen. *Le Distrait*, lifted bodily from La Bruyère, has more verve and animation in its dialogue. *Le Légataire universel* is the most amusing of all, with a sprinkling of coarseness, and even of vulgarity; the main situations cannot miss their broad effects; but they demand, in order to be enjoyed, that we do not object to sheer improbability. Still, Regnard's plays breathe a kind of genial cheerfulness, and failing higher merits that virtue should not be unduly despised.

Lesage, best known as a novelist (see Chapter XXXIV), is here a case in point. He possessed, as a playwright, just what Regnard lacked: a clear perception of the social changes that were offering comedy rich possibilities of new situations and characters. His light one-act play, *Crispin rival de son maître*, 1707, is not only brilliant and witty, but gives some food for thought: bettering Molière in the *Précieuses ridicules* he shows the servant Crispin, who impersonates his master, acquitting himself on the whole very well. This is a significant step forward in the direction of human equality. At the end of the process we shall have the servant a man of wit and talent, or a hero—Figaro, or Ruy Blas. But Le Sage is a fine observer, and not a romantic; in scene VIII Crispin goes too far and is carried out of his depth by his enthusiasm. *Turcaret* (1709), a strong, bitter comedy, with very little actual fun, moves on the fringe of what

---

[1] Jean-François Regnard, 1655–1709, born in Paris, of wealthy middle-class parents, travelled widely, was captured by corsairs and enslaved at Algiers for a time, saw the Polar Circle. Later, he led an easy life in or near Paris and wrote comic sketches, followed by highly successful comedies, among them *Le Joueur*, 1696; *Les Folies amoureuses*, 1704; *Le Légataire universel*, 1708.

will be the *drame bourgeois*. The central character is a wonderful study of the unscrupulous financier, the millionaire and new lord of society. The portrait is not unduly blackened, and the vigorous upstart is as alive and realistic as one of Balzac's or Zola's capitalists. In his powerful vulgarity there are occasional indications of largeness of mind and heart. 'Sais-tu bien que je commence à le plaindre?' the fastidious Baronne confides to quick-witted Lisette. Other figures are no less broadly and vividly sketched; and the play, too original and bold not to have shocked the public of the time, stands at the head of a long posterity on the modern stage.

Seeds of the future can also be discerned in *Le Glorieux*, a comedy by Destouches.[1] Pride of birth and rank is the theme of the play: as a principle of social superiority, it is shown in conflict with new values, mainly ethical; as an individual humour it is the source of ridiculous errors and excesses. The claim of bourgeois virtues to be granted full respect and honour is put forward; but, as will be the case for a century or more, the apology is tentative; the charming *suivante*, Lisette, who is loved on her own merits, turns out after all to be highly born. The problem of the decaying caste and class spirit is treated sentimentally, not politically; and *Le Glorieux* is very near being a *comédie larmoyante* of the La Chaussée type. Goodness of heart and family feelings are exalted, and the sinner, the Comte, is duly converted. The play is amusing, the dialogue has ease, and the verse occasional point, in lines that have become proverbial. Destouches in his Preface to his adaptation of Addison's *Drummer* has a discussion of English comedy, which he praises in general, but censures for its neglect of the unities. Indeed he was no revolutionary.

Marivaux[2] cannot be integrated fully in the contemporary French drama. Although he shows some of its tendencies, he is outstandingly

[1] Philippe Néricault, dit Destouches, 1680–1754, of middle-class origin and tastes, imitated Molière in his choice of types for character study. *Le Philosophe marié*, 1727, and *Le Glorieux*, 1732, were successful, but his other plays failed. He spent six years in England. His *Le Tambour nocturne* was an adaptation of Addison's *Drummer*.

[2] Pierre Carlet de Chamblain de Marivaux, 1688–1763, born in Paris, of a family of magistrates, after various attempts at writing composed comedies in prose for the Théâtre Français or for the Comédiens Italiens, among them: *Arlequin poli par l'amour*, 1720; *La Double Inconstance*, 1723; *La Surprise de l'amour*, 1727; *Le Jeu de l'amour et du hasard*, 1730; *L'École des mères*, 1732; *Le Legs*, 1736; *Les Fausses Confidences*, 1737, &c. He had meanwhile imitated the English *Spectator* in *Le Spectateur français*, 1722–3,

original. His chief trait is the exquisite minuteness of his psychology. The analysis of character, a constant object of the classics, could hardly be restored to the stage unless a new layer of consciousness, so to say, were tapped. This Marivaux was able to do because already the preparation for the sentimental age added to the importance of feeling and multiplied the common awareness of its shades. The age was only beginning when he wrote and, as so frequently happens with men of genius, he announced its advent rather than followed it; and his personal gift makes him an early index of an essential change in the history of the French mind.

His plays evince more variety than is generally supposed, for no two situations in them are quite alike. But a short study can best concentrate on the manner of his art, which shows up clearly in his best work.

Love had been from the first the staple of tragedy; in comedy it had played a secondary part, contributing episodes to the plot rather than forming its main support. With Marivaux love passes decidedly to the forefront. In itself it is not a plentiful source of the comic; and amusement has to be sought in the contrasts and oddities which, though not of its very substance, are incidental to its course. Of this course Marivaux chooses the first stages for his deliberate study. His interest lies almost exclusively not in the full-grown passion but in its beginnings; the surprises, hesitations, tremors that its first intimation will awake, in hearts hardly yet resigned to its presence. The subject of his most characteristic scenes is thus the realization by his characters, or the revelation to onlookers, of a particular interest felt in a person of the other sex. That these are the symptoms observed, and stressed, implies that attention is focused particularly on the psychological, and chiefly the emotional, aspects and elements of love, rather than on its properly impassioned ones; thus the plane on which the moral disturbance is viewed is shifted at one stroke to something higher and purer—although Marivaux does not ignore the part played by the senses in the complete being of love. The delicacy and dignity his plays owe to this sustained point of view are a pleasant relief to readers of the usual run of eighteenth-century comedies. As the susceptibilities of

&c. As a novelist, he published *La Vie de Marianne*, 1731–41, and *Le Paysan parvenu*, 1735–6, both unfinished.

the heart and the stirrings of feeling thus held up to observation are commonly thought to be rather an attribute of woman's sensibility, it has often been remarked that Marivaux's psychology contains a feminine strain. Doubtless his years of training owed much to the company and encouragement of women in several of the Paris *salons*; and it must be owned that his art appeals most strongly to the tender-hearted and to those who do not insist on the picture of full-blooded passion.

The finer interplay of light, incipient emotions must be rendered dramatic, so it must be expressed in dialogue—exceptionally in monologues; it must emanate for us from the attitudes, words, and acts of characters, through an inference that springs mainly from intuition. Marivaux writes for a quick-witted audience, and expects them to miss none of his hints. His plays are made up of conversations which demand of us an elementary sympathy without which the intricacies of another person's sentiments cannot be mastered. The heroes themselves are attentive and responsive interpreters of each other's words. Between them, well-bred discretion and feminine reserve make the intercourse of personalities a subtle art indeed. These exchanges of veiled avowals or refusals have been called *marivaudage*; to follow them is a fascinating task, and if we are attuned to the game, highly pleasurable. Examples of the problems thus proposed to our penetration would be, in the *Jeu de l'amour et du hasard*, the fluctuations of Silvia's feelings, the conflict between her awakened tenderness and her pride; a pride that is not only of her class—for Marivaux does not formally condemn such a notion— but of her person as well, inherent in her sense of individual value. Indeed, Marivaux raises the dignity of woman, and stands in some respects as a forerunner of modern 'féminisme' (*L'Ile des esclaves*, 1725). Another instance might be found in the ups and downs of Araminte's sympathy for Dorante (*Les Fausses Confidences*), a play whose whole action takes place in the soul of one character.

Such a technique of implicitness rests on indirect presentment, and requires a highly suggestive and allusive style. 'Finesse' of expression is sought; and as words often say more than they mean the author makes frequent use of his character's tones, to which he directs our attention; again, as terms may be shifted to exceptional values and uses, there does develop in Marivaux a kind of *préciosité*, an attempt at uncommon refinement in language. On the other hand, the stuff of his dialogue is excellent French, pure, and distinguished without being far-fetched. It can even be enlivened by touches of raciness, especially in the mouths of popular characters.

This fond portrayal of men and women in the various stages of incipient love—the sequel, marriage and all, and perhaps drama arising out of marriage, being consistently left out—is instinct with much of the spirit of poetic fancy that we enjoy in Shakespeare's comedies, and in those of Alfred de Musset (see further, Part VII). It has the 'unreality' of a world spun by the artist out of his own fancy. Some of the situations Marivaux invents as the material basis of his plots are clearly improbable. But such an assertion should be at once qualified. He is a realist in his own way. Not a few of his characters are portraits of evil, hateful people—overbearing, brutal, heartless; such a one is Madame Argante, in the *École des mères*. His charming Silvia is clearly aware of the hard facts of life. Matters of money and rank press heavily on the freedom of individuals (*Les Fausses Confidences*, *Le Legs*, &c.). His comedies do not altogether take us away from the actual. If their humour at best is rather thin, they can still move us delicately; if they seem meant for the fastidious enjoyment of an *élite*, they are sufficiently in contact with our common humanity to belong to the class of art that is alive, and will live. They are one of the most distinctive products of French literature; and when performed on the French stage with all the skill of highly trained players they take their place easily among the great achievements of the national culture.

Pierre Claude Nivelle de la Chaussée (1692–1754), far less gifted as an artist, is important as an innovator. He realized that the declining vitality of classical drama might be refreshed by satisfying at one and the same time the fondness of the bourgeois audience for a moral, and its desire to feel. He dared shift the aim of comedy from laughter to tears, which means of course that he fused comedy with tragedy. But his was not the traditional type of tragedy. The fates and misfortunes of heroes of the distant past, historical or legendary, no longer awoke a privileged response in the minds of playgoers. Though the 'ancients', by every token of criticism, had won their fight with the 'moderns', these were every day gaining more ground. The spirit of the middle class was asserting itself in literature;

and in spite of the temporary successes of counter-attacks, the day was coming when problems of actual life must be discussed for the sake of their hold upon the larger body of the spectators. La Chaussée did not in principle give up comedy; most of his plays still allowed some room for laughter; but he catered mainly for the emotions. The modern novel was being born at the same time, and laying stress decisively upon the sympathetic interest that the majority of readers would be likely to feel in the fates of characters just like themselves. The ironical name bestowed on La Chaussée's new type, *comédie larmoyante*, did emphasize that it was a development of traditional comedy. Shortly afterwards, under other influences, Diderot and his friends created the *drame bourgeois*, that linked itself up with the tragic aspect of drama; but the distinction between the two is chiefly nominal, and they show one and the same set of tendencies at work.

La Chaussée must be credited with the determination it took to offer such hybrid works to the public. They were not quite unprecedented—Destouches's *Le Glorieux*, for instance, preceded La Chaussée's first play by a few years—but they were more definitely different from the tradition than anything before them. There is little else to praise in his 'tearful comedies', except the occasional point of some neatly worded argument. His dramatic weaknesses, perhaps least apparent in his earliest attempt, *Le Préjugé à la mode*, 1735, grow more and more obvious in *Mélanide*, 1741, *L'École des mères*, 1744, *La Gouvernante*, 1747, and others; as for his adaptation of Richardson's *Pamela* for the French stage, it was an utter failure. So bent is he upon giving his audience the delicious thrills of tender emotion, and a pleasant sense of virtue, that he builds his plots on providential happenings, doing violence to hard facts, and sets the problems of the inner will, of virtue and vice, in a superficial light. Why should he bother, since most of his plays were very successful? In order to emphasize the sentimental tension of his characters he overworks the device of broken sentences and unfinished speeches. As for his verse, it reveals a sense of strain, and the *École des mères* tries the compromise of an irregular measure and a free rhyming pattern. His best suggestion, after all, may be his sensible protest against the 'fashionable prejudice', that any lasting love between husband and wife is a ridiculous proposition.

CHAPTER XXXIV

The Novel

THE novelists who made a mark during this period fall into two classes. Voltaire (see above, Chapter XXXI) and Lesage keep to the rationalist and analytical spirit of the Enlightenment. Marivaux, and still more the Abbé Prévost, are harbingers of a different age.

Lesage[1] disclaims any purpose but that of realism. In the Preface to his most successful work, *Gil Blas de Santillane*, he declares: 'Je ne me suis proposé que de représenter la vie des hommes telle qu'elle est.' Spain is the background of his novel, and no doubt he intends to lose none of the opportunities of exoticism such a theme must offer. But his object remains man in general: 'On voit partout les mêmes vices et les mêmes originaux. . . . J'avoue que je n'ai pas toujours exactement suivi les mœurs espagnoles.' In fact, the Spanish *roman picaresque*, the influence of which in France and Europe can be traced from a far earlier period, is the pattern upon which the technique of *Gil Blas* is modelled.

The book was universally acknowledged to be very amusing in the eighteenth century, and it has kept a distinguished place in post-classical fiction. It owes this to the charm of its slightly cynical wit, heightened by the deft touch of a style that cannot yet be indebted to Voltaire, but is not unworthy of being compared with his. *Gil Blas* is in several respects a younger, lighter sketch of *Candide*, with a less bitter philosophy of life. It will clothe cruel realities in transparent understatement; its softer irony has at times a distinctly humorous flavour. But it suffers from serious faults; it is both disconnected and repetitious; the interruptions of adventitious stories are too frequent, and an impression of monotony creeps into the long narrative; only certain scenes and episodes remain fully alive: such are the chapters on the hero's adventures among the robbers,

[1] Alain-René Lesage, born in Brittany, 1668, of a middle-class family, lived by his pen in Paris. He wrote for the stage (see above, chapter V) and published novels, all more or less dealing with Spain and drawn from Spanish sources: *Le Diable Boîteux*, 1707; *Gil Blas de Santillane*, 1715–1735; *Don Guzman d'Alfarache*, 1732; *Le Bachelier de Salamanque*, 1736, &c. He died in 1747.

at the beginning, in a vein not unlike that of Fielding's *Jonathan Wild*; his apprenticeship to the incomparable Doctor Sangrado; his dealings as secretary to the archbishop of Toledo, and his experiences under the Duke of Lerma at court. A good deal of the rest vanishes from our memory; and we remember only, as an after-taste, the sad wisdom of poor Domingo: 'il n'y a dans le monde que des peines'; or that disenchanted description of love: 'C'est une maladie qui nous vient comme la rage aux animaux.'

To pass from Lesage to Marivaux (see above, Chapter XXXIII) is indeed a change of air. Here the influences are not Spanish, but French and classical, with a breath from England. The point of view, as in *Gil Blas*, is that of the middle classes, but these are viewed in a favourable, not a critical, light. A tinge of sentiment is the main feature of the atmosphere.

La Vie de Marianne and *Le Paysan parvenu* were successful and influential books, and preserve most of their interest. Each has features of its own; the former tells the life, and mainly studies the character, of a woman; the latter is the story of a man. Although psychological discrimination is the staple of both, the tone of the analysis and the incidents most stressed differ from one to the other. Pathos and delicate transcriptions of feeling have more to do with *Marianne*. *Le Paysan parvenu* casts its net wider, and offers us a broader picture of society; it dwells more upon events and circumstances than on emotions; it has less of tragedy, and more of comedy. Still, their chief features are roughly common, and a general view of Marivaux's temperament as a novelist can be formed from both.

No less than in his plays, his relation to classicism remains here positive and deep-laid. The attention to detail in the description of that supreme reality, the inner world of each being, is at the core of his effort; the social surroundings, in the *Paysan parvenu*, are less important in themselves than as a setting and a field for the display of character. This dissection of motive and mood is so deliberate that the style, in both novels, shows the strain of the analytical tendency, being broken into very short paragraphs of which each one generally tackles a separate aspect of the condition within. But at the same time, although the constructive energy that should weld these pieces into one mass is able to effect the unity of a chapter, it fails to secure that of the whole book; both works are loosely conceived on far too large a scale—a lingering influence, no doubt, of the ten-volume romances of the previous century. It becomes clear, long before the end, that the author lacks matter for such an extensive plan and must cast about for artificial incidents. The story of the *religieuse*, in *Marianne*, fills the last three parts but one; the work is not finished, and Madame Riccoboni was responsible for the twelfth part; the *Paysan parvenu* comes to no definite conclusion.

The purpose of *Marianne* being truth, there was a measure of realism in the author's method; the impulses of human nature are caught and described without illusion; a Christian moralist's pessimism, though not professed, is present and felt. The pages on feminine coquetry, at the end of Part I (*Marianne*), can be quoted as an example. Jacob, the *paysan* whose life is so successful, may be a hero of a kind; he means well, and behaves generously; but one could wish for a little more diffidence in his acceptance of benefits from the opposite sex. Marivaux's moral sense is not at fault here, but he does not believe in human perfection, and makes many allowances. For this reason his didactic bent, obvious as it is, does not meet all the demands of a Puritan reader. If Richardson took hints for *Pamela* from *Marianne*—and the possibility has not been absolutely negatived—he took them with a feeling of disapproval, as the freedom of the French book must have seemed to him cynical. An English bishop, we hear, praised the first parts of the *Paysan parvenu*; but he had not read it to the end. Sentiment, kept within bounds in this later work, given a freer vent in *Marianne*, fuses with the discreet eroticism of both novels into a typically eighteenth-century mixture, the more acceptable flavour of which would lie in the sincere exaltation of kindness. 'Toute ma vie', Marianne says, 'j'ai eu le cœur plein de ces petits égards-là pour le cœur des autres.' As for social attitudes, we still have the compromises of the transition period. The haughty pride of nobility and caste is strongly censured; but Marianne feels herself inferior to her high-born lover, until she turns out to be the granddaughter of a Scottish peer. Jacob strikes root in the gentry as 'Monsieur de la Vallée', and feels the happier for it.

This chequered impression does imperfect justice to works which, though less masterly than the *Princesse de Clèves*, share with it the honour of standing at the head of the long line of modern French novels. *Marianne* especially has many suggestive pages of moral scrutiny, excellent pen portraits, and episodes of lively humour, such as Madame Dutour's quarrel with the coachman (Part II).

In the still more varied and abundant output of Marivaux's contemporary, the Abbé Prévost,[1] a masterpiece is at once to be singled out: *Manon Lescaut*.

In its unflagging progress to the end the story bears the marks of a sure artistic intuition. Being conceived only as an offshoot from the author's first work of fiction, it was spared the sprawling length and formlessness of the contemporary novel. Its spirit is one of determination, moved and moving, but calm, in telling a pathetic tale of love and death. The moralizing instinct, though indulged now and then, is kept within bounds by the sense of fate and the awe that inspire some great dramas of the world—the legend of Tristan, for instance.

Indeed, the narrative is sober, although the force of emotion is sometimes let loose. It depicts the tragedy of an impassioned attachment, proof against all better reason, judgement, principle, working itself out to a catastrophe which the hero had foreseen and dreaded from the first. The lesson of the story is the pity of it, and the degradation wrought by the unwise enslavement of one's will; as for Des Grieux's final conversion it is the perfunctory homage the author felt he owed to the ecclesiastical character he was in the end unwilling to give up.

The purpose of realism is paramount all through; not in the display of the lascivious or the sordid—though the light thrown upon some aspects of manners at the time of the French Regency is lurid enough—but in a close, courageous adherence to psychological

---

[1] Antoine-François Prévost, born in the north of France, 1697, brought up by the Jesuits, took orders, lived from hand to mouth, now monk, now soldier, wrote a novel, *Les Mémoires d'un homme de qualité*, 1728–31, broke from his convent, was threatened with prosecution, fled to England and then to Holland, published *Le Philosophe anglais ou les mémoires de Cleveland*, 1732, started a periodical, *Le Pour et contre*, 1738–40; returned to France, and was reconciled with the Church, 1734. He lived by his pen and produced other novels, among which *Le Doyen de Killerine*, 1735, &c. Exiled once more, he wandered through Belgium and Germany and translated Richardson's *Pamela*, 1742. He was pardoned and spent the last twenty years of his agitated life in France, translating more English books, among which were *Clarissa Harlowe* and *Sir Charles Grandison*. He also wrote an *Histoire générale des voyages*, 1746, &c., and various pot-boilers, and began a history of the Condé family. He died near Chantilly, 1763. *Manon Lescaut*, first included in the *Homme de qualité*, was published separately from 1753.

truth. The triumph of Prévost's clear-sighted objectivity is his study of the heroine. Manon has genuine tenderness; she is not only most attractive, she would like to be faithful. Her utter fickleness is a vice of the blood, stimulated by her total inability to face poverty. She must have luxury or at least comfort: such weakness vitiates a nature that is not in itself ignoble. So treason after treason wrings her lover's heart, through the disasters of their common lot; and each time she returns to him in a sincere abjection of grief. The despairing courage of her flight with him and her death in the desert cast a redeeming glow over the last tragic scenes. At once despicable and lovable, she was to be the ancestress of a number of figures, not all of whom are so gently though impartially drawn, in the modern realistic novel.

Short work must be made of Prévost's other lengthy novels. To take them down from the shelves of some scholarly library, and plunge, is an overwhelming, but not by any means a dull, experience. They are written with ease, and move swiftly along; they swarm with lively incidents and characters, with adventure and drama of all kinds, or with naïve or impudent—and imprudent— incursions into history, or geography; they testify to the power of an imagination that gathers material from books, facts, legends, memories, documents, sheer invention. The result is a medley that somehow lives, rousing by turns our amusement, curiosity, sympathy, wonder, and tolerant indignation, an overflowing stream that carries along with it many seeds, dropped into the consciousness of the age, to die or germinate: sentiment, pathos, the search for thrills and delicious fears, the picturesque, the exotic, the glamour of great figures and events. The desperate attempts of a writer who lived by his pen to fill volume after volume are fated to find their doom in the reader's exhaustion; and very few today will follow Prévost to the end. Of special interest, however, are his concrete descriptions of English life, manners, government, literature, in Books X and XI of the *Mémoires d'un homme de qualité*. Less brilliant but rather better informed than similar passages in Voltaire, they are evidences of an intelligent appreciation that contributed to the swelling current of *anglomanie*. We can remark finally of these novels that they are animated by the enthusiasm of 'uncorrupted' human nature scorning the artifice and insincerity of worldly life and thus making Prévost in some respects a precursor of J.-J. Rousseau.

CHAPTER XXXV

Observers and Critics

SAINT-SIMON[1] wrote his *Mémoires* from notes begun early, on things seen and heard, and intended for use when at last his political expectations materialized; but they never did, and his manuscript was the vent of his secret disappointment, likes, and glowing dislikes.

A great nobleman, he lived within the enchanted circle, near enough to the hub of events to know them from inside, but standing aloof, and taking no share in government. His keen, observant glance betrayed the independent critic, perhaps the dissenter and the opponent. The king feared and disliked him. For a time, while the duc de Bourgogne was prospective heir to the throne, and the party of the reformers seemed to be in the ascendant, he was drawn into active politics, at least the preparation for them. But the duke died prematurely, before the king, an event which set the final seal on the career of a statesman who thought he had been born under an evil star, and found a bitter satisfaction in seeing the hand of fate consistently point the same way. His friend the Regent only sent him on a meaningless embassy to Madrid, which cost him part of his fortune; after that he retired completely into his shell.

Under these circumstances there silently grew for some thirty years a unique work which, when its full text was published much later, during the romantic period, took France by storm. Perhaps it was providentially determined that the *Mémoires* should come out then; and in this, at least, Providence was kind, for at the moment of writing Saint-Simon was looking both back and forward. Some features are still pre-classical: long sentences loosely connected, often clumsily constructed; improvised expressions, slightly archaic words and phrases. But, on the other hand, that spontaneous utterance

[1] Louis de Rouvroy, duc de Saint-Simon, born in 1675, served in the army, then lived at court, as a detached observer. After the death of Louis XIV (1715) he was sent by the Regent on an embassy to Spain. Thereafter he withdrew into private life and died in 1755. His *Mémoires*, written from 1723 to 1750, consulted by a few persons during the eighteenth century, were published for the first time in 1829–30.

embodies a soul of eager impressionism; impatient of rule and the stereotyped phrase, it craves for the fresh, graphic term; it aims not at correctness, but at intensity. The vividness of his narrative or descriptive touches is at times unequalled; there is poetry in that imaginative strength; and the relation of the *lit de justice*, the epic scene in which his passion is at last glutted, the king's bastards and the parliamentarians are crushed, and the ascendancy of the peers is re-established burns with an unforgettable fire of unholy joy.

Mes yeux fichés, collés sur ces bourgeois superbes, parcouraient tout ce grand banc à genoux ou debout, et les amples replis de ces fourrures on-doyantes à chaque génuflexion longue et redoublée. . . . Moi cependant je me mourois de joie, j'en étois à craindre la défaillance; mon cœur, dilaté à l'excès, ne trouvait plus d'espace à s'étendre. . . . Je promenais mes yeux doucement de toutes parts, et si je les contraignis avec constance, je ne pus résister à la tentation de m'en dédommager sur le premier président; je l'accablais donc à cent reprises, dans la séance, de mes regards assénés et forlongés avec persévérance. L'insulte, le mépris, le dédain, le triomphe, lui furent lancés de mes yeux jusqu'en ses moëlles.

Much as the disinterested reader may enjoy such lines, and many a vicious epithet, boring to the core of an adversary's weakness, he might wonder whether so good a hater could be a trustworthy observer. Very little objectivity, indeed, is to be expected of these *Mémoires*. But their historical value is far from negligible. It is to be found chiefly in full-dress portraits, whether etched with savage relish, yet carrying within themselves the assurance of at least partial, one-sided penetration, like that of Harlay; or more com-posed, aiming at fairness, yet no less penetrating, like that of Fénelon. It lies equally in the outstanding episodes, great docu-mentary scenes, extensive and diverse, among which the death of Louis XIV is justly famous; vast frescoes in which the attitudes, gestures, and words of scores of individuals combine to form a striking study of men and women under the various strains of violent emotion, grief, and hope. The period covered by these *Mémoires* is thus, at least so far as its central focus is concerned, instructively illuminated by an unreliable but powerfully searching light. No final judgement should be passed solely on Saint-Simon's testimony; but his evidence is never to be, of set principle, entirely rejected. From the literary point of view, the only work in French that can compare with his is Chateaubriand's *Mémoires d'outre-tombe* (see below, Part VI, Chapter XLIII).

The figure of Vauvenargues,[1] who died at thirty-two, leaving an indelible impression on friends, and writings that have since steadily risen in the esteem of the *élite*, is invested with the pathos of unfulfilled destinies. In his inner nobleness, he resembles another soldier, philosopher, and stoic, Alfred de Vigny. The last years of his suffering life raised him to a spiritual heroism that Voltaire, who knew and loved him, deeply admired.

His works have more than a sentimental appeal. Their main burden is one that makes him a landmark in the intellectual history of his period. Now that reason, the Enlightenment having largely done its work, had won the right to rule over the domain of life, men began to perceive that some of their supreme needs could never be satisfied by her single agency. Vauvenargues felt that under the new light new motives of living were necessary; he probed his conscience in order to find the moral leads which conduct must follow. He is thus a moralist, but one whose work proceeds through the one sure method, fearless examination of the mind. Still clinging to reason as the indispensable guide, he took several steps in the direction of the autonomy and supremacy of the heart asserted by Pascal, and which, in its hey-day, the age of reason had been prone to forget. Along this essential line of thought the next stage will be Rousseau's.

Vauvenargues's general trend is plain in the *Introduction à la connaissance de l'esprit humain*, the *Réflexions et maximes*, and the other essays or fragments, of unequally precious substance, but almost all worth reading, and written with a talent for elegant brevity, a natural gift of virile eloquence, of rhythm and point that denote the born artist. His thinking always borders on synthesis, a fusion of the claims of reason and those of the heart. 'On honore trop souvent du nom de raison une certaine médiocrité de sentiment et de génie, qui assujettit les hommes aux lois de l'usage, et les détourne des grandes hardiesses.' From this standpoint of judicious wisdom he tends if anything to emphasize those aspects of the truth that the

[1] Luc de Clapiers, marquis de Vauvenargues, born at Aix-en-Provence, 1715, served in the army for ten years, gave up his hope of a diplomatic career on account of his health, lived poorly in Paris, and died in 1747. His *Introduction à la connaissance de l'esprit humain, suivie de Réflexions et maximes*, 1746, was republished in 1747, but little noticed. The first complete edition of his writings appeared in 1857.

fashion of the age was inclined unduly to neglect. His stress often lies on the finer susceptibilities of our nature. 'Il faut avoir de l'âme pour avoir du goût. . . .' 'Les grandes pensées viennent du cœur. . . .' 'Le désordre des malheureux est toujours le crime de la dureté des riches. . . .' Or this full confession of unashamed sentiment:

La vue d'un animal malade, le gémissement d'un cerf poursuivi dans les bois par des chasseurs, l'aspect d'un arbre penché vers la terre et traînant ses rameaux dans la poussière, les ruines méprisées d'un vieux bâtiment, la pâleur d'une fleur qui tombe et qui se flétrit, enfin toutes les images du malheur des hommes, réveillent la pitié d'une âme tendre.

In his relativism, his sense of the concrete, and distrust of dogmatic reason, he reminds one of Montaigne. 'L'effet de la science est d'ébranler les certitudes et de confondre les principes les plus manifestes.' Like Montaigne, he had his La Boétie—a friend of his youth, prematurely lost, of whom he writes: 'Je t'aimais même avant de pouvoir te connaître. . . .'

He is a perceptive critic of literature. Towards the future he opens a path, censuring the superstition of rules, defending the claims of irregular works, 'qui vous présentent . . . un tableau hardi et touchant des passions humaines'. But he clings to the best French tradition, that of many-sided, vigorous classicism, finding an example in Boileau, whom he praises discerningly: 'Ses vers sont pleins de pensées, de vivacités, de saillies, et même d'inventions de style. Admirable dans la justesse, dans la solidité et la netteté de ses idées, il a su conserver ces caractères dans ses expressions, sans perdre de son feu et de sa force. . . .'

The set of values upon which French literature had been living since the Renaissance had been gradually emptied of its contents by the use and abuse of two centuries. The critical debates of the Enlightenment reveal the uneasiness of minds that almost all kept their allegiance to the established standards, but could not help being dimly aware of their gradual exhaustion. A few critics who dared strike out for new values have won a title to our attention but their immediate influence was slight and they failed to impress themselves on the course of writing. A silent ripening of the common sensibility was to take place, before the initial stage in the vast changes summed up under the label of romanticism could fairly begin.

Houdar de la Motte whose tragedy, *Inès de Castro*, was noticed above (see Chapter XXXIII) is an interesting and original, though incomplete, critic and analyst of literature. His prefaces, treatises, discourses contain a number of paradoxes, as they were called in his time and long after, many of which appear to us in a different light. It is beside the point that his own ventures in poetry leave him among the versifiers of the period, no better, but no worse, than most, and in some secondary kinds—occasional pieces, drawing-room amusements—displaying genuine talent; or that when he wrote for the stage he forgot his bold dramatic theories. The essential fact is that as a critic he struck, on not a few subjects, the note of the future—that note which is so sure at first to grate upon all ears. The sum of those occasions would be impressive enough, were it not that he sometimes hesitated, flinched, fell back on a non-committal attitude. Steeped in the classical faith to the core, he became a philosopher in the style of the Enlightenment; as such, he would insist that reason should test the dogmas of literary tradition; and where these clashed with his eager independent sense, he blurted out heresies. But his remained a divided mind, and his rational mode of arguing was too cold to carry conviction; his fight with the conservatives was mostly a losing battle. Still, it is to his credit that he made his own and developed Fénelon's distinction between poetry and verse; that he fully recognized prose poetry, while underestimating the element of music and rhythm in all poetical speech; that he proclaimed the possibility, for instance, of writing tragedies in prose—a proposition that the *drame bourgeois* shortly afterwards, and modern drama ever since, have turned into a commonplace; that among the 'unities' he saw but one, *l'unité d'action*, that should be regarded as imperative, though he substituted for it a more properly psychological and aesthetic notion, *l'unité d'intérêt*. Of the famous and mysterious *beau désordre* of the ode, he remarked sensibly that it must 'laisser place à une liaison d'affinité et de rapport'. His championship of the moderns, against the fanatics of the ancients, fastened on the fundamental difficulty of the subject, the ingrained partiality of judgement which is the legacy of an exclusively classical education. More examples of his clear-sightedness might be adduced; but one of his good temper will do equally well: being harshly taken to task by Madame Dacier because of his ideas on the right way to translate poetry, and Homer, he answered the learned and literal lady with no less courtesy than point.

The Abbé du Bos (1670–1742) is another innovator, more considerate and cautious than La Motte, with a saner and broader outlook, but a less fruitful message for us, because practically all the paths he opened are now beaten tracks. His *Réflexions critiques sur la poésie et sur la peinture* (1739) starts from the time-honoured assimilation of the two arts. We need only mention the chief claims which his shrewd and widely read treatise has to our gratitude. He points out that the object of poetry is pleasure, not instruction; that the gratification it gives us springs from a complex of causes, among which appeals to our imagination, emotions, and senses are paramount; a good poem owes its power to *la poésie du style*—a phrase in which all these elements are summed up. The music of the lines cannot be too carefully studied; but in this the rhyme itself is only an inferior and limited factor, 'fort au-dessous de celui qui naît du rithme et de l'harmonie du vers'; besides, it 'estropie souvent le sens du discours, et . . . l'énerve presque toujours'. In a general way, rules have little to do with the actual merit of poetry: 'Les hommes préféreront toujours les poèmes qui touchent aux poèmes réguliers.' As for drama, our pleasure in this is by no means dependent on the illusion of reality—a remark that cuts at the root of the demand for the unities of time and place. Thus, the Abbé du Bos is largely stressing the values of sentiment and intuitive perception, and feeling his way to a recognition of the force of suggestion that language and imagery must yield. Such were the critical underminings silently at work beneath an immobile, intellectualized literature.

CHAPTER XXXVI

The Encyclopédie: Diderot

THE French Enlightenment worked up to a climax, the *Encyclopédie*. An age that emphasized above all the necessity for the mind to realize the world clearly would naturally find its essential task and supreme achievement in a sum of existing knowledge. Reason had established her right as the guide of human civilization; and her guidance was to be followed in a broad and impressive, almost a solemn, manner. The motives behind the undertaking were thus chiefly intellectual. But they were also practical, for the techniques of the arts and crafts were then entering, under the stimulus of science, upon the modern era of industry, and progress would be served by a full record of their instruments and methods. There was also a social purpose: the wider diffusion of learning plainly answered the anti-feudal and reforming, though not properly democratic, trend advocated by the majority of men of letters. Last but not least, the group of the *philosophes*, writers who were not a formal party in the State but to some extent acted as one, originated the plan and pressed eagerly forward with it, because it offered an almost unlimited scope to their campaign for liberalizing the public mind— that is to say, for weakening the hold of the Church, and of what they held to be superstition, upon the masses. It was never in doubt, from the first, that the venture would be animated by the purely rationalist spirit, which indeed its object—the popularizing of organized knowledge—obviously demanded.

The germ of the first scheme came from England. A Paris book-seller wanted to publish a French translation of Chambers's *Cyclopaedia*. Diderot was given charge, and substituted the more ambitious project of a new work on a far larger scale. A prospectus was issued at the end of 1750, and the next summer saw the publication of the first volume, with a preliminary 'Discours' by d'Alembert. The authors who agreed to contribute included the chief *philosophes*— with Diderot and d'Alembert, Voltaire, Montesquieu, Buffon, d'Holbach, Quesnay, Turgot, Marmontel; even J.-J. Rousseau figured among them as a specialist of music. The course of the venture was anything but smooth. A decree forbade the sale of the first two volumes (1752); publication continued more or less on the sly, friends and patrons in high places managing to have it tolerated; but d'Alembert withdrew, and Diderot bore the burden of management almost single-handed. In 1759 the interdiction was renewed. Diderot discovered that the publisher was bowdlerizing the manuscript. By 1768 the seventeen folio volumes were out, and thenceforth sold more openly and quietly. Five supplementary volumes appeared in 1779, and the plates occupied eleven more. Pirated editions in several neighbouring countries testified to the international success of the work.

Although many of its articles are not strictly technical, and bear on generalities of history, philosophy, and literature, the *Encyclopédie* cannot be analysed or appreciated here. It should be noted only that the best-known members of the team contributed in fact but little, and that not always of their best; Diderot wrote most of the text on the arts and crafts. Modest jobbers were responsible for much of the rest. These relied chiefly on pre-existing publications, so that a fair proportion of the whole is not really original, but compiled. Still, it is impossible to overstate the significance and influence of the *Encyclopédie*. It broke the spell of silence, and in the teeth of a powerful opposition, the centres of which were the Church, the magistracy, the Sorbonne, and the pamphleteers of the tradition party, it allowed the rising demand for free criticism in matters of faith and government to be authoritatively voiced. The tactics uniformly followed in the work are no doubt cautious; the dangerous elements are hidden away in corners, and neither on religion nor on political subjects is anything said openly that could be too provoking. But the general atmosphere and trend are quite plain, and the conservatives, from their point of view, had good reason to feel angry.

The *Discours préliminaire* (1751) of d'Alembert (1717–83) deserves special mention. It is a masterpiece, and no writing can be more fully representative of the Enlightenment. It sets forth the two major objects of the whole work: first, to survey the development of human knowledge, in the order of its growth, from the earliest stages of mental life to the last conquests of science; next, to deal with the present-day systems of learning and technique, explaining in each case general principles, likewise methods and routines. As was pointed out above, the latter aim coincides with a movement that led, during the French Revolution, to the foundation of the Conservatoire des Arts et Métiers, 1794, and, later, the creation of the 'Enseignement Technique'. Approaching his task with all the vigour and clarity of a first-rate mind, d'Alembert produces in effect a survey of the origin and progress of civilization—the very theme that had, a few years before, fascinated Montesquieu in the *Esprit des lois*, and lured him away from safe ground. The new survey, far briefer, is more philosophical and orderly. Our objection is that the whole plan is logical rather than experimental; Auguste Comte's classification of the sciences, in the next century, will be made definitely on the concrete basis of modern thought. The metaphysics of the 'Discours' may be described as theistic. Its rationalist enthusiasm does not hesitate to admit that one single formula might sum up the condition of the universe. Still, new eighteenth-century tolerance of a diversity of creatures is revealed in the attention paid to the complexities of things, and to the various families of man. After the sciences the arts are reviewed, with their originality and interrelations. A glowing homage is paid to Bacon, Locke, and Newton, the fathers of the English empirical philosophy that had driven Descartes out of the field; and d'Alembert, ending his clarion call to the crusaders of knowledge, happens to make a passing allusion to J.-J. Rousseau's first *Discours*, just published—the proclamation, no less ringing, of a far different gospel.

Two thinkers must be mentioned who shared the spirit of the *Encyclopédie*, whether or not they actually contributed to it. The first, Étienne Bonnot de Condillac, 1714–80, published the *Essai sur l'origine des connaissances humaines*, 1746, the *Traité des systèmes*, 1749, and the *Traité des sensations*, 1754. With a remarkable power of lucid analysis and explanation, he pushed Locke's psychology farther, showing in full detail how from the most simple sense-impressions all the faculties of the adult mind can be gradually built up. He stands for the rational endeavour of modern thought, freed from the shackles of the deductive past, and not yet aware of its own limitations. Claude Adrien Helvétius, 1715–71, the second, was no less zealous a disciple of Locke, whose doctrine he developed more particularly towards a realist system of ethics. His chief work, *De l'esprit*, 1758, was the climax of what may be called philosophical sensualism, with materialist implications. On the passive responsiveness of the young mind, he pointed out, education and the pressure of surroundings build the fabric of intellectual habits. *De l'homme*, 1772, coolly drew further consequences from those views. The same principle can be stretched to show that self-interested behaviour should be encouraged, since, serving as well the major needs of society, it must be called 'virtue'. As the first book raised a storm, Helvétius recanted perfunctorily; but the second was distinctly a relapse. The 'Utilitarians' of the next century were to refine and improve upon this somewhat over-simple scheme.

For two very different reasons Diderot[1] stands out from the body of the 'Encyclopédistes'; he had more to do than any of them with the inception and carrying on of the work; and yet, although he was its arch-promoter and supporter, he is not closely representative of its spirit. His temper was more complex, and successive aspects of it were revealed as time passed. So he requires a place by himself; he is, like Voltaire, a central figure of the Enlightenment; but he is none the less a herald, and even a part, of the next age, that of Rousseau.

Diderot's rationalistic side is not illustrated solely by the *Encyclopédie*. He had already committed himself (*La Promenade du sceptique*; *Lettre sur les aveugles*) to negative views which brought upon him the rigour of justice; he returned to the theme much later in a charming, witty dialogue, where the hard pronouncements of scepticism

[1] Denis Diderot, born at Langres, 1713, the son of a well-to-do cutler, studied in Paris, lived scantily by his pen, and spent some time in prison after publishing the *Lettre sur les aveugles à l'usage de ceux qui voient*, 1749. He was general editor of the Encyclopédie from 1750 until the end; frequented the literary 'salons'; received a benefaction from Queen Catherine of Russia, 1765, went to Russia in order to thank her, 1773, and died in 1784. His works include philosophical treatises, e.g. the *Pensées sur l'interprétation de la nature*, 1754, *Entretien d'un philosophe avec la maréchale de . . .*, 1776; essays on the aesthetics of the stage: *Discours sur la poésie dramatique*, 1758, *Paradoxe sur le comédien*, 1778; plays: *Le Fils naturel*, 1757, *Le Père de famille*, 1758; literary criticism: *Éloge de Richardson*, 1761; novels: *Le Neveu de Rameau*, 1762, *Jacques le fataliste*, 1773; art criticism: the *Salons*, surveys of the paintings at the annual exhibitions, 1759–71, &c. His *Letters* are very interesting. Several of his writings were published at different times after his death; the dates given here are, in such cases, those of composition.

are softened by tolerant humanity (*Entretien d'un philosophe* . . .). The *Pensées sur l'interprétation de la Nature*, one of his most suggestive treatises, temper the criticism of unreason by stressing the all-important study of life, in words that prefigure the theory of evolution. The *Supplément au voyage de Bougainville*, the *Rêve de d'Alembert*, are bold and pregnant ventures in ethical or scientific philosophy, away from orthodox paths. *Le Neveu de Rameau*, Diderot's most original, is perhaps as well his most masterly, work; well worthy of having fascinated Goethe, who translated into German the manuscript still unpublished in French. Beyond the wonderful bravura of the style, and the lively humour of the dialogue, these spirited outpourings of a bohemian and cynic artist have a core of rich, though tentative thought; one may read in them the audacious outline of an *immoralisme* that probes fearlessly to the depths of human nature, where the roots of good and evil are inextricably interwoven. Even the *Paradoxe sur le comédien*, one of Diderot's last writings, shows his acute analysis giving itself full play over the psychological and aesthetic problem of how much an actor is to feel in the interest of his art. The intellectual rigour of the argument, and the destruction of a sentimental prejudice, are admirable. The reader only wishes that the difference were more clearly defined between the total, vital emotion which paralyses artistic freedom, and the intellectual, imaginative feeling that moves the head but, however deep, leaves the heart cold. The former is the actor's bane, no doubt; but the latter is the very condition of his efficient playing.

No less, and indeed more plentiful, are the tokens of Diderot's addiction to the new spirit that was gaining ascendancy over thought and literature: the genius of uncontrolled, complacent sensibility. The *Éloge de Richardson* is the exultant proclamation of that faith; the English writer's novels, in which the pent-up stores of Puritan energy had been transformed into emotional effusion, are extolled with all the raptures of admiring and grateful enthusiasm: they wring the reader's heart powerfully, deliciously; they teach him how to feel, and sow the seeds of all goodness and virtue. No more significant manifesto marks the passing of France from one period of her intellectual history to another. The influence of a foreign genius upon her inner life seems paramount. But deeper than the spell cast by Richardson is the spontaneous development of France herself. The needs of the heart had been wakening for a generation, under the clamorous claims and demands of the need for light; and *Clarissa Harlowe*, in the Abbé Prévost's rather free though very readable translation, let loose the ready flow of tears. Among the writings in which Diderot gave vent to this spirit are stories of concentrated realism and pathos that seem strangely like foreshadowings of Balzac's manner: *Les Deux Amis de Bourbonne*; *Ceci n'est pas un conte*; *Sur l'inconséquence du jugement public*, &c.; the plays that illustrate the theory of *comédie sérieuse* or *drame bourgeois*: *Le Fils naturel*, *Le Père de famille* (see below, Part VI, Chapter XXXIX); and the dramatic study of a concrete ethical problem: *Est-il bon, est-il méchant?*, steeped in sentiment, but shrewd and suggestive. *Jacques le fataliste*, among the thousand contradictions of human nature, finds one single clue leading out of the maze: no principle, but the impulses of a good heart. The *Salons*, full of gushing delight over the sentimentalities of Greuze, and prone to take the 'subjects' of pictures too seriously, are yet penetrating no less than animated attempts in the still scarcely tried field of art criticism.

Diderot's works were all more or less hastily written. He composed under the strain of necessity, his mind often engrossed by painful cares. His style is unequal, not always formally correct, with a sprinkling of familiar words and phrases. These slight blemishes vanish when once we are under the spell of one of the most vivacious personalities in French literature. The flow of spirit, eloquence, wit, pathos, humour, sweeps us along in sheer pleasure, and in sympathy with a writer of genius who knew no meanness, being always, whether right or wrong, transparently sincere and completely human.

PART VI

PRE-ROMANTICISM (1760–1820)

CHAPTER XXXVII

Jean-Jacques Rousseau

WHEN a new age of French thought and literature began, during the years shortly before and after 1760, Rousseau's[1] importance as its leader and prophet was clearly revealed. To study him, however briefly, is to delineate the main features of the period that may be called pre-romantic; it is even, beyond this, to sketch the essential traits of the romantic era, in which, after many changes of fashion, we still find ourselves. So his significance far exceeds that of Voltaire, who, for all that he broke with the reign of static values, and was

[1] Jean-Jacques Rousseau, born at Geneva, 1712, was the son of a Protestant watchmaker of French origin. His mother died when he was born. He had a fairly happy childhood and an irregular youth, when he lived off and on at the house of Madame de Warens, near Chambéry. He let himself be converted to Roman Catholicism; went to Paris in 1742, mixed with men of letters, and himself tried to write, in precarious circumstances. In 1750 he won a prize offered by the Académie de Dijon with a disquisition on whether 'le rétablissement des sciences et des arts a contribué à épurer les mœurs'. He failed with another essay, *Sur l'origine et les fondements de l'inégalité parmi les hommes*, 1754, which was very successful in print. He was reconverted to Protestantism and resumed his Geneva citizenship in 1754. He stayed for some years in the house of aristocratic patrons near Montmorency and published a *Lettre à M. d'Alembert*, 1758, that condemned the stage in principle; a novel, *Julie ou la Nouvelle Héloïse*, 1761; *Émile ou de l'éducation* and *Le Contrat social*, 1762. Threatened with arrest on account of his views he fled to Switzerland, where he again suffered annoyance and had to seek shelter elsewhere. He went to England at the invitation of David Hume, but, suffering from a morbid sense of persecution, quarrelled with him and returned to France in 1767. After ten years in Paris he accepted a home on a nobleman's estate at Ermenonville, and there died in 1778. His last works include: *Lettres de la montagne*, 1764; *Rêveries du promeneur solitaire*; *Dialogues*; *Les Confessions*, written 1764–70, published 1781–8. His opera, *Le Devin du village*, was performed in Paris in 1752 with success.

spurred by the spirit of the time to an aggressive exercise of reason, was nevertheless a representative of the traditional French mind. Rationalism in Rousseau had indeed a place which must not be overlooked; but it is in other ways that he matters most; he had much more of the future in him than of the past, and at this distance in time it is easy to recognize in him the source of the ideas of two centuries, down to the latest 'philosophy of existence'. An enemy of our unsettled moods and disrupted forms, Irving Babbitt, felt justly where the root lay of what he held to be unmitigated evil, and singled Rousseau out as the false guide who, more than any other, has conducted Europe further and further away on the path of error. These are polemic views; but they are not mistaken in their estimate of Rousseau's significance.

With him sensibility decisively comes into its own; no longer as a secondary power, gaining admission in the wake of intelligence, tolerated rather than sought; but as the chief mistress of truth and virtue, to whom man owes his most precious intuitions. Pascal's considered, balanced plea for the claims of the heart becomes here an enthusiastic, paramount principle. How could such a development take place in a nation that saw itself as the lucid interpreter of rational thinking, and based its literary eminence on the supremacy of a clear, orderly ideal? The psychological revolution after the mid-eighteenth century—which preceded the upsetting of the political system by two or three decades—has often been regarded as a departure from a consecrated line, in keeping to which lay continuity and safety; as a breach of loyalty, a mental divagation, the source of endless wanderings: was not Rousseau born at Geneva, a Swiss writer of partly Gallic blood and French idiom, and was not his success in France the occasion for a powerful infusion of foreign influence? That is not the view consistently upheld in the present survey, which has, rather, discovered seeds of the new growth latent from the beginning in the spontaneous expressions of the French genius. Indeed, to all appearances, the equilibrium of the classical age had not given full play to all innate French tendencies; some, rooted in the past, had been only repressed, and were waiting their time. When, after the hey-day of classicism, inspiration dried up and form decayed, the unexhausted, fresh faculties of the national mind asserted themselves; the deeper needs of a collective soul had their way; and the accidents of circumstance only made the change more striking by favouring it. Rousseau was the instrument of fate; but if he had never written, his work would have been accomplished piecemeal by others and the course of literature would not have been very different.

Romanticism let loose did not sweep over France at once; its progress was gradual, readers still clung to the traditional habits of thought and style, even if the new accents obscurely satisfied fresh needs. In some kinds, the resistance of patterns was especially stubborn; it took poetry, for instance, half a century to shake off the trammels of conventional language; the pre-romantic age was wholly a period of transition. In vain did the action of foreign models, particularly northern, and most often English—of Shakespeare, Milton, Thomson, Richardson, Young, Gray's *Elegy*—stir the awakening perception of more intense values, of drama, grandeur, and feeling; in vain were the themes of natural scenery, night, ruins, death, exoticism, persistently treated: imitation was not yet sufficiently spontaneous to be really creative.

Meanwhile the determined attitude of criticism which characterized the Enlightenment was undermining the foundations of the political order; the absolute monarchy was losing the support, not only of the middle class, but of a large number of the nobles; economic causes and financial troubles had long been weakening the government; a dangerous spirit of revolt was spreading through the people wherever the hold of the Church and the instinctive allegiance to the old ways were shaken. In the intellectual ferment that culminated in the French Revolution, the direct influence of the philosophers and Encyclopédistes was mingled with that of Rousseau and the apostles of an emotional faith. The men of intelligence played a more conspicuous and more destructive part in the work of clearing away the obsolescent institutions of France; the men of sentiment contributed a philanthropic fervour which did much to lend the revolutionary period its peculiar atmosphere of almost uncontrollable exaltation. But Rousseau's influence was more profound, and more enduring, than that of Voltaire and was gradually instrumental in constructing the modern social framework, upon new foundations. The powerful stimulus of his thought has never weakened, but can still be seen at work in the various movements of our time. The attempts of the religious spirit to find vents outside orthodoxy, humanitarianism, our unbelieving thirst for belief, our persistent hope, and our despair, all the signs of our disquietude, can be traced to the prophet who, in anguish and sincerity, spoke as his inmost spirit prompted him. These social and philosophical aspects of Rousseau's heritage are of even greater importance at the present day than the after-effects of romanticism, the successive endeavours to re-create form, were it in formlessness, that have made up the history of literature during the last hundred years.

Rousseau began writing late; his need for self-expression was accidentally awakened. The circumstances of his youth and early manhood, though not unhappy, had already given him, with a sore consciousness, a fund of impassioned feeling that was to be turned against the conventions of civilized life. His first *Discours* on sciences and arts is a rhetorical piece of work, supporting a paradox with all the zeal of genuine conviction; the energy, the rhythmical build of the prose, point to a born writer. Far more important is the *Discours sur l'inégalité*, a forcible appeal to the head and the heart, instinct with an equalitarian ardour that fearlessly tackles the central problem of justice. Here the seeds of all the social changes that have occurred or may occur are sown, and the eloquence of the ample sentences is not pitched higher than the fervent thought. So far, Rousseau could, and did, figure as one of the *philosophes*; in spite of his emotional strain, he advocated notions of reform that more or less kept step with the theories of the Encyclopédistes, although bolder than anything to which they would subscribe. In his *Lettre à d'Alembert* the rift is becoming perceptible; attacks are freely launched against the abstract spirit of philosophical argument; the optimistic belief that tragedy does purge the passions, and comedy correct manners, is sharply criticized from the point of view of experience, and a concrete sense of character; while a fund of austere moralizing, derived from a Protestant, Genevan education, is plainly revealed. A driving force is thus brought to bear upon the ideal of culture and the idea of popularization, so dear to all *philosophes*. More serious still, an onslaught is made upon one of their leaders. Thenceforth Rousseau was distrusted by the Encyclopédistes and he felt himself a free lance, alone in the world of letters.

The full flood of sentiment is loosened in the *Nouvelle Héloïse*, a long novel in letter form, in which Richardson's influence is patent. The death of the heroine is protracted to almost as long an episode as that of Clarissa Harlowe. Passion, frankly depicted, is transmuted into pathos, and the individual's right to happiness emphatically sacrificed to an austere notion of duty. The problems of domestic life and of social obligation are treated in a spirit of unashamed didacticism. A warm expression is given to religious feelings that range from undenominational Christianity to pure deism. Nature is elevated to the rank of a universal principle, the source of all good and the guide of all healthy impulses. Vistas are opened upon the grandeur and virgin freshness of the Swiss background and the worship of a purity that dwells in the sanctuary of the hills adds a touch of pantheistic poetry to the appeal of romantic landscapes. France and Europe tasted in these earnest, often impossibly lengthy, epistles the pleasure of shedding idealistic tears, and felt the better for having wept. The book gave Rousseau the standing of a great lay teacher, a prestige that his erratic career, and the obloquy of his foes could never destroy.

The *Contrat social*, published at the same time, did little to mend matters. The threat here was not to orthodoxy, but to vested interests, and although its scope was not widely realized at first, enough was understood to make the logic of Rousseau obnoxious. Logic indeed is the salient feature of a work animated with the enthusiasm of a humanitarian heart, but which sublimates this enthusiasm into a hard force of reasoning. It purports to be a mere sketch, a fragment from a more ambitious plan that had been abandoned; and this accounts for a brevity of outline and a compression of form that are all to the good. Man is born free, and everywhere is in fetters. What are the causes, and what is the justification, of these self-imposed chains? The redoubtable subject is attacked with the decision of an audacious mind. If the book is not an actual history of society it does succeed in freeing the basis of principle and right, upon which society rests, from the obscurities and traditions which had more or less purposely been allowed to cling to it. Bound by a virtual convention that should operate for the benefit of all, all men are entitled to equal opportunities; and the wrong done to justice by the existing order is to be corrected by awakened reason. Montesquieu's study of the essential situation in the *Esprit des lois*, by the side of this, seems no more than tentative, and stops short of the core of the matter. Rousseau shows himself aware of the complexities of things. His scheme is not the fabric of a disembodied intelligence; flashes of prophetic insight play over problems that are still, and more than ever, with us, and the book, his masterpiece, still preserves a substantial interest. Only small nations, he points out, can be really free; but being weak, will they not be conquered by their larger neighbours? There is one way out of the dilemma, a federation of peoples. . . .

The *Lettres écrites de la montagne* are another instance of what his power of argument could be, when his roused passion handled the weapons of logic and facts, with a touch of irony to whet them. The working of the constitution of the Genevan republic, the compromise of Calvinistic protestantism between authority and personal interpretation, and the very notion of miracles, are assailed with irresistible vigour—a vigour which has a secret flaw in that it pretends to ignore the weakness of human nature.

The *Confessions* are a book with an appeal, proof against many faults, among which is prominent a somewhat cynical idea of sincerity. For the first time the diseased sensibility of the moderns is fully revealed, in the self-pity that clings desperately to the images of lost happiness and innocence, in the morbid pleasure of regret and remorse, and the fascination of imaginative love. An autobiography—a form that was to know a special fortune through the romantic period—it throbs with an emotion that at one stroke equals anything the egoism of the next century was able to dare. Apart from the light shed on Rousseau's personality, and the intrinsic interest of circumstances that are not always stated with strict material accuracy, the most attractive feature of the work is the manner in which sights and impressions are recaptured with all the poetry and freshness of youth.

In these *Confessions* what must be called Rousseau's persecution mania is plainly apparent. A butt undoubtedly for dogmatism, envy, and spite, but to a large extent his own enemy, he magnified the sinister intents of his adversaries, and believed himself the victim of a perpetual conspiracy, that never existed outside his own imagination. The story of his stay in England and of his quarrel with David Hume, who had befriended him—a story not included in the *Confessions*

—makes sad reading in the biographies. There never was a clearer example of a man dogged by his own faults of character; and of the inevitable clash of temperaments.

The mood is very different in the pathetic complement to the *Confessions*, the *Rêveries du promeneur solitaire*, Rousseau's last, unfinished piece of work. A kind of resignation here replaces the anxiety of self-defence: the solitary still depicts himself as a bewildered soul, surrounded by hopeless night, but he can derive some melancholy pleasure from the memories of the past, and find innocent joys in the rambles of a botanist through meadows and fields. Vain are the cures of the *philosophes* for the ills of life; their reasonings strike cold despair into the heart, and leave an ashy taste in the mouth. The only salvation lies in the renunciation of desire. Thus Rousseau's chastened soul, at the bitter end of his struggle, draws near the mystical secret of true wisdom; he adumbrates the teaching of his disciple, Sénancour, in *Obermann*. In these pages his message as the prophet of a new spiritual faith assumes its real significance.

He was not impervious to art. His musical taste, more genuine than technically faultless, secures for him a place among the modest but gifted composers of his age. As a writer, he had a natural sense of balance and rhythm, shaped by the lessons of the ancients and the modern classics. But he owed most to instinct, and to intuition. The force of his prose often lies in a cogency that is of rational origin, yet the most characteristic strain of his utterance is its imaginative sensibility. He speaks with the voice of the apostle and the poet, and it is in the infectious, seductive harmonies of his impassioned language that he appears to us as the founder of a school, and the precursor of a whole period of letters.

CHAPTER XXXVIII

Buffon

CHRONOLOGY makes Buffon[1] a contemporary of Rousseau, for the bulk of his output belongs to the latter half of the eighteenth century. Yet its background remains that of the Enlightenment. His ambition is to bring the wonders of nature within reach of all, and to inculcate a proper attitude towards physical phenomena. Living apart from the circles of the *philosophes*, a writer of noble birth who did not side with the reformers, he still took part, indirectly, in the general endeavour to spread the light of reason. The structure of the universe, as he described or implied it, was rational, and subjected to strict laws; and the supernatural element in its history was reduced to the minimum demanded by the current belief in divine Creation. He took care to maintain this minimum explicitly, bowing to the transcendent truth of Scripture and trying hard, when his account of the earth seemed to clash with Genesis, to reconcile the modern and the traditional views. His effort was obviously sincere; and his convincing assurances of orthodoxy finally disarmed the hostility that several times threatened to break out against him in high places. All things considered the outlook he popularized was the separation of the spiritual and the material orders, a kind of compromise that allowed the scientific spirit to sink quietly into the general consciousness. The *Histoire naturelle* is thus on a par with the *Esprit des lois*; it can even be compared with that far more aggressive work, the *Essai sur les mœurs*. The peculiar note of the pre-romantic age is

[1] George-Louis Leclerc, comte de Buffon, born in 1707 at Montbard, studied law and medicine, translated an English book of physics, entered the Académie des Sciences at an early age, and in 1739 was appointed head of the Jardin du Roi (Botanical Garden) in Paris. The remainder of his long life was devoted to the *Histoire naturelle*, a complete survey of nature published between 1749 and 1789, as follows: *Théorie de la terre*, &c., 3 vols., 1749; *Les Quadrupèdes*, 12 vols., 1753–67; *Les Oiseaux*, 9 vols., 1770–83; *Les Minéraux*, 5 vols., 1783–8; and seven volumes of *Suppléments*, 1774–9, one being the *Époques de la nature*, 1778. Several collaborators, including Daubenton, helped him to collect his facts. He was elected to the Académie Française in 1753, and enjoyed a wide reputation and influence in France and abroad. He died in 1788.

only to be discerned in Buffon in a complacent display of imaginative power, a glow of intellectual emotion, and an oratorical style,
that link him up with the manner of Rousseau rather than with
that of Montesquieu or Voltaire.

In principle, Buffon knew the requirements of science, and intended to fulfil them. He clearly realized the immense scope of his
endeavour, and took pains to gather information through all possible channels. Besides his tireless reading, he had correspondents in
most countries, and received reports and samples; several collaborators helped him with dissections, drawings, the description of
species, or even the writing of short chapters. Again and again he
warns himself and his reader that conjecture is not to be mixed up
with facts; that sweeping views, however tempting, must be
guarded against; he tried to keep the enthusiasm of his eager mind
within reasonable bounds. His discussions of special problems, with
the careful marshalling of evidence on this or that side, are often
models of conscientious argument. Yet the driving impulse of the
whole work is entirely his; and that he yielded as much as he did to
this impulse is both his glory and his sin. No caution could reconcile
it with genuine prudence. It prevents the *Histoire naturelle* from
rising decidedly above the premature syntheses of the pre-scientific
era, which were more useful because they stimulated the thirst for
knowledge than because they constituted lasting repositories of it.
The progress of investigation within the ensuing half-century made
Buffon's survey very largely antiquated. Today it stands only as a
great work of literature, and a landmark in the development of
French thought. That is more than enough to reward the author's
labour.

His permanent gift to his and succeeding ages was the stirring of
men's imaginations, the refreshing of their awe before the features,
large and small, of this beautiful, terrible, and mysterious world.
The mystery he felt, though he rarely emphasized the terror. The
Histoire naturelle was widely read, and very influential, in France and
abroad. We find Rousseau repeatedly quoting it. It answered the
questionings of minds sharpened, as by a second Renaissance, to a
new sense of expanding knowledge. It played a central part in the
intellectual movement of the time, opening impressive vistas into
the secrets of nature. Contemporary parallels are the growth of a

lively interest in astronomy, encouraged by the writings of Lagrange (1736–1813), and in chemistry, by those of Lavoisier (1743–94). Buffon's scheme of things was integrated with the interpretation by the *élite* of the history of our planet; and as such, it became part of the imaginative background of romantic literature.

Nowadays its appeal is largely a thing of the past. The descriptions of animals, some of which found their way into anthologies, are marred for us by an error not unlike Ruskin's 'pathetic fallacy'— that of too often regarding animals, and appraising them, in terms of human beings. The portion of Buffon's work that has worn best is the *Époques de la nature*, a reconstruction of the successive stages in the earth's history. There is grandeur in the theme, and the marked dignity of the language is not out of place. While in many respects his tentative outline of the processes of development has ceased to be acceptable—the duration of geological periods, for example, being far too short—the scheme's general agreement with the theory of evolution makes it imaginatively familiar to us. His account of the gradual rise and development of the continents, and of life, shows a remarkably intuitive approximation to what we now believe to have actually taken place.

Buffon wrote carefully, taking pains in every way with his sentences. The result is a clear, smooth, rhythmical style, full of movement, and pleasant, except that we miss the relief of an occasional departure from the uniformly noble level. He had given thought to his manner, and committed himself to a theory of good writing which was indubitably sound, but which revealed some narrowness in its allegiance to post-classical taste. A good writer, he says, should show 'de l'attention à ne nommer les choses que par les termes les plus généraux' (Discours de Réception à l'Académie française). This hierarchy of values was to be upset in France by the romantics, just as Wordsworth and Coleridge rebelled against it in England.

CHAPTER XXXIX

Drama

THE pre-romantic period was not a great, but it was a germinal, age in the field of drama. During its course many symptoms pointed to widespread dissatisfaction with the mere imitation of traditional forms, and a series of interesting initiatives was the result. Although no decisive success rewarded any of these attempts, the basis was laid for a renewal of dramatic art that has borne, and is still bearing, fruit in the nineteenth and twentieth centuries. Not a few writers still clung to the ways of the past. Comedies and tragedies of the approved type were composed in large numbers. It remained customary for a young man with talent to try his hand first at penning five acts in verse on some classical theme. Of these too docile works everything is forgotten but a handful of titles. Elements of lasting interest are to be found only in the plays that took risks, such as the few examples given here.

The more obvious subjects that the annals of Rome and Greece could suggest had been treated again and again since the Renaissance. The history of France, on the contrary, or of Europe, or of the world, had rarely been tapped. The prejudice that banned such themes was at last discarded; and within a short span events near enough to awaken emotion in patriotic hearts or encourage speculation in the politically minded became the rich matter of dramatic art. De Belloy's (1727–75) *Siège de Calais* (1765) broke the new ground with brilliant success; to justify his bold step the author claimed in his preface that 'la plupart des tragédies anglaises sont tirées de l'Histoire d'Angleterre', a significant exaggeration which reveals the growing influence of Shakespeare and the English stage on the development of French drama. The play is not without merit; some of its lines have energy and point; but it revels in the conventional style; the queer circumlocution used to convey the facts, in themselves appalling, that the besiegers' ships bombard the town unmercifully, while the besieged are reduced to eating dogs' flesh titillates our sense of the grotesque. From among its successors, one may single out Marie-Joseph Chénier's (1764–1811) *Charles IX, ou La Saint-Barthélemy* (1789), a clever appeal to the revolutionary fervour then reaching its climax, and yet the work of a genuine poet who was also a playwright able to force tension to breaking-point, if less skilful in handling a difficult theme with tact. Raynouard's (1761–1836) *Les Templiers* (1805) revives an equally damaging episode of the national past. His language often lacks point, but its sobriety contrasts with the sheer cruelty of events and becomes all the more impressive as the play proceeds.

Most arresting among such experiments are those of Népomucène Lemercier (1771–1840), a versatile writer, who was more than once very nearly, but on no occasion wholly, successful in his aims. His *Agamemnon* (1797), a curious attempt to refresh an exhausted classical subject by an infusion of psychology and lyricism, reads at times like one of the realistic interpretations of Greek stories by the 'Parnassiens' (see below, Part VIII). Its stately but compact alexandrines are enlivened by echoes of *Macbeth*, and effects borrowed from the contemporary 'novel of terror'. *Pinto* (1800), very different in style, comes nearer to being a remarkable success; it makes free play with historical fact, but adheres to the truth of manners, and gives a striking picture of a dramatic incident in the life of Portugal. It moves lightly and displays a true vein of fancy, humour, and wit, not unlike that of the elder Dumas, or even, perhaps, of Musset. Lemercier had already compromised himself by hinting that the sacred 'rules' were mere shackles; he went further, and called his *Christophe Colomb* (1809) a 'Shakespearian' tragedy. Here the unities of place and time were openly violated and the characters spoke in plain language, familiar and direct, though, one must confess, a little flat. There was a violent disturbance on the first night, and one spectator was killed: the French still took the traditions of their stage very seriously.

Shakespeare, who had been popularized in France by the translations of La Place (1745–8, incomplete) and Le Tourneur (complete, 1776–82), acted upon the French imagination like a magnetic force, revealing a range of more intensely tragic emotions. An estimable writer, Jean-François Ducis (1733–1816), who made a name as a poet, attempted to adapt for the French stage dramas that were now

universally hailed as masterpieces. The spirit of his undertaking is
more or less faithfully rendered by a critic, Auger, in 1824:

M. Ducis, avec un art qu'on eût admiré davantage, si l'on eût mieux
apprécié les difficultés de l'entreprise, a su réduire aux proportions et sou-
mettre aux lois établies par notre système dramatique les ouvrages gigan-
tesques et monstrueux du tragique anglais; il a su dégager les traits simples et
sublimes de l'alliage impur qui les déshonorait, et les rendre avec cette
force, cette chaleur, cette vérité d'expression qui associe, qui égale presque
les droits du talent imitateur et ceux du génie original. . . .

These are high claims, which no one in France would dream of repeating today; they voice the views of the transition period, when
Shakespeare was accepted, but only after radical correction and improvement. Ducis did what he could; he was obviously aware of the
grandeur and beauty of the originals, but his renderings weakened
and changed them out of recognition. His style can be truly poetical,
but even when least unfaithful he transforms Shakespeare into something utterly alien and strange. In order to read his *Hamlet* (1769)
with any patience we must forget all about the Prince of Denmark.
The meeting with the witches, in *Macbeth* (1784), is a fine piece of
impressive rhetoric; but the thane of Cawdor turns out to be almost
a sentimentalist, who feels remorse, and eventually kills himself.
Thus are the logic and the decencies of the French stage vindicated.
It was perhaps necessary that the public taste should be educated
by these timid experiments up to fuller sympathy with the Elizabethan drama, the day of which was no longer distant.

The most fertile initiative, judged by its later if not its most
immediate consequences, was Diderot's. He was aware of La
Chaussée's example, and eagerly admired the English precedents of
Lillo (*The London Merchant*, 1731) and Moore (*The Gamester*, 1753);
still, he added breadth to their significance, and his own position
may be regarded as independent. From the logical point of view of
the philosopher, he argues, there must be four main types of drama:
the two chief aspects of life, characterized respectively by the predominance of laughter and tears, are separated by a line of social
cleavage, since our mood and our attention, in a theatre, are quite
different, according to whether the plane upon which the action
proceeds is one of familiarity or of majesty. Consequently, traditional comedy and tragedy can be further divided into 'La comédie

gaie, qui a pour objet le ridicule et la vie; la comédie sérieuse, qui a pour objet la vertu et les devoirs de l'homme. La tragédie qui aurait pour objet nos malheurs domestiques'; and 'la tragédie qui a pour objet les catastrophes publiques et les malheurs des grands' (*De la poésie dramatique*). The first and the last have been tried to satiety; but fresh and wide possibilities are open to the second and the third, in which we recognize at once the *comédie larmoyante* and the *drame bourgeois*. Have Molière and his successors put all the diseases of character on the stage, and do the comic writers complain that they are short of subjects? Let them realize that an infinite field of interest lies no longer in merely psychological types like the 'Liar' or the 'Miser', but in the 'conditions', the professions, the trades, the human relations, which shape and mould so much of the actual figures of men. In this study, the sources of ridicule and of pathos will be inseparably mixed; indeed the hard distinctions imposed by critics between dramatic genres are artificial; the union of laughter and tears is the law of experience, and the *comédie larmoyante* naturally, if the author feels so inclined, shades off into the *drame bourgeois*.

In order to illustrate this ambivalent kind, the very prototype of modern French drama, Diderot wrote two plays of unequal value. *Le Fils naturel*, though performed later, was composed first; it indulges all the sentimentality that was becoming fashionable, and clearly aims at showing that in the conflicts of middle-class persons situations may yet develop comparable to those of Greek tragedy. Humour is conspicuously absent; but the action works up to a really moving tenseness, and great issues of conscience are thrashed out in impassioned, eloquent language. *Le Père de famille* is still more openly edifying, and its high-wrought ecstasies of emotion would be slightly exasperating, if it were not that some social problems are boldly and frankly presented. But on the whole Diderot the theorist of drama is more remarkable than Diderot the dramatist. His *Entretiens sur le fils naturel* are very suggestive criticism, in the form of literary dialogue. The impact of these ideas was particularly felt in Germany, where his influence was joined to that of Richardson and Lillo.

In France, an outstanding sign of the leaven at work was the *Philosophe sans le savoir* (1765) by Sedaine (1719–97). Pathos here is handled with fine discretion, and glints of humour lighten the austere interplay of bourgeois honour and sentiment. This modest masterpiece is almost free from rant, and in a variety of ways it anticipates the spirit of the best nineteenth-century drama.

Meanwhile, post-classical comedy was also represented by several plays in which the symptoms of renewal were very few. They were equally lacking in original talent, and the brilliant output of one writer alone easily eclipses the work of a whole generation.

A pushing, mercurial man, Beaumarchais,[1] soon captured the new spirit of comedy, all the more easily, indeed, as its social tendencies agreed with his own feelings. In the *Essai sur le genre dramatique sérieux*, published with his first play, *Eugénie*, he claimed to follow Diderot's lead, inveighing against 'les règles, cet éternel lieu commun des critiques, cet épouvantail des esprits ordinaires'. But when he struck a highly successful vein in his *Barbier de Séville*, his work was hardly 'intermédiaire entre la tragédie héroïque et la comédie plaisante'. Except for the political allusions and skits that give many retorts a frankly revolutionary edge, it is comedy of the traditional type, but it glows and sparkles with the most lively wit. The Spanish setting is superficial, owing much to *Gil Blas*, and the subject is indebted to the *École des femmes*; but the character of Figaro is a triumph that, along with the scintillating dialogue, has secured for the *Barbier* a permanent place in French repertory. In the *Mariage de Figaro*, even more of a classic, the thrusts at social privilege grow more aggressive, and the shadow of the impending Revolution looms larger. Yet the play's gaiety and youthful zest are irresistible. It may rely too much on the machinery of a complicated plot, but several of its characters are drawn with the hand of genius. The action continues that of the *Barbier*, and Figaro's significance develops as his resourcefulness bids open defiance to the arbitrary power of authority. Chérubin's calf-love is painted with exquisite delicacy, not without a spice of perversity; and Bridoison the worshipper of form is an immortal, though incidental creation. Altogether the comedy is a most clever variation on the approved type, a pointer to the future in spirit rather than technique.

[1] Pierre Augustin Caron, known as de Beaumarchais, 1732–99, a watchmaker's son, led an adventurous and upon occasion a rather unscrupulous life, at one time a man of business, at another a political agent, or, again, a writer of pamphlets and plays. His attempts at drama were mostly failures, but two were resounding successes: *Le Barbier de Séville*, 1775, and *Le Mariage de Figaro*, 1784.

The emergence of the *mélodrame* is the last feature of interest in the development of eighteenth-century comedy. It betokens a lowering of the level of dramatic taste, but also a more widespread interest in the drama, bound up with the wide expansion of the reading public. But this decidedly low dramatic kind has further roots, in the dissatisfaction with the worn devices of the theatre, whether comic or tragic, that had brought about the appearance of the *drame bourgeois*; and in the universal thirst for sentiment. Its fortunes are by no means unworthy of notice, as it drew large audiences from the Revolutionary times to a far later age, and even today cannot be said to be wholly extinct, though much of its vitality was transferred, at the beginning of the twentieth century, to the film. During the romantic period it entered into association with more dignified literary forms, and contributed to the development of a school of drama that did not disdain violent sensational effects. Among the writers of *mélodrames*, Guilbert de Pixérécourt (1773–1844) deserves special mention. His first triumph, *Victor ou l'enfant de la forêt* (1797) was based on a novel by Ducray-Duminil (1761–1819). *Caelina ou l'enfant du mystère* (1800), founded on another work by the same writer, was still more successful, and is a fair specimen of his art. The construction is skilful, and the thrills come off satisfactorily. The good are rewarded, the villains punished, in the most providential manner. But the characters are mere sketches, and the dramatic devices are of the crudest. Pixérécourt claimed that his 120 plays, half of which were melodramas, totalled between them some 30,000 performances. It is interesting to note that he dramatized Mrs. Radcliffe's *Udolpho*, with mediocre success. By that time the worthy lady's terrors were already outdone in France; and such as they were, they were too subtle and psychological for Pixérécourt's manner.

CHAPTER XL

The Novel

THE abundant fiction of the pre-romantic period is rich in quality and reveals widely differing tendencies. Some of these link up most clearly with the analytical tradition of the past, while others pave the way for full-fledged romanticism. Mid-way come the works of writers who appeal to the emotions in a spirit of reserve, and with a more or less serious intent.

In giving first place to a consideration of this group it is well to bear in mind that Richardson's works, eagerly read in Prévost's translation, together with Rousseau's *Nouvelle Héloïse* were to invest the French novel with an ethical dignity that not even Marivaux, among previous authors, had managed to secure for it. During the second half of the eighteenth century this novel of emotional and ethical appeal entered decidedly upon its modern career, as the most complete and interesting image of life, to be enjoyed without reservation by the most respectable of readers. It was, of course, recognized that by rousing the passions the novel might incur the objections of moralists, but a writer could well be on his guard against such a risk, and it had also to be taken into account that fiction was an agreeable as well as a fit means of conveying instruction. Some contemporary novelists of this type were far from unexceptionable, but many more managed to redeem the fair name of their craft.

Shortly after 1750 the *Contes moraux* (1755–61) of Jean-François Marmontel (1723–99), a younger friend and disciple of Voltaire, showed how the latter's wit and irony could be united, in delightfully written apologues, with the tender charm and complacent sweetness of reawakened sentiment. In the following years the manner and also the title were widely imitated.

With Florian (1755–94) we are still close to Voltaire, who befriended him—one more token of the patriarch's liberalism, as no two tempers could be more different. Possibly owing to a mere analogy of sound, his name calls up in the French mind ideas of a flowery style and insipid themes. The association, in fact, is not unwarranted; but if *Galatée* and *Estelle* flatter a taste for conventionally pastoral scenes, we can still enjoy this amiable writer's sincere idealism. His *Fables* have a charm and piquancy, that keep well on the right side of explicit moralizing. His contemporaries liked Florian for himself; we find in him the sophisticated interest of an old-world naïvety and kindness.

During this age a whole school of novelists, mostly women, wrote very successful books that managed, at one and the same time, to move, to edify, and to instruct both young and old. These works shade off into children's literature, a very praiseworthy order of production that a short history may disregard. The names of Madame de Genlis (1746–1830), Madame Cottin (1773–1807), Madame de Souza (1761–1836), of Berquin (1749–91), for example, remained familiar to young people during the greater part of the nineteenth century. They are now known only to the specialist, because a new inspiration, born chiefly of the scientific movement, has transformed the horizons that beckon to the youthful imagination.

Meanwhile the ingrained love of moral analysis for its own sake, the quest for the truth of a privileged subject, the mind and heart of man, that had been from the first prominent in French fiction, were asserting themselves as much as ever. Restif de la Bretonne (1734–1806) claimed to be Rousseau's disciple, and his professed object was ethical: in fact, he was carried away by his vigorous, independent temper to realism of an extreme and most original kind. Of his immense output, written at top speed with careless ease, and largely set up by himself, some parts have survived, and are today scanned with refreshed curiosity: *Le Paysan perverti*, 1775; *La Vie de mon père*, 1778; *Les Contemporaines*, 1780–5; *Monsieur Nicolas*, 1796–7. These stories have no style, yet gain possession of us through their absolute spontaneity and our sense of their perfect adherence to fact. It matters little that such candour should reach and at times exceed the limits of cynicism; or transcend the decencies, as it does with genuine unselfconsciousness. The picture of some levels of life, especially low-class or rustic, is of unique value; but the light thrown on the play of mood and motive in unsophisticated beings, for whom no complications exist outside nature, is even more precious.

Pierre Choderlos de Laclos's (1741–1803) *Les Liaisons dangereuses* (1782) is a great book, but one of the saddest ever written. It tells in full detail, by means of letters, how two women, who mean to be honest but have an enemy in themselves, fall a prey to an unscrupulous libertine. It is interesting to study the contrast between Richardson's seducer in *Clarissa*, and that of Laclos. Lovelace is a fiction of the brain, the dramatic nightmare of a Puritan's imagination, with a conscience, which he must kill. Valmont is the quintessential rake, ironical and clever, naturally heartless, no less real for being utterly selfish. The closing in of the snare on the victims works with cool logic. Here again the cynicism is shocking, but the moral aim is incontrovertible. The spare, sober style is in the best tradition of classicism.

The strictly pre-romantic strain is prominent in the work of a third group of novelists, beginning with a writer to whom modern criticism has often been unfair, Bernardin de Saint-Pierre.[1] A disciple of Rousseau and still more an impassioned student of nature, he devoted his main work to an eloquent commentary upon what he thought to be her benevolent intentions, revealed at all turns in the order of the world. Nature herself was to him only the cloak of the divine will, and his deeply religious philosophy is in deliberate reaction against the materialism of the eighteenth century. The spirit of his remarks upon the beauty of the universe, and the interrelation of rock, weed, flower, and bird is thus an anticipation of Ruskin, with whose prose poems his far less magnificent but still often inspired pages may not unworthily be compared. Even omitting his worst mistakes, which are the fruit of his unscientific mode of thought, many of his interpretations are coloured with a naïve excess of anthropomorphic optimism. The mutual adaptation he glorifies is seen very differently by us nowadays in the light of Darwinian selection and the *élan vital*, but in spite of this his minute analysis

---

[1] Bernardin de Saint-Pierre, 1737–1814, born at Le Havre, entered the army as engineer, and travelled widely in Europe. He was sent on a mission to Mauritius, where he spent three years. His publications included *Voyage à l'Île de France*, 1773; *Études de la nature*, 1784; *Paul et Virginie* (in the 1787 edition of the previous work); *La Chaumière indienne*, and *Vœux d'un solitaire*, 1790; also a number of works, among them *Harmonies de la nature*, which appeared posthumously.

shows an intuition and a glowing perception that a biologist might not entirely despise; while his language alone is of great evocative value.

It is no satire to say that the *Études de la nature* are mostly a work of imagination; and the imaginative as well as the descriptive strains are happily blended in the novel of *Paul et Virginie*, which stirred the reading world at the end of the century, in the turmoil of the Revolutionary years. All the charms of sensibility, the sad pleasures of melancholy, are here turned to artistic uses. These may provoke our impatience, as being too obvious, and too futile, or even cheap, yet their mixture of human warmth, sincerity, and unashamed pathos is enough to melt the wariest hearts. The prospect of death as the sure and ultimately redeeming end of virtue and innocence is not a literary device, but the faith of a religious mind. The book's moral tone and its worship of nature are echoes of Rousseau; but the author showed originality in situating his tale of simplicity, purity, and unmerited disaster in a primitive, distant isle, and so adding a spice of exoticism to the fresh beauty of Rousseau's Swiss mountains. The landscapes, the picturesque life, the luxuriant vegetation of Mauritius are evoked by a man who knew them well, and could write. With a shade more concentration and restraint, a more careful avoidance of commonplace his striking success would have been a masterpiece.

Sénancour's[1] *Obermann* is in a class by itself. It was published in 1804, and hardly noticed until it was discovered by Sainte-Beuve (1833); but it had already appeared in an earlier form, with the title *Aldomen*, in 1795. It thus antedates all the other direct studies of the pre-romantic mind.

It is not a novel, but a confession, in the form of letters, some short, others long, written to a fictitious correspondent whose answers are occasionally implied, never given. The whole constitutes a spiritual diary of unique sincerity and interest. The life described, which is that of the author himself, is one of brooding and meditation,

[1] Étienne Pivert de Sénancour, 1770–1846, born in Paris, was intended for the Church, but took refuge in Switzerland, where he was deeply influenced by the scenery and by the manners of the people. He published *Aldomen ou le bonheur dans l'obscurité*, 1795; *Rêveries sur la nature primitive de l'homme*, 1799; *Obermann*, 1804; *L'Amour selon les lois primordiales et selon les convenances des sociétés modernes*, 1806. After the restoration of the monarchy he took part in politics.

with very few external incidents. He is a prey to incurable melancholy; in fact, doubt, self-diffidence, and the loss of the freshness without which the discovery of the world lacks all zest, have eaten into his vital energy, even before he could feel the full taste of experience. This is the main aspect of the *mal du siècle*, made fashionable by Chateaubriand's *René*, a tale published in 1802 with the *Génie du Christianisme*, in 1805 by itself. Sénancour was the first exponent of this romantic malady, but his name did not remain attached to it: his style was too argumentative and cold in the expression of ideas. Nurtured on the philosophy of the eighteenth century, and sharing its religious scepticism, he was not able to forge for himself a new instrument; his vocabulary is often vague, and his thought wrapped in a veil of curiously blurred abstraction. Besides, *Obermann* lacks firmness of texture; its development is desultory to an excess, with frequent repetitions, and not a few arid passages. That in spite of such faults, the book should have gradually won the warm esteem of an *élite*, and impressed Matthew Arnold, during his susceptible youth, as strongly as it did, is due to outstanding merits. Candid beyond anything written before or immediately afterwards, it sounds the note of a desolation that is strangely searching and moving. It has none of the special rhetoric of romanticism. A generous and noble personality reveals itself frankly, without pose, and with the fullest avowal of its contradictions and weaknesses. The blight of a difficult and dramatic transition in the moral world is upon it, and succeeding generations can still recognize themselves in the picture. When the emotions are roused, the style is transformed and acquires a rigour, a terse power of suggestion, that invest it with genuine poetical force. This is specially true of the scenes and descriptions in which nature is the central theme; most of all, of the episodes that deal with the sublimity, the untouched charm, or the magnetic mystery of mountains. In the French literature of the Alps there are pages here that go far beyond Rousseau, to a restrained, evocative force that surpasses the sensuous, romantic appreciation of nature, and belongs to the symbolist art of the future. With all its imperfections, *Obermann* bears the sure marks of greatness.

Benjamin Constant's[1] *Adolphe* is a short masterpiece which brings

---

[1] Benjamin Constant de Rebecque, 1767–1830, born at Lausanne, a descendant of Huguenot refugees, was naturalized French in 1794. He turned to politics during the

all the analytical power of the classical intelligence to bear on the morbid theme of a disunited self, soon to become a favourite with romantic literature. It is thus a work of synthesis which sums up the past and foreshadows the future. Nothing could be more lucid, close, and sober than this study of an irresolute and divided character, unable to rise above the dead love that poisons it, and in its wrangle for freedom with the innocent heart it has conquered, breaking it to death. The hopelessness of mere passion as a lasting principle of moral life, when change is the law of feeling, and of a struggle with society, when the individual rebel is not braced up by an iron will, could not be more forcibly illustrated. A high, serious purpose, along with the sanity of the most chaste art, thus saves the story from sensationalism and at the same time reveals a full knowledge of the disease it probes so firmly; the bitter outcries and the vagaries of the writers of revolt are anticipated in the restrained account of a subdued drama, played against a background of nature which is introduced only at brief moments. The conclusion is pessimistic, but not negative, since a clear realization of the fate that, on the human plane, lies in character, leads up to a prospect of salvation through fortitude, goodness, and spiritual humility. The moving tale is a landmark in the development of the modern psychological novel.

The *roman noir*, by way of contrast, the form of fiction that answers to melodrama, was wholly free from analysis and sought to enhance emotional appeal by drawing upon the mysterious and the weird. It was encouraged by foreign influences such as those of Mrs. Radcliffe, Lewis, and Maturin. Here, again, more dignified developments were to follow beginnings which, with Ducray-Duminil (1761–1819), for instance, keep within a modest sphere of definitely popular literature.

ascendancy of Napoleon, and after the restoration of the monarchy was an eloquent supporter of the liberal cause; his works include a novel, *Adolphe*, written in 1807, published in 1816; *Cours de politique constitutionnelle*, 1818–20; *De la religion considérée dans sa source, ses formes et ses développements*, 1826–31; and numerous pamphlets and speeches.

CHAPTER XLI

Poetry

THE poetry of the pre-romantic period shows very little of the sense of the future so clearly stirring in much of the prose. Apart from Chénier, the poets of the age show general mediocrity; even their more acceptable strains have since assumed the doubtful appearance of fading flowers. The difference is easily accounted for, when one remembers how particularly strong was the resistance of the post-classical conventions—with their characteristic tone and style —to any suggestion of change. French poetry then possessed all the elements of a 'poetic diction'; choice of subject, treatment, imagery, phrasing, and rhythm, were cast in a mould which the majority of readers resented every attempt to break. It was visibly a condition of their poetic pleasure that the tradition should be respected; that generalities, fitly dressed in the cloak of abstraction, adorned with antitheses, epigrams, and set elegances, should meet the expectant habits of mind and ear. England, where the post-classical canons of versification had exercised less authority, was gradually liberated after the highly significant initiative, in 1798, of Wordsworth and Coleridge. France had to wait longer. It was not till 1820, when Lamartine was writing, that the head-springs of lyricism appeared to be cleared of persistent obstruction.

It was André Chénier's[1] miracle to refresh and reinvigorate classicism, by bringing it back to its source—the enthusiastic love of ancient models, a close friendship with nature, the intuitive sense of pure form. He was thus, spiritually, a man of the Renaissance; and being even more endowed than Ronsard with intellectual fervour and verbal felicity, he would have been, if his career had not been

[1] André Chénier, the son of a French consul, was born at Constantinople in 1762 and brought up in Paris. He studied at the Collège de Navarre, served in the army, travelled, and occupied a post at the French embassy in London. He was actively engaged in the Revolution, on the side of the moderates, and in 1794 was arrested and executed. He published very few poems during his lifetime. His literary remains were only gradually brought to light, and the first full edition appeared in 1907–1919.

cut short, a greater poet. He owed this privilege to the mystery of temperament, and to the accident of birth: he was born in the near East, his mother was a Levantine woman; his earliest instincts developed under the Greek sun. Of the Hellenic spirit he had not the austere simplicity of its first phases; his affinities lay with the graceful sensuousness of the Alexandrines. His complete works, revealed by degrees in the nineteenth century, resemble the site of some old sanctuary of faith and art, strewn with exquisite marble fragments; the tantalizing charm of mere sketches, short paragraphs, or single lines fills a reader with wonder and regret, and only a few poems brought to perfection allow us to take his full measure.

Like Ronsard, again, he had philosophical ambitions, but time was refused him to do more than outline the long poems—*Hermès, L'Amérique*—in which he intended to survey the vast developments of the physical and moral sciences during the eighteenth century. Of that century he was the heir, making his own the general trends of the Enlightenment; his imagination, revelling in the themes and images of pagan mythology, was alien to those of Christianity. It is difficult to fancy that he would have produced a very substantial body of original thought in poetry or in prose, with mature years. His *Elegies* and erotic poems have warmth and loveliness, but rarely arouse any deep-felt sympathy, because they deal exclusively with physical attraction. The *Jeu de Paume*, an important political ode, has fine passages, despite its somewhat laborious and artificial construction. André Chénier's best compositions in verse were classed by himself under the name of *Bucoliques*; they are episodes from the common stock of Greek legend, variations on themes treated by the authors of pastorals or idylls. Some, consecrated by the choice of generations, such as *L'Aveugle, Le Malade, La Jeune Tarentine, Hylas, La Mort d'Hercule*, are visions of the glory of a faded world, with its grandeur or, more often, its naïve simplicity and naturalism: they are bathed in the divine purity of young light and mellowed by the wistful tenderness of a fresh though reminiscent art.

Of this art the feature that strikes and delights us most is its infallibility. The care Chénier lavished upon his lines can well escape our notice; it appears only on a study of the many corrections and changes in his successive texts. He wrote the most facile verse, with full attention to the dangers of facility. The outcome of his inspired effort is a plenitude of sense and sound, a sureness of rhythm and a majesty of form that stamp hundreds of his fragments with the beauty of triumphal music. This melody and harmony were his by instinct, and no devices can account for them. That he opened the way to the freedom of romantic prosody is a hard-lived fallacy. He used the technique of his immediate predecessors, the post-classical poets; but the powerful swell of a truly lyrical, sometimes an epic genius, instils animation and life into the soulless measure used by his contemporaries. The variety of his breaks can be arresting; but the easy sweep and grand rolling movement of his alexandrines remain our most admiring impression.

André Chénier paid generous tribute to many poets who were famed during his short life, but one hardly dare mention their names in the same breath as his. Most members of that generation —the last before the romantic—had merit and talent of some sort; still, only the specialized historian of literature would try nowadays to recapture even part of the glow with which their works were then read. It matters little that Écouchard-Lebrun (1729–1807) should have been honoured, and somewhat crushed, with the appellation Lebrun-Pindare. His most reputed odes (*A Buffon*; *Le Vengeur*) have vanished from the anthologies for schools, where they preserved a ghostly life till the end of the nineteenth century; his many witty epigrams still have some sting. Marie-Joseph Chénier, 1764–1811, André's brother, besides writing for the stage, made a mark with poems of personal feeling, like *La Promenade* (1805); Legouvé, 1764–1812, with shrewd understanding of the fashionable mood, published a treatise in verse on *La Mélancolie*. Saint-Lambert, taking due note of the popularity of Thomson's *Seasons*, followed their general outline in his *Saisons* (1769), and Roucher (1745–94) exploited a similar theme in *Les Mois* (1779). But what could a pretence of personal emotion or a close description of nature avail, when the 'dull brain perplexed and retarded' what might have been genuine flights of poetry? Thomson's precision is alive with a fire that Saint-Lambert, plodding and reasonable, utterly lacked; Roucher's catalogue of rustic labours is tedious. Delille (1753–1813), again, managed greatly to impress his age. He stood for learning as well as art, translated Virgil's *Georgics*, and was a professor of Latin; and certainly, no one could turn out more skilful or more regular alexandrines than his. From his *Jardins* (1780) to his *Trois règnes de la nature* (1809), he ranked as an authority on those beauties of gardening and landscape that the century thought it had discovered; his fall was the greater for his prolonged supremacy, and the romantics made ruthless fun of his well-behaved raptures.

In others our partiality—for what age can be impartial?—finds more to like; their claims to remembrance are still valid, and, if one may prophesy, will remain so. Casimir Delavigne (1773–1843), in the first of his political *Messéniennes* (1815), combines rhetoric with really warm feeling, nervous form, and imaginative power. Though less original than Chénier, he affords a further proof of the creative energy that still lingered in classicism. Millevoye (1782–1816), a precocious writer who died prematurely, gave a slight but sincere and moving sketch of a truly personal inspiration in, for instance, *Poésies*, 1800. He was already a romantic in the direct emotional utterance of his later *Chants élégiaques*, although his language still shows some of the blight of convention. Chênedollé (1769–1833) waited too long before he let his heart speak freely and simply: his *Essais poétiques* (1820) came out at the very same time as the *Méditations* of Lamartine. Népomucène Lemercier's (1771–1840) *L'Atlantiade* claims our respect in several ways: he goes beyond the romantic era and links up with the objective and cosmological poetry of the mid-nineteenth century. Another victim of early death, Gilbert (1751–80), before bewailing his fate in lines that left a mark on the sensibility of the time, gathered up his strength and turned his self-pity to bitter satire in *Le XVIIIᵉ Siècle* (1775) and *Mon apologie* (1778). He probed to the quick some of the shames of an age when reason and feeling, having assumed the dignity of first principles, no longer needed to be practised. Parny (1753–1814) almost succeeded in melting to liquid grace and sweet harmonies the language of a poetry stiffened by convention and tradition. But his melody lacked the deeper notes of the heart; his inspiration is that of a superficial, elegant, and pleasure-seeking love.

CHAPTER XLII

Madame de Staël

A REMARK often passed on Madame de Staël,[1] not without some slight admixture of irony, is that her genius had something virile in its robustness. It is none the less fair to point out that no writer, in her age of sensibility, laid more stress on the claims of the heart. If as a critic she stands, in a position of eminence, on the threshold of the French romantic period, she owes it not to any superior subtlety of aesthetic discrimination, but to her fine perception of issues that the sharpest minds had largely failed to see and feel. For years literature in France had been heading for renewal, and progress was governed by profound changes in the mental outlook of the nation. It was left for Madame de Staël to realize the fact more fully than had been done before, and to formulate it in terms of the comparative psychology of human groups. This was her creative contribution to the thought of her time; and her work was not so much an example of the literature of the new era as an interpretation in advance, sufficiently well founded, when once the dust of controversy had cleared, to meet the demand for a justification in principle.

The starting-point of her book, *La Littérature dans ses rapports avec les institutions sociales*, is an idea that was already current, indeed a common-place. But her treatment of the theme is so broad, and involves such decisive preferences of taste, that it becomes a signal

[1] Germaine Necker, born in Paris in 1766, was the daughter of a Swiss financier and diplomat who played an eminent part in French politics, and of a Protestant mother from Geneva. She married the Swedish ambassador, Baron de Staël. In 1789 she published *Lettres sur J.-J. Rousseau*, followed by *De l'influence des passions sur le bonheur des individus et des nations* in 1796; *De la littérature considérée dans ses rapports avec les institutions sociales*, 1800. She was hostile to Napoleon, and until his fall was banished from Paris and lived mostly at Coppet, near Lausanne. After two novels—*Delphine*, 1802, and *Corinne*, 1807—she wrote *De l'Allemagne*, which was printed in 1810, destroyed by the police, but republished abroad in 1813. She remarried in 1811, and died in 1817. Her circle at Coppet, from 1804 to 1814, was an active centre of liberal thought and literary discussion, frequented by Benjamin Constant, A. W. Schlegel, Sismondi, &c. She wrote other works (*Dix années d'exil*, &c.) and letters, which were published posthumously.

expression of a new faith. The very basis of the classical tradition is destroyed, when the unity of art is broken down into a variety of racial and cultural groups, each of which claims a right to an artistic form adapted to its needs. The eighteenth-century belief in progress is brought to bear on the long-standing issue of the moderns against the ancients, with the result that because of its depth of Christian feeling the poetry that has flourished since the Renaissance appears as appealing far more to the heart than the masterpieces of Greece and Rome. The school of poets whose ideal is apparently to bring together only such words as have been associated before, is charged with failing to satisfy the need for genuinely personal utterance, without which writing misses the indispensable value of originality. This is practically equivalent to the famous attack that, at the very same time, the authors of the *Lyrical Ballads* were launching against English poetic diction. Madame de Staël asserts that there are two worlds of thought and art: the South and the North. In the former all emphasis is laid on clarity, order, and elegance of form; in the latter there prevails the inextinguishable love of the indefinite, which grants full scope to the search for emotion and mystery. She definitely commits herself to the superiority of the latter: 'Toutes mes impressions, toutes mes idées, me portent de préférence vers la littérature du Nord.' All the possibilities of regeneration are contained in the inspiration that French poets have, in fact, instinctively, for some time, been seeking abroad, especially in England. What matters is not perfection of phrasing, but 'ce qui agrandit l'âme et l'esprit'.

So, the unique fecundity of Shakespeare's example is defined with an energy and a sureness of perception that leave the half-hearted appreciation of previous critics far behind; and Milton is no less aptly praised. No doubt the immense scope of such an inquiry severely taxes the authoress's knowledge; her description and judgement of Italian and Spanish literatures are especially sketchy. None the less, owing to its wealth of suggestive views, the book is remarkable; and it is no mean merit to have defined so well, at so early a stage, the essence of the romantic frame of mind: 'le sublime de l'esprit, des sentiments et des actions', which is a result of 'le besoin d'échapper aux bornes qui circonscrivent l'imagination'; and the craving of souls 'à la fois exaltées et mélancoliques, fatiguées de tout ce qui se mesure, . . . d'un terme enfin, à quelque distance qu'on le place'.

De l'Allemagne is even more certainly an epoch-making work, though it is not, perhaps, a great one: it does not superadd the supreme grace of style to the abounding interest of the thought. The general distinction between South and North is here deliberately forced to a particular application, namely that France and Germany stand in complete moral, intellectual, and literary contrast as the two extreme types of their kinds. Madame de Staël's courageous and outspoken thesis is that the civilization of the former, having developed and borne fruit at an earlier date, is now in need of being fertilized from German sources. It needs the inwardness, the imaginative ardour, and the emotional enthusiasm which these can supply and to which distinguished French writers had lately been turning.

Toutes les fois que, de nos jours, on a pu faire entrer dans la régularité française un peu de sève étrangère, les Français y ont applaudi avec transport. Jean-Jacques Rousseau, Bernardin de Saint-Pierre, Chateaubriand, &c., dans quelques-uns de leurs ouvrages, sont tous, même à leur insu, de l'école germanique, c'est-à-dire qu'ils ne puisent leur talent que dans le fond de leur âme.

Not only is the best means of a necessary and salutary renewal said to lie in the influence of Germany but, yielding without reserve to the promptings of her hereditary impulses, the authoress evinces the warmest sympathy for the characteristic features of the German genius, which she presents in a most favourable light. Deeply religious, thoughtful, hardworking, true, and loyal in their life, manners, activities, and institutions, the men and women whom Carlyle in the next generation was to praise with very similar zeal have, she asserts, created a philosophy, a poetry, a learning, a system of ethics that should be models to Europe and to the world. The object of her book is to establish these high claims by a detailed survey of 'l'Allemagne et les mœurs des Allemands; la Littérature et les Arts; la Philosophie et la Morale; la Religion et l'Enthousiasme'. Leaving out the unguarded excess of many appreciations, the value of this sympathetic and, on most points, fresh information, to even the cultivated French public, cannot be exaggerated.

No less essential a merit of the book is its noble advocacy of that genuinely cosmopolitan spirit, that European point of view, which the next hundred years were repeatedly to discover, to extol in principle, and to ignore. If intellectual nationality is to be transcended, Madame de Staël must be ranked permanently among the prophets of international culture. At the same time, all Frenchmen, and many Germans, will agree that her image of Germany was incomplete and misleading in its simplified and sentimental idealization. A more accurate and a better-shaded notion of the facts had to be purchased by Europe at the cost of experience. Moreover, her idea of the spiritual rebirth that lent profundity to the romantic movement in France, was unduly coloured by her somewhat dogmatic theory of the exclusively 'Southern' and 'classical' quality of the innate French genius. The present book has tried to point out that from the very beginning there was a latent romantic tendency in the consciousness of the French people. When Madame de Staël qualifies her own thesis by remarking: 'Rien ne peut être comparé à nos trouvères et à nos troubadours, et c'était peut-être à cette source que nous devions puiser une littérature vraiment nationale', she is playing with a then fashionable theme, for the popularity of the 'genre troubadour' was a contemporary phenomenon of taste; but she draws nearer than perhaps she knew to a truer view of what happened to the French consciousness, in its eventful development from the Song of Roland to Victor Hugo.

As a novelist she is interesting, without being in the first rank. She lacks the restraint of a consciously artistic purpose. Constructed more or less on the pattern of Richardson and Rousseau, *Delphine* and *Corinne* are prolix and diffuse. The former tells a pathetic story in the form of letters, and conveys the lesson that conscience is not enough to make a woman secure; what she is and means to be is essential, but not sufficient; a good name before the world must be preserved, for it is an element of wisdom that no sensible person can properly ignore. *Corinne* strings affairs of the heart together with sight-seeing episodes and scenes of Italian manners, painted very much in the unblushing spirit of a guide-book. The sentiment is over-strained, and the lack of humour sometimes appalling. A genuine sense of the problems that beset a woman's life, and of her almost inevitable dedication to suffering, is the best feature of both works. The authoress makes no bones of declaring soundly that women are generally better than men, and she manages to prove her point, although the difference is minimized by the fact that her men are womanish to a degree. The reader is left with the impression that genuine passion is always respectable and that it creates a legitimacy of its own, though more often than not this is doomed to disaster; and herein lies the direct link between these two books and the properly romantic novel, especially that of George Sand.

CHAPTER XLIII

Chateaubriand

PERIODS of literary history are, of course, mainly abstractions; in fact they all overlap, and merge into each other. With Chateaubriand[1] one need no longer speak of preparation: the tide of romanticism has risen, and has reached its full. His long life indeed took him as far as the ebb-years, when a new phase could be expected. Still, while he is in some respects the arch-romantic, he should be studied, not with the men of the twenties, but as the last product of the transition. He was a relic from the time before artistic as well as political revolutions were common happenings. He carried the spirit of the old world into an era which he but incompletely accepted; a supporter of moderate liberalism, he opposed Napoleon, but harked back to the monarchy; a conservative in taste no less than in doctrine, he reconciled the ardours of romance, and even a feeling for the evocative possibilities of the language which anticipated the symbolist experiments, with a sense of construction and order, based on the ancient humanities; bold as were the flights of his imagination, he never gave up in principle the traditions of classicism. Considered in the round, his affinities would rather link him up with André Chénier, as a writer who had vigour enough to rejuvenate an exhausted invention, and to thrust out towards the future without

[1] François-René de Chateaubriand, born at Saint-Malo, 1768, lived for some time, after his school years, in the country at Combourg, his father's home. He joined the army, tried his hand at literature in Paris, then went to America in 1791 as a means of avoiding the Revolution. He returned on hearing of the king's arrest and fought with the army of the *émigrés*. He sought refuge in England in 1793, and remained till 1800, teaching French for a living. He published an *Essai sur les révolutions* in 1797, followed by *Atala*, 1801; *Le Génie du Christianisme*, 1802; *René*, 1805; *Les Martyrs*, 1809; and the *Itinéraire de Paris à Jérusalem*, 1811. After Waterloo he was created a peer, and was successively ambassador in Berlin, London, and Rome, and for a time foreign minister. After 1830 he sided with the opposition. A collected edition of his writings, 1826–31, contained *Les Aventures du dernier Abencérage, Les Natchez, Voyage en Amérique*, &c. Later publications included the *Essai sur la littérature anglaise*, a translation of *Paradise Lost*, 1836, and the *Vie de Rancé*, 1844. He died in 1848. His *Mémoires d'outre-tombe*, written throughout the greater part of his life, were published after his death by instalments; a complete text was first printed in 1948, one century later.

breaking from the past. The main difference is that he had a wound in his soul, which Chénier had not: the incurable anguish of a diseased sensibility.

His personality is everything; greater than his books, except in so far as he is himself the theme and substance of his works. These, if one leaves out the immature *Essai sur les révolutions*, can be classed under three heads. The chief items in the first group would be *Atala*, *René*, *Les Martyrs*, and *L'Itinéraire de Paris à Jérusalem*. *Atala* and *René* are landmarks in the history of literature but their appeal has very perceptibly waned, and the magic of the style can no longer conceal their intrinsic defects from our sophisticated age. The short tales, and especially *René*, are instinct with what was shortly to be called the *mal du siècle*; the heroes and heroines are sick with a thoughtful melancholy; they are crushed by experience before they have actually suffered it; their hypersensitiveness deprives them of the power to meet the demands of life. This malady, the growing-pains of the modern mind subjected to the strain of rapid changes, shaken by repeated shocks to religious faith, and to social and moral values, had been revealed to the cultivated classes of Europe by Goethe's *Werther*; Sénancour's *Obermann* had described it with unsurpassed penetration, but had hardly been read; Chateaubriand encountered it in the inmost promptings of his sad, morbid, and unsettled heart; and transmuted it into the pages of glowing beauty in which he evokes the grandeur and charm of nature, the pathos of human fate. As confessions the tales are deeply moving; but they also serve a didactic purpose, being originally offshoots from the *Génie du Christianisme*, intended as proof that our corrupt nature demands the support of religion. The influence of Richardson and Rousseau, perhaps even that of Mrs. Radcliffe, can be traced in the craving for dramatic effect that heightens with rather cheap thrills the emotion of plots in themselves psychological. The death of Atala, the scene in which Amélie takes the veil, and the secret shame of her guilty love, are too complacently emphasized: great art should show more discretion. Another weakness of these works, as of the *Natchez*, the *Voyage en Amérique*, &c., lies in what was for long, and to some extent is still, the main source of their strength: the exotic background that the writer has so skilfully, but somewhat unscrupulously made the counterpart of his visions and dreams. All artists are creators

of illusion; and we should be ill advised if we censured Chateaubriand for having made far more impressive use of his American
experiences than chapter and verse warranted; still, the uneasy sense
of exaggeration and make-believe, mixing with our enjoyment,
rather disturbs it; taking much from books, he might have more
freely acknowledged his debt, and not pretended, implicitly or explicitly, to guide us along his actual footsteps through 'the Floridas'.
In the same way his prose epic, *Les Martyrs*, however masterly as a
semi-legendary evocation, is a clumsy attempt at the historical, and
imitates Homeric similes with forced obstinacy. That the *Itinéraire* is
largely unconscious or conscious fiction is also evident; and we
cannot conquer a pedantic preference that *voyages imaginaires* should
bear special labels. But what magnificent settings for picturesque
fancies!

The second group of Chateaubriand's works would be composed
of the *Génie du christianisme*, and various tracts. Although his political
thought has dignity and shrewdness, it may be neglected here. The
Génie appeared at a time (1802) when the French society of the
Empire was feeling its way to a restoration of faith that was morally
needed and politically desirable. Thus the welcome was eager for a
book that did not appeal to cold reason, but invested belief with
prestige, poetry, and beauty, and so provided the public with an
effective excuse to indulge their latent hankering after religious
emotion: the imaginative, aesthetic and practical claims of the Catholic Church were illustrated eloquently and brilliantly by a writer
who had sown his wild oats of scepticism, and of whom the lessons
of grief had made a sincere convert. The work is not one for the historian or the philosopher; it should be read as a poem of emotional
apologetics, strong on its chosen ground, and on no other. That it
wanders away into somewhat diffuse argument about every aspect
of spiritual life is no fair objection, since the point it makes is that
religion lies at the core of all things human.

With the third group we come to what, in spite of some inequalities, is Chateaubriand's masterpiece, the *Mémoires d'outre-tombe*.
Beside this one may place the *Vie de Rancé*: the story of another life
than his own, but full of an instinctive, silent and pathetic reference
to himself. In the *Mémoires*, the tale of what he was and what he did
from his earliest years broadens out again and again into general

vistas of events and of men, lit with flashes of tragic, meditative, or ironical reflection. At the heart of it is the poignant sense of the passing of time and the fragility of each prop to which our longing for permanence clings. And yet, a recoil from life, the nostalgia of death, the hope of supernatural immortality, all are mingled with this bitterness, in a conflict of emotions no less true than it is illogical. Another contradiction lies in the mixture of inordinate pride, characteristic arrogance, and an almost puerile vanity with a Christian humility which is not entirely verbal; and of rooted selfishness and constant self-pity with genuine tenderness. Nothing in its dumb or direct appeal can be more sincere. This is in every way the author's most genuine book, and the one that will remain proof against the change of fashion.

In all his work, and in the *Mémoires*, perhaps, with more power and a surer taste than anywhere else, Chateaubriand is the born writer and poet. The terse vigour and the grandeur of his evocations of destiny could be matched for instance in Hardy's *Dynasts*; but Hardy's verse lacks the felicity and the enchanting harmonies of Chateaubriand's prose. From the beginning, from the picture of the virgin forest in *Atala*, it grew plain that the music of Rousseau and his school was here acquiring a more concentrated and original accent. 'Bientôt elle' (the moon) 'répandit dans les bois ce grand secret de mélancolie qu'elle aime à raconter aux vieux chênes et aux rivages antiques des mers. . . .' Rousseau's lyrical passages compared with this sound almost like eloquent rhapsodies. As he matured, Chateaubriand's instinct fastened more and more upon such intensely evocative phrases, that in their vividness equal Michelet's style, and in their indefiniteness are anticipations of symbolism. It is refreshing to find, on the other hand, that the *Mémoires* can play at times upon a very different string, that of humour.

PART VII

ROMANTIC LITERATURE (1820-50)

—————————— ✦ ——————————

CHAPTER XLIV

The Romantic Mood

THE objection to general labels in literary history has been so strong for some time that the epithet 'romantic' is criticized by many, though wholly avoided by few. Yet if this name were banned another, probably still open to criticism, would have to be sought. The basic fact in French literature between 1820 and 1850 is the relative predominance of a mood with which, for better or worse, one particular word has constantly been associated. The mood was already far from new. In incipient or ill-defined forms it might have been encountered in groups and individual writers from the early stages of French history; it had even been obscurely incorporated with the strong synthesis of classical thought; and before the middle of the eighteenth century it began to assert itself, gaining a vitality that promised to make it the chief characteristic of the coming age. After the turmoil and immediate sequels of the Revolution, a nation shaken to the depths and only now recovering her mental balance allowed it to assume prime importance among artistic impulses, not easily and at once, but by degrees, and at the cost of a struggle. The success of Lamartine's *Méditations* on their publication in 1820 is symbolic, for it represents the acceptance, notwithstanding a resistance that never wholly subsided, of a new source of literary inspiration.

If by that date the mood was no longer novel, it was richer and fuller than ever before. All its elements, and the fondness for emotion which lay at its core, had existed during the previous age. Sensibility in the latter part of the eighteenth century had already been a fashion, a craving, and almost a mania; now it reappeared allied to imaginative thrills in a manner that increased and refreshed its appeal. But a difference existed, in the proportions of the mixture, the strength of each separate element, the homogeneity of the blend, and the power it showed of forcing itself upon the accepted conventions of expression. Literature tended more and more to turn for inspiration to the far-distant in space and time, to the Middle Ages, their quaintness and vigour; to the foreign and the exotic, the strange and the mysterious; to night, ruins, the symbols and images of death; to the wild and the primitive; to nature, untouched, with all its grandeur as well as its soft, luxuriant glow. The new tendencies had for years been at work in the subconscious, shaping the instinctive need of melodious verse and evocative phrasing. The outcome of this gradual, silent, and in the long run irresistible action, the true preparation for romantic poetry, was the creation of a literary form capable of communicating the new mood. Among important external causes the Revolution may be singled out, for though it by no means destroyed the ascendancy of the old literary types, it showed that everything human could be cast into new moulds.

The temper of romanticism thus composed of emotions, longings, preferences, and instincts did not exclude ideas; it did, however, make less allowance for them than classicism had done; and the shift in literature from properly intellectual patterns was distinct. The English poets and Shakespeare were by this time widely read; the names of Byron and Scott were soon added in fresh glory to those of Milton, Thomson, Gray, and Ossian. Germany was slowly coming into her own; after the Swiss Gessner, Goethe's *Werther*, and now his first *Faust*, as well as the works of Hoffmann and Bürger, were stirring a sense of the fantastic; and the cultured class was initiated into the original qualities of the Italian and the Spanish genius. From all these stimuli there resulted a broadening of the public taste, a keener perception of the freedom of art, a more eager search for dark, bizarre, or pathetic effects. A feeling that vagueness was preferable was in the air; the hard outlines of things seen, shown, or said, in the clear-cut presentment of the traditional French style, began perceptibly to melt; more frequent appeals to intuition and a

more suggestive method of writing toned down the insistent definiteness of the language. But while readers and writers were becoming
ever more receptive to foreign influences, no actual principle of
imitation was laid down, and it was left for Madame de Staël to
deduce from all these symptoms that a change in the national allegiance was desirable, from the spirit of Southern to that of Northern
literature. There was no complete expression of the romantic doctrine, with the one signal exception, in the particular field of drama,
of Hugo's preface to his *Cromwell* (1827). The literary battle was
fought by the writers on grounds that, at bottom more or less
similar, seemed separate and diverse; there was often a sense of
brotherhood within groups, but not a really coherent movement.
Besides, in the central mood itself, many varieties could of course
be detected, as one or another of its constituents was emphasized by
individual temperaments. These differences were all the more pronounced, because the independence of the artist was universally proclaimed. The discipline of opinion, of academies, of a predominant
scale of values, had been a feature of the classical period; the gradual
decline in the vitality of that faith had for long left its sway unshaken;
but now the spell was broken, and each writer was taking the law
into his own hands. Sentiment is personal; its expression individual.
Hence the relative unity of French romanticism includes a number
of important divergences, that in some cases might almost seem to
destroy any community of purpose. But lyricism was the gainer; it
set its stamp on almost the whole body of contemporary literature.
    The lack of stability in the political and social order contributed
still further to diversify the literary scene. The after-effects of the
Revolution were making themselves felt in a chronic agitation and
frequent changes. Conflicting trends severed the conservative,
mainly idealistic, forces supporting the restored monarchy and the
Church, from the liberal, matter-of-fact, and still largely rationalist
bourgeoisie, and the new, lyrical fervour of the romantic poets was
thus at first more often inspired by devotion to 'the throne and the
altar' than by a democratic warmth inherited from the revolutionary
years. That confusion was mirrored in the division of the press, then
growing more influential, with the birth of the cheap newspaper
(Émile de Girardin's *La Presse*, founded in 1836), and with the new
reviews, literary no less than political (*Revue des Deux Mondes* and

Revue de Paris, both founded in 1829). The most important daily in matters of literature was *Le Globe* (1824), where a brilliant critic, Sainte-Beuve, soon made a mark, and which tended to give romanticism a positive burden of somewhat reformatory, if not revolutionary, zeal. Indeed the second revolution, in 1830, discouraged reactionary efforts, and the humanitarian spirit of reform and improvement was thenceforth in the ascendant. Its increasing hold upon the masses coincided with a rise in the standing of the man of letters. Early in the period, the majority of readers were still outside the reach of the most representative writing, and it was only by degrees that the spread of education widely extended the circles to which a Victor Hugo or a Balzac could appeal. This development owes its special significance to the fact that, the age of patrons now being decidedly over, literature as a career had to be self-supporting. So the many-sided process, at once intellectual, political, and economic, led to what may be regarded as the most marked feature of the period; and after 1830 various lines of thought and literature can be seen converging towards a spirit of seriousness, a more eager desire to spread social or philosophical views. The romantic mood in the first place was the result of a psychological urge for freedom of expression; and the burden for which expression was sought was purely emotional. When a positive content was given to writers' feelings, and their works tried to become a means of persuasion, French romanticism returned to a sense of moral responsibility, to which the previous ages of the national thought had been generally faithful.

CHAPTER XLV

Poetry

I. LAMARTINE[1]

THE enthusiastic welcome given to the *Méditations* has been again and again tested by succeeding years, and the poet's voice, heard then in its freshness, keeps its hold upon new generations. But we must confess that the book is unequal. A rhetorical manner creeps into some pieces; moralizing arguments, too often, remind us of the didactic poetry of the eighteenth century; novel as the inspiration is, it allows passive, ready-made phrases to appear that bear the stamp of the artificial vocabulary of that age. An essential difference, however, is that whatever the subject of each piece, it is treated in close union with the poet's sincere feeling. Intellectual debates are transferred to the domain of sensibility, where values are really measured, beyond a merely emotional response, in terms of life. As if in accordance with that inner sensibility, the words are not associated only by a rational process; they are notes of music, soft, flowing, liquid, and evocative, as well as logical tokens; their solid nucleus of sense tends to melt into liquid sounds. Their succession thus resembles a musical theme, that speaks to the intelligence, the imagination, and the heart, in miraculous and enchanting harmony. Even when

[1] Alphonse de Lamartine, born at Mâcon, 1790, the son of a country gentleman, spent his childhood at the family home of Milly; after his schooling, he lived at the manor-house of Saint-Point. He travelled in Italy, married an Englishwoman, and filled diplomatic posts at Naples and Florence. The success of the *Méditations poétiques*, 1820, made him famous. Next appeared the *Nouvelles méditations* and *La Mort de Socrate*, 1823; *Le Dernier Chant du pèlerinage d'Harold*, 1825; *Harmonies poétiques et religieuses*, 1830. After a journey in state through the Near East, he published *Jocelyn*, 1836; *La Chute d'un ange*, 1838; *Recueillements poétiques*, 1839. From 1833 he had been engaged in politics. His prose *Histoire des Girondins*, 1847, stirred public feeling on the eve of the Revolution of 1848, when he became foreign minister and a leader of the Republican government. The last period of his life was saddened by a long struggle against financial worries, to relieve which he wrote, among other works, *Cours familier de littérature*, 1856–69; *Histoire de la Révolution de 1848*, 1849; *Confidences, Raphaël*, 1849; *Graziella, Le Tailleur de pierres de Saint-Point*, 1851, &c. He died in 1869. His letters have been published.

rhetorical, the poems of this collection did strike chords of meditative sentiment. The melancholy with which a deep-felt bereavement
then suffused the poet's moods naturally pitched his accents in elegiac
tones, and the whole book breathed a searching appeal to sympathetic affinities. A bond was thus woven between the author and his
readers, more intimate and personal than French poetry had ever
before experienced. Today, in spite of the hardening of fibre which
the abuse of such appeals and the repeated shocks of our dramatic
age have inevitably induced, there still lives a spell in most of these
poems, and chiefly in the purely lyrical ones, so flowing in their
effortless but penetrating melody, and where the landscape evoked
is so perfectly attuned to the emotion: *L'Isolement, Le Vallon, Le Lac,
L'Automne*. Lamartine was clearly aware of the nature of this communication: 'Le public entendit une âme sans la voir, et vit un
homme au lieu d'un livre. Depuis J.-J. Rousseau, Bernardin de Saint-
Pierre et Chateaubriand, c'était le poète qu'il attendait' (Preface,
1849).

His inspiration did not substantially alter with the successive stages
of his output; it was not the result of a deliberate choice, but the imperious bent of temperament. Still, we are struck with a sense of
growth as we pass from the first to the *Nouvelles méditations* and to
the *Harmonies poétiques et religieuses*. The lines are more smooth than
ever; the beautiful, delicate, or grand images arise and spread out
more serenely; thought and language flow more evenly, with no
rhetorical strain. Along with the Catholic themes, the fond evocation of Church rites, and the expression of a royalist faith, which the
poet owed to the traditions of his family, there appear accents of a
freer idealism; moving with the times, Lamartine's belief broadens
out to a religion of the spirit, and a democracy of the heart, with
which his noble share in the politics of a tempestuous age (1848)
remains for ever associated. Apart from these subjects, the impressions of everyday life awake lyrical echoes. More prominent becomes the fondness of a mind dwelling on memories of childhood.
Elegies of love and death recede into a background of mellow sadness; with a keener thrill and a more clinging affection, the poet's
remembrance fastens on the cherished scenes of his youth, his home,
his parents, especially the mother to whose tenderness and intuitive
gifts he proclaimed himself so deeply indebted. These idylls of the

countryside, in a typical setting of hills, vineyards and woods, flooded by the golden glow of simple happiness, have an idyllic charm second to none in the literature of any nation; and when, near the end of his life, Lamartine returned to the same theme of reminiscent grief, distilled by the years to a rarer, more poignant essence, he wrote *La Vigne et la maison*, and gave French poetry one of its most exquisite gems.

Yet his greatest vein is not that of emotional lyricism, in which with Paul Verlaine he is supreme among nineteenth-century poets, but a philosophical fervour in which emotion and thought are inseparably fused. *Jocelyn* has beautiful episodes, but suffers as a whole from an over-heated, hectic sentiment, and some diffuseness. There is a happier blend of harmony and meditation, a serene strength, in the *Mort de Socrate*, an admirable dream of pagan idealism bordering on Christianity; and while the *Chute d'un ange* generally is a fine failure, there is a vigorous concentration in some of its parts, especially the *Huitième Vision*, where the idea of God is grandly expressed in lines as compact and faultless as marble. Expression indeed is one of Lamartine's most wonderful gifts. That he possessed facility is one fact; that he sometimes indulged it imprudently is another; and critics have censured him for the sin of habitual negligence, beyond all truth and fairness. He had an artistic conscience, and to the ease of his invention were superadded the labour and the tact of the attentive craftsman. His music, the fluidity of his verse, are natural, but they are careful; though his favourite is the alexandrine, he handles the various forms of the ode as well as the writers who staked everything on their metrical cleverness. In general, his meditative song is as just and aptly worded as it is harmonious, and reconciles opposite qualities because it is truly inspired.

He should stand as an argument against generalizations and the slur often cast on the poetry of his fatherland. With him there begins an age when a normal feature of French literature is its genuinely poetic vein. He came under various influences, acknowledged Ossian as one of his masters, wrote his first lyrics in the stanza and the rhythm of Gray's *Elegy*, admired Byron generously; but when all has been said the fact remains that his genuine lyricism is fed almost exclusively from national sources; he was deeply, typically French, rooted in old provincial ground, writing from an unsurpassed fund of the language at its purest and freshest. The miracle is that his language recovered an imaginative and evocative virtue that had seemed worn out and lost; but the decline had been the fault of men and mental fossilization, not of the popular genius.

The prose of Lamartine has most of the merits of his poetry; it is warm and eloquent, periodic but supple, graphic, and musical; less guarded than the verse, it lets itself go more freely, with the result that it suffers from over-facility, especially in the hasty works of his last years. Ardour and impressiveness are to be found in all he wrote, and a range of beauty that can reach the sublime, but which keeps successfully on a more familiar plane. His historical books are largely improvised, but the *Cours de littérature* is interesting; and the *Confidences, Raphaël, Graziella, Le Tailleur de pierres* have many moving scenes of sentimental autobiography, not unmixed with fiction.

2. VIGNY

In most respects the poetic temperament of Vigny[1] shows a striking contrast to that of Lamartine. He was no creator of spontaneous harmonies; with him the idea and the words did not flow together of themselves into a form that was the inevitable pattern of their union. He fought hard to mould the language to his needs, and was sometimes vanquished in the battle; forced, inappropriate phrases occur in most of his poems. The sum total of his slow, scarce output is a single volume, and not a bulky one at that. But it is all of value, and contains a dozen masterpieces, any one of which has such originality and concentrated significance that it might in itself suffice to make a writer's fame. The language, forged and polished, has an exceptional density, each syllable being packed with meaning. What is thus conveyed is the burden of an earnest, intensely meditative

[1] Alfred de Vigny, born at Loches, 1797, of an old family, entered the army at the Restoration, left it at thirty, married an Englishwoman, and lived a retired life in his manor in the west. His first *Poems* were published in 1822, after which came *Éloa*, 1824; *Poèmes antiques et modernes*, 1826 and 1837; *Poèmes philosophiques*, 1843–54; *Les Destinées* and the prose *Journal d'un poète*, posthumous, 1864 and 1867. He died in 1863. A novel, *Cinq-Mars*, was published in 1826. His adaptation of *Othello* was played in 1829, that of *The Merchant of Venice* was published in 1839. His original works for the stage include *La Maréchale d'Ancre*, an historical drama, 1831; *Quitte pour la peur*, a comedy, 1833; *Chatterton*, his most successful attempt, 1835. *Stello*, 1832, and *Servitude et grandeur militaires*, 1836, are made up of short stories and moral disquisitions.

mind; of thought steeped in the emotions of a sensitive heart, and waking a thousand human echoes. Whatever slight strain may subsist here and there, disappears under the spell of this impressive utterance, which is carried along by the rhythm of simple, grand lines. No verse in French is fuller, more weighty, more unforgettable than that of Vigny at his best. And with its strength, it can have charm, a haunting beauty.

Themes of several kinds unite in the texture of this one volume. The properly romantic mood prompts imaginative renderings of the past, Biblical or pagan; while the social preoccupations of the present appear in frequent allusions to contemporary problems. But few scenes are limited to dramatic incidents or to the distant civilizations evoked with such vivid picturesqueness; moral and psychological issues are never out of sight. Vigny's last series of poems, *Les Destinées*, frankly gives first place to philosophy. No doctrine is thrust upon the reader; what is emphasized is the searchings of a thinker open to all the anxieties of the modern age. Although no longer finding support in dogmatic religion, he is keenly aware of the spiritual dignity of profoundly sincere thought; he feels the sadness of man's fate, but turns pessimism into food for unbreakable courage. Bitterness and violence are shunned; a quiet, proud but not haughty resignation, a tender compassion, are the characteristics of these pieces. Their restrained pathos and their calm sublimity rank them with the most noble poetry in any language.

Among the earlier poems, *Éloa*, in which Vigny's inspiration is most sustained, has admirable passages, and bears throughout the stamp of genius. In *Le Déluge* and *La Fille de Jephté* he voices the protest of the modern conscience against the pitilessness of the Old Law; while *La Femme adultère* reverently calls up the forgiveness of Jesus. Of the poems on subjects from legend or history, the happiest in its treatment is *Le Cor*, an epic evocation of the death of Roland, punctuated with dreamlike melancholy by the huntsman's horn in the distant woods. A light, sensuous grace invests the pagan sketches, and their elegant form reminds us of Chénier. Still, the direct and poignant note of the later poems has a more irresistible appeal. There is a Dantesque spirit in the powerful *terza rima* of *Les Destinées*; the inspiration of *Le Mont des oliviers*, somewhat similar, opposes the intuitive sense of justice to the hard obstinacy of heaven's decree;

La Mort du loup teaches the grim lesson of stoicism; *La Bouteille à la mer* symbolizes the redeeming virtue of heroic manhood, the pure devotion to science; and *La Maison du berger*, one of the greatest of all French poems, fuses aching love, the recoil from the unfeeling beauty of the earth, and the passion for a dedicated solitude, in a piercingly sad idyll of latter-day disillusion, no longer comforted by the fallacy of nature's response to man's need of sympathy in the universe. In spite of occasional flaws, Vigny's manner is very near to the purity of finished art, as may be felt by comparing it with that of Matthew Arnold, a most careful poet somewhat akin in spirit. That essentially romantic fancy, *The Scholar Gipsy*, is closer than Vigny's *Maison du berger* to the perfection of classicism; but Vigny's imagery is no less seductive, its blending of sound and sense no less winning, it is freer from any admixture of adventitious humanism, and its philosophical scope is broader.

Vigny's record as a dramatist and novelist is distinguished. On the stage, his adaptation of *Othello* (1829) is not only closer to the text than any previous French attempt, but it illustrates and in its preface aptly defines the free Shakespearian pattern of modern tragedy. His prose drama, *Chatterton*, sets an essentially romantic problem, the conflict of the artist and society, in an atmosphere of genuine realism. His novel, *Cinq-Mars*, is one more proof of his original initiative; while loosely following the example of Scott, it raises historical fiction to a higher plane by the addition of a symbolic significance. It is difficult to do justice in a few words to the suggestive power of his prose in *Stello* and *Servitude et grandeur militaires*, or to the nobility of his simple self-revelation in the *Journal d'un poète*.

3. VICTOR HUGO[1]

The greatest French poet, though essentially romantic, showed a suppleness of genius that freed his work from the inevitably

[1] Victor-Marie Hugo, born at Besançon, 1802, the son of an officer, followed his father abroad, studied in Paris, wrote verses early, published the collected *Odes et ballades* in 1828, and *Orientales* in 1829. He adopted the views of the romantics and was hailed as leader of the new generation. Meanwhile his one-time royalist feelings shifted more and more to liberalism. Further collections of poetry: *Les Feuilles d'automne*, 1831; *Les Chants du crépuscule*, 1835; *Les Voix intérieures*, 1837; *Les Rayons et les ombres*, 1840, were no less successful. He engaged in politics and sat in Parliament, first as a Deputy,

cramping bonds of doctrines and schools. The usual remark, that he developed with the century, evincing the features of its successive periods, is not strictly accurate: he was in advance of his times, and preceded rather than followed them.

His earliest attempts held out no such promise of the future. The *Odes et ballades* hardly break with the tradition of eighteenth-century lyricism. But they display an ease and vigour that raise the author to a very high level of original power. His handling of the classical types of metre and stanza is brilliant; while his images, instead of repeating the approved models, are continually fresh and arresting. In the ballades especially, a lively imagination plays over the medieval or exotic themes with intense vividness, and produces bolder, richer, and more varied effects of language than French poetry had yet known. In the *Orientales*, where Greek independence, a subject then very popular, has a conspicuous place, the colour is still more profusely applied. Such performances did indeed reveal a poet of outstanding quality; but they were no more than a practical application of the more superficial tenets of romanticism; as poetry they introduce no revolutionary principle.

In the next volumes, from *Les Feuilles d'automne* to *Les Rayons et les ombres*, the spell of the past is vanishing; the same central inspiration had already, in Lamartine's *Méditations* and *Harmonies*, opened new paths. The titles themselves indicate that imagery and music

and then as a *pair de France*. When Napoleon III seized power he retired to Jersey, then to Guernsey, and for eighteen years lived the life of an exile. The *Châtiments*, 1853, were bitter attacks against the dictator. In the *Contemplations*, 1856, the main inspiration was personal, centring on the loss of his daughter, drowned with her husband. The disasters of the Franco-German war, and the fall of the Second Empire, called him back to France; he was in Paris during the siege, and patriotic poems fill the *Année terrible*, 1872. The *Légende des siècles* came out in three instalments, 1859, 1877, 1883, and embodied a chiefly epic inspiration. A figure of national importance, he lived till 1885. The poems of his last years, *L'Art d'être grand-père*, 1877; *Les Quatre Vents de l'esprit*, 1881, &c., are eclipsed today by the posthumous volumes that have appeared at intervals: *Toute la lyre, La Fin de Satan, Dieu*, &c. During the first part of his career he had written actively for the stage, putting forth the theory of romantic drama in the preface to *Cromwell*, 1827; winning more or less disputed successes with *Hernani*, 1830; *Marion de Lorme*, 1831; *Le Roi s'amuse*, 1832; *Ruy Blas*, 1838, and meeting with signal failure in *Les Burgraves*, 1843. His prose novels, the chief of which are *Notre Dame de Paris*, 1831; *Les Misérables*, 1862; *Les Travailleurs de la mer*, 1866; *Quatre-vingt-treize*, 1873, remain in the forefront of nineteenth-century French fiction. Other side-issues to his works: notes on his tours abroad, pamphlets and speeches, letters, &c., are far from negligible.

have now become the medium of poetic utterance. The melody of Hugo's line is by no means that of Lamartine's; it is not so fluid, and a more nervous, varied, and spontaneous rhythm replaces Lamartine's musical regularity. But already at this stage the most notable trait is the poet's individual vision, and his fondness for the vague and the mysterious. The aim of such an art cannot be fully described in merely romantic terms; it implies a straining after values that were later to be defined as symbolist and impressionist. The poet's gaze, probing dim vistas, grows more and more to resemble a philosopher's interrogation; and his lyrics become, as it were, a meditative and prophetic brooding upon the darker problems of life. Vision and meditation were to remain their characteristic features from which their most striking beauties, as well as some of their typical faults, are derived. The visionary power adds depth and mystery even to the familiar aspects of nature:

> L'étang, lame d'argent que le couchant fait d'or,
> L'allée entrant au bois comme un noir corridor . . .
> Dans les prés, dans les eaux et dans les vallons verts,
> Retrouver les profils de la face éternelle
> Dont le visage humain n'est qu'une ombre charnelle;
> Quand le bruit du vent coupe en strophes incertaines
> Cette longue chanson qui coule des fontaines . . . .
>
> ('A un riche', *Les Voix intérieures*)

> . . . Les feuilles qui gisaient dans le bois solitaire,
> S'efforçant sous ses pas de s'élever de terre,
>   Couraient dans le jardin;
> Ainsi, parfois, quand l'âme est triste, nos pensées
> S'envolent un moment sur leurs ailes blessées,
>   Puis retombent soudain. . . .
>
> ('Tristesse d'Olympio', *Les Rayons et les ombres*)

Such passages are rife with the 'mental materialism' that Emerson held to be typical of English thought: they signal the decisive end of the tradition of intellectualist thinking with which two classical centuries seemed to have identified French literature. Declared symbols are now handled with a sureness, an authority of imagination, that belong to a new era, and bring romanticism a long stage beyond its initial range:

Toutes les passions s'éloignent avec l'âge,
L'une emportant son masque et l'autre son couteau,
Comme un essaim chantant d'histrions en voyage
Dont le groupe décroît derrière le coteau.

('Tristesse d'Olympio')

This last poem is one of Hugo's best-known masterpieces; many others show the same purity and sustained pathos. But on an average the high quality of these volumes is no longer a matter of unexceptionable artistry. The writer stakes all on a vigour and directness that preclude the possibility of very thorough polishing; the rhyme is still most often rich; the wording always easy, maybe somewhat prosaic. Imaginative content is stressed more than perfect form.

The supreme achievements of Hugo's poetry are scattered through *Les Châtiments*, *Les Contemplations*, and *La Légende des siècles*. In the first series a fever of political and moral indignation makes the poet burningly eloquent, at times somewhat shrill, but it can inspire gems of lyrical beauty, like 'Le Manteau impérial'. A truly epic grandeur appears in evocations such as 'Ô Soldats de l'an deux', and 'L'Expiation'. The *Contemplations* owe their particularly poignant appeal to the grief of an intimate tragedy. Under the stress of this purifying emotion the last shreds of rhetoric vanish, and the cry of the suffering soul approximates to the *poésie pure* that was to become the motto of a later age ('A Villequier'). At a time when Hugo was already engaged upon the mystic quest and thrilling experiences that henceforth filled his inmost mental life, nothing can be truer than the humility of these words to God, from a heart crushed by the loss of a beloved daughter:

Ô Dieu! Vraiment as-tu pu croire
Que je préférais, sous les cieux,
L'effrayant rayon de ta gloire
Aux douces lueurs de ses yeux?

Si j'avais su tes lois moroses,
Et qu'au même esprit enchanté
Tu ne donnes point ces deux choses,
Le bonheur et la vérité,

Plutôt que de lever tes voiles,
Et de chercher, cœur triste et pur,
A te voir au fond des étoiles,
Ô Dieu sombre d'un monde obscur,

J'eusse aimé mieux, loin de ta face,
Suivre, heureux, ùn étroit chemin,
Et n'être qu'un homme qui passe
Tenant son enfant par la main.

At the same time, the free lyricism of the *Contemplations* gives full play to a cast of imagination that for choice calls up strange, anguished visions:

Et je reste parfois couché sans me lever
    Sur l'herbe rase de la dune,
Jusqu'à l'heure où l'on voit apparaître et rêver
    Les yeux sinistres de la lune . . .

('Paroles sur la dune')

Le crépuscule étend sur les longs sillons gris
Ses ailes de fantôme et de chauve-souris . . .

('Pasteurs et troupeaux')

But it is the *Légende des siècles* that has left the deepest and most permanent imprint on the reading public of France; while in epic breadth of conception it ranks with the great poems of the world. The humanitarian and optimistic faith to which Hugo's mind, in spite of public or private disasters, ·obstinately clung, fuses into a coherent whole disconnected themes, historical, legendary, or symbolic. Heroic figures and tragic episodes are evoked with wonderfully suggestive force, and ages of civilization live again. 'La Conscience' is one of the best-known examples of those cyclopean frescoes; but an idyllic relief to their sombre sublimity is provided by poems such as 'Booz endormi'. Occasionally the visionary and the dreamer are too much in evidence; the spacious canvas gets a little confused, and vigour and eloquence succumb to declamation. Much of the best and some of the worst of Hugo's output are here side by side.

The *Quatre vents de l'esprit*, and the posthumous publications: *Toute la lyre, La fin de Satan, Dieu*, &c., which in many cases date from the middle period, are no less unequal. The poet's qualities of

facile, forceful expression are hardly ever in abeyance, and his inexhaustible genius surprises us again and again with admirable fragments; but his critical faculty has too often remained dormant.
Wordiness creeps in under cover of unguarded enthusiasm. Pieces
of two very different kinds still arrest us: short lyrics of old age, intensely moving in their simplicity and resignation; or the triumphs
of a seer who grasps the absolute fearlessly, and can find ready images
for the deepest spiritual convictions. To Hugo the personification of
Evil will finally be conquered by the unquenchable compassion of
human love; and the revelation of the divine will lie in man's
exalted consciousness of being at one with the underlying purpose
of the universe. This faith is not dogmatically uttered; it shows itself
wise enough to bow before the mystery that only death may solve:

> Veux-tu dans la lumière inconcevable et pure
> Ouvrir tes yeux, par l'ombre affreuse appesantis?
> Le veux-tu? Réponds.
>   Oui, criai-je.
>   Et je sentis
> Que la création tremblait comme une toile;
> Alors, levant un bras, et d'un pan de son voile
> Couvrant tous les objets terrestres disparus,
> Il me toucha le front du doigt, et je mourus.
>
>   (*Dieu*)

If, in spite of so many inequalities, and superficial failings of temperament, that some fastidious readers cannot forgive, Victor Hugo
is very generally regarded by the French as their supreme singer, he
owes it to the force of his imagination, his power of pathos, and the
magnetism of his vision; to his incantation, and his command over
all the resources of language and music; to the width of his scope,
and the variety of his rhythms. He owes it, further, to the humanity
of his genius, that encompassed and made his own all the joys and
the drama of life, and to the courage of his thought, that faced the
inscrutable and, a direr necessity, the commonplace, in order that he
might not fail in his high conception of the poet's task. His art has
faults, but at his best he is above art. Whatever foreign critics may
like or dislike in him, it must be admitted that he gives the lie
decisively to the charge of a limited range, still often upheld against
the poetry of France.

The preface of his unperformed play, *Cromwell*, 1827, more finally than the prefaces of the *Odes*, made Hugo the leader in principle of the new school. The scope of this manifesto is broad and ambitious. Civilization has known three ages; lyric poetry corresponded to the first, the epic to the second; drama is called for by the third, in which the conflict of good and evil, stressed by Christianity, is predominant. Modern drama must be such as to include tragedy and comedy, the beautiful and the grotesque, in one synthesis. It must not be bound by the so-called unities of place and time, but need accept only that of action. Verse should still be its medium; but the French alexandrine, in order to cope with such heterogeneous matter, must be free in its structure and movement. The language must not submit to the conventions that impoverished eighteenth-century diction. Shakespeare, of course, is the supreme example of this modern dramatic type.

This compound of arbitrary and sound views was illustrated by a series of plays that were successful, in the teeth of stubborn opposition, until the loud failure of *Les Burgraves*, 1845, ended Hugo's career as a dramatist. In spite of striking beauties, and the royal gift of imagination, only two of them have been added to the permanent repertory of the French stage. These exceptions are *Hernani*, the fire and the glamour of which still fascinate the most sophisticated audience, and *Ruy Blas*, a picturesque and remarkably accurate picture of seventeenth-century Spain, with a fourth act of excellent bravura and humour. The other plays, though quite as good in parts, are less successful in concealing their secret hollowness; they are the products of a brilliant creative force, which can animate moving episodes, strong contrasts, telling antitheses, but which cannot endow the forcible outlines of men and women with the solidity of three-dimensional characters. Their intense lyricism saves them from mediocrity and at the same time seals their doom as genuine dramas. Their language has a fiery energy which destroys the very passion it expresses. Still, they are at the least well worth reading.

Hugo the novelist fares rather better than the playwright. The broad canvas on which he works lends itself pliantly to the exuberance of invention; the accumulation of detail gives substance to the chief characters. The imaginative force of the narrative triumphs over the resistance of even the coolest minds. His novels have a purpose: historical, moral, social, or all at once. Their insistent, vibrating style, and the frequent intrusion of the author's reflexions and digressions may awaken a sense of strain; but they have kept their hold on others than schoolboys; and the grotesque, swarming, medieval crowds surging round the huge cathedral (*Notre-Dame de Paris*), the symbolic fight of man with the fury and the wiles of the sea (*Les Travailleurs de la mer*), the epic allegories of vice, suffering, and regeneration in the background of modern society, of its cruelty and indifference (*Les Misérables*), have an appeal that secures for them a place among the French books that live.

4. MUSSET[1]

Twenty years younger than Lamartine, thirteen than Vigny, eight than Hugo, Alfred de Musset might have seemed destined to be the arch-romantic; he was brought up in the atmosphere of the new literature, imbibed its influences, French or foreign; he had no need to open a path, the road lay clear before him. Perhaps for that very reason he felt no attachment for a fashion he sincerely shared at first, but for which he had not had to fight. After making the most of its resources, and adapting to its trends such of his inborn tendencies as did not clash, he dropped all show of allegiance, and followed the bent of his own genius.

His first poems are an interesting medley, in which two very distinctly different elements are closely associated. On the one hand,

---

[1] Alfred de Musset, born in Paris, 1810, of well-to-do parents, was a brilliant student, turned early to poetry, and frequented Nodier's and Hugo's circles. He published a translation of de Quincey's *Opium Eater*, 1828; *Contes d'Espagne et d'Italie* in verse, 1830; *Spectacles dans un fauteuil*, 1832 (*La Coupe et les lèvres*, 'poème dramatique'; *A quoi rêvent les jeunes filles*, 'comédie', &c.); *Rolla*, a poem, 1833. Having failed on the stage with *La Nuit vénitienne*, he wrote dramas and comedies intended solely for reading but which were eventually almost all performed (*Fantasio*, *Les Caprices de Marianne*, *André del Sarto*, 1833; *Lorenzaccio*, 1834; *On ne badine pas avec l'amour*, 1834; *Barberine*, 1835; *Il ne faut jurer de rien*, 1836, &c.). From the end of 1833 to 1835 he had a stormy love-affair with George Sand, breaking with her at Venice, before a final estrangement in Paris; the direct echo of these events is heard in a prose novel, *La Confession d'un enfant du siècle*, 1836, and in poems of a new inspiration (among them *Les Nuits*, written 1835–7), later collected in *Poésies nouvelles*, 1852. The *Lettres de Dupuis et Cotonet*, 1836–7, marked an open breach with the romantics. His last period was filled with writings of various kinds, the prose *Nouvelles* being collected in 1840, and the *Contes* in 1854. He died in 1857.

the tales told in the *Contes d'Espagne et d'Italie* flaunt a romanticism
of the fancy, a matter of whims, insolences, and cruel realism, and
brilliantly handled, with some fastidious scorn of syntax, by a gifted
young poet. Stories of love, jealousy, revenge, and death—all in
southern settings—are narrated with a cool, witty, rather cynical
composure. The spirit of Byron is constantly present in the background, though Musset will not confess to it; frequent allusions are
made to things English, and Shakespeare is quoted again and again.
The verse moves jauntily, often running on from line to line. At
moments of deeper emotion, the manner changes to a heart-felt
eloquence, the language soars, and the rhythm swells into the sweeping movement of full, vigorous lines that call up the best tradition
of poetic dignity and force. This impression of a latent classicism is
borne out by the shorter pieces, and here the other aspect of the
poet's temperament is conspicuous. They are in excellent drawing-
room verse, madrigals, epistles, love lyrics that match any effort of
the masters of *petits vers*, and they are supremely elegant, sensuous,
caressing, or biting; and except for the new-fangled dandyism, and
a vein of almost boyish humour, all might be taken from an anthology of the two previous centuries.

Musset was to remain witty to the end of his life; but wit falls to
second place when the new note is heard. 'Ah, frappe-toi le cœur,
c'est là qu'est le génie', he had already written to a friend; and his
greatest poetry grew from bitter experiences, of which his unfortunate passion for George Sand was the main but not the only occasion. Even before that crisis, he had given the revolt of a sensitive
soul against a life of pleasure a striking expression in his strange
drama, *La Coupe et les lèvres*. This is sincere romanticism, though
influences and echoes from Byron, Shakespeare, and Goethe jostle
in the highly imaginative treatment of the symbolic plot, to which
it is undeniable that the author's inmost self has contributed. The
hero voices the indictment brought by all his fellow sufferers from
the *mal du siècle* against a world out of joint, and the ghost of his
past errors kills the happiness to which his purified self was trying
desperately to rise. The burden of conflicting, half-articulate thought
breaks down the structural instinct of an art born for logic and
balance; but all through the confused play there are vivid moments
of moving eloquence and beautiful poetry. This was the purge of

Musset's genius; from the baptism of actual suffering he emerged, shortly afterwards, in quieter possession of his mature powers both of pathos and of charm. The romantic ardour sends up one more glow in the historical drama, *Lorenzaccio*, the nearest approach to a successful French play on the Shakespearean model. It is a vivid, realistic picture of Florence under the Medici; a searching study of a complex character, tied to a self-imposed duty of heroism, bringing dishonour upon himself in the means chosen to fulfil it, and reaping from his sacrifice the bitter confirmation of his pessimistic view of man; here, again, something of Musset's most intimate experience has been incorporated.

These avowals are even plainer in the *Confession d'un enfant du siècle*, which is one more tragedy of two fond hearts and of the madness that mixes with impassioned love, and destroys it. As a study of the romantic imbalance characteristic of the opening years of the nineteenth century, and here traced to the spiritual shock of Revolution, and to the loss of faith, it tends to have a wider significance; but this is narrowed by the stress laid on the personal story. This itself is told movingly, though with some excess of declamation.

The distilled essence of Musset's full knowledge of the best and worst of life forms the rich substance of his finest lyrics, which a kind of serenity in suffering raises to an exalted beauty. The classical dignity fused in the *Nuits*, in the *Lettre à Lamartine*, the *Ode à la Malibran*, parts of *Rolla*, or the *Espoir en Dieu*, with the deepest thrills of romantic intensity, is the synthetic triumph that French poets had been seeking instinctively from the earliest time of classicism, and which had been reached only in rare moments of perfect consummation, such as Racine's and Corneille's best passages.

Even more striking are an inspiration, strong, nervous, eager, and yet poised and elegant; a brilliant ardour controlled by faultless tact; ample periods that take no thought of their structure yet chance infallibly on the right balance and on appropriate words and images; a music that is no more than the vestment of emotion, securing the beauty of flawless rhythms and rhymes. More than either Lamartine or Hugo, for all that he is no greater poet, Musset has these patches of truly noble eloquence.

After the unmerited failure of his first attempt at drama, *La Nuit vénitienne*, Musset wrote plays only for readers. By degrees, both before and after his death, his dramatic works found their way to the footlights, and now, whether read or acted, their distinguished place is no longer in doubt. They are essentially original, though their features and charm invite comparison in some measure with Shakespeare's and Marivaux's comedies, with the poetical fancy of the former, and the fine, delicate psychology of the latter. Signs of haste and uneven treatment keep them within the class of incomplete, second-rate masterpieces. Their light, dexterous touch, their witty, springy, youthful dialogue, are free from the heavy tradition of classical comedy; Beaumarchais's style was equally sparkling, but his invention did not show such poetry, or such profound understanding of the feminine character. The range of these plays is wide. *André del Sarto* is a drama of subdued, concentrated pathos, not unworthy of being compared with Browning's searching monologue. *A quoi rêvent les jeunes filles* is a delightful *jeu d'esprit* about young girls who fall in love and whose wise, indulgent father reminds us of Prospero. *Les Caprices de Marianne*, with the same brilliance, raises more serious problems, suggestively sketched. *On ne badine pas avec l'amour*, in spite of some farcical scenes, tends to the dramatic treatment of weighty issues, but stops short of welding incongruous elements into a rounded whole. *Le Chandelier* is cleverly managed, and appeals to tenderness as well as to the sense of fun. Nearly all Musset's plays contain an echo, which can be more or less clearly caught, of his meditation upon his own varied experience of life.

5. OTHER POETS

Among such minor poets of the age as have left more than a name, a few kept their allegiance practically unchanged to the old ideal of verse writing.

Viennet, 1779–1868, owes his survival, paradoxically, to his long, courageous battle against overwhelming odds. For half a century he insisted on the integrity of classical principles, and wrote historical epics, which few read, and still fewer liked: he is a useful pointer to the decisive victory of romantic taste. Auguste Barbier, 1805–82, again, had a gift for forcible political satire, and the vigorous rhythm of his short stanza—an alexandrine and an eight-syllable line, a metric combination imitated from Chénier—is well suited to convey his scathing ironies and indictments (*Iambes*, 1831; *Il Pianto*, 1833). A perfectly definite form, a nervous eloquence, a language polished and hard as steel, in spite of occasional awkwardnesses, answered the general mood of reaction, moral and physical, and of nervous exhaustion, from which a vast number of French people was suffering after the tension of the July Revolution (1830). The underlying emotion was so strong and so sincere that the soul of classical poetry was revitalized; but this one brilliant reversal of the course of literature must remain an exception. *Lazare*, 1837, describes the dark fate of the English miners and factory labourers, before the conscience of the nation rose and cleansed her soil of the worst evils. Pierre-Jean de Béranger, 1780–1857, counted for more than a generation as a great poet, and his popularity was almost unrivalled. He owed these rewards, that we must think excessive, to persistent affinities between the traditional French temper and qualities that he very distinctly possessed, but which are not in themselves poetical: neatness, light and deft phrasing, easy, short, well-marked rhythm. Béranger's chansons have humour and a touch of sentiment; they appeal discreetly to national emotions; sometimes they even reach imaginative impressiveness: all this was enough in their hours of relaxation, for readers who could enjoy romantic effects, but did not yet actually demand them.

Far more numerous were the poets inspired by Rousseau, by English and German poets, and by the early work of Lamartine and Hugo. Their number and quality safely establish the proposition that French poetry by that time, however erratic its course might have been in the past, was commonly attuned to the emotional tone of literature. Brizeux, 1806–56, for instance, is a most sincere representative of the 'regionalist' school that was the offshoot of the romantic revival. He was a native of Brittany, steeped in the austere beauty of a land of granite and oaks where the simplicity of life, through a naïve Christianity, preserves so many traditions of a pagan past. He felt her soul threatened by modern civilization, and clinging passionately to the memories of his childhood he distilled his love and his grief into the idylls of his best book, *Marie*, 1836. The writer's touch is not quite safe, the form is sometimes less pure than the inspiration it reflects; but many episodes are delineated with unfailing truth, and a gentle pathos that endears them to French readers.

Marceline Desbordes-Valmore, 1786–1859, had an untutored gift
for the free, harmonious expression of feeling; her *Élégies*, *Romances*,
&c., published from 1820, owe nothing to Lamartine, whose fluidity
she equalled, without his nervous strength. Her poems grew in concentration and reserve; some, among the last, are worthy of the high
reputation that such good judges as Sainte-Beuve thought she deserved. Sainte-Beuve, 1804–69, was himself an original poet, who
managed his talent more cleverly (*Joseph Delorme*, 1829; *Consolations*,
1830; *Pensées d'août*, 1837; *Livre d'amour*, 1843, &c.). He had all that
Marceline Desbordes-Valmore lacked: keen literary consciousness,
self-criticism, ingenuity. As his inspiration was slight, he husbanded
it in short poems whose merit lay in their careful realism and
an emotion that was left implicit. The label *intimiste*, later attached
to this manner, calls up a vein of homely truth akin to that of Cow-
per and Wordsworth, whom he knew. In his best moments he has
accents of a deep poignancy; but on an average his art is only tentative, and imperfect. Victor de Laprade, 1812–83, in his *Psyché*, 1841,
Poèmes évangéliques, 1852, &c., added features of his own to the common romantic stock; and his dignity, soberness, and taste for broad,
imaginative, and philosophical themes make him a precursor of the
Parnassiens.

Romanticism is not a school, but a lasting attitude of the modern
mind; while the period of its ascendancy, in a narrow sense, may be
assigned the approximate limit of 1850, it survived in a wider sense,
presiding over the fluctuations of literary taste to the end of the century—and beyond. Two romantics of the first generation were
definitely harbingers of the next, looking forward to a still more
distant future. Maurice de Guérin, 1810–39, died before his rich
promise could be fulfilled. He was of a profoundly religious nature,
a devout Christian, and at the same time a pantheist, intensely and
delicately in sympathy with the life of the elements. His *Journal* and
Lettres, are the records of a charming, unselfish personality, with a
strain of heroism. His impressions of nature are almost as finely
accurate as those of Dorothy Wordsworth; but they show a stronger
grasp of their object, being a philosopher's as well as a poet's. His
idealistic sense of language ignored the barrier convention had
erected between the rhythm of inspired prose and that of poetry;
his few regular poems are musical, fresh, and tender; but even more

original and striking are the two prose fragments, *Le Centaure* and *La Bacchante*, in which a sure divination is active, re-creating the mystery of early Greek art, and conveying it by means of the suggestive melody of words. The technique of the symbolists is here anticipated.

More outstanding is the importance of Gérard de Nerval, 1808–55, a wonderfully gifted dreamer, who put an untimely end to his erratic, unsettled life. Of his work, both verse and prose, a good deal is hastily written, and second-rate; the rest deserves to be treasured among the prophetic books of the century. Some of his poems, above all the series of sonnets called *Les Chimères*, unerringly enclose the very essence of the allusive technique that symbolism was to extract from the overt art of the romantics. Ideas merge into 'images', to which the subtle music of the lines lends overtones; and the whole wealth of dim significance has none the less a compactness that remains true to the classical ideal. In the opening lines of *El Desdichado*, the sense of fatality is all the more powerful for their mysteriousness:

> Je suis le ténébreux — le veuf — l'inconsolé,
> Le prince d'Aquitaine à la tour abolie:
> Ma seule étoile est morte, — et mon luth constellé
> Porte le soleil noir de la Mélancolie. . . .

Baudelaire himself wrote nothing more superbly marble-like than *Vers dorés*:

> Souvent dans l'être obscur habite un dieu caché;
> Et, comme un œil naissant couvert par ses paupières,
> Un pur esprit s'accroît sous l'écorce des pierres.

The prose stories, *Les Filles du feu*, are medleys of sentiment, humour, and fancy all bathed in the soft light of that land of blue horizons and lovely memories, the 'Île de France'. The charmingly written *Sylvie* is a gem of tender, rustic realism and the wistful poetry of the might-have-been. Nerval's rare union of talents was unjustly eclipsed for two generations, but it has at last emerged to the fond admiration of French readers.

CHAPTER XLVI

Drama

IN a short outline such as the present, a brief mention should be sufficient for the drama of the romantic age. New plays were constantly performed, and reputations made, but from the point of view of aesthetics, the conditions of the stage were not such as to favour innovation, while the public of the early nineteenth century, for the most part, clung to traditional habits and standards. As a result, tragedies, comedies, and *mélodrames* continued to be written on the old pattern, or with the most timid adaptation to recent initiatives. Of the abundant output, hardly anything has survived outside the records of historians. We find it difficult to realize how successful Michel Pichat, 1790–1828, Frédéric Soulié, 1800–47, and similar playwrights were in their time. From that generation the name of Eugène Scribe, 1791–1861, has been preserved as the very symbol of an artifice that mistook itself for art and was widely accepted as such. Scribe staked everything on his skilfully constructed plots, and won repeated triumphs. His influence for long bolstered up the declining prestige of a purely formal ideal; and to the young bloods who had fought at the first night of *Hernani*, he was the very type of the glorified Philistine. A somewhat similar significance attaches to François Ponsard, 1814–67, whose *Lucrèce*, 1843, was hailed as a masterpiece by the many theatre-goers who had long objected silently to the strained intensity of Hugo's drama.

Meanwhile the romantics themselves had been writing plays which embodied their conceptions of drama (see Chapter XLV above) with varying success. But even at their best they failed to establish the undisputed and lasting authority they had aimed to win for the new type. Whether the very essence of a romantic mood may not clash with the severe objectivity which is, or purports to be, the law of dramatic creation, is of course in itself an issue, which some contemporary critics were not slow to raise. But however that may be, most of the important romantic poets were also noteworthy for their experiments in the field of drama. Vigny, Hugo, Musset, and shortly before them, Casimir Delavigne, were playwrights as well as poets, but their dramatic works had not quite enough autonomy, solidity, and substance to constitute a self-contained literary development: they are appendages to their poetry, instinct with the same spirit, expressing the same temperament; it is not as dramas, in the purely technical sense, that they possess their chief interest and they do not therefore require separate study. Musset's creation of a French Shakespearian comedy (see above) is alone an exception, deserving very special credit. The plays of Alexandre Dumas père (*Henri III et sa cour*, 1829; *La Tour de Nesle*, 1832) are, like his novels, lively shoots from the main trunk of romanticism, equally skilful and ingenious, and no more profound.

CHAPTER XLVII

The Novel

THE new spirit in literature was a powerful stimulus to the creative imagination generally, and perhaps even more to the writing of fiction, but some inner necessity of the period demanded also that one of the chief factors of interest in any fictitious image of life should be its resemblance to the truth. And so it happens that an important element of realism in the novel dates from a period which at first sight would appear to be hostile to any such tendency. In fact, the more important novelists of the time show an unlimited diversity of tempers and talents. Some are poets, passing naturally from lyrical self-expression to more or less impersonal narratives in prose. The novels of Lamartine, Vigny, Hugo, and Musset have already been mentioned. Other novelists, among them Stendhal and Balzac, the most eminent of the group, make their romanticism one element in a very different whole; they are testimony to the fact that at the very core of the era of fervour the next era is already taking shape, in which the supreme aim of art will be the study of reality.

I. STENDHAL

The prime importance of Stendhal's[1] work was not fully appreciated till the end of the nineteenth century, but any lessening of his reputation is unlikely now. The main features of his personality are original. He shared most of the literary views of the romantics, felt

[1] Henri Beyle, in literature Stendhal, born at Grenoble, 1783, studied mathematics, took some part in the French expeditions to Italy, central Europe, and Russia, lived for seven years at Milan, then in Paris, was appointed consul at Trieste, then at Cività-Vecchia. He died in 1842. His literary activities, mostly unsuccessful, include the various essays, criticism, and travel literature: *Rome, Naples, et Florence*, and *Histoire de la peinture en Italie*, 1817; *Essai sur l'amour*, and *Racine et Shakespeare*, 1822; *Promenades dans Rome*, 1829; *Mémoires d'un touriste*, 1838; and the novels: *Armance*, 1827; *Le Rouge et le noir*, 1831; *La Chartreuse de Parme*, 1839. A number of posthumously published works include his *Journal*, 1888; *Vie d'Henri Brulard*, 1890; *Souvenirs d'égotisme*, 1893; *Lucien Leuwen* (a novel), 1894, &c.

no respect for the Académie, laughed at passive tradition, sharply criticized the classics, Racine included, whose prestige he traced to the mere conservatism of taste; his pamphlet, *Racine et Shakespeare*, not only extols the free creativeness of the one in contrast with the regularity of the other: he also denounces the very idea of a permanently settled type of art. What is romanticism, he asks, but the insistence that modern readers shall be given what pleases them; what is classicism, but the obstinate effort to offer them what pleased their great-grandfathers? His continual stress was on the demands of the present, but at the same time he refused to be bound by any orthodoxy, even a revolutionary one; fierce independence was the breath of his nostrils; and his instinctive mood is very far from the enthusiasm of the romantics. He reveals himself in his likes and dislikes, of which he makes no mystery, as a spiritual heir of the age of Enlightenment; dry, critical, rather cynical, and without any doubt supremely intelligent. He is full of Voltaire, far more than of Rousseau; and his novels are indebted to *Candide*. But his sense of social wrong is quickened and sharpened by the Revolution, and what followed; his ironical criticism of the France of 1820, clinging to the shadow of the old order, of the world of official faith and traditional rites in which Chateaubriand lived, of the new bid the ruling classes were making for power, is far more searching and concrete than that of the *philosophes*; more bitterly even than Rousseau, he is the talented outsider with a grudge against society. So what he says is clear-cut, with no hint of the vague or evocative, even in his sketches of natural scenery. Intellectually he bestrides his period: his roots are in the eighteenth century, and he reaches forward to the restored rationalism, the scientific and positive spirit of the mid-nineteenth.

In his work he appears to us first as a critic of manners and the arts. He stands wholly for frank, intelligible values and will allow of no make-believe, in conduct or style. Rhetoric and verbiage are unpardonable; the briefer the utterance, the better. His ideal is that of the Italian Renaissance, when energy ran riot, in good or evil, and great passions engendered high deeds. The carefree life of the Italian cities is still to him a joy and a source of longing. He views the French character, its strong and weak points, with the detachment of the cosmopolitan. He has something of Voltaire's pungency, but without his light, flashing touch. In his lucid analysis, *De l'amour*, he proposes the image of 'cristallisation' for the changes wrought by incipient love in the lover's very perception. The phrase is useful, but the book as a whole misses the finer shades of such a theme. Of painting, architecture, music, he spoke often with gusto, even with warmth, and not without freshness and acumen; yet his taste could be erratic and perverse. His impressions of travel abroad or in France have a piquant interest, and contributed to educate the curiosity of the cultivated public. He was never a popular writer, but his initiatives, though not his freaks, left some trace on the mind of his age.

His novels were the real cause of his influence, not upon his own age, but the next. *Le Rouge et le noir* is in several respects a great book, though not quite a masterpiece: too long, unequal, dry, its technique elementary, its art careful, but rarely inspired. From the supremacy of Napoleon, and the soldier's red-coated prestige, France, we are shown, has entered years when the ascendancy shifts back to the black garb of the priest. On which colour will the hero's calculating ambition stake his future? The theme has breadth, and allows of a satirical survey of society. Julien Sorel's cult of energy leads him from the army to the Church, to worldly triumphs, and finally to a murder, which he pays for with his head. Meanwhile he has seduced two women, whom he tortures pitilessly. This outline does scant justice to the relative humanity of a rank egotist, who could find some excuse for his actions in the hardness of his early fate. Stendhal's psychology is clear, disillusioned, and penetrating, except that he makes insufficient allowance for our illogicalities. One of the women is a credible and moving figure, the other a self-willed, haughty person. There is pungent irony and graphic truth in not a few scenes and characters. After this book *La Chartreuse de Parme*, as often happens, is more mellow, and altogether less vigorous. One justly famous episode is the chaotic account of Waterloo, as seen by the eyes of the hero. The rest—the picture of the intrigues at a small Italian court—has thrilling chapters, but moves slowly.

The first critic to discover Stendhal's genius was no less a writer than Balzac: he praised the *Chartreuse* glowingly; did it not largely answer his own idea of the novel? The temper of realism was there in fact, plainly enough; and, no less, the display of imagination. The complicated plot, the unceasing adventure, remind us of the old picaresque story. These appendages of an art that at bottom was bound by the trammels of the past, were easily forgotten or forgiven. When Stendhal's example bore fruit, in the discipleship of his spiritual successors—Taine, Bourget, Gide—this was due fundamentally to his determined intellectual honesty and his respect for truth. His work, with us, does not pander to susceptible sensibilities, or uncompromising artists: his faults of construction and style are patent. But his books are still at the present day nourishing food for the mind, with an influence upon each succeeding generation of writers.

2. BALZAC[1]

The imposing mass of Balzac's output belongs to the latter half of the romantic period, and is still distinctly typical of this, despite the fact that it already reveals the main features of the succeeding age. It has survived changes of taste, and the criticism of four generations, and may surely now be considered an imperishable picture of the world which surrounded the author, as he intended it should be, as well as a monument to a labourer's single-minded devotion to his task. He was a vigorous but incomplete artist, unaware of the full extent of his problem; style, upon which he lavished incredible care, was to him only a matter of continual labour and revision; and at times the manner in which the *Comédie humaine* is written is its weakest point. It has the virtues of its faults: deliberateness, abundance, a technical wealth and precision, without marked pedantry, and a profusion of concrete descriptive detail that makes the background of every plot full, picturesque, and convincing. But this very thoroughness may at times grow heavy. Our attention is not usually focused on the externals of life to such an extent unless some special moral or poetical significance is in question; while the reason for Balzac's

[1] Honoré de Balzac, born at Tours, 1799, studied at Vendôme and in Paris, set up a printing business, and from 1829 laboured at literary composition, with short intervals of travelling. His books were soon successful, but the burden of debts, of ever renewed and unfortunate schemes to pay them, made his life a ceaseless struggle. He died in 1850. Some chief items in his series of novels, *La Comédie humaine*, would be *La Peau de chagrin*, 1831; *Louis Lambert, Le Colonel Chabert, Le Curé de Tours*, 1832; *Eugénie Grandet*, 1833; *Le Père Goriot, La Recherche de l'absolu*, 1834; *César Birotteau*, 1837; *Les Paysans*, 1845; *La Cousine Bette, Le Cousin Pons*, 1847, &c.

meticulousness is seldom anything but an over-conscientious sense of duty to the object described. Worse still are his occasional over-emphatic phrases and somewhat trite images. But these are trifles which slip from our minds. We are held fast by the story, and this in its turn is inseparable from the astounding verisimilitude of the background and the characters. Balzac's descriptions and portraits are justly famous. They are as fresh, graphic, and striking as those of Dickens, but they keep more firmly to real life, and allow less play to the imagination. The store of impressions from which these lines, colours and characteristics of things and persons could be drawn in such plenty, for more than twenty years, must have been inexhaustible. The ceaseless exertion of writing can hardly have left time and strength for the study of reality, and the critics are no doubt justified in asserting that Balzac had already assimilated the world when his literary life began. The vast and varied picture presented in these fifty-odd volumes embraces society as a whole, including such rarely studied aspects as the life of the country people, not only those of the castle and the manor-house, but those of the farm, although the city middle classes, trading or professional, are given most prominence. The Paris boarding-house (*Le Père Goriot*), or the priest's home in *Le Curé de Tours*, the characters of Goriot, Chabert, Grandet, or Birotteau are so vivid in the remembrance of French readers that they are used involuntarily as tests and types in our apprenticeship to life. That a dominating passion may lead to pathetic dramas and conflicts no one will doubt who has read *La Cousine Bette* or *La Recherche de l'absolu*. The liveliness and individuality of the character-drawing in no wise resemble the relatively cold, objective method of the scientific novel of the next period; we have here a quiet gusto not far removed from humour, as in the following sketch, an average specimen of its kind, of Mademoiselle de Pen-Hoel, a Breton gentlewoman:

Cette demoiselle était une sèche et mince fille, jaune comme le parchemin, . . . ridée comme un lac froncé par le vent, à yeux gris, à grandes dents saillantes, à mains d'homme, assez petite, un peu déjetée et peut-être bossue; mais personne n'avait été curieux de connaître ni ses perfections ni ses imperfections. Vêtue dans le goût de Mademoiselle du Guénic, elle mouvait une énorme quantité de linges et de jupes, quand elle voulait trouver l'une des deux ouvertures de sa robe par où elle atteignait ses poches. Le plus étrange cliquetis de clefs et de monnaie retentissait alors sous ces étoffes. Elle avait toujours d'un côté toute la ferraille des bonnes ménagères, et de l'autre sa tabatière d'argent, son dé, son tricot, autres ustensiles sonores. Au lieu du béguin matelassé de Mademoiselle du Guénic, elle portait un chapeau vert avec lequel elle devait aller visiter ses melons; il avait passé, comme eux, du vert au blond; et quant à sa forme, après vingt ans, la mode l'a ramenée à Paris sous le nom de 'bibi'. (*Béatrix*)

Humour, indeed, is often an ingredient of Balzac's realism, and tones it down, as is exemplified by *Les Paysans*.

His is genuine unpretentious realism, without the drabness of the professedly realist school. How far his mood still tingles with romanticism, we feel when we dwell on the imaginative and dramatic interest of his plots. The life he sets out to paint is not only the familiar image of small daily happenings; it moves us also by its adventure, romance, and pathos. His art often makes room for the heroic, the thrilling, and the mysterious, in *La Peau de chagrin* and *La Recherche de l'absolu*, for instance; while *Le Père Goriot*, *Pierrette*, or *Le Colonel Chabert* are examples of the moral tragedy that can develop from the most simple happenings.

His psychology, again, is clear-sighted and rather pessimistic. It could also be called subtle, if he would more often consent to take things for granted, and thus spare the fastidious reader's squeamishness. Many of the feelings he probes are simple, yet he comments upon these as fully as if they were rarer or more complex—a straightforward technique gradually abandoned by the more sophisticated writers of the next period. But it would not be correct to call this absence of the corresponding scruple in Balzac a sign of superficiality. His plain, direct statement of what takes place in his heroes' minds and hearts throws a revealing light upon them, and earns him a place in the long line of the French analysts.

But more than this, and for all that the more severe conventions of the modern novel were unknown to him, Balzac remains one of the greatest and most satisfying of French novelists, with a creative range which to this day is unsurpassed.

3. GEORGE SAND

Though her once great fame has declined, George Sand's[1] work is almost certain to endure, for its talents and virtues, even when unfashionable, make a perennial appeal to the imagination and the heart. Its very ease and plenty are its worst weakness; no part of these many volumes shows the finish of perfect writing; on the other hand, hardly any part fails to rouse our interest and pleasure. Too much may be made of the development clearly perceptible as her novels succeed one another. The first are exultingly, at times crudely romantic. _Indiana_ and _Valentine_, make a glowing apology for the independence and initiative of feminine love; the rights of woman are upheld on social and moral, rather than political planes; marriage, as an institution moulded by binding customs, is frankly criticized; thrilling adventure, and somewhat flushed sentiment, are lavishly and recklessly added. The second group, which would include _Mauprat_ and _Le Meunier d'Angibault_, is more directly revolutionary in theme, laying stress on manifold aspects and consequences of an inequality that corrupts the health of the community and destroys the happiness of the individual, and denouncing orthodox religion as too often in league with selfish evil. Lastly, such rustic idylls as _La Mare au diable_ and _François le champi_ are content with a quieter atmosphere, and so win the preference of many readers.

In fact, all these various trends are more or less present from the beginning, and the ·writer's whole. output bears the stamp of one creative temperament. The temperament is exuberant, even irritating at times; nevertheless it silences all but the most bigoted criticism and arouses a sympathy for the woman behind it which is not easily destroyed. There is in George Sand generosity, and nobility

---

[1] Aurore Dupin, born in Paris, 1804, spent her childhood at Nohant, in Berry, married baron Dudevant in 1822 and parted from him by mutual agreement in 1830. She lived in Paris, writing novels, and collaborated for a while with Jules Sandeau, whence her _nom de plume_ of George Sand. _Indiana_, 1831, made her famous, and then came _Valentine_, 1832, _Lélia_, 1833, _Jacques_, 1834, _Mauprat_, 1837. She shared A. de Musset's life in 1833–5. After this, under other influences (Lamennais, Pierre Leroux, &c.), she wrote socialist novels: _Consuelo_, 1843; _Le Meunier d'Angibault_, 1845, &c., followed by tales of country life: _La Mare au diable_, 1846; _La Petite Fadette_, 1849; _François le champi_, 1850, &c. Her last years, spent at Nohant, were given to more detached fiction: _Le Marquis de Villemer_, 1861, &c. She died in 1876. Her autobiography (_Histoire de ma vie_) came out in 1854–5.

of purpose, as well as a slight streak of sentimentality which leaves her pathos unimpaired. Her imaginative grasp of incident and scene is sustained; her tales have human substance; she can describe landscapes or more immediate environment in lively or impressive fashion. Her eager idealism, kept up till the end, is gradually relieved by the vein of instinctive realism, not unmixed with humour, that gives her work its most distinct claim to originality. Her profusion of archaic phrases and provincial idiom, in *François le champi*, for instance, is a little artificial; but the charm and the truth of her country stories are altogether superior to the brutality of most of the heavily documented 'naturalism' that tried later to improve on her sober, finely pencilled sketches. Her fluent, abundant style is often accused of laxity; yet its animation and piquancy can fix and hold the attention; at times, even, it becomes condensed into passages of genuine force. Several of her characters are no more than the conventional types of fiction, but she also created not a few unforgettable figures, especially women. Her lucid yet not pitiless account of her imprudent passion for the attractive and morbid Musset and of her cruel experiences (*Elle et lui*) shows far from despicable gifts of psychological analysis; though these are exercised without the pretentions of modern psychological fiction. Finally, no one can question George Sand's right to a place among the gifted tellers of tales who turns, for instance, to her late, unpretending novel, *Le Marquis de Villemer*.

4. OTHER NOVELISTS

The story-teller's gift is the main reason for the continuing popularity with young (and many older) people, of Alexandre Dumas *père* (1803–70; *Les Trois mousquetaires*, 1844; *Vingt ans après*, 1845, &c.); and uncritical readers will not cavil at the writer's happy knack of making history serve the turn of romance. Moreover, these old favourites have many positive merits, such as fertile invention, liveliness, a measure of rough justice to characters taken from real life; the cleverly caught atmosphere of stirring times; and, lastly, a fund of good humour that notwithstanding the melodramatic episodes prevents the wild plot from being taken too seriously. This is, after all, the manner of Walter Scott, handled by a not unworthy follower.

At a time when newspapers of the modern type were being

launched Eugène Sue, 1804–59, contributed with Alexandre Dumas to start the vogue of the *feuilletons*, or novels published by instalments, and usually detachable from the main sheet, in the daily papers. Sue's 'popular' stories: *Les Mystères de Paris*, 1843; *Le Juif errant*, 1844–5; *Les Sept Péchés capitaux*, 1847–9; *Les Mystères du peuple*, 1849–57, are somewhat crude, and stand very near the borderline of literature; but they deserve mention because of their vigour and the vivid depiction of the Parisian underworld. In his humanitarian feeling and powerful drama, this author is not unlike a coarser Dickens.

With Jules Sandeau, 1811–83, the later romantic novel is perceptibly moving towards realism. By degrees more serious claims are urged, where once the emphasis had lain wholly on eager or rebellious passion. *Catherine*, 1845, begins as an insipid, rather conventionally written tale of rustic love, but ends on an unexpected note of common sense, courage, and resignation to duty.

Sainte-Beuve the poet has been mentioned, and his importance as a critic will be discussed later. His novel, *Volupté*, 1834, is distinguished, and original, but tentative, and remains an exceptional near-masterpiece. The subject is treated with extreme care and intuitive delicacy, but in the light of modern psychology its development seems a little wordy and off the point. The genuinely impressionistic style has much poetic charm, in spite of awkward phrases and passages that jar.

Mérimée's[1] personality is many-sided. His earlier writings were fundamentally romantic, and it is with the romantics that he must be considered. But, like Gautier, he soon grew to be a precursor of the next period, to which his mature years fully belonged. He shared the romantic love of intensity, which indeed with him often turned

[1] Prosper Mérimée, born in Paris, 1803, the son of an artist, was himself a man of wide culture. His first publications were two literary hoaxes: *Théâtre de Clara Gazul*, 1825, and *La Guzla*, 1827. They were followed by chapters with an historical background: *La Jacquerie*, 1828, *Chronique du règne de Charles IX*, 1829, and a series of short stories, culminating in *Colomba*, 1841 and *Carmen*, 1845. He was appointed inspector of historical monuments in 1841, and did much in his reports and special studies to revive an interest in old French architecture and religious painting. His historical works include *La Guerre sociale*, 1841; *La Conjuration de Catilina*, *Les Cosaques d'autrefois*, &c. He also translated several Russian novels. During his later years he was closely connected with the court of Napoléon III. The *Lettres à une inconnue*, *Lettres à une autre inconnue*, and his *Correspondance inédite*, &c., were published after his death, 1870.

to violence; but he invariably clothed his highly coloured themes, and his vivid pictures of persons and situations, in the quiet garb of sober art. His self-possessed, slightly sardonic attitude was apparent at the outset in his first successes, faked translations from fictitious Spanish plays and Illyrian poems. In his historical novel, the *Chronique du règne de Charles IX*, though not yet fully master of his talent, he revealed a brief, dramatic, and objective technique that had more to do with the grim power of realism than with the facile impressiveness of romantic effects. Realism, indeed, is an almost constant feature of his writing, but even when this was the result of deliberate effort it implied no departure from the literary ideal then prevailing. Where he did contradict this ideal and thus ally himself more closely with an opposed aesthetic was in his actual conception of the writer's craft. With him, everything so clearly serves an end of precision, balance, and measure that a reviving classicism may be felt exerting its sway. Thus, once again, we find writers of the generation that followed 1830 recoiling instinctively from the excesses of the romantic mood, and, apparently in obedience to some compensatory urge, searching for a synthesis.

Apart from his remarkable essays in history, archaeology, and art criticism, Mérimée is above all a writer of short stories, and one of the supreme representatives of the art. He did not exhaust the possibilities of the genre, though the effects he made it yield are so well within its compass that one is tempted to think they embody its very essence. But the art of the short story is supple, lending itself to various forms of treatment, and other writers have practised it with results that are equally fascinating without being less natural. The *nouvelles* of Mérimée are triumphs of concentration, point, and impassibility. His absolute refusal to give any sign that he shared the emotion he wishes to excite enhances what one may call the realism of his subjects, most of which are not only dramatic, but involve some cruelty (*Matteo Falcone, Tamango, Carmen*, &c.). He can condescend to a thriller, such as *La Vénus d'Ille*, one of his finest achievements; and play upon the chords of the supernatural, as in *La Vision de Charles IX*, but there is a grim and slightly bitter humour about this severely restrained technique when applied to what is odd or absurd in life. The economy of the narrative, its directness, its simplicity, and the unfailing brevity of the style, multiply so to say the potential charge of every line. Mérimée's other masterpieces include the rather longer nouvelles, *Colomba* and *Carmen*, which are unsurpassed in French for their wide appeal to our sense of life's rich substance; and it was Mérimée the artist, with an eye for the characteristic and the picturesque, who filled in the Corsican and Spanish backgrounds of these works, or the background of sixteenth-century France in the *Chronique de Charles IX*. But the continual expression on this writer's countenance is one of self-mockery, and well-bred scepticism. In *Colomba* we even find him affecting to despise the watchwords of his own art: 'couleur locale, . . . caractère. Explique qui pourra le sens de ces mots, que je comprenais fort bien il y a quelques années, et que je n'entends plus aujourd'hui'.

CHAPTER XLVIII

Historians and Thinkers

THE romantic mood, by quickening the imagination, stimulated the concrete vision of the past. On the other hand, the spirit of the nineteenth century was one of greater interest in nature and society, and scientific and intellectual studies took on a spiritual significance they had never known before. Literature and knowledge became even more intimately related than they had been during the Enlightenment; the writer felt that his sense of the world, even in spite of himself, was largely shaped by the views that formed part of the mental horizon of all; the scientist realized that to meet the needs of a wider public he must use clear and pleasant language, and reconcile technical accuracy with style. History and philosophy thus entered definitely into the general background of the artist in words; the thought, indeed the obsession, of the eras through which mankind had passed, was reflected in a curiosity that attached to recent as well as distant periods. Moreover, there was a general impression that discussion of the deeper problems of the individual and the group might help to solve the conundrums that the teachings of dogmatic religion had failed to answer. The prevailing metaphysics, and chiefly the disciplines that in the light of ultimate principles deal with issues of conduct and social behaviour—ethics, psychology, political economy, sociology—were definitely integrated in the field of literary invention, nourishing the roots of most works, and directly contributing to the flavour of not a few. It was at a later date that a reaction set in among specialists against imaginative history, and the documentary ideal tended to cancel the alliance which had obtained in literature.

Michelet's[1] writings are chiefly historical, but it would be wrong to

[1] Jules Michelet, born in Paris, 1798, the son of a printer, knew poverty and hardship in youth. After a brilliant career as a student he taught in various schools and at the École Normale Supérieure, then was appointed head of the historical department of the Archives Nationales, and a professor at the Collège de France. He translated Vico, 1827; published *Histoire romaine*, 1831; *Histoire de France au moyen âge*, 1833–44; *La*

appreciate his work simply as history. Its originality and its greatness lie in the fact that it is essentially of the nature of poetry, though such poetry is, of course, not subject to the laws of regular prosody. Nevertheless, the word here is not misapplied. Michelet was fully conscious of the part which rhythm plays among the deeper constituents of his manner, and says somewhere: 'La fatigue et la privation de sommeil blessaient en moi une puissance, la plus délicate de l'écrivain, je crois, le sens du rythme. Ma phrase venait inharmonique. . . .'

Each writer who is at all a poet has his own individual sense of rhythmic movement. It is enough, for instance, to think of Ruskin's organ-like prose, with its ample, periodic tempo, to realize the difference. Michelet's is all in quick, short thrusts of nervous impression and intuition. When he lets himself go, he writes in brief snatches, heaving with repressed energy, at times rising to climaxes; and the illuminating power of these flashes is unequalled. They reveal the tenseness of a highly emotional temper, aiming by no means at logical statement, but possessed by the urgency of a vision that must be expressed. Immediate communication being thus an almost physical need, he makes everything subserve it—impassioned fervour, the music of words, their weight and order, the mental urge with which language pulsates, and even more the figures of speech that appeal to the imagination. These, along with rhythm, are Michelet's favourite means of suggestion: his images, strong, vital, charged with the creative force of his visionary mind, set on his writings the stamp of a genuinely poetic utterance.

He was a son of the people, ardently sharing the democratic zeal of the Revolution, in whose afterglow his childhood was bathed. To him the story of the past was a moving tale of long oppression, and of the birth-throes of deferred justice; not the bitterness of the social partisan, but the pity and love of the idealist were his animating emotions: he lived for that cause, suffered for it, and in the dignity of his disinterested career was to the young a prophetic voice. It was only gradually that he worked his way to the problems of the

Révolution française, 1847–53; *Histoire de France des XVIe, XVIIe et XVIIIe siècles*, 1855–67; *Le Peuple*, 1846; *La Bible de l'humanité*, 1864; *L'Oiseau*, 1856; *L'Insecte*, 1857; *L'Amour*, 1858; *La Femme*, 1859; *La Mer*, 1861; *La Montagne*, 1868. After 1848 he was removed from first one official position, then another, because of his ardently liberal views and his political influence with the young. He died in 1874.

present. His *Histoire romaine* illustrated the view of evolution he owed to Vico; the history of Rome shows the growth of a people's will to live within a set of natural conditions, and the legends which surround it must be interpreted in that light. The *Introduction à l'histoire universelle* hailed the final triumph of liberty. French history was next tackled, in successive volumes on the medieval period, the Revolution, and the intervening centuries, and it is by these works that Michelet's credit as an historian must stand or fall. Although based on an eager study of documents, his method fails to satisfy the scruples of present-day specialists. The compass of the undertaking is too large for a single investigator, and the writer's passion destroys all possible claim to judicial impartiality. What keeps the surveys alive is their dramatic vividness, the intuitive grasp of scenes and characters, the forcible picture of events. If the play of light and shade is governed by an artist's sense of contrast, more than by the cold judgement of a scientist, the past is raised again to life, and invested with convincing actuality by the magic of the style. Michelet amply justified his formula, of history as resurrection.

Of his other writings, a few grapple directly with political and religious issues, like *Du prêtre*, *De la femme*, *De la famille*, and inevitably raise the dust of controversy; more often, as in *Le Peuple* and *La Bible de l'humanité*, his generous championship preserves serenity through nobleness. *L'Oiseau*, *L'Insecte*, *La Mer*, &c., which have a special appeal for present-day readers, are mature studies, truly poetical disquisitions on the animal and the physical worlds, in which intuitive sympathy displays a wonderful gift of divination. His romantic manner has not aged because it transcends the mere glow of an active imagination and a susceptible heart; it is instinct with a desire for truth in which spiritual elements predominate. He has moods of a searching and subtle intensity which anticipate the impressionist and the symbolist trends of the later years of the century.

In a group with Michelet may be placed Augustin Thierry, 1795–1856, whose idea of history was somewhat similar. His *Conquête de l'Angleterre par les Normands*, 1825, and the *Récits des temps mérovingiens*, 1840, aim at presenting a vivid image of the past, which does not exclude the glamour of general theories, for instance, the development of medieval England by the long struggle of the Norman and the Saxon; while in the history of France, as he interprets it, the relations of conquering and conquered races are no less essential. His books are still esteemed for their narrative power, though their scholarship is no longer regarded as sound. A work more closely approaching the historical novel of Scott is *L'Histoire des ducs de Bourgogne*, by de Barante, 1782–1866. Of Thiers, 1797–1877, with his lucid, artificial picture of the network of political causes and effects (*Histoire de la Révolution*, 1824–7; *Du Consulat et de l'Empire*, 1840–55); of Mignet, 1796–1884, and Henri Martin, 1810–83, a mere mention, while necessary, should be sufficient.

More stress should be laid on another school, that of the philosophical historians. Edgar Quinet, an original and interesting thinker, 1803–75, expressed himself variously, without ever achieving really fruitful concentration. His metaphysical epics in prose: *Ahasuérus*, 1833, or verse: *Napoléon*, 1833, *Prométhée*, 1836, are among the curiosities of literature. A translator of Herder (*Philosophie de l'histoire de l'humanité*, 1827), open to German influence, he dealt with the history of ideas chiefly in *Le Génie des religions*, 1842, and his action on the youth of the forties was parallel to that of Michelet. Guillaume Guizot, 1787–1874, who played a prominent part in French politics, was a student and admirer of English institutions (*Histoire de la Révolution d'Angleterre*, 1826–7) as examples of liberalism and representative government; the volumes of *Mémoires relatifs à l'histoire de France et d'Angleterre* which he collected and published, 1823–40, have won for him the gratitude of many scholars. His main work, *Histoire de la civilisation en Europe*, 1828–60, is a landmark in the progress of what is now termed 'sociological' history. More famous in the same field is Alexis de Tocqueville, 1805–59, whose epoch-making study of *La Démocratie en Amérique*, 1835–40, for the first time placed before the French public the full analysis of the working of a modern democracy, and was welcomed by the Americans themselves. In *L'Ancien Régime et la Révolution*, 1856, he corrected over-simplified views of the complete break which the Revolution was held to have caused in the deeper life of the French nation.

Meanwhile other thinkers were tackling the philosophical, social, and religious issues which were now, after the Revolutionary upheaval and the attempt at a reconstruction, clearly facing the nineteenth century. Neither Victor Cousin, 1792–1867, nor Jouffroy,

1796–1842, gave philosophy the abstruse and technical character that makes it the preserve of the specialist. Philosophy as they saw it was a higher wisdom, which from the thought of ages distilled for the layman the broad principles upon which life can be based. The spiritualism of Cousin, a synthesis of the systems of the past, and the idealism of Jouffroy, that tended to make lucid expression a test of truth, were within the grasp of all cultivated readers, a salvation from pessimism for minds shaken by the crisis of dogmatic belief. Socialist tendencies, again, that had been present and active in the fever of the French Revolution, reached a peak during the romantic period. Count Claude-Henri de Saint-Simon, 1760–1825, a bold and pregnant thinker, whose *Nouveau christianisme*, 1825, was a leaven to European thought and for a while fascinated Carlyle, threw out germinal hints of industrial organization, the association of workers, and a new distribution of wealth. The names of Fourier, 1772–1837, and Proudhon, 1809–65, are inseparable from the tentative growth of the national forms of French socialism before the impact of the dogmatic teaching of Marx. The widespread influence of these three writers and propagandists favoured the new sense of social obligation which then appeared in the mental background of French literature, and to which George Sand gave a signal expression.

Lastly, the powerful personality of Lamennais, 1782–1854, stands at the head of a religious movement that told on the conscience of the age, and in the thirties and forties acted as a magnetic force on the thought of many writers. A Breton priest of high spirituality and generous heart, he strove to shift the axis of religion from a personal to a social basis, so that in the quickening of charity and love the war of classes should be appeased, and Christian belief revitalized. He was condemned by Rome, and submitted, but he poured the turmoil of his emotions into the *Paroles d'un croyant*, 1824—a pathetic book, of singular eloquence and beauty, that left its mark in the liberal spirit of what may be called the left wing of orthodox believers.

Nearly all the romantic poets of note were literary critics, to the extent at least that, being conscious of their break from tradition, they felt the need to explain and justify their new departures. Victor Hugo's manifestos, which have already been noticed, were of special interest. Sainte-Beuve, a distinguished poet who imagined himself to be a failure, developed into a very prominent critic, but the years after 1850 were the period of his most fruitful activity and greater influence: he belongs to Part VIII.

The critics of academic reputation and professional character did not all condemn the romantic principles. Abel-François Villemain, 1790–1867, *Cours de littérature française*, 1828–9, may count as a liberal; he kept an open mind on the progress of foreign literatures, especially English and Italian, and, following in the footsteps of Madame de Staël, supported the claims of various national groups to express their original genius in different and equally legitimate ways. Philarète Chasles, 1798–1873, was an enthusiastic student of English and American writers; his articles were a lively initiation into the works and personalities of not a few. On the contrary Désiré Nisard, 1806–88 (*Études sur les poètes latins de la décadence*, 1834), with shrewd irony tried to crush the heretics under the precedent of Latin writers. These, he pointed out, were great until their classical practice degenerated under the corrupting strain of romantic tendencies. Gustave Planche, 1808–57, and Saint-Marc Girardin, 1801–73, vehemently or with elegant composure denounced the errors of the new school, and recalled the saving virtues of traditional orthodoxy.

CHAPTER XLIX

The Realistic Mood

REALISM was the predominant trait of French literature during the period immediately following the romantic age. This may seem no more than an instance of the rhythmic succession generally apparent in phases of artistic development, and perhaps most clearly observable in the most intellectual art, that of writing. Romanticism from its nature tended to emphasize aspects of description and characterization which correspond primarily not with what is but with what might or should be: it was imaginative, and it was sentimental. Now the tendency of the imagination is to re-create rather than to produce a close likeness of the object evoked. The world of its construction is not that of actual experience but of desire and dream. As for feeling, its inner law is to expand as far as human nature will allow; to select, and feed upon, all that is most intense, so that the image of life and of the world evoked under its stimulus will most often be pitched in a key distinctly higher than that of average happenings. But the appeals of imagination, however sympathetically the reader may respond to them, soon cease to give pleasure, by causing fatigue and awakening the fear of excess; they call into play the instinct of sanity and the search for corrective actuality that are the fundamentals of realistic art. The reaction against romanticism is instinctively in the direction of sober reason; and it was this silent shifting of temper that grew perceptible as early as the French forties, and reached its full force about the middle years of the nineteenth century. Two interrelated and often quoted episodes, the failure of Hugo's *Burgraves* on the stage and the triumph of Ponsard's *Lucrèce*, 1843, were only two among many signs of the change.

At the same time, the drift to realism was determined by positive as well as negative influences. The generation that came to adult thinking about 1850 could not fail to be deeply impressed by the decisive emergence of the physical and moral sciences. The impetus which the century had gathered from its beginning was becoming irresistible; and gradually, year after year, the general background of notions upon which man's vision of the universe rested was further upset. Among the most far-reaching changes may be mentioned the undermining of dogmatic faith by the inroad of exegesis upon tradition; the rise of the theory of evolution to the size of an interpretation of cosmic history, especially after the translation of Darwin's *Origin of Species*, 1859; and the development of Auguste Comte's philosophy into a system that claimed to dismiss all *a priori* principle. The name of 'positivism', given to the last body of ideas, at once suggested a form of literature to correspond which would above all stress the factual side of life and assign a leading part to observation.

In the wake of realism a similar and more radical movement, naturalism, soon emerged, founded on documentary evidence and professing to employ the methods of scientific inquiry. The naturalist was not simply a more uncompromising realist; some aspects of reality drew him more than others; while his doctrine largely coincided with that of Flaubert, its spirit and atmosphere were perceptibly different; the major influence upon him was not Comte, but Taine; the determinism he proposed to illustrate was chiefly physiological. He clung to a pessimistic belief in the decisive part played by the body, its demands and impulses, in our common behaviour; his approach to his characters, their actions and their motives, was strongly scientific.

But the origin of the realist mood is not so simple as this would indicate. To some extent, while opposing romanticism, it was its heir and successor, and sprang from the very core of its being. If the inmost quality of aesthetic principles is that they can be tested and known by the objections they rouse, it is of interest to note that the early realists were condemned by the conservatives on much the same grounds as the romantics had been; they were charged with being spiritual descendants of the romantics, but descendants who had improved on the sins of their parents. The striving for intensity had recourse, among other means, to the stark truth of naked facts. There is no more powerful call to imagination than a literal accuracy in the description of what is strong, violent, or unpleasant, and correspondingly difficult to realize. In one way, the emotion excited by the sadness or the grim squalor of the human condition contradicts the imaginative glow that an idealization of life strives to produce; but in another way it is a parallel and comparable emotion, and may be born of a similar desire to make the image of the world vivid, striking, and true. In fact, most romantic writers moved at times on the border of realism; and many realists, whether aware of it or not, were very largely inverted romantics. It has already been pointed out how difficult, and indeed how vain an attempt it would be, to try and divide the work of such great writers as Balzac, Stendhal, or Mérimée between the two successive schools of art, to both of which they belonged in spirit. No more significant proof could be adduced from the history of literature in support of the thesis that romanticism, having once flooded the whole field of modern thought, did not withdraw like an ebbing tide, leaving the sands dry; it filtered gradually through to the deeper layers of sensibility, so that all the phases and fashions of literature since that time have been more or less, in diverse ways, variations upon it, and still embody much of its substance.

CHAPTER L

Poetry

ONE great poet, Baudelaire,[1] transcends the spirit and the labels of his age. His work is obviously steeped in the realistic mood, though he disdained the epithet, and refused to be bound by what in some quarters was hardening into a doctrine. His connexion with romanticism, on the other hand, remains vital; but he reaches forward no less than back; he is a precursor of symbolism, and more, for at times he goes even farther and anticipates post-symbolist developments, thus constituting in himself an epitome of nineteenth-century poetry.

The realism of his *Fleurs du mal* is bitter, insistent, and can be gruesome. We may acquit him of any cynical intent to shock the reader merely in order to satisfy an itch for scandal. His insolent pictures of vice and crime are deadly earnest. His purpose is complex. He was determined to show things as they are; and this resolve fastens naturally on aspects of life ignored by conventional art. Moved by a disgust that does not spare himself, since his knowledge is gathered from experience, the poet evokes images of debauchery and all the excesses that welter behind the decent veil of civilization, and the flowers of the poet's hot-house are defiant, sinister, and poisonously scented. This brutal reaction against shallow idealism is stimulated by the craving for self-expression, and the avowal of a despair that has probed the unfathomable vanity of pleasure. Thus a positive

[1] Charles Baudelaire, born in Paris, 1821, had an unhappy childhood after his father died and his mother remarried. He studied in Lyons and Paris, and was sent on a voyage to India which was interrupted at Mauritius and Bourbon. Back in Paris he lived on a small capital in difficult circumstances. From 1841 onwards he wrote poetry. He published art criticism (*Salons*) on the Exhibitions of 1845 and 1846, and for a while, in 1848, tried political journalism. He translated the works of Edgar Allan Poe (5 volumes, 1858–65) and in 1857 published *Les Fleurs du mal*, which led to his being prosecuted and fined on grounds of immorality. Later, he published *Les Paradis artificiels*, 1860; *Richard Wagner*, &c., 1861; and *Petits poèmes en prose*, in periodicals. From 1844–66 he lived in Brussels, where he was taken ill. He was brought back to Paris, and died in 1867. His complete *Correspondance générale* was published from 1947–53.

meaning steals into the grim denial of every kind of faith; we are shown the horror of our unregenerate selves, and implicitly told to digest it and learn.

Do such didactic hints ever turn to definite lessons, and does the spirituality that undoubtedly lurks in the *Fleurs du mal* ever assume the full character of religious moralizing? The strong pessimism that is the core of Baudelaire's thought is akin to the motive of many orthodox teachers; theologians have written prose equivalents to these poems. A Christian essence is undoubtedly concealed by the morbid feelings of a soul sick unto death, and whose vitriolic irony is the only relief to its crushing sadness. It might be objected that the temper of that soul is hardly compatible with the milk of kindness, whether human or divine. Still, the book has genuine accents of tenderness and some moving utterances of a chastened heart.

At the time it was published its bitterness was more than public taste could tolerate, and Baudelaire was prosecuted. He was supported by an *élite* of the critics, and his already growing fame rose steadily thenceforth. Even the readers whose ethical dislike could not be mastered had to acknowledge the magnificent power of the poet. The romantic fire is here held in check by the imperious will of an artist who commands all the serene self-possession of classicism. The majestic sweep of his full lines and robust quatrains at their best is unsurpassed in the whole range of French poetry; the packed terseness, the perfect wording, the faultless rhythm and rhymes lift the *Fleurs du mal* to the range of high emotion fused with grand music. Unfortunately this level is not sustained, and the masterpieces are interspersed with inferior poems.

A further virtue, elusive and rare, is added to this beautiful synthetic quality. Baudelaire's mind and his ear were intuitively attuned to the subtle values of suggestion that were soon to become the conscious aim of symbolist art. It is not only that to the poet distant echoes link up all sense-impressions, so that the domain of style is widened by the possibility of associating them, and making use of one to evoke another ('Correspondances . . .'): 'Les parfums, les couleurs et les sons se répondent . . .'; nor that allegories are transmuted into symbols by being enriched with an expansive, an unlimited pregnancy:

Le Poète est semblable au prince des nuées
Qui hante la tempête et se rit de l'archer;
Exilé sur le sol au milieu des huées,
Ses ailes de géant l'empêchent de marcher;

('L'Albatros')

but the magic of strange, untried images, of syllables and rhythms
that speak a mysterious tongue, conveys a meaning that is not entirely susceptible of expression:

Loin des sépultures célèbres,
Vers un cimetière isolé,
Mon cœur, comme un tambour voilé,
Va battant des marches funèbres.

('Le Guignon')

The spells unite to create an enchantment that speaks to the imagination, the senses, and the intellect, in a language richer than that
of any other kind of poetry:

Ma douleur, donne-moi la main; viens par ici,
Loin d'eux. Vois se pencher les défuntes Années,
Sur les balcons du ciel, en robes surannées;
Surgir du fond des eaux le Regret souriant;
Le Soleil moribond s'endormir sous une arche,
Et, comme un long linceul traînant à l'Orient,
Entends, ma chère, entends la douce Nuit qui marche.

('Recueillement')

Signs, too, are evident of a search for *équivalences* that goes
beyond the average practice of symbolism itself, and points to the
radical transpositions of 'modern' poetry. They occur in, for instance, 'Avec ses vêtements ondoyants . . .' or 'Le serpent qui
danse . . .':

Sur ta chevelure profonde
Aux âcres parfums,
Mer odorante et vagabonde
Aux flots bleus et bruns,

Comme un navire qui s'éveille
Au vent du matin,
Mon âme rêveuse appareille
Pour un ciel lointain. . . .

> Et ton corps se penche et s'allonge
> Comme un fin vaisseau
> Qui roule bord sur bord et plonge
> Ses vergues dans l'eau. . . .

Baudelaire's prose writings, such as the *Petits poèmes en prose* and *Les Paradis artificiels* (containing his translation of part of De Quincey's *Opium Eater*) are no less instinct with the future than his poems. His complete translation of Poe's *Tales* is characteristic of his eager response to the fanciful, the mysterious, and the weird.

Baudelaire, a good judge of poetry, much admired Théophile Gautier[1], a lesser poet than himself but a pattern of the virtue he most esteemed, faultlessness of technique. A poet's instruments being language and rhythm, we can only have praise for Gautier's handling of these. His shorter pieces, and especially *España* and *Émaux et camées*, have a firmness of texture, an exactness of wording, a clinching power of phrase and measure which command admiration. From the romantic heritage Gautier preserved the love of colour, exoticism, and the picturesque; he gave up and denounced sentiment, humanitarianism, and a tendency to slipshod eloquence. Poetry to him was before all a craft which should allow no ideal but technical perfection; the intrusion of a philosophical or social purpose warped its aim; beauty of form was its object, and beauty was sufficient. It was now that the claims of art became paramount, and it was Gautier who founded the school of 'art for art's sake', a development clearly to be recognized in French and other literatures of the middle and later years of the nineteenth century. In France it was not wholly a novelty; it had certain links with tradition, and with classicism in some aspects. It even had more recent precedents, for Gautier considered himself a follower of the Hugo of the *Orientales*. His practice did indeed to some extent fuse and reconcile the principles of the romantic and the classical doctrines; its synthetic quality delighted

---

[1] Théophile Gautier, born at Tarbes, 1811, studied painting in Paris, joined the romantics, and became one of their warmest supporters. He struck an original note, and his cult of form made him a harbinger of the next age and a figure of considerable influence. His output, as extensive as it was varied, included poems: *Poésies*, 1830; *Albertus*, 1832; *La Comédie de la mort*, 1838; *España*, 1845; *Émaux et camées*, 1852; novels: *Mademoiselle de Maupin*, 1835–6; *Le Roman de la Momie*, 1858; *Le Capitaine Fracasse*, 1863; criticism: *Les Grotesques*, 1833; *Histoire du Romantisme*, 1874, &c.; accounts of travel in Spain, Russia, and Italy; art criticism: *Salons*; verse comedies, dramas, &c. He died in 1872.

perceptive readers; and proof abounds that it was more influential than Baudelaire's, which baffled imitation. Nowadays, much as we admire Gautier, we do not surrender quite so fully to the magnetism of his art. We are more inclined to expect poetry, even at the cost of some of its exactness, to rely more on inspiration, without which its range of imagery would be restricted and its evocative force weakened.

Yet with all their hardness of outline, many of his unpretending lyrics are little gems; here, for instance, is part of one of the earliest, on the dragon-fly:

> Bois qui chantent, fraîches plaines
> > D'odeurs pleines,
> Lacs de moire, côteaux bleus,
> Ciel où le nuage passe,
> > Large espace,
> Monts aux rochers anguleux;
>
> Voilà l'immense domaine
> > Où promène
> Ses caprices, fleurs des airs,
> La demoiselle nacrée,
> > Diaprée
> De reflets roses et verts.

Among his more ambitious attempts 'Albertus' has brilliant verve and wit; but that 'moral poem'—a hardly justified epithet—is merely an ironical fanciful apologue in the manner of Musset and through him of Byron. The *Comédie de la mort* descants on the theme of the *danse macabre*. Some poems (*Ténèbres, Thébaïde, Melancholia,* &c.), written shortly after 1830, are in a more serious vein; the poet confesses his growing distaste for existence with an unashamed and moving sincerity—a warning to us not to conclude rashly that because he usually repressed his sensibility he had none. But the *Émaux et camées* contain the best work of this gifted poet. The slight, jewel-like lyrics enshrine brief thoughts and impressions in exquisitely chased words. Of this kind, however limited its range, modern poetry has few better examples.

His prose work is plentiful and important, with a very wide range of subjects. His novels include: *Mademoiselle de Maupin*, whose fighting preface, against the French equivalent for Victorian reticence, is an historical landmark; *Le Capitaine Fracasse*, a spirited descendant of Scarron's *Roman comique*, &c. His criticism, in *Les Grotesques*, has the merit of reviving some unjustly forgotten reputations. He was one of the most fertile writers of the mid-nineteenth century, who brought the conscience and the talent of a genuine artist to his many and varied tasks.

Théodore de Banville, 1823–91, was Gautier's chief follower in the doctrine of 'art for art's sake'. He carried his master's respect for technique to almost intemperate lengths, and in his zeal displayed not only brilliant cleverness but the very acrobatics of metre (*Odes funambulesques*, 1857), &c. His *Petit traité de versification française*, 1872, formulated principles he had himself abundantly illustrated. Still, it would be unfair to give him credit only for verbal and rhythmic feats; in reviving the claims of Greek culture to remain the permanent source of all beauty, and in reintroducing the old French verse forms, from the ballade to the rondeau, he set examples that were to remain influential through the latter half of the century.

The worship of art and the cult of Greece were both essential factors in the personality and writings of Louis Ménard, 1822–1901: *Poèmes*, 1855; *Les Rêveries d'un païen mystique*, 1876. The markedly poetic prose of the latter is interspersed with sonnets of austere and forceful grandeur. He was a thinker of rare originality who left his mark on several problems of comparative religion, scholarship, and even practical science. Recognition, when at last it came to him, was fully deserved.

Louis Ménard was also one of the Parnassiens, a group of poets whose common link was one of negative tendencies even more than positive tenets. They were prominent during the sixties and seventies, and owed their label to the collections of new verse published as the *Parnasse contemporain* in 1866, 1871, and 1876. Their numbers grew with the successive issues of the publication, and one of them, Leconte de Lisle, whose vigorous personality had singled him out from the first, became their acknowledged leader.

Although Leconte de Lisle took an important share in formulating the aims of the Parnassiens, the doctrine was mainly derived from Gautier, whose place among the chiefs of the movement was that of a somewhat retiring elder, and whose dogma of the supremacy of art naturally entered into the gospel of 'impassible' poetry. The

Parnassiens were at one in deriding the sentimental effusiveness of the romantics and the laxity of their style, whereas the new doctrine laid stress on the endless care to be given to form and to precise, clear-cut expression. Ideas, moreover, with a value that was impersonal, were to be the matter of expression, as distinct from moods, which were purely subjective. Thus was restored an ideal of severe intellectuality and correctness; and the claims of science, philosophy, and thought were again recognized. In fact, with the important exceptions of a far stronger emphasis upon art and a ban on didactic literature, the Parnassien conception of poetry was not very different from that of the eighteenth-century post-classicists.

Leconte de Lisle[1] owed his love of Greek literature and the Hellenic spirit to innate tastes and to the influence of his friend Louis Ménard. But even in his first collection of verse, *Poèmes antiques*, this eager worship is clouded by a menacing sense of spiritual downfall. More openly through the succeeding volumes the images of an ancient and vanished glory become merged in a deeply pessimistic survey of doomed human hopes. Such sentiments, it is true, are characteristic of a period when the discovery of man's solitariness and the soulless ascendancy of science were casting a gloom over life, but the poet's inspiration is sufficiently sincere and profound to rise above the plane of the accidental. His allegorical lyrics dramatize the death of the many religions that from the earliest times have informed, sustained, and, he avers, corrupted man's dreams. His oversimplified and partisan denunciation of all Churches and his total condemnation of the Middle Ages show superb talent, but few readers will sympathize with their shrillness of tone. More subdued and moving is the modern, haunting sense of the transitoriness of things and the anguished realization that no firm support exists to which man, so desperately in need of permanence, can turn. Death is the inevitable end of the cosmos, as of each being, and holds out to suffering life the only comfort to which it may reasonably aspire.

[1] Charles-Marie Leconte de Lisle, born at Saint-Paul, Réunion, 1818, of a Breton family, spent most of his childhood and youth in the island. From 1845 he settled in Paris, and was for a time politically active, besides supporting with radical circles the movement for the abolition of slavery in French colonies. His publications include *Poèmes antiques*, 1852; *Poèmes barbares*, 1862; *Poèmes tragiques*, 1884; translations of Homer, Hesiod, the Greek tragic writers, &c.; his *Derniers poèmes* came out the year after his death (1894).

Meanwhile Nature stretches across the stage a magnificent veil of painted appearances, able to charm and soothe the very eye that sees through them. In spite of Leconte de Lisle's consistent effort to spare his feelings the shame of public display, a virile emotion throbs in all his significant pieces. The ecstatic memory of the Eden-like splendour of his native island adds a poignancy to his evocations of her sights and scenes, filled with regret for a lost paradise ('Le Bernica', 'La Fontaine aux lianes', 'Le Manchy', 'La Ravine Saint-Gilles', 'L'Aurore', 'L'Illusion suprême', &c.) He has a genius of which we are continually aware for bringing to life before our eyes a land, an age, a civilization, in a manner comparable with that of Victor Hugo's *Légende des siècles*. It is particularly vivid in his descriptions of what he could only know imaginatively—primitive races or cults, Indian, Hebraic, Egyptian, Scandinavian—and these are evoked with an accuracy of detail that is the fruit of conscientious reading and study, and defies even the searching of critics.

It would thus be mistaken to expect actual impersonality and resolute coldness from this professedly impassive poetry. The very pieces in which Leconte de Lisle haughtily asserts his scorn for romantic effusions are revelations of his own heart ('La Mort d'un lion', 'Les Montreurs', &c.). Nor would it be fair to tax him with a purely negative philosophy. He adopted when young, and never renounced, the political and social tenets of a radical humanitarian. The expressions of his ultimate belief are not atheistic but pantheistic, and the intuition of a mysterious presence in the universe which strikes us in the endings to 'Midi' and 'Le Bernica' is the same in spite of their apparent contradiction:

> Viens! Le soleil te parle en paroles sublimes;
> Dans sa flamme implacable absorbe-toi sans fin;
> Et retourne à pas lents vers les cités infimes,
> Le cœur trempé sept fois dans le néant divin . . .

and:

> Mais l'âme s'en pénètre; elle se plonge, entière,
> Dans l'heureuse beauté de ce monde charmant;
> Elle se sent oiseau, fleur, eau vive et lumière;
> Elle revêt ta robe, ô pureté première,
> Et se repose en Dieu silencieusement.

As these lines well testify, Leconte de Lisle's rhythm is ample and vigorous, with a majesty of utterance that reminds one of Baude-laire's. The energy may be felt as a tension, and because of its almost constant presence his poetry has been accused of monotony. His pre-ference is, certainly, for the stanza of four alexandrines with crossed rhymes and a strong lilt, but variations on this pattern are not infre-quent; he handles softer, flowing melodies very successfully ('Les Roses d'Ispahan', &c.); he is a master of the *terza rima*, as of the sonnet, and poems in shorter measures introduce a welcome change. His ear was true and subtle, and the care with which each element of his language and verse is chosen and kept free from every kind of blemish sets his poetry apart, among the most genuine examples of the faultless workmanship demanded by the doctrine of *l'art pour l'art* and Parnassian principles. However passing fancies may vary, his place in the forefront of French poets is permanent.

Born in Leconte's tropical island (La Réunion), his younger friend and disciple, Léon Dierx (1838–1912), was elected by his peers *prince des poètes* after the master's death (*Poèmes et poésies*, 1864; *Les Lèvres closes*, 1867, &c.). Though his earlier work was too plainly imitative, he developed a much more individual manner; and such poems as 'Les Filaos' and 'Soir d'octobre' will survive any present neglect.

Sully-Prudhomme, 1839–1907, began as an orthodox Parnassien, but his original temperament soon asserted itself. He was at his best in the analysis and expression of delicate shades of thought or feeling, but his philosophical cast of mind led him more and more to the dis-cussion of abstract problems. Poems of the first type include *Stances et poèmes*, 1865; *Les Solitudes*, 1869; *Les Vaines Tendresses*, 1875; of the second, *La Justice*, 1878; *Le Bonheur*, 1888. His bent is also evident in a translation of the first book of Lucretius into French verse, 1866, and such treatises as *L'Expression dans les beaux-arts*, 1890. To nine-teenth-century readers his usually neat and elegant phrasing was sufficient compensation for some occasional awkwardness or dryness. The present day is less tolerant and charges him roundly with pro-saism, yet some modification of this verdict seems possible. There is enough rhythmic and imaginative life in his psychological pieces to make many of them cling to our memory; nor are *La Justice* and *Le Bonheur* the sheer failures they are sometimes pronounced to be. Sonority and images frequently add a force of suggestion to their very real power; and the argument ends by abdicating, as it should, before the humble obstinacy of the heart. Here is the appeal of the thinker, sick unto death of his vain quest, to the charity of the moonlight:

> Quand saurai-je mourir, si ce soir je ne l'ose?
> De la molle nuée où tu t'ensevelis,
> Douce lune, à mon front forme un coussin d'oublis,
> Dût ma pensée y faire une éternelle pause!
> Laissons l'âme en un songe oublier ses douleurs,
> Comme l'étang s'azure en déposant sa vase . . . .

And the voice of our better self, that collects our saving dreams, answers:

> Dors vite, car l'ombre où tu plonges
> A déjà des pâleurs de lait!
> Moi, je vais suivre au vol les songes
> Et pour toi les prendre au filet;
>
> De l'Orient qui s'illumine
> Je vais cueillir les fins rayons
> Pour en tisser la mousseline
> Où j'arrête ces papillons.
>
> Et bientôt ton angoisse obscure
> Ne sera plus qu'une langueur
> Mêlée à ma douce piqûre
> Qui les fixera sur ton cœur. . . .

François Coppée, 1842–1908, who dedicated his earlier poems to Leconte de Lisle, was also a Parnassien to begin with. His reputation was greater than that of Sully-Prudhomme in his lifetime and has since known almost the same decline. He had at first the Parnassian care for wording, correct rhythm, and rhyme; but he poured a paradoxical matter into this fastidious form. From the *Reliquaire*, 1866, through the *Intimités*, 1868, to the *Poèmes modernes* and *Les Humbles*, 1869, he developed in a few years to an *intimisme* which far outdid that of Sainte-Beuve. The final stage, symbolized by the famous elegy, 'Le Petit Épicier', 1872, butt of many parodies, is resolute realism, instinct with sympathy and social pity. The feelings are sincere, and served by the discretion of the technique, and the pathos can be moving; but it has lapses into sheer vulgarity which inevitably provoke ridicule. Still, his plebeian idylls are morally honest, and preferable to the slightly snobbish elegance of his first pieces. His best achievement is probably the *Promenades* and *Intérieurs*—brief sketches from life in the lanes of suburban Paris. The description is tellingly spare and sharp, and the sentiment is kept within bounds. Coppée also wrote a number of plays in verse, for the most part successful.

Madame Louise Ackermann, 1813–90, in her *Poésies philosophiques*, 1872, expressed the revolt of the modern mind against a traditional faith that left the heart unsatisfied. Her pessimism has sincere and vigorous accents; but compared with Vigny's grand lines hers lack the imaginative concentration of genius.

Louis Bouilhet, 1821–69 (*Les Fossiles*, 1854), a friend of Flaubert, wrote one short masterpiece, 'Vers à une femme', which entitles him to a place in any survey of French literature.

CHAPTER LI

The Novel

IT was during this period that the novel finally established its ascendancy among literary forms, for with its unlimited possibilities as a picture of life it offered the widest scope to the spirit of realism.

There is some measure of good fortune in the fate of Champfleury, 1820–89. He began writing just when the demand for a closer truth in the background of fiction was coming to a head; and as a critic he was sufficiently alert to take his stand as a representative of the new ideas in his *Réalisme*, 1857, an interesting medley which deserves a place among the significant books of the period: consequently he is to some extent a pioneer, although his sketches of provincial life are still rather timid and his style lacks point. He has the gift of sympathy with his modest heroes (*Les Bourgeois de Molinchart*, 1854); and his amusing tales of schoolboys and their tricks (*Les Souffrances du Professeur Delteil*, 1856) at once had the honour of an English translation.

Flaubert's[1] position as the leader of French realism cannot be challenged. But his development must be seen as a painstaking progress towards a mastery of himself and his art that was a deliberate feat of will power. His first writings show every symptom of exuberant romanticism. His determination to eradicate these impulses was an intellectual one, inseparable from a search for recovery after a severe nervous breakdown. It is thus only natural that the victory should have been won gradually, and at the cost of some loss in the easy expansion of temperament. Great as his work is, Flaubert never

---

[1] Gustave Flaubert, born at Rouen, 1821, studied law in Paris, soon began to write, and thereafter spent most of his life at Croisset, near Rouen, with occasional intervals of travel in France or abroad. Works published during his lifetime include novels: *Madame Bovary*, 1846, for which he was prosecuted, and acquitted; *Salammbô*, 1862; *L'Éducation sentimentale*, 1869; *Trois contes*, 1877; and *Bouvard et Pécuchet*, unfinished, posthumous, 1881; and also a philosophical allegory, *La Tentation de Saint Antoine*, first published in 1874 and several times recast. His *Œuvres de jeunesse*, *Notes de voyage*, *Correspondance*, &c., were published at various dates after his death in 1880.

created any of those happy masterpieces that grow like fruit on trees. His letters keep us a party to the laborious maturation of his books, that were several times recast and rewritten. The stages in the process are worth studying; but only the final forms can be considered here.

Madame Bovary owes its place as a landmark in literary history to external circumstances no less than to its striking merits. The author's prosecution and acquittal were a signal defeat of official censorship, that had chosen its battleground badly. The novel has harsh features, but in the light of present-day tolerance it is, for better or worse, unexceptionable. A romantic ardour still glows at the core, melting and fusing the elements of a drama that shows texture, coherence, and composition. The language has life, imagery, rhythm, and rises at times to subdued eloquence; while moments of poetry relieve the sadness and squalor of the painful story. There is a racy humour about many of the episodes; and the figure of Monsieur Homais has justly grown proverbial. Nevertheless, the reader is continually aware of the author's deliberate restraint and objectivity: the rich study of provincial manners, with its fearful picture of retribution, to us almost reminiscent of Hogarth or Richardson, is carefully devoid of any attempt merely to amuse or edify. One may fully appreciate the discretion of the method yet still regret the absence of a touch more of human feeling to soften the pitiless narrative. The style has pleasing firmness, but in spite of all the polishing it is not immune from occasional blemishes. Flaubert's ideal of perfection was acquired, not inborn.

Salammbô is a setback on the path of deliverance from romanticism. Flaubert seems to have been carried away by the intoxication of his exotic and dramatic theme. His literary conscience spends itself on an excruciating and hopeless attempt to make the tale entirely acceptable to the historian and the archaeologist. But scholars have picked a thousand holes in his learning; worse still, the heaped-up details exhaust our attention and the gorgeous colouring dazzles our imagination. So insistent are the scenes of barbaric cruelty that one can hardly avoid suspecting the author of an obscure streak of sadism. But many elements went to the composition of this grim fabric—an unflinching and professedly realistic image of what human civilization could be at no very distant period of the past.

The *Education sentimentale*, in its revised text, is Flaubert's most significant work. The book is also the single full illustration of his doctrine. Ruthlessly exorcized, the joy of creative invention is apparently dead. The story is jotted down in short desultory fragments, with the cold accuracy of a police report, and without apparent continuity or dynamic purpose. But the stripped, severely matter-of-fact style has the cumulative impressiveness of an impartial statement. The dry bones begin to throb and live; the vacillating hero's innumerable disappointments are not only a source of ever-renewed comedy, one senses a remote but genuine sympathy behind the dismal tale of his struggles; and in the end the persistence of his calf-love invests him with a kind of unheroic dignity. As a whole the novel is moving, and its thoroughly pessimistic philosophy contains some seeds of respect for the naïveties of human nature.

In *Bouvard et Pécuchet* the artistic faults of *L'Éducation sentimentale* are even more apparent, and shorn of their redeeming features. The interminable account of the mishaps of two egregious, persevering fools who keep knocking against the stubborn angles of things amuses at first and then becomes tedious. It is a savage indictment of lower-middle-class stupidity; but the stupidity has its revenge in the unguarded monotony of the narrative. As social types the heroes are barely individualized; office clerks are, after all, men; these are caricatures. The popularization of science may make half-crazy brains lunatic; but sciolism seldom reaches such a degree of pompous silliness. The book is, however, more than amusing: as an allegorical satire and an exposure of the harm done by raw, undigested knowledge it serves a justifiable purpose.

Flaubert's finely balanced art reached full perfection in those late short stories, *Trois contes*. The realism of *Un Cœur simple* is no less spare than that of Maupassant, but the author's silent sympathy vitalizes it and renders it moving. In *La Légende de Saint Julien l'Hospitalier* the sober tone and style produce an almost symbolist sublety of suggestion.

The strange philosophical rhapsody, *La Tentation de Saint Antoine*, attacks its boldly conceived theme in the grand manner, though the development still shows some uncertainty and repetitive excess, and to compare the book with Goethe's second *Faust* is a damaging honour. As in some Breughel painting, the wildest shapes of man's imaginings march past Anthony, shocking and bewildering him. They are here not monsters and devils but gods and demi-gods, the numberless figments of the primitive instinct of worship. From this orgy of rank superstition one set of symbols emerges, those of modern science, while Christianity, with doubtful success, struggles to preserve its traditional privilege of superiority. There are fine, imaginative passages of poetical exegesis, and others, again, of bland irony, in the manner of Renan.

The brothers Edmond (1822–96) and Jules (1830–70) de Goncourt were an interesting pair who stamped themselves indelibly on the development of French realism. They never courted popularity and never obtained it, but their private fortune placed them above want and they did not pay the whole price of aggressive independence. During the younger brother's short life, and after their very first venture, the share of each cannot be distinguished in their works. Their initiative was remarkable. As novelists, historians, and playwrights they opened up new paths; while beyond their artistic achievements they added resources that are now common property to the study of the past and the present. To some extent they followed the examples of Balzac and Flaubert, and their own practice was soon paralleled and outdone by that of Zola and the 'naturalists'. But if their actual priority is not absolutely clear in the complex of literary actions there should be no doubt of their courage and their intuitive sense of what was inevitably coming.

For a broadly conceived history of manners, with the main stress laid on art, they made abundant use of documents till then too much neglected: letters, pictures, engravings, all the material background of life, decoration, and furniture; their works in that line are still reputed and read (*Histoire de la société française pendant la Révolution*, 1854; *L'Art du XVIIIème siècle*, 1859–75; *La Femme au XVIIIème siècle*, 1863, &c.). In their plays (*Henriette Maréchal*, 1865, &c., and dramatizations of most of their novels) they aimed at fusing the dignity of the stage with the liveliness of everyday dialogue. Almost from the first each novel was devoted to some modern problem, making vital use in its treatment of the concrete knowledge gathered from observation and documents, and by no means restricted to the outward frame of existence. The Goncourts did not succumb to the obsession with externals so often characteristic of the 'naturalist' school; they were psychologists, with a penetrating attention to the hidden workings of the mind which preluded the psycho-analysis of modern times. *Renée Mauperin* is an understanding portrayal of contemporary youth; *Madame Gervaisais* is a study of religious mania; and *Manette Salomon*, an arresting picture of studio life and manners, lays bare the gradual estrangement between an artist and his wife. Most impressive of all is *Germinie Lacerteux*, a cruel drama, told with compassion and restraint, of a humble being's fall into degradation and misery. Of the works written by Edmond alone *Les Frères Zemganno* probes the deeper layers of brotherly affection while *La Fille Élisa* deals with prostitution and solitary confinement.

The Goncourts are not only realists, students of society and the heart; from their early training as painters, and their artistic culture, they preserve an exquisite sensitiveness of eye which lends striking gifts of colour and suggestion to their language. Their vibrant style and their manner of revealing an object by capturing its successive phases in a series of quick flashes are very much a verbal form of the impressionist method that was even then making its way into painting. The scientific mood that inspired and sustained the literature of fearless truth can thus already be seen, in some of its most representative works, in process of transformation to the mood of poetic evocation, the eager search for 'correspondances', which was to be typical of the next, the symbolist age. All these novels have purple patches that often delay the action, but few readers will withhold admiration from a brilliance so productive of enjoyment. Many are descriptions of landscape not only of such consecrated scenes as the forest of Fontainebleau but—another instance of the originality of these two—of the suburban districts of Paris. These are vividly evoked, with all their sordid picturesqueness.

Jules Barbey d'Aurevilly, 1808–89, cannot by any means be called a realist. He is a belated romantic, a fierce opponent of the political and intellectual trends of his age. Democracy he hates; rationalism, the ascendancy of science, he tirelessly denounces. As a critic of society and literature he flaunts the banners of his stubborn, defiant faiths—traditional monarchy, the Catholic Church, the classics, and the great lyrical poets of the early nineteenth century. His onslaughts against his many and powerful enemies command our esteem, but though eloquent, and sometimes penetrating, they lack the essential fairness of a balanced judgement. His novels, which have a better chance of survival, show imagination, a love for impassioned characters, a fondness for the substance or the shadow of the supernatural, and a warmth and vigour of style that may at times exceed the bounds of wise discretion but do not exclude the charm of gracefulness and even of wit. He was most finely inspired by the hopeless struggle of the 'Chouans' to revive the dying embers of the royalist and religious cause in Revolutionary France: *L'Ensorcelée*, 1854, and chiefly *Le Chevalier des Touches*, 1864, are impressive and truly dramatic. His short stories, *Les Diaboliques*, 1874, would not be unworthy of Mérimée, though they fall short of Mérimée's in concentration, and their warmth of sensuality is rather unexpected in so professedly orthodox a writer.

Jules Vallès, 1832–85, cannot be passed over. He was an arch rebel whose political violence served his reputation with many but disserved it with more. With the lapse of time his talent can be appreciated on its own merits. He was moved to write by the bitterness of his grievances no less than by the fervour of his social faith; and from both extremes of feeling a cynical frankness of manner developed that gives his work a strong flavour of realism. But however desperately he clings to hateful experiences, his imagination is that of a poet; it soars in the brief images that time and again raise this matter-of-fact style to striking power. His life of poverty, his hand-to-mouth struggles and beginnings as journalist or writer, the prominent part he played on the revolutionary side in an unsettled period, are the themes of his autobiographical trilogy: *L'Enfant*, *Le Bachelier*, *L'Insurgé*, 1879–86, published as *Jacques Vingtras*, the name of one character. The first two are indictments of family tyranny and oppressive educational methods; while the last is a dramatic record of the Paris 'Commune', its heroism and its frenzy.

With Daudet[1] the labels of criticism prove more than usually

---

[1] Alphonse Daudet, born at Nîmes, 1840, began life as an usher in a school, but went early to Paris, where he published poems, articles, wrote for the stage, and was very successful with short stories (*Lettres de mon moulin*, 1866) and other novels: *Le Petit Chose*, 1868; *Tartarin de Tarascon*, 1872; *Contes du lundi*, 1873; *Fromont jeune et Risler aîné*, 1874; *Jack*, 1876; *Le Nabab*, 1877; *Les Rois en exil*, 1879; *Numa Roumestan*, 1881; *L'Évangéliste*, 1883; *Sapho*, 1884; &c.; his best play is *L'Arlésienne*, 1872. He died in 1897.

misleading; however substantially founded, the epithets commonly attached to him, 'realist', even 'naturalist', fail to convey the more significant originality of his art. He is, no doubt, wide awake to reality; his southern mind and senses are keen upon outlines and characters. But his manner is no less supple than it is sharp; his gift of intuitive perception is almost feminine, and his touch tender or mocking. Tenderness and mockery are often fused, and from their union is born the very shade of humour which the English prefer, and to which in their fondness they will sacrifice all others. Some analogy of spirit has often been traced between Daudet and Dickens, and, among the French novelists of his age and school, Daudet met with the kindest reception in England. His eager sensibility, which at bottom is that of a poet, flashes out into a lively, agile, half impressionistic style; and though the natural clearness of his thought and his fine instinct of measure reveal his kinship with the classics, he heard the call of modernity, and learnt to trust a little too much the charm of the discontinuous.

It is permissible to feel that the smaller part of his work in bulk is the more characteristic, and his most enduring claim to be permanently read. It deals in a mood of loving familiarity and indulgent satire with the physical aspects, the moral and social features of southern France. Rather than *Numa Roumestan*, or the *Contes du Lundi*, the masterpiece is the *Lettres de mon moulin*, a set of very early sketches in which an astonishingly sure hand has mixed fun and sentiment in happily discreet doses. The popular *Tartarin* series is an amusing skit, but after the initial volume the irresistible verve grows somewhat stale. His other novels are full-dress studies of 'Second Empire' society, rich in picturesque scenes and individual characters, and displaying a talent that still lives successfully on a fund of observation, but they attempt too ambitious a canvas, and the strain is evident. The sentiment is apt to deteriorate, and the appeals to comedy or drama are not always effective. Yet *Le Petit Chose*, partly autobiographical, *Jack*, *Fromont jeune et Risler aîné*, *Les Rois en exil*, *Sapho*, have very moving episodes, and keep a place among the books that old readers remember with affection and the younger generation are willing to tolerate. Whatever judgement may be passed upon them, all will agree that they use the French language with remarkable ease and purity.

With Zola[1] the strictly 'naturalist' movement came to a head;
though if lack of reticence, of which the naturalists are accused, is the
main test, this has been much more complete since their day. What
should count more is definite and genuine artistic purpose; in Zola's
work this was at once unmistakable. His devotion to the *roman ex-
périmental* filled his life with the dignity, as well as the somewhat
fanatical obsession, of a single, long-sustained, and partly miscon-
ceived effort. He had chapter and verse for each item of his technique.
The word 'science' is written large over his whole undertaking; and
yet its use was not wholly justified. Zola's doctrine was based on
doubtful analogies and hasty conclusions. A psychologist, Taine (see
below, Chapter LIII), had said that 'Le vice et la vertu ne sont que
des produits comme le vitriol et le sucre'. A biologist, Claude Bernard, argued that medicine should be ruled by trial and experiment,
like physiology (*Introduction à la médecine expérimentale*, 1865). A
doctor, Lucas, had stressed the part played by heredity in man's life.
Zola's theory of the novel was a combination of these three theories.
Character being a product of organic and hereditary factors, he
asserted, a novelist's study of character must be closely similar to the
medical diagnosis of a case, or, in other words, to the discussion of a
physiological problem. On the strength of this he planned a series
of novels—twenty volumes eventually—which under a collective
label, the *Rougon-Macquart*, would follow the direct or distant effects
of an original taint on the various branches of a family. In this way
ideas interesting in themselves, but which should have been tested
and probably modified before being incorporated with the body of
solid knowledge, became the hard-and-fast basis of an aesthetic doctrine. To yield to enthusiasm in this way was to take risks; the risks
have materialized, and the *Rougon-Macquart* novels remain today as
no more than the imposing mass of an ambitious but insecurely
built monument.

There are fine failures, among books as elsewhere. Zola's works,
in spite of the flaw at their core, cannot be dismissed as hopelessly

---

[1] Émile Zola was born in Paris in 1840. His early writings were in a romantic vein,
but he was converted to realistic views, and adopted the scientific determinism of a
biologist, Claude Bernard. After some attempts he planned a series of novels illustrating the influence of heredity on the generations of one family: *Les Rougon-
Macquart, histoire naturelle et sociale d'une famille sous le second empire*. They were published in a score of volumes from *La Fortune des Rougon*, 1871, to *Le Docteur Pascal*.

unsound. They were very widely read for a whole generation, in France and abroad, and have not entirely fallen out of favour. One reason for this was the courageous part the writer and journalist played in politics during his last years, but his novels have more intrinsic merits. Art is more essential than the doctrinal background of a novel; and Zola's art has eminent virtues. His determination to tell the whole truth without flinching is responsible for the frankness with which he presented some of the disgusting or brutal aspects of experience. Objection to this was at one time very vocal, but has now been practically silenced. He has no lasciviousness or downright obscenity; his most nauseous pages are far less unhealthy than the salacious descriptions that have sometimes more easily passed muster since he wrote. The philosophical or ethical support he adduced for his plain speaking and the rhapsodical fervour which, as a kind of compensation, suffuses his gospel of democracy, labour, and progress (*Fécondité*, &c.), have not generally been thought to mend matters very much. He might thus seem to have won complete success in nothing that he attempted systematically. But while his painstaking survey of industrialized France is no longer regarded as an important contribution to sociology, and the genealogical tree of his characters at the end of the series leaves us perfectly unconcerned, we can still be impressed by his strikingly realistic picture of the modern world.

His documentary method stood him in good stead whenever the document was vivified by imagination. His study, for instance, of the gin-shop as a social plague, and of the havoc wrought by liquor (*L'Assommoir*), remains unforgettable; his descriptions of the inner life of a coal-mine (*Germinal*), or a big store in full swing (*Au bonheur des dames*), have not been surpassed. Indeed, it has gradually become obvious that his chief and most undoubted claim is one to which he himself attached little importance. The romanticism of his early years never ceased to colour his vision and emotions; even when factual narrative was his purpose he was carried away by his imaginative energy; and grandiose scenes, processions of human beings, and pageants of facts began to take shape before his mind's

1893, the most successful being *L'Assommoir*, 1877; *Germinal*, 1885; *La Débâcle*, 1893. Later series were *Les Trois Villes: Lourdes*, 1894, &c., and *Les Quatre Évangiles: Fécondité*, 1899, &c. He took an active share in the political struggles connected with the Dreyfus case, and died in 1902, having tried his hand at poetry, short plays, and criticism.

eye. Some of his epic descriptions, such as the rush of fate, sweeping national disaster onward (*La Débâcle*) or the frenzy of suffering multitudes hoping wildly for a miracle (*Lourdes*), have a beauty that is not fastidious and refined but powerful and moving. His style may lack delicacy and distinction, chiefly when he tries to achieve them, as in *Le Rêve*, but he is far from an indifferent writer: he has pathos, graphic power, and eloquence; and time and again this author can quicken his reader to thrilled appreciation of a reality that comes straight from his vivid imagination, and not from his well-stocked memory or his carefully kept commonplace book.

To his contemporaries Zola was the undoubted head of a school. Several of his professed disciples, such as Paul Alexis and Céard, broke with him when public taste rebelled decidedly against the peculiarly uncompromising realism of *La Terre* (1888). But other and greater followers kept within his circle, and today appear as rivals to the master.

Maupassant[1] owed the distinctive quality of his work, and its lasting success at home and abroad, to the relative limits as well as to the vigour of his temperament. He had adapted a natural gift, perfected by dogged labour, for the literary form of the short story, which demands a rich complex of talents though perhaps not the highest creative faculty. It would be unfair not to give him credit for his full-length novels: *Pierre et Jean* and *Bel-Ami*, especially, though spread over a broader canvas, manage to preserve the main characteristics of the *nouvelle*, but they add nothing essential to his total achievement. The concentration and the economy of the tale that works itself out within ten to fifty pages, define the scope of the instrument which he wielded with such astonishing mastery. A simple subject, which can be developed significantly in a brief narrative; stress laid exclusively on indispensable circumstances, and on

[1] Guy de Maupassant, born near Dieppe, 1850, of a family that claimed nobility but lacked wealth, became a clerk in government offices in Paris (the Navy and Education). Befriended and advised by Flaubert, he worked hard to become a writer and first made his mark with *Boule de suif*, one of the stories in *Les Soirées de Médan* (1880), a volume representing the naturalist school. His own publications include poems; several collections of stories: *La Maison Tellier*, 1881; *Mademoiselle Fifi*, 1883; *Les Sœurs Rondoli*, 1884; *Contes et nouvelles*, 1885; and full-length novels: *Une Vie*, 1883; *Bel-Ami*, 1885; *Pierre et Jean*, 1888; *Fort comme la mort*, 1889, &c. *Sur l'eau*, an interesting diary of a Mediterranean cruise, was published in 1888. He died in 1893.

the salient features of a few characters, often striking or at least picturesque; a background reduced to a few outlines, graphic enough
to evoke a social group, a situation, or a landscape; and a decidedly
concise style, a series of bare statements, sparingly worded and
severely objective, devoid of all emotional commentary or intrusion
of the writer's feeling: these are the rules. So deliberate and impersonal is this art, bent on intensifying every effect by a manner of
absolute unconcern, that the richly satirical or ironic flavour of the
tales closely resembles the most sardonic humour.

However successful, these tactics of complete self-effacement fail
to hide Maupassant's own personality. His choice of subjects alone
is revealing. Naturalism, a doctrine of which he grew more clearly
conscious under Flaubert's guidance, is the key to his view of fiction.
He is determined to tell the whole truth; and as the conventions of
society and language have banned important aspects of life, he
singles out themes that clash violently with the well-meant lies of
cheap, rose-coloured idealism. His stories are not only resolutely
unsentimental but free from all romantic stretch of imagination;
under the transparent cloak of respectable phrasing they frequently
border on indecency. In the general hypocrisy of manners, he seems
to hint cynically, everything can be said provided no *i* is dotted.
Systematic triviality, a desire to show existence in its actual drabness, especially when surrounded with the pompous vulgarity of the
lower-middle class or the sly miserliness of the Normandy peasants,
are thus the ordinary motives behind his naturalistic 'slices of life'.
These are charged, it must be owned, with a high flavour of unvar-
nished reality; wherever the scene may be laid, the characters introduced are their own, natural, unself-conscious selves, in looks, garb,
gestures, and talk, and strike us as being samples of the most common, if not always the most average, humanity. An element of implicit fun is thus added to the truth of the picture; and the plain,
unmoved style, classical in its direct simplicity, produces in us a sort
of intellectual amusement in which feeling seldom has any part.
But Maupassant's lack of sensibility represents a triumph of will,
and a pretence, from which he allowed himself occasionally to
be free. Repressed emotion is more than once felt or divined;
pity flickers in his bitter pessimism, the revolt of the heart against
man's hard condition. Or, again, the dramatic tone of some

stories may be heightened by a straining after the gruesome and the fearful, which confesses to a mind haunted by the thrill of the supernatural.

Such are the main constituents of these masterpieces of compressed comedy, tragedy, and satire, full of the grotesqueness and the sadness of things, and conveying both so suggestively and with such cool composure, in faultlessly impassive words: *Boule de suif, La Maison Tellier, Histoire d'une fille de ferme, Miss Harriet*, &c. With Mérimée's tales, they are the high-water mark of a genre on which Maupassant has left his stamp so unmistakably that despite his apparent cruelty and occasional indelicacy his influence can be widely traced in the world literature of the last half century. Yet if technical perfection is a great asset for a writer, it does not include all other virtues; the art of Maupassant is admirable, but one can admire without loving it supremely. His poignant sense of life leaves out too much of life's poetry, of its finer shades, and of what is unutterable in both its sweetness and its misery; one may prefer Chekov or Katherine Mansfield.

Huysmans[1] stands apart in a very original relation to naturalism. He took the doctrine to heart, and obeying his half-Dutch instincts, fully open to the need for objectivity, he gave a rigorously accurate and somewhat dull account of his distressing military experiences ('Sac au Dos', in *Soirées de Médan*). His early novels (*Les Sœurs Vatard*, &c.), which treat of the most sordid aspects of life, are as objective as Maupassant's, and full of the same repressed despair. But already one senses that the author is finding the cruelty of life hardly bearable, that the bitter sense of duty done in painting the truth will not long sustain his energy, and that the warmth and sensitiveness already perceptible in his style will sooner or later break out in revolt. The coming change was obvious in *A rebours*, a strange book that describes a man's desperate attempt to escape the nauseating monotony and mediocrity of our fate by recourse to a general policy of artificiality. The hope of new zest for jaded, over-civilized minds and senses lies in consistently running contrary to the course followed

---

[1] Joris-Karl Huysmans was born in Paris in 1848 of Dutch parents. His early works include poems, realistic novels (*Marthe*, 1878; *Les Sœurs Vatard*, 1879; *Croquis Parisiens*, 1880, &c.), and art: *L'Art moderne*, 1883, &c. A marked change in his outlook was apparent in *A rebours*, 1884, and *Là-bas*, 1891, and developed into the mystical Catholicism of *En route*, 1895; *La Cathédrale*, 1898, &c. He died in 1907.

by nature and society; and the very type of artifice being art, it is chiefly as an artist that the hero tries to put this theory into practice. This might have a surface kind of kinship with the hedonism of the aesthetes, and the school of Walter Pater; but a spirit of earnestness at work here points to an eager search for religious and spiritual values. The hero fails in his attempt, but it was plain thenceforth that Huysmans had abjured the gospel of naturalism.

The stages of his return to the devout Catholicism of his childhood are told in *En route*, and *La Cathédrale* gives full scope to the mystical and enthusiastic ritualism that was the mainstay of his faith. These books have stimulated and deepened the interest taken by the cultivated public in early Christian architecture, painting, and music, especially plainsong. Besides this historical significance, what keeps them alive is the individuality of their style. Huysmans now lets himself go, and writes with the whole range of his instincts. Of his naturalist manner he still keeps a frank realism that reminds one of the concrete raciness of a Breughel; but in all other respects he is now an idealist, and a symbolist. His language, surprisingly rich, and free, sometimes hardly correct, and dotted with technical and dialectal terms, is glowing and inspired, raising the expression of ardent and rapt states of feeling to a vivid intensity that is truly poetical. Its power of conveying the sensations both of ordinary and mystical experience is essentially creative, and the badge of a born writer.

Another born writer, like Huysmans an artist, but gifted with a creative as well as a critical talent in the field of painting, wrote a novel that clashed even more decidedly with the naturalist standards, and has been held ever since to be a masterpiece. Eugène Fromentin, 1820–76, made a mark with impressions of Africa (*Un Été dans le Sahara*, 1857; *Une Année dans le Sahel*, 1858) and a volume of art criticism, *Maîtres d'autrefois*, 1876; but these distinguished books are eclipsed by the outstanding quality of his single story, *Dominique*, 1863. This links up boldly with the most genuine tradition of French classicism and with *La Princesse de Clèves*. The psychological drama has the same quintessential purity; it develops on a similar plane of subtle analysis, discreet, implicit notations, and nobility of soul; the subdued pathos is instinct with reserve; and a scrupulous acceptance of duty is the spirit of the whole, though never professed. Yet there are indications that the romantic fever, though checked, is not purged away. Moderate realism is at work in the fine truth of the country atmosphere and the rustic episodes; while the exquisite distinction of the style and the charm of the landscapes betray the touch of the painter. This is a book in which French literature can feel a legitimate pride, and which it may pit against any foreign idyll.

CHAPTER LII

Drama

ROMANTICISM was the most marked incident in the development of French literature. Rooted as it was, and more than it knew, in a distant past, and announced more recently by a long series of symptoms, it most nearly approximated, among such episodes, to the quality of a thorough change, bringing with it a principle of complete renovation. But just because its promise was in fact so wide, it could not be fulfilled at one stroke. The social complexity of the French nation, and the psychological diversity of its types, precluded such a consummation. The taste of the middle classes, whose power was growing more firmly established in spite of all political disturbances, was on the whole conservative. They might learn to tolerate, rather grudgingly, the experiments of romantic poetry, but they never gave it a really joyful assent, and they clung silently to their deeper preferences, as the over-valuation of Béranger significantly shows. The genuine supporters of the new literature were mostly artists and intellectuals; to some extent it also had the benefit of the prestige that usually attaches to novel fashions, once they have gathered sufficient impetus. It took a slow maturation, prolonged throughout the nineteenth century, to make the conquests and achievements of the romantic poets a possession and almost an instinct of the mass of the nation. Thus it was only in the second romantic age, as the Symbolist period may be called, that the potentialities of the first became an actual and permanent feature of the French literary temper.

Of all literary kinds, drama, in the success of which collective appreciation and the taste of the average man count for so much, offered the most stubborn resistance to the declared and open change that had been threatening. When realism won in its turn, its spirit was no more easily or immediately incorporated in the practice of playwrights than that of romanticism had been. Almost till the end of the century the stage accepted no more than a partial and timid infusion of this spirit, and the distinctly modern French drama dates only from the foundation of the Théâtre Libre. The atmosphere then became one of bolder innovation, and the decline of the naturalist movement coincided with the progress of Symbolism.

But in the meantime, the encouragement of the Second Empire public was reserved for those dramatists who were content with a rather timid compromise, or even for those whose standards remained purely conservative.

Eugène Labiche (1815–88) relied happily on the fund of accepted observation from which traditional comedy had drawn its matter. He wrote some hundred odd plays, single-handed or with collaborators, and all without originality, unless we are prepared to dignify by the name of psychological discovery the single remark that we love those to whom we have done good and hate those who have done good to us (*Le Voyage de Monsieur Perrichon*). Still, his lively, good-natured wit and genuine, light-hearted gaiety made the French laugh for some thirty years (*Un Chapeau de paille d'Italie*, 1851; *La Poudre aux yeux*, 1861; *Célimare le bien-aimé*, 1863; *La Cagnotte*, 1864; *La Grammaire*, 1867; *Le plus heureux des trois*, 1870, &c.). If there is any cathartic virtue in thoughtless merriment, free from the mere scurrility of coarse farce, his typical brand of French comedy deserves not to be overlooked.

Comedy with Émile Augier[1] gathered more substance, and showed the final victory of the hybrid type recommended by Diderot, in which serious and even tragic elements, as in life, could enlarge the scope of amusement and satire to a survey of man's condition under some of its aspects. Many of his plays are really *drames bourgeois*, and while he acknowledged in his ethical intent the influence of Dumas, his social criticism should be regarded as original and independent. His limited realism is sincere and cleverly managed; without unduly stressing a definite purpose, against which the habits of the public would have rebelled, he touched not a few weaknesses of the contemporary scene, in a way that told effectively on minds and manners. At a time when the power of money and freedom in sexual

---

[1] Émile Augier was born at Valence in 1820. After some attempts at poetry he wrote comedies, first in verse, then in prose: *Gabrielle*, 1849; *Le Gendre de Monsieur Poirier*, 1854; *Le Mariage d'Olympe*, 1855; *Les Effrontés*, 1861; *Le Fils de Giboyer*, 1862; *Maître Guérin*, 1864; *Lions et Renards*, 1869; *Madame Caverlet*, 1876; *Les Fourchambault*, 1878. He died in 1889.

behaviour were being openly flaunted, he depicted these irregularities in ways that were rendered all the more diverting and convincing because the action was served by the measure and the finely shaded truth of his portraits. *Madame Caverlet* helped to convert French opinion to the need for re-establishing legalized divorce, while a particularly happy blend of comic invention and keen observation made *Le Gendre de Monsieur Poirier* one of the most successful plays of the age.

Although younger by a few years than Labiche and Augier, Alexandre Dumas *fils* developed a manner of his own more quickly and soon became a leader among the realist dramatists. He is by preference a moralist, who stands for the reaction of sanity, backed by the wisdom of experience, against the sentimental illusions of romanticism. His attitude was already clear in his first play, based on his very popular novel, *La Dame aux camélias*. His later plays were variations on that theme, and at the same time lashed the materialism of a bourgeois society more and more under the spell of money. He was a master of the technique of play-writing, with a skill in handling his weighty subjects which allowed him to moralize with impunity; his tempered realism never exceeded the limits a respectable audience was prepared to accept. But the novelty of his theses has largely faded, and his writing is not sufficiently brilliant to win much favour at the present day.

Tragedy of the traditional kind had been sinking into mediocrity and neglect, in spite of the short-lived triumph of Ponsard (see above, Part VII, Chapter XLVI) and the genius of the tragic actress, Rachel, who drew crowds to her performances of classical masterpieces. Victorien Sardou, 1831–1908, was the chief representative, for more than forty years, of a more modern type of tragedy that avoided Hugo's truculence while still assimilating something of the romantic and the realist tendencies. He had many gifts—facility, animation, and a good sense of the theatre: he could provoke both laughter and emotion, and the style of his dialogue is far from indifferent. His successes were many, in England and America as well as in France, but his artistic ideals were never high, and he contributed little to the renewal of drama. Some of his comedies, *Divorçons*, 1880, for instance, and *Madame Sans-Gêne*, 1893, are remembered; like some of his tragedies, such as *Patrie*, 1869, *La Tosca*,

1887; while his talent for appealing to the imagination survives in his opera libretti.

From the realistic and naturalistic novel to realism and naturalism in the drama the step was obvious. Balzac, Flaubert, the Goncourts, among others, tried their hands at play writing. One man, Becque, made the venture a striking achievement.

The naturalism of Becque reaches far deeper than the rather superficial plane to which the doctrine was often confined. His determination to paint the truth is not reflected in the choice of low characters, vulgar or shocking situations, and brutal language; and the pessimism of his picture, by being kept independent of these facile resources, is only the more starkly penetrating. *Les Corbeaux* deals with the conspiracy of selfishness and greed against a middle-class family condemned to hardship by the death of the bread-winner. *La Parisienne* is a scathing but cool and ironical study of the sexual corruption that can fester beneath the cloak of upper middle-class respectability. There is not a word in either play that is not decent, and appearances are cynically maintained by even the worst characters. Both plays are vigorous and sad, though the theme and the plot of the latter allow an amusing wit to flash out. Becque has been thoroughly faithful to his artistic and moral purpose; he has ignored all the compromises and devices which appeal to the sentiment, the prejudices, or the cowardice of the public. *Les Corbeaux* rejects the convention of a dramatic finish; the play ends in the grey atmosphere of an insignificant incident. *La Parisienne* concludes on a note of unmitigated sarcasm. The severe discipline and classical sobriety of this art have won the just admiration of the discerning, but Becque was never a popular success.

The Théâtre Libre (1887–96), founded by André Antoine, exerted a very important influence during its short life. It educated the taste of a public that clung to habits and instinctive preferences; it produced new dramatists and new types of drama, including foreign masterpieces, and it also helped to introduce foreign techniques to the French stage. Its work began when the tide of naturalism was already subsiding; and before long it extended its activities to further the rise of the symbolist spirit.

CHAPTER LIII

Thinkers, Historians, and Critics

FRENCH thought during the third quarter of the nineteenth century was so closely associated with the salient features of realism that a sketch of the literary movement cannot altogether ignore the contemporary philosophy. The scientific and positivist tendencies whose nodal point was the work of Auguste Comte had a parallel in the aesthetic theories of Flaubert and Zola. This must not be interpreted wholly in terms of the effect of the former upon the latter, since both were deeply and independently rooted in the intellectual and social circumstances of the time, but it is safe to assert that the novelists, and even the poets, did reflect the attitude of the philosophers, and to some extent drew their general inspiration from them. A sense of their significance stimulated writers to theorize about their art, even if it did not entirely guide their views.

Auguste Comte, 1798–1857, was by no means an artist. His inclusion in a short history of literature is due to the fact that, directly or indirectly, the *Cours de philosophie positive*, 1839–42, and among other writings, the *Système de politique positive*, 1852–4, entered into the mental background of the years that saw the transition from romanticism to realism. His 'positive' insistence upon the observation of facts as the main object of science was the chief source of the method formulated and put into practice by the naturalistic writers; the theory of the *trois états*, theological, metaphysical, and positive, as the key to the whole development of human thought, confirmed the inference that the study of society was the task which fate had assigned to modern art, and the 'religion of humanity' roused excitement and sympathy even abroad, in the mind of George Eliot for instance.

Taine,[1] who had received the training of a specialized philosopher,

[1] Hippolyte Taine, born at Vouziers, 1828, entered the École Normale Supérieure and formed unorthodox philosophical opinions. He failed in the competitive examination and gave up teaching for literature. His works include *La Fontaine et ses Fables*, 1854; *Voyage aux Pyrénées*, 1856; *Vie et opinions de Thomas Graindorge*, 1857; *Histoire*

felt most strongly, among the men of letters, the impact of the positivist system of thought; but the fact that he also possessed the sensibility of a poet made him the finest of the artists who dealt in abstract ideas. The union of conflicting abilities in a complex temperament broadened his range, but prevented him from being appreciated at his full value. To a large part of the public he was an *idéologue*; while the professional thinkers and historians ended by mistrusting his glowing imagination and his subjective views. When a balance was struck, and a new generation thrashed out his various claims, he appeared as one of the significant French writers of the late nineteenth century. His treatise *De l'intelligence* is a landmark as the last in a series of attempts, which the progress of philosophy has now apparently condemned, to reconstruct the higher powers of the mind exclusively on the basis of sense impressions. The Bergsonian movement was soon afterwards to reorient psychology completely. But for a while Taine's influence on the current notion of the inner life gave a new lease to the analytical and rationalist study of character always more or less favoured by the French novel.

Of whatever errors and simplifications Taine the thinker, who took sides and fully committed himself, may have been guilty, the shrewdness and originality of Taine the critic must be acknowledged. His action was deep and lasting. Too much has perhaps been made of his over-systematic turn of thought. He laid strong emphasis on the basic connexion between a book or a painting and the material and moral conditions in which it was produced. But 'la race, le milieu, le moment' was not a rigid formula whose mechanical application would account for all individual talent, and by itself solve the problem of aesthetic valuation. It was a group of preliminary questions, that might usefully be asked when the ground was being prepared for judgement. Such queries have entered into common practice, and Taine's method, freed from its exaggerations, has left a permanent mark on all the varieties of criticism. Again, his historical study of *Les Origines de la France contemporaine* may have been justly censured as the work of a biased, conservative mind, but it is founded on a conscientious use of documents, and remains a piece of honest

de la littérature anglaise, 1864; *Philosophie de l'art*, 1865; *Essais de critique et d'histoire*, 1866; studies of the art of Italy, Holland, Greece, &c.; *De l'intelligence*, 1870; *Notes sur l'Angleterre*, 1872; *Les Origines de la France contemporaine*, 1871–94. He died in 1893.

scholarship, though it is not to be followed without caution. Exception has also been taken repeatedly to the *Histoire de la littérature anglaise*. Yet the brilliant generalizations of this work are not, as has so often been asserted, radically wrong; they contain at least an important measure of truth; and what matters more, the appreciations of individual writers are always interesting, and mostly just, though occasionally wide of the mark; the author's specialized knowledge and his understanding of his subject were somewhat inadequate. *La Fontaine et ses Fables* is much more than a suggestive paradox; the *Notes sur l'Angleterre* set forth an image of Victorian England that offered to many French readers something very like the character of the people. Taine as an historian of art has written illuminating pages, stressing with persuasive vigour not only the relation of each artist to his milieu, but his individual temperament as well. The truth is that this so-called system-monger was endowed with fine and penetrating perceptions, and could express them in beautifully evocative language. He was second to none in his feeling for natural scenery; and a grand philosophical poetry suffuses the descriptions of the *Voyage aux Pyrénées*. The *Vie et opinions de Thomas Graindorge*, finally, is a very distinguished addition to that scantily recognized branch of French literature, authentic humour.

Renan,[1] like Taine, was both a scholar and an artist; and although his manner was very different, he incurred much the same penalty for having sometimes, in the judgement of the learned, sacrificed scholarship to art. The shock and scandal of his break with the Church have long subsided; nowadays objection to his work is more frequently directed to the very suppleness of his temper, his reliance on intuitive perception, and the dangerous relativity he introduces into

---

[1] Ernest Renan, born at Tréguier, 1823, the son of a master mariner, was brought up by his mother and sister. After a period in a seminary in Paris he turned to philological studies, abandoned his intention of entering the Church, and lived by teaching. He wrote *L'Avenir de la science*, 1849 (published 1890); travelled in Italy, married, and went on a mission to Palestine; was appointed professor of Hebrew at the Collège de France. In 1862 he was suspended from his chair, but he was reintegrated in 1870, and became head of this institution in 1884. He died in 1892. His publications include *Histoire générale des langues sémitiques*, 1848; *Études d'histoire religieuse*, 1857; *Essais de morale et de critique*, 1860; *Dialogues et fragments philosophiques*, 1876; *Ma sœur Henriette*, 1882; *Souvenirs d'enfance et de jeunesse*, 1883. His chief work is *Les Origines du Christianisme*, 6 volumes from *La Vie de Jésus*, 1863 to 1881. His *Drames philosophiques* (*Caliban*, *Le Prêtre de Némi*, *L'Abbesse de Jouarre*, &c.) were published from 1878 to 1896.

the very notion of moral truth. Cardinal Newman, in England, met with reproaches of a somewhat similar kind. In the heyday of his liberated youth, Renan poured into *L'Avenir de la science* enthusiastic visions of the happiness man would reap from an exclusively rational discipline of thought and life. His more mature writings revealed a mellower mind, the sense of a relative and complex reality, a desire for delicate fairness in judgement, an instinctive belief in the persuasive virtue of charm as an asset to style. He abandoned his intention of taking orders but never lost his reverent faith in the spirituality of religion, or his living sense of the soul which animates belief; his attitude to the personality of Jesus was an infinitely respectful admiration and love, short of devotion to a Being who was actually divine; his effort to interpret the development of Christianity was not the stern inquiry of a rigid historian, but the vision of an imaginative thinker who saw further than texts, testimonies, and documents strictly allowed. Thus his ultimate fate as an historian somewhat resembled that of his opposite number, Taine: he was charged with following the preferences of his subjective sensibility, instead of confining himself to the rigorously scientific inquiry of the professional student.

Even the scholars who have pointed out the dangerous conjectures to which Renan allows his investigation of religious problems to lead him, or the ambiguity of a standpoint which clothes disbelief in the garb, tones, and phrases of belief, have praised his liberalism, his sensitive and penetrating approach to the reading of character, and his flowing, soft and transparent style. Although his fame rests mainly on his success in humanizing the treatment of some of the most knotty questions of biblical lore, the cultivated public at large has been lastingly won chiefly by some side-issues of his work: his delightful autobiography, *Souvenirs d'enfance et de jeunesse*; his touching homage to the unobtrusive figure of his sister, *Ma sœur Henriette*; and his discerning *Essais de morale et de critique*. The *Prière sur l'Acropole*, a beautifully written appraisal—actually part of the *Souvenirs d'enfance*—of the respective shares of Celtic mysticism and Greek aestheticism in modern culture, is a piece for anthologies; but there is more substance in the *Dialogues* and the *Drames philosophiques*, serene and suggestive expressions of a many-sided wisdom, playing freely and fruitfully round some of the highest questions of ethics or social morals.

Among historians of a more severe type, conceding less to intuition and psychological interpretation, Fustel de Coulanges, 1830–89, must be given a leading place. Not that he was destitute of the imaginative sense that, when documents have yielded their facts, allows the architectural need of the mind to have its way in a theory: *La Cité antique*, 1864, *La Monarchie franque*, *La Gaule romaine*, &c., are now classed with those very suggestive and useful books that give a powerful impetus to the philosophy of history, but cannot emulate the all-but-final solidity of more modest studies. Fustel de Coulanges erected syntheses, and modern research has not spared his general views. But he did build on as safe a basis as he could, and the example of his method remains precious, even if his conclusions do not all stand. His conscientiousness is reflected in the sobriety and the terse vigour of his style.

The nineteenth century, a strikingly creative age in French literature, also witnessed the rise of criticism to the status of a fully acknowledged literary kind. On the one hand, an ideal was gradually evolved that stressed the need for learning and objectivity, and tended to make the critic a brother to the scientific historian. On the other hand, critics who belonged to the class of talented men of letters were extending their hold upon the public, and in the conflict of professional and lay opinion an entirely different conception of the function of criticism was gaining ground. The deciphering and re-expressing of a writer's temperament in terms of a reader's sensitive perceptions was becoming a recognized art, that not only threw light on original works, but sometimes added to their number books whose origin may have been derived, yet which were worth enjoying for their own sakes. Many names might be adduced on one or the other side, some standing half-way and trying to strike a compromise. The full-grown impressionist manner hardly developed before the Symbolist period. At the end of the realist age Paul de Saint-Victor (*Les Deux Masques*, 1880–3) was a brilliant heir of the romantics, as well as a precursor of subjective criticism; while Émile Montégut, 1826–95, was a discerning critic of English and American books.

Sainte-Beuve[1] owes his high standing as a critic to his exceptionally

[1] Charles-Augustin Sainte-Beuve, born at Boulogne in 1804, studied the classics there and in Paris. After a period as a medical student he joined the staff of a new and influential paper, *Le Globe*, formed friendships with the romantics, Hugo and Vigny,

successful handling of a method that is in itself obvious enough, and that could have been, indeed was, attempted by others. It consists in penetrating a writer's personality thoroughly, and expressing it in human no less than in aesthetic terms. It is thus mainly a process of psychological and intuitive perception. But it is very definitely based on a preliminary process of exploration, which takes full note, besides the works themselves, of all relevant biographical data, letters, memoirs, &c. Neither method was at all a novelty when Sainte-Beuve wrote, and they have both been used repeatedly ever since, though more often separately than together. Their fruitful combination is not rare, however, for this is the pattern that every responsible monography on a literary subject follows, or pretends to follow. What makes Sainte-Beuve a prince of critics is that he was so richly gifted in both directions. The touch of his feelers, so to speak, probing the features and the quality of a literary object, is infinitely delicate, supple, and insinuating; his valuations are almost always just, and take full account of the finer shades that make a work of art unique. That he brought to bear on an investigation which was primarily intellectual a sympathetic imagination and a tact which are of a piece with inventiveness, and that such re-creation is only a slightly different kind of creation, is plain enough. As regards the earlier process, which leads up to this act of divination, we can see in Sainte-Beuve's complete assimilation of his subject's moral and physical characteristics many resemblances with the doctor's art of diagnosis. The critic who began life as a medical student brings a scientific care to his examination of a literary case, giving even character and habit of body their full significance. Thus, his industry and power of observation provide for his aesthetic analysis the solid foundation that distinguishes it from mere impressionism; and in an often quoted phrase he has aptly compared his manner to that of a scientist, writing 'a natural history of minds'.

and published his *Tableau de la poésie française au XVIème siècle*, 1828; poems (see Part VII, chap. XLIV) and *Volupté*, a novel (see ibid., chap. XLVII). He collected his critical essays from *Le Globe*, *La Revue de Paris*, *La Revue des Deux Mondes*, as *Critiques et portraits littéraires*, 5 vols., 1836–9; *Portraits littéraires*, 1884; *Portraits de femmes*, 1864; and wrote an *Histoire de Port-Royal*, 1840–8. He taught for a time at the École Normale Supérieure, and entered the Senate in 1865. His *Causeries du Lundi*, which to begin with appeared in various papers, were collected in 15 vols., 1849–61, his *Nouveaux Lundis*, 1861–6, filled 13 volumes. He died in 1869. Several other works were published posthumously. His *Correspondance générale* is in course of publication.

The achievements of his method are imposing. The survey of *French Poetry in the XVIth century*, a landmark in the development of romanticism, stressed the analogy of that movement with the Pléiade, and revived the fame of Ronsard and his group. The *Histoire de Port-Royal* is a masterpiece in which the subject and the author's temperament are in perfect unison, for Sainte-Beuve was particularly well qualified to render with lucid sympathy the spiritual gropings and perplexities of the fervently religious. His history of the Jansenist movement finds its natural centre in the portraits of the men and women who devoted their lives to meditation and teaching; and the small band of apostles has for its background a rich prospect of the intellectual and political society of the time. The critical essays which compose the bulk of Sainte-Beuve's work (*Portraits, Lundis,* &c.) range widely over three centuries and more of French literature and life. He chooses not only writers for special study, but personalities of all kinds, many of them figures of minor importance. Indeed he seems almost to prefer character to art. His easy, flowing, and lucid style allows him to follow the outline of each figure, and as it were to caress it, with a faithful sympathy that leaves room for the piquancy, now and then, of not unkindly satirical strokes. The occasions for these studies are generally provided by the daily events of the literary world—such as the recent publication of letters, or memorials, or new editions, &c. In sum, Sainte-Beuve's gallery of portraits testifies not so much to ingenious scholarship as to the inexhaustible curiosity of a great analyst and word-painter. It has added much to the knowledge of the cultivated public, and corrected many errors of ignorance, forgetfulness, injustice; and the author's judgement has only occasionally been at fault, in his rather niggardly appreciations of some of his most eminent contemporaries.

André Chevrillon, 1864–1957, added considerably to the artistic and philosophical appreciation of great writers, especially English, as well as to the knowledge and intelligence of British civilization, in books that derive largely from the tradition of Taine.

PART IX

SYMBOLISM (1885–1914)

CHAPTER LIV

The Symbolist Venture

ALTHOUGH realism and naturalism were largely a reaction against the romantic movement, they were in part a development from it. In the change to symbolism, the law of opposition and contrast acted more radically. The groundwork on which the realists had with temporary success based themselves remained firm and unshaken; science kept its validity as the best method for the pursuit of truth; only it appeared to many writers that the pursuit of truth was not the business of literature; or, rather, truth assumed for them a quite different aspect. What was interesting, and allowed the artist to express himself most satisfactorily, was not the hard outline of matter-of-fact experience but the vague, elusive aura which somehow surrounded it to the meditative eye of a sensitive onlooker. The temper of literary creation was thus decisively altered, and a new ideal of art was erected, in the light of new values. Imagination and sensibility had recently been at some discount, if not wholly starved; they now reasserted themselves, and triumphantly shook off the ascendancy of rationalism. Their rebellion was in itself no novelty; during the hey-day of romanticism they had been in power; and important affinities thus made symbolism, essentially, a return to romantic instincts, linking them up, at bottom, with the emotion and imaginings in which literature had revelled some half-century earlier.

Indeed it was romanticism again, but with a difference. Intensity had been exploited as far as the public seemed willing to bear it, and there was no question of reverting to quite the same range of effects. But feeling could spring anew in the rich field of subtle, half-obscure shades; a precious instrument, suggestion, was at hand, offering unlimited possibilities of a rare enjoyment which was due quite as much to the gradual elucidation of what was implied as to the direct interpretation of a plain appeal. Realism continually made an appeal to the intellectual sympathy of readers, with hard, brutal descriptions that roused, at best, the bitter joy of seeing things as they are; such food needed a strong stomach; it might be healthy, but it left an after-taste of sadness; the whole entertainment lacked music, and provided something of the cold satisfaction of watching a theorem properly demonstrated. At the back of the symbolist movement was the very general longing for values which, being dim, offered a wide field to imaginative perception and allowed for enchanting harmonies of sound and sense. A new period of literature developed because a sufficiently large number of writers of talent felt these needs more or less consciously, and because a majority of the *élite* could be induced to sympathize with them.

Symbolism can thus be considered historically as a more thorough fulfilment of the promise of romanticism. But from the aesthetic point of view it was revolutionary, and the boldest example of initiative to be found so far in French literature. A study of its whole course from the origins to the last quarter of the nineteenth century may have revealed a certain number of hints and symptoms, especially during the Renaissance and the pre-classical period, or within the romantic age itself. From the time of the troubadours there had been 'precious' and 'difficult' writers, striving to convey something that words could not easily compass. There had been a Maurice Scève, a Théophile, a Saint-Amant. Victor Hugo and Baudelaire had been immediate and significant precursors. Still, the sum total was not substantial enough to qualify the usual assertion that the French mind from the first had obeyed a more or less constant craving for clear thought and lucid expression; that it had, to speak generally, set up and followed an ideal of coherence, order, and intelligibility. But here, now, was a movement purposely upsetting this scale of values, stressing the superiority of pregnant hints to plain statements; poets were staking everything on music, from

which little that was definite could be gathered, but which induced a
pleasantly open frame of mind. It was not only that the concrete, the
full-blooded raciness of facts and emotions, had recently been flood-
ing literature, in which a tendency to the refining process of abstraction had for centuries obtained. That had been an irruption due to
the romantics, and made worse—or better—by the realists. But the
break with the past was now more grievous, and indeed unpardonable: French writers were obsessed by mere shades and subtle modes
of feeling; they renounced the light, so long sought and cherished,
and they actually turned to the dark. The vague and the obscure
were coming into their own, with a downright denial of the national
tradition which had seemed inconceivable. Was symbolism, then,
a kind of intellectual apostasy, the forsaking of the inmost spirit of a
collective personality? Our reading of the psychological growth of
French literature tends to forbid any such conclusion; a rarefied
strain, and a tendency to imply rather than to state precisely, had
been present in it from the first; the classical striving for absolute
clarity of expression, which was dictated partly by a search for the
more distant and elusive aspects of the truth, was never wholly
divorced from a sense of underlying mystery. The symbolist phase
was not the humiliating self-renunciation of an exhausted people
pandering to insincere, superficial, and foreign tastes; it was the
achievement of a spiritual destiny that had been largely, but never
completely, moulded by a strong preference for one aspect of the
mind's powers. If symbolist poetry had not been the expression of an
instinctively French inspiration, it would be hard to explain how it
could have started a liberating movement that influenced Europe
and the world, or why other nations chose to seek in Verlaine and
Valéry supreme examples of a beauty with which, for the most part,
they were already familiar.

This profound autonomy and truth of the symbolist movement
by no means excludes the presence and action of foreign influences;
these should, indeed, be remembered all the more because they were
tokens of the inner needs of French sensibility. It was because of the
widespread dissatisfaction with the brutality of naturalism, and the
cold objectivity of the Parnassiens, that the appeal of great foreign
masters of the literature of idealist emotions penetrated to the subconscious layers of the French mind, with such galvanizing effects.

Studies of comparative literature do well to draw attention to the various foreign influences on the French mentality of this period— to the English romantic poets, the philosophy of Carlyle and Emerson, the pessimism of Schopenhauer, the mysticism and fraternal spirit of Russian novels, no less than to the Pre-Raphaelite painters, Turner's dreams of light and mist, Wagner's music, and before long the Scandinavian writers. Impressionism in French painting dates from about the same time, and although it was essentially an independent growth, it had, like the symbolist poetry, many foreign affinities.

The romantic poets had freed language and metre, pulling down the barriers of conventional dignity that in the past had restricted the use of words, and making verse itself more supple. Some of the symbolists went farther, demanding complete artistic freedom and seeking effects of melody and expressiveness beyond the limits of traditional prosody. Others used their liberty more sparingly, and sought in music only the regularity of a haunting but rather monotonous song. Still, the way was opened for the practically unlimited vagaries of more recent poets. When Verlaine wrote:

> De la musique avant toute chose,
> Et pour cela préfère l'impair,

he was putting an end—or trying to put it—to the rule of even numbers, and shifting the centre of the art of poetic suggestion from thought to sound. Nothing remained for his successors but to draw the natural conclusions from the principle of total independence, and to measure the value of each initiative by its result. Already the set habits of language as a means of logical expression had been banned by Mallarmé; his example was not lost on the writers who chose the label of 'Décadentisme' in order to emphasize their defiant attitude, and as 'Décadents' formed the left wing of the young army of the 'Symbolistes'. The wing was never very numerous, but it impressed the critics beyond its actual strength.

The origin of the name 'Symbolisme' can be definitely traced. In the years of ferment that followed 1880, there were many attempts to find a descriptive label for the new kind of poetry, a banner, as it were, under which a large but disorderly troop of poets, with confused and ill-defined needs, might rally. In 1886 one young poet, Jean

Moréas, proposed the word 'Symbolisme', which was accepted, and became a shibboleth for the friends, a target for the foes, of the movement. What it purported to signify was that indirect expression should become the central principle of art. A 'symbol' was a sign, or system of signs, the suggestive powers of which exceeded its direct connotation. A vague atmosphere of half-mysterious or semi-mystical meaning lingered about the term, from its religious or esoteric use; and to the young enthusiasts of this generation it echoed the appeal of the more precious, new-fangled forms of art, of pictorial aestheticism, for instance, and the music of Wagner. But leaving out these overtones, the heart of the message was that poetry, and literature generally, should aim at conveying, through the natural affinities of words with emotions and imaginings, dim, indefinite shades of meaning far beyond the trite and narrow scope of plain phrasing.

In the history of French literature to date symbolism represents the last movement with an influence sufficiently wide and pervasive to justify its selection as the major feature of a period. Not that its ascendancy was universal or undisputed. The thirty years over which it is conventionally accepted as having presided were a medley of currents and cross-currents, in which no general discipline of art was even relatively dominant. Nevertheless, Symbolism left a deep mark on the age as a whole, and stamped itself upon many writers who were opposed or indifferent to it. It did not die after 1914, but in its broader spirit still lives on, a diffuse but active leaven. Whatever may happen in the future, its transient fortune will not be forgotten in the literary memory of the French nation. The same cannot be said of the following period, from which, probably, we have not yet emerged. The historian of the inter-war years, and of those we are now living, is faced with a hopeless search for clues that are so far invisible, and that time alone can reveal, if they do indeed exist.

CHAPTER LV

Symbolist Poets

NOTHING is more remarkable in the years leading up to the symbolist movement than the importance attached by a number of small groups to the free, uninterrupted play of the imagination. These groups came into being independently, and at first had practically no influence on literary development. It was only after 1880 that the critics, and in some cases the leading symbolists themselves, called attention to their significance. Their influence was gradually recognized, and at a later date, when the Symbolist age itself had ended, similar small movements were among the complex of causes responsible for the latest phase in French literature, the Transition, of which the 'surrealist' movement is only one aspect.

Gérard de Nerval and Baudelaire exercised a more distant but still perceptible influence upon the growth of symbolism. As for the occasional examples of suggestive poetry in the pre-classical age of the seventeenth century, the case was rather that the new literature drew attention to them than that they provided models or encouragement for it.

Isidore Ducasse, 1846–70, born at Montevideo of a French father, wrote and published in Paris, under the name of Comte de Lautréamont, a prose poem, *Les Chants de Maldoror*, 1868–9, which waited half a century for its original power to be discovered. This work of a very young man is both turbulent and turgid; a chaotic outpouring of rhetoric, satire, and images with all the freedom of uncensored expression. Striking phrases and grand visions are scattered among bizarre thoughts and crude fancies; a genuine lyrical gift gathers the medley into the eloquent stanzas of a prophetic, defiant hymn. The aesthetic or intellectual value of the whole would be slight but for the audacity of this uncontrolled self-revelation and a Byronic flaunting of the revolt of man. The 'Surréalistes' were to claim Lautréamont as their direct precursor.

Rimbaud's[1] deep and lasting influence on French literature far exceeds the confines of the symbolist movement; he was one of the arch-rebels whose aim for more than half a century has been the upheaval not only of poetry, but of art, ethics, and logic. His work has been overlaid with so much commentary and discussion, that he has himself become a symbol, and the central figure of what has justly been called a myth. His scathing indictment of traditional thinking and writing severed the remaining links with the past, that both romanticism and realism had left untouched. His desperate effort to make literature the outlet of the immediate experience of heart, mind, and senses, has turned it into the creative exploration of the inner world. The *sonnet des voyelles* has given a charter to the *vision colorée*, and opened the way for some of the boldest attempts to enlarge the field of imaginative art. He stirred the sense of the half-mystic power of language, and refreshed with a totally new meaning the old belief in the magic value of words. His iconoclasm was an infuriated idealism, and a sanity lives in the poison of his most deadly ironies. It is possible to regard him as a landmark on the road to the moral suicide of the race, or as a harbinger of thorough rejuvenation.

In the uncertainty of our present, transitional age it is only natural that Rimbaud's imperfect utterances should attract the impassioned attention of revolutionaries, thinkers, and artists. To those who read poetry for the sake of its accomplished beauty there is little promise in his outpourings, though dictated by a most genuine, impatient need to vent the burning truth within. The bitter flavour of revolt gives an incomparable tang to his earliest pieces, written in fairly regular lines, wielding a spell of suggestive music that puts them, with a more ferocious power, on a line of descent from Baudelaire. *Une Saison en Enfer* is a strangely far-reaching confession, which abjures all meretricious blandishment of style for the sake of absolute sincerity.

[1] Arthur Rimbaud, born in the Ardennes, 1854, showed a fiercely independent nature from boyhood. He began to write very early, got to know Verlaine, and had a strong influence over him, though ten years younger. He accompanied him to England and Belgium but broke with him after a quarrel in which he was shot and wounded. Hardly over twenty he gave up literature, led a wandering life abroad; he died in 1891. We have recovered his first poems; *Une Saison en Enfer*, prose and verse, published by himself, 1873, re-edited 1895; *Les Illuminations*, poems and *poèmes en prose*, written 1874-5, published 1885; and sundry additions since his death.

Les Illuminations are a fusion, with a resultingly free pattern, of entirely liberated verse and poetic prose, a form which may be held to have inspired and guided the 'verset' of Claudel. Their flashing sentences and paragraphs have indeed something of the luminous effect of an ancient, decorated manuscript, as well as an arresting visionary quality. Their lack of either superficial continuity or any underlying connexion in logic represents both a final stage of literary experiment and the first example of what was to be *surréalisme*. But if impressive they are obscure and repay only the most enthusiastic perusal.

In Rimbaud the decadent mood is no less conspicuous than his symbolism; in Charles Cros, 1842–88 (*Le Coffret de Santal*, 1873); Tristan Corbière, 1845–75 (*Amours jaunes*, 1873), and Maurice Rollinat, 1844–1903 (*Les Névroses, Dans les Brandes*, 1883), it is predominant. Of the trio Corbière is the most vigorous and attractive personality. His bitter, explosive verse is full of clumsy prosaisms, but it also contains unforgettably graphic passages. This instinct of defiant rebellion is coloured, in Cros, with irony; and in Rollinat, with a macabre sense of anguished terror.

Verlaine and Mallarmé, the two poets who brought symbolism to its full accomplishment, were early enough in date to count also as precursors.

Verlaine[1] had admirable gifts, and wrote some pieces of unequalled exquisiteness. If he just fails to rank with the very greatest French poets, this is due to his somewhat limited inspiration. But pure poetry owes nothing to subject; and in its simplicity the best of Verlaine equals the highest art.

Even with his fine sense of literary values he did not at once discover his own virtue of spontaneous, lyrical utterance, but when once

---

[1] Paul Verlaine, born at Metz, 1844, studied in Paris, and became a clerk in a municipal office. He published *Poèmes saturniens*, 1866; *Les Fêtes galantes*, 1869; *La Bonne Chanson*, 1870, and after being compromised in the Paris 'Commune' he fled to England and Belgium. His friendship with Rimbaud (see above), their quarrel, the drama that followed, and Verlaine's imprisonment for two years, filled the period 1872–5. While in prison he wrote the *Romances sans paroles*, 1874. After one more stay in England, he published *Sagesse*, 1881, which was very successful. He tried farming and teaching at one period, and also lectured in France and abroad. His last years were poor and irregular and he died in hospital, 1896. His late works include *Les Poètes maudits, Jadis et naguère, Parallèlement*, &c.

he did, his sure instinct, or possibly no more than his good fortune, enabled him to keep it free from the artificiality that is the bane of the most genuine spontaneity, as soon as it becomes conscious. His first volume of verse, the *Poèmes saturniens,* in which the Parnassien influence is strong, contains imitations of Baudelaire, Leconte de Lisle, and even of Hugo, that show the skill of a born writer. Despite all this talent it would still be no more than a 'derived' book, were it not for an evocative quality beyond that of the Parnassiens. Some pieces, indeed, have a power of delicate, indefinite suggestion that already points towards Symbolism. *Fêtes galantes,* which came next, contains several masterpieces of airy, fluid music (*Clair de lune, En sourdine,* &c.), where the careful melody flows without the slightest jar, and at the same time reveals a sure union of manner and temperament. But the atmosphere, reminiscent of Watteau and eighteenth-century charm, is the one dear to contemporary art, still obsessed with the images of the past. The lighter, ten-syllabled line is often used for its musical effect, and Verlaine is also plainly aware of what can be done with short measures. The step towards the simple expression of sentiment, his most characteristic note, is decisive in *La Bonne Chanson,* lyrics of married love that are among the poet's finest work. These two volumes, with *Romances sans paroles* and *Sagesse,* which followed, contain the final achievement of his talent; new accents of despondency, and humble compunction, mix with others that almost remind one of Blake's *Songs of Innocence.* Every reader familiar with his whole work must know how quick and disastrous the fall was from this pure quality to the cynicism of the subsequent volumes. The art is still alive, but the inspiration is hopelessly vulgar, or utterly lacking, even in the poems of religious repentance.

Verlaine's reputation is thus exclusively, but beyond all question securely, dependent on the first part of his work. There, we enjoy the thrilling simplicity of naked emotion, conveyed in the most genuine words, with a liquid harmony of sound and mood that few have ever reached, and none surpassed. That the tone of sadness should be more frequent than that of joy agrees only too well with the truth of sensitive experience. But the remnant of rhetoric in the confessions of the romantics has been purged away; the appeal to emotional sympathy is purified and as it were excused by the shedding of all pride and pretence, and the candid revelation of the poet's soul. That such candour should soon have been degraded to shamelessness is a highly useful warning to the sentimental; but the final degradation does not destroy the appeal. Above all, however, the unique quality of so many of Verlaine's lyrics is due to their fluidity, their use of language as a veil, through which the inner world may be at one moment clearly glimpsed, and at another miraculously suggested. 'Prends l'Éloquence et tords-lui son cou', Verlaine wrote in his short *Art poétique*, composed about 1874, published in 1884; and he followed his own precept with such exquisitely musical effect in *La lune blanche luit dans les bois*; *Donc, ce sera par un clair jour d'été*; *Il pleure dans mon cœur*; *Le ciel est, par-dessus le toit*; *Le son du cor s'afflige vers les bois*, as to inspire the lovely settings of Hahn and Fauré, which have become inseparable in our memory from the poems themselves. Verlaine's work is thus a triumphant proof that French poetry possesses the very qualities so often denied it. Yet it is also true, from the fact that he has some analogy with Villon, that his symbolism links us with old precedents in French literature.

Mallarmé's[1] artistic effort and concentration, on the contrary, though his literary career was parallel with Verlaine's, grew more and more intense with time. But his originality increased at the cost of the element of balance, without which a writer's contact with the public is inevitably endangered. The esoteric character of his work was finally so pronounced as to become proverbial. The short volume of his poems is none the less a precious monument to the high purpose and rare quality which was the common aim of the Parnassiens and the Symbolistes. Few readers are so familiar with his style, and so well trained in the interpretation of riddles, that their enjoyment is not marred or ruined by its density and allusiveness. But fewer still do not feel that some of his poems are superb master-pieces, and that most of the others do at least contain sublime moments, and communicate an intoxicating sense of visionary

[1] Stéphane Mallarmé, born in Paris, 1842, spent some time in England, then taught English for thirty years in provincial French schools and in Paris. He published *L'Après-midi d'un faune*, 1874; a translation of Poe's poems, 1888; *Vers et prose*, 1893; *Divagations* (criticism), 1897; and his complete *Poésies* appeared in Brussels ,1897. His home in Paris was frequented by most of the distinguished writers of the time, and his personal influence profoundly felt. He died in 1898.

energy. This is sufficient to make his name last, as well as to make him the cult of an *élite*. For actual popularity he did not care, nor is this ever likely to be his fate.

The characteristics of his manner, elaborated through years of unceasing labour, can be plainly described, for no writer's doctrine was ever more fully rooted in his temperament. Beauty to him, not success, was the single purpose of an artist's devotion to his task. The unpardonable sin was to sacrifice any of the just aversions of a fastidious taste to easy intelligibility, or to the commonplace preferences of even the cultivated public. The poet's idiom should be his own creation, and free from all fossilized patterns of expression. The most severe economy and compression would ensure the greatest wealth of content; and the more indirect the utterance, the stronger its mental stimulus. Explicit logic and syntax had to go, if the repeated shocks of broken construction are to rouse and reward attention. Things must be hinted, not said, and suggestion must be the standard method. The music of the lines was a quality even more suggestive than words and images, and although Mallarmé's musicality was not like Verlaine's, being more varied and nervous, less continuously flowing, the two leaders of French symbolism were agreed upon that essential part of their programme.

The devout Mallarmean would probably feel himself bound to recommend the most obscure poems as his favourites; but one may still mention the relatively lucid *Apparition*, *Soupir*, *Les Fenêtres*, *Tristesse d'été*, *Brise marine*, or the sonnet: *Sur les bois oubliés quand passe l'hiver sombre*, &c. As for *L'Après-midi d'un faune*, usually regarded as Mallarmé's supreme achievement, its suggestive power is wonderful, but its shimmering, voluptuous fancies are not to be probed for a solid core of meaning. Mallarmé's experiment was certainly not fruitless, and should be admired as a fine struggle against the imperfection of that all-too human instrument, language, with which the noblest poetry has to deal; his greatness is that he was not utterly defeated in the attempt, and his half triumphs are glorious beyond complete ones. It must, however, be remarked that his influence did much to lure French poetry into a half-century of implicitness, from which the near future may recoil with disapproval: symptoms are not wanting that would betoken a long-delayed return to a simpler intelligibility.

Mallarmé's prose poems—and practically all his prose is poetic—closely resemble his verse, in their compression and evocative force, and in their difficulty. That his lecture, *La Musique et les lettres*, should have been patiently heard in 1894, at Oxford and Cambridge, by mixed audiences in which the purely academic element of professors and undergraduates was in the minority, speaks well for English courtesy.

But Symbolism must be emphasized as a profound movement of the French mind and French poetry and not merely the craze of a few exceptional writers. Only a few of its important disciples can be mentioned here. They were, broadly speaking, less advanced in their views than Mallarmé and even Verlaine, and they illustrate the far-reaching effect and the fertility of what was in fact a spontaneous revolt of French idealism against the realism of the preceding age. They also show how strongly the Symbolists were indebted to foreign sources for their literary, aesthetic, and spiritual ideals. A significant fact of the period was the parallelism and the fecundity of a vein of Belgian literature which showed strongly national traits, but was at the same time so closely associated with French symbolism as to be inseparable from it, for even then France was giving as much as she was receiving. But in most of the symbolists, however wide may have been the field of foreign influence, there prevailed a habit of intellectual discipline, a fund of instinctive attachment to definiteness of expression, that linked up the movement with the inmost spirit of French tradition. The determined break with the past, a break so pronounced that it is possible to speak of a partial denationalization, came later with surrealism.

Foreign elements are conspicuous in Jules Laforgue, 1860–87, born of Breton parents at Montevideo, like Lautréamont, and whose short adult life was largely spent in Berlin. This strong infusion of cosmopolitanism seems rather to have encouraged his spiritual independence than given him any one decided bent. His *Sanglots de la terre*, 1883, first published in 1901, the *Complaintes*, 1885, and the *Imitation de Notre-Dame de la Lune*, 1886, are of far more interest than his humorous fancies in prose, *Les Moralités légendaires*, 1887. They are deeply pessimistic, full of self-mockery and sarcastic criticism of life, with a particularly bitter flavour that is due to the fatigue and disgust of a jaded sensibility facing a world grown old. Their prosodic interest is that they carry the liberation of French verse almost to the final stage. Far more than to symbolism, Laforgue belongs to the Décadents; and his ironical vein, as well as his *vers libre* herald the further developments of the twentieth century.

Another determined rebel was Villiers de l'Isle-Adam, 1838–89, who lived longer than Laforgue or Rimbaud. He hated the society in which he moved, and maintained contact with several of the most advanced symbolists, serving as a rallying-point for the new idealism. After his early poems he wrote almost always in prose, a prose that was at will ironical, as befitted his satirical purpose, or impassioned, to clothe an exalted vision of what had been or what might be. He had sufficient command of his feelings to make satire amusing, as *Tribulat Bonhomet* and the *Contes cruels* testify. The dream and the mysticism are undeniably striking and eloquent, but turn too often to vagueness and confusion. Of this class *Axël*, published posthumously, 1890, rouses hopes of greatness that are not fully realized; but no more vigorous refusal to be content with the moral or aesthetic realism of the age came to comfort the hearts and warm the imaginations of the symbolists.

Jean Moréas (Papadiamantopoulos), 1856–1910, was born in Greece. He learnt French at an early age and came to Paris, where he joined the controversy against the Parnassiens; it was he who wrote the *Manifeste littéraire de l'École Symboliste* (*Le Figaro*, 18 September 1886). His first poems (*Les Syrtes*, 1884, &c.), true to the spirit of the new school, and to Verlaine's *Art poétique*, were mainly a search after freedom of metre. But a contrary tendency appeared in his *Pélerin passionné*, 1890, and became increasingly evident. He founded the École Romane, with Maurice du Plessis, Charles Maurras, and others; their openly avowed principle being to return to the traditional pattern of an explicitly formal type of poetry. This was the first definite check to symbolism; without losing its prestige, it lost its claim to be one of those general movements that are for a while irresistible. Finally, the *Stances*, 1899–1901, more genuinely than any of his other collections, reflected the personality of Moréas. They are very short pieces, of two, three, or four quatrains, embodying the essence of impressions or moods. Their neat, compact phrasing and regular lilt bear the stamp of a classical temperament, not very original, but in its artistry firm and elegant.

The importance of Gustave Kahn, 1859–1939, is due to his initiative. Towards 1885, what has been called *vers libre* was in the air; and
Rimbaud's contribution to its decisive emergence has been mentioned. But Rimbaud was a solitary talent, with few contacts and, at
first, very little influence. It was left for Kahn, in agreement with
Laforgue, to tackle the problem directly, and bring it to the full
attention and consciousness of poets and the public. His *Palais
nomades*, 1887, is the first complete break with what for many centuries had been the numerical basis of French prosody; and ten years
later he emphasized the significance of the new departure in the Preface to a new edition of his book. Rhythm, he points out, is a supple
adaptation of each line to the inflexion and shade of the mood expressed, the number of syllables being immaterial. This revolutionary
principle was used sparingly at first. But the door was opened to
unlimited freedom; a vast intermediary field was discovered between
regular 'poetry' and 'prose'. Mallarmé at once recognized its scope,
and the possibility it must entail for each poet to create his own
metre. Claudel's 'verset', to take one example, was to be a natural
outcome. In other respects Kahn's practice, which can best be studied
in the *Livre d'images*, 1897, did not prove very fruitful; his ear,
though subtle, was not very creatively attuned to the melody of
words; and in his lyrics the inner conflict of simplicity with preciosity
is frequently evident.

It is interesting to note the large number of foreign-born writers
among the active followers of the movement. Stuart Merrill, 1863–
1915, and Francis Vielé-Griffin were Americans, though one element
in the latter's mixed ancestry was French. Merrill sought consciously
to fuse with the aims of Symbolism the musical values that appealed
to him intimately, not only, as Baudelaire had pointed out, in Poe,
but in the whole tradition of English poetry (*Poèmes*, 1897; *Les
Quatre Saisons*, 1900; *Une Voix dans la foule*, 1909). Vielé-Griffin was
tempted by the same harmonies, and laid even more stress on the
fluidity of *vers libre*; but his allegiance to the properly symbolist
example did not destroy his originality, or the fervent joy and love
of life which contrasted with the drooping melancholy most often
characteristic of the French venture (*Cueille d'avril*, 1886; *La
Chevauchée d'Yeldis*; *Fleurs du chemin et chansons de la route*, &c.).

A 'literature of French expression' has developed in several countries where a native culture with affinities to that of France has flourished, on soil that ethnic elements, history, and traditions have made more or less congenial. A complete survey could not leave out Belgian, Swiss, and French Canadian writers, who are undoubtedly part and parcel of their own national life, but who are also, on the spiritual plane, united by language or artistic influences to a foreign growth. The scope of the present work is too limited to include them, with the exception of the great Belgian writers whose sympathy with the symbolist doctrines was instinctive, and who were in close touch with the movement in its hey-day.

Vigour and a rich vein of realism have long been features of Flemish art. They were conspicuous during the last quarter of the century in the work of Camille Lemonnier, 1844–1913, a robust personality and an original disciple of the French naturalists. He was the leader of *La Jeune Belgique*, an influential review, strictly devoted to a literature not unlike that of the Parnassiens in spirit. Shortly after 1880 the magnetic appeal of symbolism reached Belgium. Its mouthpiece was another review, *La Wallonie*, founded by Albert Mockel, 1866–1945, who was both a gifted poet (*Chantefable un peu naïve*, 1891, *Clartés*, 1902) and an able defender of the new literary ideal (*Propos de littérature*, 1894). Another poet, Georges Rodenbach, 1855–98, lived in Paris and became identified with French symbolism. The dramatic melancholy of his writing (*Le Règne du silence*, 1891; *Les Vies encloses*, 1896; *Bruges la morte*, prose, 1892) was to some extent re-echoed in 1904 by Charles van Lerberghe, 1861–1907, in the more philosophical visions of *La Chanson d'Ève*.

Maurice Maeterlinck, 1862–1949, a writer of international fame, was no less well known in England than in France, and only the chief aspects of his work need be mentioned. The poet (*Serres chaudes*, 1889, &c.), as the far more numerous readers of his prose would expect, continued by the most simple means to stir the emotions and to awaken a sense of life's mysteries. The dramatist turned to deliberate and striking use the power of suggestion contained in elementary dialogue and repeated phrases (*La Princesse Maleine*, 1890; *Pelléas et Mélisande*, 1892; *Intérieur*, 1894; *Aglavaine et Sélysette*, 1896; *Monna Vanna*, 1902; *L'Oiseau bleu*, 1909). The moralist and essayist borrowed his favourite themes from a meditation on human life (*Le Trésor des humbles*, 1896; *La Sagesse et la destinée*, 1898; *Le Temple enseveli*, 1901, &c.), or from a penetrating study of the obscure consciousness of animals and plants (*La Vie des abeilles*, 1901; *L'Intelligence des fleurs*, 1907; *La Vie des termites*, 1926; *La Vie des fourmis*, 1931, &c.). He has made idealism a cherished possession of numberless readers, not only by the spell of his style but by the fearless intellectual sincerity he brings to bear on the darkest problems of destiny.

Émile Verhaeren, 1855–1916, less familiar to the English or French public, was a native of the northern part of Belgium; he represents the Flemish temperament with intense vigour, but transcends it, his rich culture having steeped him in the Latin influences which contribute so much to the complex originality of Belgian literature. Still, to read him is to feel carried away by a generous temperament overflowing with primitive energies. In the somewhat sophisticated atmosphere of Symbolist poetry, Verhaeren creates a contrast by his almost popular inspiration. His rhythms and harmonies are simple, but they seize upon us with the irresistible authority of a force of nature; they are the signs of a movement of the poet's soul, of a genuine craving for expression. Freedom of imagery and of versification count for much, in typical symbolist fashion. Impressions are conveyed by the sound and the emotional value of the words, independently of any literal value: statement and syntax are sacrificed to suggestive music. Most of modern poetry was soon to be written on that principle; but how disappointing the effect, too often! Here we have burning vision and a genuine outpouring of sensibility, but an infallible instinct keeps both under control; the lyricism of Verhaeren, true and free as it is, never passes the limit of intelligibility; our consciousness, soothed into relaxing some of its logical demands, still preserves its dignity.

Periods are clearly marked in the development of the poet's manner. Nostalgia and a quiet despair prevail in *Les Soirs, Les Débâcles, Les Flambeaux noirs*, 1887–90. In *Les Campagnes hallucinées, Les Villages illusoires, Les Villes tentaculaires*, 1893–5, the ravages of toil, and the inroad of industry upon the dying world of the villages, are called up with profound sympathy; *Les Visages de la vie, Les Forces tumultueuses*, 1899–1902, rise to higher themes of acceptance and love, and an intuitive assurance of the permanence of life. The confident serenity of married love pervades the *vers libre* of *Les*

Heures claires, 1896. The powerful glimpses of the history of the world in *La Multiple Splendeur* and *Les Rythmes souverains* remind one of Hugo's *Légende des siècles*. Symbolism, in Verhaeren's work, is an abundant and substantial stream, if not of the most intellectual kind.

With Albert Samain, 1858–1900, the music and voluptuousness of a somewhat enervated symbolism languished and came near to dying of its very perfection. His emotions were sincere, but he could not give new life to the age-old themes of lyricism. His melodies are honeyed, but cloying (*Au jardin de l'infante*, 1893; *Aux flancs du vase*, 1898, &c.). There is more individuality in the aristocratic talent of Henri de Régnier, 1864–1936, who was too fastidious to remain a Symbolist when symbolism became so fashionable as to develop conventions of its own. His subjects are often very close to those of Samain, but he brings a saving measure of discretion to their treatment, and the poetry that results is a fine harmony of classical regularity with a delicate dose of freedom in the handling of the metre. His fancy is naturally wistful, dwelling for preference on images of pre-Revolutionary France, such as the fading glories of Versailles (*Les Jeux rustiques et divins*, 1897; *Les Médailles d'argile*, 1900; *La Cité des eaux*, 1902, &c.). His prose novels have the same fondly imaginative quality, and even his pictures of contemporary life have an air of the past (*La Double Maîtresse*, 1900; *Les Amants singuliers*, 1901, &c.).

Symbolism was even more definitely a phase in the development of three writers who, having assimilated the lessons of the school, turned them into elements of their independent art. The personal traits in the figure of Francis Jammes, 1868–1938, are very prominent indeed; he took care to cultivate them as fully as was compatible with his manner of almost naïve simplicity. Living away from Paris in his native province of Béarn, he chose its landscape and people for his theme, and the routine and incidents of village farming. The spirit was one of moderate realism tempered by a gentle, idealistic sentimentality. From the half-pagan atmosphere of his first works he turned increasingly to a heartfelt acceptance of the Catholic faith. His poems (*De l'Angélus de l'aube à l'Angélus du soir*, 1898; *Clairières dans le ciel*, 1906) are in a free alexandrine metre. His stories should also be mentioned (*Pommes d'Anis, Clara d'Ellébeuse*, 1899; *Le Roman du lièvre*, 1903). Charles Guérin, 1873–1907, subtly and discreetly harmonized his return to the relative regularity of verse by concentrating on the moods and emotions of the inner life; his premature death cut short a very promising career (*Le Semeur de cendres*, 1901; *L'Homme intérieur*, 1905). Paul Fort, born in 1872, is one more proof of the fecundity of the symbolist spirit, of its breadth and variety, when once the arbitrary fashions induced by its narrower interpretations have been transcended. Here an apparently paradoxical association has been attempted, with very fair success, between a sophisticated mode of poetry, and a simple, indeed a popular, inspiration. In the many series of his *Ballades françaises*, 1897–1940, the symbolist influence is evident in the evocation, through free snatches of song, shorter or longer, as the theme allowed, of France herself, her past and her present, the figures and incidents of her history, the features of her land and her people. The supreme value of the metre is the supple manner in which it adapts itself to the familiarity and raciness of the tone; and in order to conjure away the spell of traditional, broken verse the lines, though syllabically regular, are printed in one continuous paragraph, like prose. The best known of these ballades, a term which must be dissociated from the meaning it bore of old with Marot, and recently with Hugo, is one that has been dramatized, the *Roman de Louis XI*. Paul Fort's connexion with the symbolist movement is also exemplified by his creation of the Théâtre d'Art, 1890, and of the magazine, *Vers et prose*, 1905.

The Comtesse de Noailles, 1876–1933, a Rumanian princess by birth, but brought up and married in France, was a poetess of ardently romantic inspiration, who was infected by the general enthusiasm of the Symbolists. She first chiefly expressed an almost pagan rapture before the intoxicating charm of nature—the aristocratic nature of the gardens of the 'Île de France' (*Le Cœur innombrable*, 1901; *L'Ombre des jours*, 1902); and next the sufferings of a human heart bruised by life and death (*Les Vivants et les morts*, 1913; *Le Poème de l'amour*, 1924). Her voice had the impassioned candour that was becoming characteristic of a woman writer's enfranchised sensibility, and that man's sophisticated fastidiousness had learnt to avoid.

CHAPTER LVI

The Novel

THE novel, as was natural, was not so readily influenced by the symbolist spirit as poetry; its more substantial links with reality necessitated a large measure of direct statement as opposed to imaginative freedom. But fiction has always shown itself the most supple of literary forms, with an unlimited power of adaptation to all the varieties of manners and moods. In fact, there were symbolist novels well before symbolism grew conscious of itself; and it is in a novel by Villiers de L'Isle-Adam, written before 1890, that a critic has seen the typical expression of the symbolist spirit (see *Axël's Castle*, by Edmund Wilson, 1931). During the years 1885–1914, when the output of French fiction was more abundant and varied than ever before, the presence and the action of symbolism can be observed like a leaven in that abundance and that variety, stirring to fuller life a substance already quickened by the imagination. Even writers whose intellectual attitude appears to continue the realism of the preceding age—as for instance Bourget—show a freedom of conception and a sense of inner problems which owe much to the symbolist rebellion. But symbolism is a more decisive element in the later novelists of the period, such as Loti and Alain-Fournier.

Paul Bourget, 1852–1935, clearly inherited his attitude to fiction from the naturalist age, and did indeed confess his indebtedness to Taine. He was serious, earnest, and philosophical, drawing upon a solid fund of observation, and writing with a purpose. But that purpose was not to show what is, but to teach moral and social lessons. The naturalist had been obsessed by the material world, its rankness, violence, and unsavoury features; Bourget sets out primarily to be a psychologist, less concerned with describing what men do than with discovering the reasons for their actions. That attention should be thus focused on inner motives was in keeping with the neo-idealism the symbolists claimed to reassert; it befitted an age on whose intellectual formation Bergson was soon to be such an important in-

·fluence. From poetry the young writer turned to penetrating, conscientious studies of minds and manners (*Essais de psychologie contemporaine*, 1885), which helped greatly towards the more discerning appraisal of Stendhal and Baudelaire. His novels are full diagnoses of moral cases: *Cruelle énigme*, 1885, *André Cornélis*, 1886, were not unnoticed; *Le Disciple*, 1889, which attracted considerable attention, widened the study of a sentimental incident into a survey of the conflict between the duties of life and a purely intellectual allegiance to science. After *Cosmopolis*, 1893, Bourget was increasingly preoccupied with social obligations, and his novels took on a decidedly religious and conservative complexion (*L'Étape*, 1902; *L'Émigré*, 1907, &c.). His *Physiologie de l'amour moderne*, and his book on America, *Outre-mer*, 1895, merit special mention. The interest and sincerity of his critical thought preserve his work from oblivion, in spite of some ponderousness and the occasional stiffness of his style.

Élémir Bourges, 1852–1925, is an example of the symbolist revival of imaginative writing. His retiring life was devoted wholly to the slow maturation of a few books: novels, *Le Crépuscule des dieux*, 1884; *Sous la hache*, 1885; *Les Oiseaux s'envolent, les fleurs tombent*, 1893, &c.; and an allegorical epic in prose, *La Nef*, 1904 and 1922. The latter is one of those ambitious attempts, the type of which remains Goethe's second *Faust*, to graft a cosmic philosophy upon old legends. The myth of Prometheus, freely interpreted, becomes the starting-point of a grand spiritual drama, in which the problems of man's destiny are figuratively expressed in a spirit of anxious doubt and hard-won stoicism. The rhythmic prose, exalted and inspired, has a beauty not unworthily reminiscent of the high poetry of Shelley's *Prometheus Unbound*. But here the comparison ends. *La Nef* is no supreme masterpiece, but a mass of chaotic fragments, which a consistent purpose vainly struggles to build into a work of art. A rich mine for anthologies, it exhausts the patience of the reader, and remains an admirable failure. The novels, semi-historical with a large element of fiction, are more firmly knit. They are powerfully written, in a style that is braced and glowing; and the stories are full of pathos and tragic pity. Bourges is a distinguished writer, little known to the general public, yet an arresting figure. He was bent upon widening the scope of French Symbolism, and broadly cosmopolitan in his tastes, influenced alike by Victor Hugo,

Saint-Simon and the 'memorialists', Shakespeare and the Elizabethans, Shelley and Wagnerian music.

Two brothers, Jérôme, 1874–1953, and Jean, 1877–1952, Tharaud, were successful authors of what might be called the novel of culture —a literary form born not of the rough instinctive energy of temperament, but of a talent and a taste fashioned by the intelligent study of literature. Not that their work is purely imitative and without originality: it is original in preserving its strength and avoiding the defects which a high degree of awareness often entails. Their manner has a classical quality free from the tameness now generally associated with passive discipleship to the classics. Positive virtues were within their reach, and they very deftly made the best of them. Their highly distinguished art has a leaven of romanticism and symbolism especially apparent in their appeal to the imaginative curiosity of their readers and their vivid images of, for instance, the civilizations, races, and landscapes of the world. They are also competent story-tellers; their plots are nearly always skilfully constructed, and their characters are well drawn (*Les Hobereaux*, 1907; *La Maîtresse servante*, 1911). Some of their chief novels revive historical episodes (*La Tragédie de Ravaillac*, 1913; *Quand Israël est roi*, 1921). More often they depict exotic milieux, and they frequently touch on social problems, such as the Jewish groups of central Europe or the Near East, and French Morocco (*La Fête arabe*, 1912; *L'Ombre de la Croix*, 1917; *Rabat ou les heures marocaines*, 1918; *Marakech ou les seigneurs de l'Atlas*, 1920; *La Rose de Saron*, 1927, &c.). The wealth of concrete impressions that they handle is set off by the exact soberness of a style uniformly clear and elegant, preserved from the sin of overemphasis by the fine artistic tact that was, in its minute delicacies, common to both.

The authoress whose works after the year 1905 were signed by her own surname of Colette belongs to a very different category. Intuitiveness is the outstanding quality of her style, and the almost classical sobriety that her manner has gradually acquired has not dimmed her fresh, exquisite sensitiveness. Her gift was revealed at the beginning in a series of sketches that dealt with a young girl's varied schooling and experiences (*Claudine à l'école*, 1900, &c.), and which to a large extent owed their slightly cynical candour and perversity to the author's collaborator, her first husband, Henry

Gauthier-Villars, or 'Willy'. After separating from him she turned to ingenuous confessions of emotional and sensuous experiences, marked by extreme delicacy and subtlety. The staple of these books is autobiography, of a decidedly free and imaginative kind (*Sept dialogues de bêtes*, 1905; *Les Vrilles de la vigne*, 1908; *La Vagabonde*, 1910; *L'Envers du music-hall*, 1913; *L'Entrave*, 1913; *Mitsou*, 1917; *Chéri*, 1920; *La Maison de Claudine*, 1923; *La Naissance du jour*, 1928; *La Chatte*, 1933, &c.). For the right-minded reader these minute studies of the ways in which we can be alternately caressed and wounded by contact with nature and with life contain only the pagan sanity of truth, served by a wonderfully acute perception of the physical world, and a divining sympathy with all tender, obscure existences, especially children, flowers, and cats. Of all her portraits of human creatures, drawn with or without a model, her masterpiece is that of her mother. She sees love in the mystery of its intoxication and torment, ever quickened and threatened by a premonition of inevitable change. The deep note of quiet despair and resignation is thus often audible, mingling with an ecstatic delight in nature, the seasons, and our capacity for sensuous enjoyment.

The lesson of the transitoriness of human bliss is as old as the hills, and one may wonder whether anything is added here to the wisdom of Omar Khayyam. But Colette's unpretending style has the pure charm of spontaneity. Her writing is capriciously feminine, and in its freedom audaciously ignores the ordered progress of academic expression; it may at times overstep the dividing line between sincerity and desultoriness or care and preciosity, but a natural coherence keeps it almost always close to the object; and there is a perpetual pleasure and refreshment in the unexpected light that it sheds on the ebb and flow of our consciousness. She died in 1954.

Pierre Loti[1] is no longer, as he was for a whole generation thirty years ago, a favourite of the public. His theme of exoticism, after such abundant and more than century-old treatment, has grown somewhat stale, and today his sober descriptions are eclipsed by a more

---

[1] Julien Viaud, 1850–1923, born at Rochefort, became an officer in the French navy, visited foreign lands, and under the pseudonym of Pierre Loti conquered a large public with novels of a descriptive, romantically emotional character: *Aziyadé*, 1879; *Rarahu*, 1880; *Le Mariage de Loti*, 1882; *Mon frère Yves*, 1883; *Pêcheur d'Islande*, 1886; *Madame Chrysanthème*, 1887; *Ramuntcho*, 1897; *L'Inde sans les Anglais*, 1903; *Les Désenchantées*, 1906; *La Mort de Philae*, 1909; &c.

intrepid curiosity, a fuller exploration of out-of-the-way scenes, and a more eager intensity of colouring. The elegiac emotions in which his vision of the world and of life is steeped are too insipid for sophisticated readers, and too dangerously near sentimentality for an era of anguish and all-too-real horrors. But the quality of his art is such, that after the inevitable eclipse of his reputation a just revival may be expected.

His enjoyment of all that is picturesque, quaint, and magnificent is never lured into anything cheap or declamatory. This is another aspect of his more positive virtue of quiet good taste. The amorous episodes almost inseparable from the subject of a young Westerner's experiences in the East are handled with a minimum of complacency and with reserve. The charm of each land is felt and rendered aptly and sensitively. Loti is, however, at his most readable in the novels with a more thoroughly familiar theme, the landscape of Brittany, the innate austerity and spirituality of the Breton race, of the sailors, fishermen, and peasants whose lives, under grey skies or on stormy seas, are upheld by such a deep, silent sense of duty. *Mon frère Yves* and still more *Pêcheur d'Islande* will probably remain the author's best claim to remembrance.

The very atmosphere of Brittany is nostalgic; and Loti's brooding, pessimistic sensibility, ever haunted as it is by the sadness of decay, change, and death, is the intrinsic feature of his work. His pity extends to all suffering creatures, whether men or animals. Akin to romantic emotion, it is unashamedly indulged, but kept within the bounds of transparent truth. The sentiments expressed so nakedly in *Le Livre de la pitié et de la mort* are likely to appeal only to congenial spirits, for they dwell upon the painful or gruesome aspects of life and death with a determination that frequently excites disapproval. For a mature writer to bemoan the hard condition of man's fate is indeed puerile; but how human!

French literature is often said to be, more exclusively than any other, written for adults. The statement must be qualified, even as applied to the past; and it is less founded at present than it ever was. A case in point is *Le Grand Meaulnes*, 1913, by Alain (Henri-Alban) Fournier, 1886–1914. The book is well fitted to delight every reader, old or young, but it is also a prominent example of a vein that has been cropping up for some half-century, namely stories in which the chief interest lies with youthful characters, and it comes as a very welcome refreshment. In minds sated and depressed with the natural-istic novel it provokes a sense of wonder which blends intimately with simple, pleasant images of rustic life; and the subtle essence dis-tilled by this original mixture is a call to nobleness—the magic spell of a high ideal. The art of the novel is not flawless; but its pure charm, its happy fusion of gentle realism with the half-mysterious, has endeared it to numberless readers. As in the English novel of adventure, for instance, in R. L. Stevenson's *Kidnapped*, the influence of which is here perceptible, we enjoy a stirring atmosphere of romance and heroism, never completely divorced from actuality, but free from the bitter cynicism without which French writers too often seemed to feel no picture of life had a chance to be accepted. Alain Fournier died in the First World War; so did Émile Clermont, 1880–1916, whose *Amour promis*, 1910, and *Laure*, 1913, had already singled him out as a brilliant example of the idealistic novelist whose particular bent is for analysing the spiritual development of his characters.

CHAPTER LVII

Drama

THE conservative forces in French criticism were pitted for a time against the extension to drama of the symbolist spirit, though this had won acceptance in other fields of literature. The majority of hard-headed playgoers sided with the critics and refused to be persuaded or bullied into enjoying plays in which a dreamy unreality and imaginative suggestion claimed to be sufficient sources of dramatic suspense. This collective hostility found a centre in a robust, doggedly narrow-minded journalist, Francisque Sarcey, 1827–99, who for long defended with tooth and nail what he considered the hall-marks of a good play, namely, a satisfactory plot, firmly knit structure, and a clear conflict, with the chief stress laid on the crisis of the action, or *scène à faire*. Yet the ramparts were being gradually undermined; they fell, not at one stroke, but piecemeal; Sarcey's death, towards the end of the century, was a symbol of the final defeat of the past.

A word has been said above (Part IX, Chapter LV) of the Belgian writer, Maeterlinck, who is such an essential figure in French symbolism that neither he nor the movement can be studied unless their connexion is fully recognized. His genius brought to full development the far-reaching potentialities of the implicit—the effects to be drawn from what is hinted rather than what is said. The new dramatic art was glaringly opposed to the long-standing classical tradition, in which the problems of the heart were expected to be explicitly thrashed out. To a large extent, symbolist drama ceased to be a matter of language, to become one of omens and pregnant silences. That such a method tallied exactly with the general trend of symbolist poetry and fiction, is obvious enough. Mallarmé in his *Divagations*, describing his idea of what the stage should be, had given an exact forecast of Maeterlinck's manner. However brief and disputed the actual ascendancy of symbolism may have been, it left an ineffaceable mark on play-writing, as on every province of literature.

With Maeterlinck, Claudel is the most eminent representative of French symbolist drama. He belongs, however, to the age that followed, when the doctrine was interpreted more freely, and as a result had an even wider following. Symbolism itself in its early years produced few dramatists, but in the field of the drama generally, during the years 1885–1914, the number of talented playwrights was surprising. Among them not the least successful were those who were content to please by the old ways, or by compromising timidly. Henry Bataille, 1892–1923, Henry Bernstein, 1876–1953, Maurice Donnay, 1859–1945, Henri Lavedan, 1859–1940, George de Porto-Riche, 1849–1930, penned endless variations on the theme of the eternal triangle—the wife, the husband, and the lover; but they made no serious addition to the substance of dramatic art, and are of interest chiefly as reflections of the temper and tone of contemporary society. Others, in varying degrees, did try to reinvigorate the drama, but the diversity of their attempts is a clear sign of the confusion of the age. The naturalist impulse was not quite spent, and could still prompt hard, pitiless studies of life; and, on the other hand, the essence of Symbolism was revealed in many ways with an intermixture of foreign influences, among which Wagnerian music and Scandinavian plays were the most active. François de Curel, 1854–1929: *La Nouvelle Idole*, 1899; Paul Hervieu, 1857–1915: *Les Tenailles*, 1895; Eugène Brieux, 1858–1939: *La Robe rouge*, 1900, wrote problem plays that reached dignity and power but too often lacked the unmistakable appeal of genuine drama. An exception may be made for Jules Renard, 1864–1910, whose bitter, realistic attitude to life found a concentrated expression in terse, relentless studies of characters and situations: *Le Pain de ménage*, 1899, and *Poil de Carotte*, 1900, &c. Comedy was flavoured with biting irony in the typically French skits of Georges Courteline, 1860–1929: *Boubouroche*, 1895; and in the shrewdly amusing farces of Tristan Bernard, 1860–1947: *Triplepatte*, 1905, &c. It is impossible to omit Edmond Rostand, 1868–1918, or to forget the resounding success of *Cyrano de Bergerac*, 1897. Such a triumphant display of wit, verve, bravura, and sentiment, and of the brilliancy still dear to the traditional French temperament will not succumb to highbrow disdain, but *Chantecler*, 1910, was and remains a gigantic failure. Joséphin Péladan, 1858–1918, stands less for the dynamic quality of symbolism than for the affinity of its inferior forms with mystification. Alfred Jarry, 1873–1907, in his *Ubu Roi*, 1895, a student's farce with much sting in it, is a defiant example of the anarchic spirit that appears when aesthetic values are upset.

During this period of some thirty years, under the stir of an intense dramatic production, the taste of the French public was silently maturing and feeling its way towards its present-day, far broader tolerance of unfamiliar types, whether foreign or native. The greatest importance of the theatrical life of the time lay in the initiative of pioneers and reformers, who put their theories into practice and brought new life to the stage. Antoine's Théâtre Libre (Part VIII, Chapter LII) had served the cause of naturalism; Paul Fort's (Part IX, Chapter LV) Théâtre d'Art, 1890–3, performed symbolist plays, and profoundly modified the conventions of stage production and the habits of the public by dropping the realistic background for one that was imaginatively reconstructed; from 1893 Lugné-Poë at L'Œuvre popularized the philosophical symbolism of Ibsen and Björnson, simplified every appeal to the spectator's eyes, and supported, in a general way, intellectual and experimental drama.

CHAPTER LVIII

Thinkers, Essayists, and Critics

NEVER was a French philosopher, with the exception of Descartes, better entitled than Bergson[1] to be studied, by the side of men of letters, as an integral part of a literary age. He was widely read, not only by the specialists, but by the cultivated public. His direct influence was felt in the circles of French, not to speak of European, thought and letters; and his work found itself in striking harmony with the artistic trend of the period. Lastly, he was himself an eminent writer, with a right to consideration on this ground alone.

The seduction of his infinitely supple style, as smooth and clear as water—a comparison that would be trite, if it were not indispensable—carried and conveyed to the most stubbornly intellectualist reader a sense of mental life that was in itself revolutionary. The master-images of a thinker are far more than illustrations of his thought; they are his thought itself, in its concrete and unformulated, that is to say, its primitive and truly genuine form. The image of the 'stream of consciousness' has had an extraordinary fortune; it has invaded the world, not only of philosophy, but of literature and art. It is no less than a universally valid expression of man's central experience, which at one stroke establishes a new view of mental activity through all its channels. The natural unity and the fluidity of an unbroken flow, the course of which is only artificially divisible, were substituted for another image, a mosaic of parts laboriously adapted to one another by the engineering feat of a mechanical mind. Psychology, in its early stages, had seen its object in the light of the physical sciences; sense impressions were atoms, which a combining process would build into ideas. With the new image, the whole became the original, and the parts derivative. The intellect's

[1] Henri Bergson, born in Paris, 1859, of a Polish father and an Irish mother, entered the École Normale Supérieure, was naturalized French, taught in several schools and universities, and in 1900 was appointed professor at the Collège de France. He died in 1941. He published *Essai sur les données immédiates de la conscience*, 1889; *Matière et mémoire*, 1896; *Le Rire*, 1900; *L'Évolution créatrice*, 1907; *Les Deux Sources de la morale et de la religion*, 1932, &c.

function was to perceive the parts, and to erect upon that perception a systematic theory of their working; the function of intuition was to perceive the whole, and to reach in that contact an assurance that was at least half-mystical. That William James in America and Bergson in France developed this notion of the inner life at practically the same time, and independently of each other until they discovered their agreement, is common history. How that view met and confirmed the philosophical needs of the symbolist aesthetic is obvious enough. The novel was transformed within the span of one generation. The revelation in France of Freud and the subconscious followed the diffusion of Bergson's thought; and it was not long before the monumental work of Proust incorporated the one movement while illustrating the other.

On this psychological basis Bergson proceeded to develop his complete philosophy. The problem of moral liberty appeared a false issue, wrongly raised under the influence of rationalist, *a priori* thinking. We can say our decisions are 'determined' only if we ignore the unity of our consciousness, and on an external plane they follow our motives as an effect does a cause. Our freedom becomes indisputable as soon as it is grasped in our inner continuity. Memory is not the material registering of impressions on the brain, but an essential attribute of psychological life, and the very stuff of the mind. In the reality of our experience, duration is the genuine fact, the pulsation of our spiritual existence: to conceive of time only in terms of the spatial time of watchmakers and historians is misleading. From the world within the vision passes on to the universe around us, and there also development is seen as an expanding process, not as a mechanical combination of parts. Evolution appears as a dynamic growth; creative energy—the *élan vital*—whose origin is mysterious, while its nature is much more spiritual than material, has responded to nature's profound stimulus and given birth to an infinite variety of organs and functions. Discovery and intuition, again, prevail in the wide field of ethics and religion: the 'closed' morals of the codes, enforced by the group, are utilitarian sets of rules, devised so as to preserve it from destructive perils; religion, on the other hand, is 'open', a series of revelations that have given prophets and apostles, in all lands and periods, a common assurance of mystical affinity with the things of the spirit.

Another example of the fertility of Bergson's intuitive perception is *Le Rire*, a most suggestive study of the significance of the comic, though not of the physiological, nature of laughter.

French philosophy, generally speaking, had been an intellectual effort to analyse, to understand, and to explain. The success of the Bergsonian doctrine was the confirmation of a far-reaching revolution, and the opening of a new era of thought. It is one more aspect of the fundamental change we have already had occasion to mention, a change which can also be observed in both the symbolist and the post-symbolist spirit in French literature, which had its initial phase in the romantic movement, and which had some roots, but only roots, in the national past. Bergsonianism is now apparently receding, but it has been lastingly assimilated; and the present age can be regarded either as the first period of a new cycle in the spiritual destiny of modern France, or as a transition towards an unknown future.

Bergson's influence was deeply felt by the young from the beginning of the twentieth century. But it was not at once a decisive element in literature. To a large extent the outstanding thinkers of the symbolist age were untouched by it, and their personalities link up either with the past or with different movements. The main characteristic of the period remains its essential diversity, the variety of temperaments, instincts, tendencies, and opinions. Each age of literature is a world in itself.

Two influential writers, Romain Rolland and Péguy, can none the less be seen as the nucleus of a distinct group. Not only were they both, at bottom, ethical thinkers, but there was a fundamental similarity in the way they reacted to contemporary life. The age of symbolism was also that of Decadence, so-called; as a result of a hundred years of more or less destructive criticism, there prevailed in the circles of the *élite*, and more generally in the cultivated classes, a sense of uncertainty and even of anarchy as to moral and social problems. The English 'Yellow Nineties' were a parallel to a largely similar period in France, the responsibility for the weakening of ethical purposes being, in England, often laid upon the French example; but it seems fairer to make allowance for a general crisis of the western European will, and for tendencies common to both civilizations. Rolland and Péguy, among others, keenly felt the threat to the balance and sanity of their time, and allowed didactic themes, diverse but ultimately converging, to dominate their books.

Romain Rolland[1] makes an immediate impression of ethical fervour and of democratic and humanitarian sentiment, coloured with the idealism of the French Revolution. The last was the source and inspiration of his historical dramas, most of which were not performed, but which, under the general title of *Tragédies de la Foi* and *Théâtre de la Révolution*, were meant as examples of a dramatic art actually written for the people. This part of his work shows much of the spirit of Michelet. Although no believer himself, he was profoundly aware of the vital necessity of faith, whether religious or human, as an incentive to the heroism he exalted in his lives of Beethoven, Michael-Angelo, &c. About 1910 he was known primarily as the author of *Jean-Christophe*, the initial work of the series of *romans-fleuves*, or successions of novels which more definitely than Balzac's *Comédie humaine* or Zola's *Rougon-Macquart* are designed to unfold, throughout numerous episodes, a story with one central theme, which may be personal, such as the destiny of one hero or one group, or, again, historical. The ten volumes of *Jean-Christophe* follow the life and growth of a musical genius, a composer, born in the Rhineland, and thus representing a union of the best strains in intellectual Germany and France, the crisis of a restless generation, the hope of a new civilization for Europe, &c. His zeal was becoming decidedly pacifist, he had to withdraw to Switzerland, and during the 1914–18 war he offended French susceptibilities in the pamphlet *Au-dessus de la mêlée*, 1915. Henceforth he was not only an exile but a spiritual rebel, taking an interest in the mysticism of the East and in the Russian Revolution. After 1920 he was largely reconciled with his compatriots; and among his other novels the trilogy of *L'Âme*

---

[1] Romain Rolland, born at Clamecy, 1866, entered the École Normale Supérieure, went to Rome as fellow of the École Française; then for some years taught art history at the Sorbonne. In 1914 he was not fit for active service; moreover his outspoken pacifism made it necessary for him to reside in Switzerland for many years. He died in 1945. His publications include historical plays: *Le Triomphe de la raison*, 1899; *Danton*, 1901; *Le XIV juillet*, 1902, &c.; biographies of spiritual heroes: *Beethoven*, 1903; *Michel-Ange*, 1905; *Tolstoï*, 1911; musical studies: *Musiciens d'aujourd'hui*, 1908; *Musiciens d'autrefois*, 1909; a defence of pacifism, *Au-dessus de la mêlée*, 1915. He was a contributor to Péguy's *Cahiers*, in which he published the ten volumes of his *roman-fleuve*, *Jean-Christophe*, 1904–12. This was followed by a trilogy, *L'Âme enchantée*, 1922–7. Other novels were *Colas Breugnon*, 1919; *Clérambault*, 1920. A biography of Péguy appeared in 1948.

enchantée, a powerful study of impassioned love, showed him in a less controversial light.

It is difficult to make any guess about his future literary standing. His wide success in the early century did much to keep Péguy's *Cahiers* going. Since that time he has lost much ground, but has never fallen into oblivion. The political associations of his name and writings recommend him to some circles, and inevitably disserve him with others. It is hard to believe that so much nobleness of feeling could ever lose its appeal permanently. But the glowing and pathetic idealism of his books lacks the support of faultless art. His manner is insistent, with a self-revealing candour that is not always free from rhetoric. His eloquent sincerity has some fresh poetic accents and can undoubtedly rouse emotion; but the tone is marred by traces of the commonplace, and somewhat heavy attempts at humour. Some episodes are almost hectic. It is probable that only some parts of his work will survive; but that is the common fate. They might include the truly moving *Vie de Beethoven*, 1903, and the simple, poignant story of *Antoinette* (*Jean-Christophe*, vol. 6).

Like Rolland, Péguy[1] was a born moralist. But a more vigorous temperament made him a thorough rebel, and a free lance who struck out for himself in every direction. The only definite influence he felt was that of Bergson. He always called himself an independent believer, but a time came when he realized that he was a Christian.

Armed with a dogged certainty that he was right, secure in his contact with the deepest sources of old French patriotism, and his provincial simplicity and integrity, he made war on the cankers that were destroying the life of France: a corrupt civilization, an ethical anarchy. He determined to be an apostle and a reformer, keeping to the path of rigid, disinterested honesty. All his works sprang from this elementary determination, which had the force and the obstinacy of fanaticism. Thus, into a world in which literature was

---

[1] Charles Péguy, 1873–1914, born at Orléans in modest circumstances, studied there and in Paris, entered the École Normale Supérieure, left it to write, opened a small book-shop near the Sorbonne, and started a periodical, the *Cahiers de la Quinzaine*, 1900. In its 238 numbers he published his own works and those of many beginners, several of whom made a mark. He was mobilized in 1914, and killed at the beginning of the battle of the Marne. His writings, besides a number of prose articles or pamphlets, include a poetical drama, *Jeanne d'Arc*, 1897; *Le Mystère de la charité de Jeanne d'Arc*, 1910; *Le Porche du mystère de la deuxième vertu*, 1912; *La Tapisserie de Notre-Dame*, 1913; *Ève*, 1913, &c.

mainly commerce, cynicism, and advertising, and where politics were a self-seeking game of hollow cleverness, he determined to introduce one modest but conspicuous exception, the *Cahiers*, which would serve to restore the business of writing, printing, editing, and selling books to a more decent level. He knew what hard-working poverty meant, and in his capacity of editor of the *Cahiers* he set himself to fight for justice to the suffering many and oppose those who exploited the sacred cause of the people; his socialism was a religion, not a career. His lesson of genuine tolerance, and of respect for original talent, was signally fruitful; the *Cahiers* proved a nursery for several coming writers. The campaign against politicians and frauds was naturally less effective; Péguy the polemist is scathing, but the demon of denunciation sometimes lures him past all sanity and fairness. Nevertheless, he left French prose the richer for some brilliant pages of impassioned eloquence. His chief claim to national gratitude was his contagious idealism; the combined effect of his life and his death made him one of the spiritual teachers of France.

The prophetic value of his writings leaves the question of their artistic worth unsettled. His prose has nerve and weight, and habits of emphasis that do not exceed the privilege of a writer with an axe or axes to grind. The problem of his poems is more difficult. They are original hybrids of drama, reflective epics, and religious psalmodies. The first impression is strange, and not altogether pleasant. Unmetrical utterances cut at unequal lengths move forward with a slow urgency, more spontaneously than ordinary free verse. They are cousins to the *verset Claudélien*, but more plodding, more incisive, and less poetical. They are full of an energy that finds vent in constant repetitions; the idea first expressed, however simple, is charged with far more force than can be liberated at one statement. The diction is so resolutely bare of ornament, even of variety, as to seem almost elementary. But before long we realize that this monotonous chant has a compelling attraction, and for all its sobriety it is often both imaginative and deeply poetic.

> ... Les nuits toutes ensemble
> Se rejoignent, se joignent par-dessus les bords du jour, se tendent la main
> Par-dessus les jours, font une chaîne et plus qu'une chaîne,
> Une ronde, une danse, les nuits se prennent la main
> Par-dessus le jour, du matin au soir,

Du bord du matin à celui du soir, se penchent l'une vers l'autre.
Celle qui descend du jour précédent se penche en arrière,
Celle qui monte
Du jour suivant
Se penche en avant,
Et les deux se joignent, joignent leurs mains,
Joignent leur silence et leur ombre
Et leur piété et leur auguste solitude
Par-dessus les bords difficiles
Par-dessus les bords du laborieux jour.

> (*Le Porche du mystère de la deuxième vertu*)

We have here a nearer approach to metre, and suggestive diction, than is usually the case, but the passage is none the less typical of Péguy's poetical style.

In Maurras[1] we have an example of the negative influence of symbolism. Symbolism repelled him and confirmed his own natural preferences. He was a southerner, born and bred under clear skies, steeped in knowledge and love of the Mediterranean spirit, which counted for so much in the national history and character. French ways of life and government, religion and traditional art, he considered, all fitted harmoniously together into a constructive pattern of logic and order. Romanticism was the poison that had tainted philosophy and literature; the symbolist infatuation was a new attack of the romantic malady. The vague fancies and fads of the north had obscured the healthy search for a beauty founded on the immortal lucidity of the classics. The French Revolution, a disaster contemporary with the romantic blight, had left the social body a prey to unending convulsions. An evil prophet, Rousseau, had been the source of a continuous stream of error and decadence. The time had come to make a stand against all these evils which were interrelated aspects of one and the same disease. The monarchy must be restored, or the

---

[1] Charles Maurras, born in 1868 at Martigues (Provence), studied at Aix, then lived in Paris, writing articles, essays, and poems. He travelled in Greece, took an active interest in political controversy, shared in the founding of *L'Action française*, which he permeated with his monarchist ideas, and was co-editor of its daily paper. He was several times threatened with prosecution. In 1940 he supported the Vichy government, and was imprisoned at the Liberation; in 1952 he was freed and sent to a hospital. He died in 1952. His works, for the most part a mixture of literary and political criticism, include *Anthinéa*, 1901; *Les Amants de Venise*, 1902; *L'Avenir de l'intelligence*, 1905; *La Musique intérieure* (poems), 1925; *Un Débat sur le romantisme*, 1929, &c.

nearest possible substitute for it set up in the person of a strong, able leader; public morals must be reformed on the traditional basis of the family; the influence of German philosophy and poetry must be exorcized; while art was to be redeemed from its feverish incoherence by the example of classical balance. Finally, it was the duty of all right-minded citizens, irrespective of belief, to co-operate in maintaining the salutary authority of the Catholic Church.

Whether this doctrine was a sensible plan of practical action, or merely a dreamer's craze, it possessed enough inner strength, and found sufficient backing in the course of events, to win the status of a recognized social theory. Maurras's books were read, and left their mark upon the mind of the age. What concerns us is their literary value. The poems (*La Musique intérieure*) are distinguished exercises on the Parnassien model and that of the École Romane. Their rhythm and phrasing are felicitous, but the condensed nature of their thought, which is not unlike that of Valéry, is at times responsible for a somewhat unclassical obscurity. The prose is undeniably elegant, telling, and forcible, even brilliant. The vigour and brilliancy are subdued, but we are continually aware of their presence, which, indeed, gives the lie to some of the author's own militant teaching. This style has not the pure seventeenth- and early sixteenth-century ring. In spite of its appeal to reason it betrays an ardour, an imaginative glow in which Rousseau and Chateaubriand have had some part. No one wrote in exactly this manner before the age of romanticism. The decrees of partisan feeling are indeed, in all art, ironically vain.

Barrès[1] was another writer with a doctrine, one which coincided at several points with that of Maurras; but his nationalism was not that of the *Action française*; and although a champion of patriotic

---

[1] Maurice Barrès, 1862–1923, born in Lorraine, studied at Nancy, came to Paris and soon began to write: *Sous l'œil des Barbares*, 1888; *Un Homme libre*, 1889. He engaged in politics, joined the 'Boulangiste' movement, stood for Parliament (elected 1889, several times defeated, re-elected), and later opposed the revision of the Dreyfus verdict; wrote actively for the newspapers, especially during the First World War, and was a leader of the Nationalist party, in or out of Parliament. Meanwhile he had published *Le Jardin de Bérénice*, 1891; *L'Ennemi des lois*, 1892; *Du sang, de la volupté et de la mort*, 1894; *Les Déracinés*, 1897; *L'Appel au soldat*, 1900; *Leurs figures*, 1902; *Amori et Dolori Sacrum*, 1903; *Le Voyage de Sparte*, 1906; *Colette Baudoche*, 1909; *Le Secret de Tolède*, 1911; *La Colline inspirée*, 1913; *Chronique de la grande guerre*, 14 vols.; *Le Génie du Rhin*, 1921, &c.

unity, he was from the first an arch-individualist. How those tendencies were superficially reconciled, or remained in conflict till the end, is the problem of his very interesting career.

There cannot be any doubt as to the order in which they appeared. His first writings, down to the turn of the century, are variations upon the theme of that outstanding duty, the cultivation of one's own personality. To dwell intently upon our powers of feeling, to broaden and deepen them, to nourish them with all that life, passion, books, art, travel, can offer, is the task upon which we must concentrate, valuing each event or circumstance, each new contact, in terms of its fitness to enrich our sensibility. Perhaps the most typical expression of this view is *Le Jardin de Bérénice*, where a refined hedonism is flaunted with almost cynical candour. The complacent emphasis with which the atmosphere of delicately veiled eroticism is sketched somewhat recalls the manner of Sterne. As a side-issue, the author extolls the fresh, unspoilt characters he has discovered among the people. This points to the change from an inward obsession to a kind of altruistic interest, and heralds the emergence of Barrès's second period. Here the master book is *Les Déracinés*—a strong, doctrinaire demonstration that the worst fault of French teaching is to sever the profound links between the individual citizen and his native district —a 'regionalism' that naturally broadens into thorough nationalism. The theme remained at least in the background of all Barrès's further writings, even in his vivid impressions of foreign lands. It would be unfair not to accept this political awakening as genuine; it was the main reason for an active life that had coherence and dignity, and his faith breathes in the *Cahiers* into which he poured his spontaneous thoughts to the end. But one feels instinctively that the deepest urge was the first; the fervent preaching of the national religion was the sublimation into an almost opposite principle of an egotism that had exhausted its power of feeding upon itself.

Barrès's vigorous and original talent was highly self-conscious, and his search for hardly compatible qualities gave his style or styles an air of artifice that sometimes borders on artificiality. His *culte du moi* books are fastidiously written, elegant, and keenly impressionistic, often ironical or jaunty. The change is striking to the 'Romans de l'énergie nationale', which are laboured, eloquent, and at times somewhat ponderous. His weak construction has been criticized, and justly, for his novels are bunches of episodes. Yet his work contains brilliant or arresting pages, well worth inclusion among the best examples of French prose. What prevents his being classed with the very first writers is the slight flavour of dilettantism that allows the reader to be moved to admiration, but hardly obtains an actual hold upon his heart.

The reputation of Anatole France[1] was perhaps exaggeratedly high during the first quarter of the twentieth century, but after his death the revulsion of feeling exceeded all limits of fairness. A more sober view may be that, if he was not one of the greatest French writers, he was still an eminent representative of such elements of the classical tradition as managed to survive the eventful course of nineteenth-century literature. And he possessed both personality and charm.

Like Barrès, he gave early critical indications of his ironical frame of mind, and before long also of a fighting spirit; and though he kept aloof from active politics, the trend of his thought was open and unmistakable. His outlook remained fundamentally unchanged. But with him satire of existing persons and conditions was compatible with a plea for fairer and more liberal standards of public conduct. This is a different problem from that of Barrès. Anatole France had expressed the scepticism of a mind too clear to be hoodwinked by existing conventions or hopes of substantial improvement. *Les Opinions de Jérôme Coignard* remind one of Voltaire's *Candide*. The book is no less thorough in its indictment of human nature, but it is less bitter, more mellow in its sense of relative values, and we feel that something of Renan's gentle spirit has fused with the sharpness of eighteenth-century rationalism. Coming after it, the radicalism of the *Histoire contemporaine* and of *Crainquebille* is unexpected, but

[1] Anatole-François Thibault, whose pseudonym was Anatole France, 1844–1924, was born in Paris, the son of a bookseller, and was for many years a publisher's reader. He wrote poetry: *Poèmes dorés*, 1873; a play, *Les Noces corinthiennes*, performed 1902; criticism: *La Vie littéraire*, 4 vols., 1885–92; memories of his early life: *Le Livre de mon ami*, 1885, &c.; novels: *Le Crime de Sylvestre Bonnard*, 1881; *Thaïs*, 1890; *Les Opinions de Jérôme Coignard*, *La Rôtisserie de la Reine Pédauque*, 1893; *Le Lys rouge*, 1894; essays: *Le Jardin d'Épicure*, 1896. Political and social satire is a prominent feature of the *Histoire contemporaine*, which has many allusions to the Dreyfus case: *L'Orme du mail*, *Le Mannequin d'osier*, 1897; *L'Anneau d'améthyste*, 1899; *Monsieur Bergeret à Paris*, 1901. A similar vein of social criticism crops up in *L'Affaire Crainquebille*, 1902; *Sur la pierre blanche*, 1905; *L'Île des pingouins*, 1908; *Les Dieux ont soif*, 1908; *La Révolte des anges*, 1914. A *Vie de Jeanne d'Arc* appeared in 1908.

it is not an artificial growth; and something very like philanthropy, as we know, had been a part of the make-up of Voltaire himself. The explanation seems to be that in Anatole France we have the natural development of a mind which, having in the first place adopted an attitude of sheer negation, found this in the long run impossible to maintain; and the accent in his advocacy of Leftist theses, in his democratic, pacifist, and indeed socialistic declarations, removes all doubt. This was a thinker who had committed himself to the acrid pleasure of pessimism, but who could not resist the appeal of generosity, even at the risk of succumbing to illusion.

Nevertheless, from first to last the tone of his work is one of mocking and ironical criticism. We are seldom, if at all, deeply stirred by *Thaïs*, or *Le Lys rouge*; the author remains cool, and interlards description and narrative alike with satire. His studies of characters in the grip of passion, whether the animating principle is sensual love or religious fanaticism, do not wholly satisfy us; the sketches of fashionable or bourgeois circles, of snobbish women, military boobies, or political adventurers in the *Histoire contemporaine* are often very diverting, but never genuinely creative. His most felicitous characters are those in whom his own personality can be glimpsed, such as the trio of scholarly, helpless, old-world cousins to Parson Adams and the Vicar: Sylvestre Bonnard, Jérôme Coignard, Monsieur Bergeret; or the poor, simple Crainquebille.

Such figures possess originality, and these agreeably amusing books are lightly and skilfully written. Anatole France, in the wake of a long line of predecessors, is manifestly able to provide the finesse which for several years had characterized French social satire. In his style, smooth, easy, and lucid, he expresses everything with discretion and a masterly handling of understatement. His pastiche of eighteenth-century diction is never pedantic, only graceful, sparing in its use of antiquated phrases. This simple determination to write a prose equal to the best classical models, and to yield to none of the conventional symbolist adornments, is the most genuine quality of the art of Anatole France. As moralist and critic he is at his best in *Le Jardin d'Épicure* and *La Vie littéraire*. It is possible, finally, to take exception to the derivative nature of his thought, for he adds nothing really new to rationalist philosophy; and one may deplore his fondness for erotic allusions.

The end of the nineteenth and the beginning of the twentieth centuries saw a marked increase in the number of French critics. The growth of the reading public, the number of books published, and the success of the better-class periodicals, favoured an activity which was, at any rate in theory, directed towards guiding the choice of readers. In fact, though the good critics were enjoyed, their very multiplicity weakened their influence, and with the decline in the authority of standards judgement became increasingly free and individual. Subjective methods of criticism continued to gain ground, and this at the very moment when, in academic circles, the aesthetic rulings and values shown by the study of literary history to have been imposed by tradition and convention were being codified and strengthened.

The leader of the conservative critics was Ferdinand Brunetière, 1849–1906: *Le Roman naturaliste*, 1883; *Les Époques du théâtre français*, 1892; *L'Évolution de la poésie lyrique au XIXème siècle*, 1894. His method was a complex of rationalism and scientific theory. He accepted Sainte-Beuve's individual analysis, but he also laid stress, as Taine had done, on social factors and the evolutionist point of view. In addition, he was concerned to demonstrate two theses: the *évolution des genres*, a view perhaps unduly supported by biological analogies; and the theory that men's literary preferences are dictated by the national character. With such foundations, the judgements at which he arrived were not unnaturally dogmatic, and likely to be swayed by ethical considerations.

Gustave Lanson, 1857–1934, was the undisputed master and lawgiver of literary history. Whatever excesses some of his disciples may have committed, he himself was fully aware of the real nature of the creative process, and he had an instinctive appreciation of original quality. His *Histoire de la littérature française*, 1894, which was widely used abroad, still retains its solid worth, increased by all the later spade-work he has largely inspired. His *Manuel bibliographique de la littérature française moderne* is indispensable.

Pierre Lasserre, 1867–1930, Julien Benda, born 1867, and 'Alain' (Émile Chartier, 1869–1949) are not so much literary historians as professional and rationalist critics. The first created some stir with his indictment of French romanticism, which he treated from its origins and throughout its aesthetic and moral developments (*Le*

Romantisme français, 1907) as the modern disease of the French mind, and a threat to the sanity of the national intelligence. The second is an uncompromising opponent of the anti-intellectualist movement in all its aspects, from symbolist poetry to the Bergsonian philosophy (*Belphégor*, 1919; *La Trahison des clercs*, 1927, &c.). Alain was primarily a teacher, a formative influence on generations of young men; but he was also a stimulating critic, whose intellectual honesty, clear-sightedness, and energy were felt far beyond his schoolroom, for instance in his thought-provoking *Système des beaux-arts*, 1920, and *Mars ou la guerre jugée*, 1921.

Some critics fall into a third category because they were primarily essayists who practised the appreciation of books as a diagnosis of personalities. They brought to their task an intuition which was the joint product of their own creative gift and of the writer's temperament. Such 'impressionists', who recounted 'the adventures of their minds among masterpieces', linked up in a direct line with Sainte-Beuve. Anatole France was one (see above); so was Jules Lemaître, 1853–1914 (*Les Contemporains*, 1885–99; *Impressions de théâtre*, 1888–1920), one of the most complete and best examples of a critical faculty nourished on the delicate perception of shades of meaning and of art. He reflects the whole, rich image of the literary development of his age with a sound and subtle impressionism that in itself becomes a kind of objectivity. In Rémy de Gourmont, 1858–1915, we find a more retiring analyst of books and ideas (*Épilogues*, 1903–10; *La Culture des idées*, 1900; *Promenades littéraires*, 1904–13, &c.). He was a student of artistic forms, relativist in his approach, though admitting the claims of individual tastes; and before all intelligent and liberal. Émile Faguet, 1847–1916, again a penetrating analyst, discussed French writers and periods of French life and thought in an easy, spirited, non-academic manner. Sound common sense was not the least feature of his criticism (*Politiques et moralistes du XIXème siècle*, 1891–1900; *Le XVIIème siècle*, 1889; *Le XVIème siècle*, 1893, &c.).

CHAPTER LIX

The Mind in Flux

THE upheaval caused by two great wars has not unnaturally been accompanied in most nations by a sense of disruption and unrest. Things are in a continual state of change, and all rhythms beat quicker. Fate had placed France at the heart of the military struggle. She was deeply shaken, and her literature inevitably bears the marks of her sufferings. It is not less creative, but it is agitated and unstable, more divided and multiform than ever before. Uneasiness seems to be its very essence, a disquietude that is haunted by the dim sense of an unpredictable future. The only appropriate label for it is the non-committal one of transition; while an attempt to classify and study its various aspects in really systematic order would be unwise. Moreover, critical appraisal of all but the most outstanding writers is hardly possible, for individual values have not yet stood the test of time. For this reason our book must conclude with tentative lists rather than premature estimates.

This lack of stability takes many forms, and France shares her consciousness of it with western Europe. Her economic system and her public organization are challenged by a foreign revolution, that has mastered large parts of two continents and may have the will to conquer more. Apart from this momentous danger, France, like England, has entered upon a cycle of social changes destined ultimately to make her democracy more real. But in the meantime, between the liberalism of yesterday and the present-day interpretation of the limits of social security, she is a prey to a painful conflict of general principles. At the same time her relative situation in the world is altering with the growth of giant empires, the progress of new-born nations, and the crisis of colonial ascendancy. Material civilization is developing so rapidly in the wake of scientific discovery and industrial improvement that even a few years can alter our surroundings and ways of life. Traditional beliefs have been uprooted, and no faith seems sufficiently strong to re-coordinate man's spiritual background. As a result the twentieth century in its middle period appears to have lost its bearings, and to be drifting rapidly towards the unknown. Under the stress of these conditions, the words anxiety and anguish are by common consent stamped with a new appositeness.

The crisis is philosophical, religious, and social, and two main influences have contributed to make it also one of aesthetics. The discovery of the subconscious, and the idea which this implies of a dim or dark lining to all thoughts and emotions, have altered the significance and the methods of analysis and description. At the same time, and for largely the same reason, artistic techniques have been transformed boldly and radically. In all fields 'modern' art is separated from that of tradition by sharp differences, which have increased to such a point that it seems impossible the breach should ever be healed.

What was regarded fifty years ago as the normal development of complementary tendencies, within a fairly regular and predictable cycle of change, has been violently wrenched from that course, and recent departures have cut at the root of habits that thought themselves eternal. No less than the pictorial arts and music, literature, and especially poetry, has wandered away towards totally new paths. To readers of mature age, and perhaps to more of the younger ones than will care to admit it, up-to-date writing in verse is largely difficult or unintelligible.

Such is the unsettled state of the present. The mind is in flux, and the arts, and primarily literature, reflect its doubts and conflicts. Nevertheless, it is encouraging to note that talent is not becoming perceptibly scarcer, and a prudent hope may be entertained that the turmoil of extreme and often wild views will before long subside into a compromise pointing to an acceptable and newly stable age. A few symptoms would already seem to indicate this, but it is more reasonable to abstain from conjecture.

CHAPTER LX

Heirs of Symbolism

In its more precise, and as it were local sense, the Symbolist movement has easily recognizable time-limits; by 1914 its career, as the central force of a literary age, was over. It had failed to unify and co-ordinate within one discipline the instincts of the majority of artists. Other influences took the lead, though none of these rose to undisputed supremacy, and the resulting period was one of diversity, confusion, or conflict. But the spirit and inspiration of Symbolism, if diffused, never ceased to be active, and its stimulus can be detected throughout the whole course of French literature to date. Many of the greater writers, who had grown up in its atmosphere, revealed their inner adherence to habits and preferences of the heart and of the imagination that bore the distinct mark of the movement. Valéry, Giraudoux, Gide, Claudel testify in various ways to its lingering fecundity, and can, with no artifice, be considered together, not as symbolists, but as heirs of a mode of thinking that has significantly contributed to the substance of their individual temperaments.

The early poems of Paul Valéry,[1] republished as *Album de vers anciens* (1913), make his derivation from Mallarmé quite plain. His prose style, too, has occasional twists and mannerisms that are no less revealing. But never was the evidence of discipleship less depreciatory of one who was a master in his own right. The sense of Valéry's originality is in spite of all overwhelming.

[1] Paul Valéry was born at Sète, 1871, studied at Montpellier, and then held various posts in Paris. His interests were literature and mathematics. A few poems which he wrote at this time were printed in reviews and show the influence of Mallarmé. He then for many years wrote only prose (*Introduction à la méthode de Léonard de Vinci*, 1895; *Une Soirée avec Monsieur Teste*, 1896, &c.). Some years later he again wrote poetry (*La Jeune Parque*, 1917; *Le Cimetière marin*, *Odes*, &c., collected as *Charmes*, 1922), and he also revised his early poems (*Album de vers anciens*, 1920). Finally he was engrossed by prose works: *L'Ame et la danse*, *Eupalinos ou l'architecte*, 1923; *Variété*, 5 volumes, 1924–44; *Rhumbs*, 1926; *L'Idée fixe*, 1932; *Regards sur le monde actuel*, 1933; *Tel quel*, 1941–3, &c. He died in 1945. His occasional writings (prefaces, letters, articles, &c.) are all worthy of study.

Valéry had the audacious wit to point out that since all speech was more or less obscure, his poetry was by no means particularly difficult. 'Rien ne m'attire que la clarté', he wrote. 'Les ténèbres que l'on me prête sont vaines et transparentes, auprès de celles que je découvre un peu partout.' The paradox should be taken with a smile. We may agree that he does not set himself deliberately to embarrass the reader. But his eager pursuit of certain values made the consequence in a measure unavoidable; and he accepted it quietly. When the occasion demanded a normal degree of clearness, as in the charming poem, *Cantate du Narcisse*, intended to be set to music and sung, he managed to be transparent, and we were grateful. But compression is not a feature of this piece, and it is obviously compression that gives him his favourite effects. It drives away all the dross of poetry, reduces it to pure gold, and strips it of the appendages necessarily involved when language is used as a means of making the associations between ideas explicit. We are expected to supply missing links, to catch undeveloped allusions; material data are to be gathered under a veil of abstraction; our mind is to be agile in seizing hints, and must piece together a silent commentary far longer than the text. *La Jeune Parque* is the eminent example of such high enticing mysteries. None of the proposed elucidations of the poem is entirely satisfactory; but they go a long way to dissipate the darkness, and agree sufficiently among themselves to redeem the honour of the human intellect, as well as Valéry's good faith.

Was the game worth playing at such cost? The answer must surely be Yes, for the prizes are moments of beauty which could not have been realized otherwise. The concentration and tenseness in which the whole piece is maintained were probably the necessary condition if poetry of this richly allusive quality, and fragments of such rare beauty, were to be produced. The poem develops under the pressure of a controlled inward meditation, with a music at once ample, flowing, and majestic. The verse, as the old image has it, springs the more smoothly for being forced like water in a jet. The masterly movement of the lines bespeaks a subdued tenseness, which no one has the heart to deplore, even if the reader's need for occasional relaxation of mental effort is so violently disallowed, that sooner or later it becomes impossible to follow the poet's meaning.

Such accents are so striking in their sovereign beauty that readers
may well accept the challenge they present:

> Tout-puissants étrangers, inévitables astres
> Qui daignez faire luire au lointain temporel
> Je ne sais quoi de pur et de surnaturel;
> Vous qui dans les mortels plongez jusques aux larmes
> Ces souverains éclats, ces invincibles armes,
> Et les élancements de votre éternité,
> Je suis seule avec vous, tremblante, ayant quitté
> Ma couche; et sur l'écueil mordu par la merveille,
> J'interroge mon cœur quelle douleur l'éveille,
> Quel crime par moi-même ou sur moi consommé? . . .

Or this, from *Fragments du Narcisse*:

> La voix des sources change, et me parle du soir;
> Un grand calme m'écoute, où j'écoute l'espoir.
> J'entends l'herbe des nuits croître dans l'ombre sainte,
> Et la lune perfide élève son miroir
> Jusque dans les secrets de la fontaine éteinte . . . ,
> Jusque dans les secrets que je crains de savoir,
> Jusque dans le repli de l'amour de soi-même,
> Rien ne peut échapper au silence du soir. . . .

If all French symbolism were like this it would be easy to forgive
the symbolists their faults. We enjoy a sense of urgency and of fullness in these splendid, expanding harmonies, which resemble the
ecstatic largo of some inspired composer. *Charmes*, also, is mostly
first rate, for instance *Au platane* and *Cantique des colonnes*; but many
of the tricks of the *Cimetière marin* border on triumphs of ingenuity,
worthy of the *trobar clus* of the old troubadours. The body of
original poetry enshrined in this small volume has justly aroused
enthusiasm in France and in other countries. But it takes genius to
write successfully in this way, and to be forgiven by the reader for
the effort exacted of him.

Valéry's prose is a fit and a relatively simple instrument for the
expression of penetrating thoughts. What he has to say is the austere
product of a mind too resolutely intelligent to cater for emotion of
any kind. There is Attic grace in the Socratic dialogues of *L'Ame et
la danse* and *Eupalinos*; *Regards sur le monde actuel* show a philosopher's

detachment yielding to political pessimism; while *Monsieur Teste* appeals more pleasantly to the common man, and possibly to the English reader in particular. Here we have what is, to a large extent, a humorous self-portrait; and the study of an absent-minded scholar trying to deal with the practical and domestic situations of life is a French, intellectualized parallel to the unworldly, naïvely picturesque heroes of traditional British fiction.

The personality of Giraudoux[1] is, as it were, made up of features from different worlds. The predominant ones are typically French, and traditional. Classical culture is the foundation upon which his clear thinking, his natural elegance, and the finely shaded artistry of his manner are built. At the same time, this writer, who is in many ways a spiritual heir of Voltaire and the eighteenth century, shows himself permeated by the essence of modern imaginative art: his work is deeply tinged with symbolism; his refinement and the 'precious' originality of his style clash with the sober purity of the genuine classics. While French of the French, typical of the most intimate strains in the temper of his nation, he plainly reveals cosmopolitan influences; a specialized student of German literature, and also a lover of Shakespeare, he rises above exclusively patriotic preoccupations. His humour has a whimsical quality that seems to have roots beyond the Rhine and the Channel; while he is keenly aware of the values of the French genius, he avows a cool, open-eyed perception of the failings of France; and no one has more boldly tackled some international parallels in terms that to be impartial must cease to be orthodox. The work which resulted from this happy mixture of somewhat conflicting elements was never wholly popular, but it charmed the cultivated public, and won a durable hold upon the French love of literary elegance.

The books that filled his relatively short career are varied and

---

[1] Jean Giraudoux, born at Bellac, 1882, entered the École Normale Supérieure, made a special study of German literature, travelled, fought in the First World War, joined the diplomatic service, and played a semi-political part in the Second War. He had published essays and novels: *L'École des indifférents*, 1911; *Simon le pathétique*, 1918; *Amica America*, 1919; *Elpénor*, 1919; *Suzanne et le Pacifique*, 1920; *Siegfried et le Limousin*, 1922; *Bella*, 1926; *Églantine*, 1927; *Jérôme Bardini*, 1930; *Combat avec l'age*, 1934, &c.; critical essays: *Littérature*, 1938; *Pleins pouvoirs*, 1939; plays: *Siegfried*, 1928; *Amphitryon 38*, 1929; *Judith*, 1931; *Intermezzo*, 1933; *La Guerre de Troie n'aura pas lieu*, 1935; *Électre*, 1937; *Ondine*, 1939; *Sodome et Gomorrhe*, 1943; *La Folle de Chaillot*, 1946, &c. He died in 1944.

many-sided, but all characterized by a highly individual manner. His novels must not be judged by any standard but their own; they are conceived and planned with absolute freedom, oblivious of conventions of plot-construction or character-drawing; each one is unique in itself, to be viewed only as a passing mood of the author's fancy; its standpoint and tone should be accepted as an experiment in the wider art of fiction, amenable to no other criterion than that of our pleasure. Read in this light, for instance, *Bella* turns out to be a political satire, propped up by the mere sketch of a love story; a half-humorous, half-serious account of an episode in the then recent history of France, the rivalry between two famous statesmen. The case—for the author quite unmistakably takes sides—is amusingly presented; but what matters most is the earnest criticism of the French Parliamentary routine. This is perhaps a specimen of the better type of the Giraudoux novel; in *Suzanne et le Pacifique*, on the other hand, the theme is predominantly fictitious, and the fun rather forced.

These books stand or fall by their style, of which the salient feature is a constant refusal to think and write passively within the accepted grooves. This insistence upon novelty assumes many forms, the most frequent being the breaking of the usual associations of words in favour of new ones whose strangeness at once reveals the freshness of shrewd observation or witty paradox. A special feature of the trick is the surprise that can be created by giving a concrete literal sense to the stock metaphors of our language, long ago worn out and unperceived. These lively, repeated shocks are a delight to most readers, and an occasional irritation to not a few; their effect is closely similar to that of the Renaissance conceits, and it must be confessed that the trick has given a new lease of life to what was formerly known as *préciosité*. Giraudoux may at times have abused his stylistic mannerisms, but they gave the body of his output an artistic brilliance that baffles imitators.

Some of Giraudoux's other writings show him able at will to temper his wit with the gravity of a political or philosophical thinker. But his best work, by which he will live, is his contribution to dramatic literature. Here again he has quietly ignored the most approved technique of the theatre, and his attempts are all more or less inspired by the free spirit of the symbolist stage. No precaution is taken to prevent the characters from speaking in the master's own, individual manner. Most of them are mere sketches, and develop hardly at all; while the plot itself is reduced to an unsubstantial out-line, and genuine dialogue is sacrificed to long speeches. Yet these fanciful plays act well, and can keep a responsive audience spell-bound. They shift us bodily on to a poetical sphere, where truth and reality have wings, and golden sense, mixed with paradox, trans-figures into intoxicating surprises the commonplaces of life, history, or ethics. Audacious views are expressed, which only the exceptional talent of a wizard can make acceptable and accepted, and at the end we realize that beneath its wit and artifice Giraudoux's work is packed with significance. Two particularly successful plays of this type are *Siegfried* and *La Guerre de Troie n'aura pas lieu*. The former dares to paint in genuine colours the psychological conflict of France and Germany; the latter, with clear-sighted wisdom, reaches the inmost roots of the obstinate plague of war.

André Gide[1] insisted that he should be judged primarily as an artist. This view is hardly fair to him, for as an artist he does not reach his full stature. His books are very interesting and suggestive, rather than literary masterpieces; and unlike his friend Valéry, he never concentrated fully on any one artistic purpose.

The impression one gathers from his first writings is that of an acute mind, which makes effective use, in revolt, of a preoccupation with ethical and psychological problems, due to his mainly Protes-tant upbringing; but his searchings of the heart strike us as hardly genuine, and for all his obsession with the imagery and the language of Biblical religion, he is too much of a sceptic to be truly religious. Life mellowed him; in his middle and later years he did write moving pages. Still, emotion is not his game; and the best that was in him is of a piece with his diffident attitude towards the easy indulgence

[1] André Gide was born in Paris, 1869, of well-to-do parents, and educated irregu-larly. He mixed with symbolist writers, published *Les Cahiers d'André Walter*, 1891, poems, prose essays: *Le Traité du Narcisse*, &c.; then travelled in Algeria for his health. After this his works included *Paludes*, 1895; *Les Nourritures terrestres*, 1897; dramatic fragments: *Saül*, 1896, *Le Roi Candaule*, 1900, *Le Retour de l'enfant prodigue*, 1907, and later *Œdipe*, 1930, &c.; novels: *L'Immoraliste*, 1902, *La Porte étroite*, 1909, *Les Caves du Vatican*, 1914; *La Symphonie pastorale*, 1919; *Les Faux-monnayeurs*, 1925; *Corydon* (dialogues), 1920; an autobiography, *Si le grain ne meurt*, 1926, and his *Voyage au Congo*, 1927; *Retour du Tchad*, 1928; *Retour de l'U.R.S.S.*, 1936; his *Journal*, which covers the period 1889–1942, with an additional chapter, *Et nunc manet in te*, published posthumously; also several other items of interest. He died in 1951.

of feeling. His refusal to be cheaply won by half-deceptive sympathies broadens into an uncompromising sincerity, a decision to face the facts, that is a tonic to the young. Much of his influence on the *élite* of a generation was derived from no other source.

In many ways he takes after the eighteenth-century leaders of the Enlightenment. The main aspect of his thought is ethical, and undoubtedly negative. The idea of personal freedom is written large over most of his work. A further notion that a positive aspect should be added to the destructive one, and new values of belief or at least of conduct erected in place of the old, does occasionally enter his mind; and it may assume moral or social forms, as in his campaign for the more humane treatment of colonized peoples; nevertheless man's essential duties, in his view, are to himself. Several books, and a number of pronouncements or hints, convey the lesson of freedom; among others, *Les Nourritures terrestres*, *L'Immoraliste*, *Les Faux-monnayeurs*, set stress on the central or secondary items in what may be called a hedonism, rising by degrees to a Greek ideal of full individual growth: the first emphasizes the readiness with which the promises of life should be welcomed—a somewhat Pater-like lesson; the second shows the rebellious attitude that experience forces upon a soul chained by rigorous constraints; the third illustrates the conflict between generations, the stifling hold of the family, and the anarchy of the young. But Gide is many-sided: another novel, *La Porte étroite*, develops in an atmosphere of idealistic devotion to spiritual duties; the heroine destroys her own happiness and her lover's for the sake of an almost fanatical other-worldliness. This may have been meant simply as a cautionary tale; but Gide, if he disagrees with his Alissa, profoundly respects her. This book and the *Immoraliste*, he tells us, are complementary. Indeed the enfranchisement of his critical mind left him attached to a balanced view of wisdom; in his ethics, as in his aesthetics, he held to a truly classical measure and roundness. His symbolist, and so half-romantic, beginnings (*Le Retour de l'enfant prodigue*, &c.), did not last long, though some of the mental habits of symbolism lingered with him to the end. His images of life are always more significant than realistic.

Other than a doctrine of absolute honesty, no systematic teaching can thus be derived from his work; he was, as we mostly are, divided against himself, insecure, and tossed by conflicting tendencies. He was aware of this, warned his readers against making him a prophet, and sought a refuge in his allegiance to truth and to art; but there again he was baffled, because truth to him was often doubtful, and art was no natural, happy instinct; he had been inoculated with the Puritan poison, and vainly tried to purge it from his system. The pathos of his fate was his long fight for a serenity that he could not achieve. For all these reasons it would indeed be unwise to choose him as a spiritual guide, though a fertilizing influence can be recognized in his books, and his candid self-scrutiny, and the frankness of his confession, can be admired and imitated. The free avowal of his erratic sexual impulses is not, as was charged against him, defiant cynicism; neither is it an act of spiritual humility; there again he was torn between opposite impulses, and never unified his theory, any more than he did his practice. His remorse at the thought of the wrongs of which he was guilty towards his wife reminds us of Carlyle's far less justified compunction; but *Et nunc manet in te*, touching as it is in its painful effort to be just, does not move us profoundly; coarser elements mingle with his genuine affliction, and such clear-sightedness, even though belated, should have borne fruit in action.

Intellectually Gide has strength, and the history of his mental development will be of lasting value. His mind was widely in contact with the issues of his time, and his criticism of the errors and prejudices that ran riot is highly useful. His views of political and social matters are independent and shrewd, though he feared to commit himself radically. His appraisal of books, paintings, and music shows keen perception. Neither the novelist nor the dramatist in him is quite eminent, though some of his plays, as, for instance, *Bethsabé*, have high merit; but he is distinguished in both fields, and as an essayist and a rationalist thinker he stands at the forefront of his age.

His most solid claim as an artist is his style, with which he took great pains, holding decided views. One may give him full credit for virtues that never were common, and which the trend of his time was making scarcer. He had formed an ideal of classical correctness and elegance; and he fulfilled it to an extent that made him a model for his less-guarded contemporaries. But his taste was not infallible; he was not free from mannerisms, and the archaic turns are often slightly pedantic. It is possible that his *Journal* will prove to have been his best work. It is written with comparative spontaneity. Its many thumbnail sketches of men, objects, and landscapes are remarkable for their sharp precision and at times, also, for their imaginative power. *L'Immoraliste* and *La Porte étroite* are probably his most signal approaches to great fiction. The expert humour of *Si le grain ne meurt* may owe something to his wide acquaintance with English literature.

In Paul Claudel[1] we have a frequent rebel against the world of his day, a prophet of an uncompromising, and to many repellent, dogma, but a figure of singular bulk and authority, one of the most powerful in contemporary French literature. The very essence of symbolism is conspicuous in his work; an essence vigorous but modified by two factors which, being complementary to each other, give the resulting mixture an exceptional originality. One is a cosmopolitan culture that includes, not only the influences usually associated with French symbolism, such as the literature and spirit of England and Germany, but others that range from the Americas to the Far East. On the other hand, Claudel is fully steeped in the spiritual traditions of Old France. Nothing can be more deliberate and conscious than his attachment to the country and the people, his realization of, and sense of participation in, their permanent and unchanged features. Like those of Péguy, but even more deeply and passionately, his instincts and his thought are rooted in the soil and the life of the provinces, where so much of the drama of French history has been enacted. Thence the peculiar atmosphere of his writings: a keen, ever-present sense of the modern world, its diversity and problems; and along with this, a sensitive awareness of values that time has weakened or tends to efface, but in defence of which the man, the believer, and the artist eagerly rise. At the core of the feelings that prompt and sustain Claudel's inspiration, even more so than his patriotism or his reverence for the monarchy, is his

---

[1] Paul Claudel, b. north-east of France, 1868, d. 1955, entered the diplomatic service, and was successively consul and ambassador, his last posts before retiring being in Tokyo, Washington, Brussels. After a profound experience of religious illumination, he adopted orthodox Roman Catholicism. His publications include poems: *Cinq grandes odes*, 1910, &c.; an *Art poétique*, 1903–4; dramas: *Tête d'or*, 1889; *L'Annonce faite à Marie*, 1890–9; *Partage de midi*, 1906; *L'Ôtage*, 1911; *Le Soulier de satin*, 1929; *Christophe Colomb*, 1930; *Jeanne au bûcher*, 1939, &c.; lyrical farces: *Protée*, 1920, &c.; essays: *Positions et propositions*, 1928, &c.; also translations of Aeschylus for the stage.

allegiance to the most orthodox form of the Roman Catholic faith. His religious conversion remains the outstanding experience of his life. Claudel's inspiration is thus, in its essence, conservative though fed from so many sources. When it comes to form, he is a bold innovator.

The poet is striking; but Claudel's poetry is fused with prose in a union that is practically constant, and not to be looked for in any privileged place. His usual utterance is a kind of chant; and he has adopted a rhythmic pattern that suits the evocative quality of his style. Among his better-known poems, the *Cinq grandes odes* are of unequal merit, the first two being rather obscure, while the last three, and the *Processionnal*, far less cryptic, are quite as fine. The author seems to make no mystery of his changed aim:

> Et je voudrais compasser un grand poème plus clair que la lune qui brille avec sérénité sur la campagne dans la semaine de la moisson,
> Et tracer une grande Voie triomphale au travers de la Terre. (Ode III.)

In his dramas, his outstanding title to fame, the animating spirit is a resolute and fearless contradiction of doctrines of worldly wisdom. They disdain to achieve their purpose by the ordinary methods of realistic drama, preferring rather the significance that a partly imaginary universe can lend to their action. Satirical touches continually recall the familiar outline and plane of everyday experience, without destroying the imaginative symbolism of the subject, the characters, and the language. This essentially free technique may to a large extent have found example and encouragement in Shakespeare, and Calderon, and Maeterlinck; but in the last resort these plays have no complete parallel in any literature. Their magnetism consists chiefly in the dramatic emphasis accorded to characters whose complete other-worldliness and reassuring self-sacrifice are the outward expression of a stern religious enthusiasm, and of an exacting form of spirituality which is both pessimistic and instinct with mysticism. Only Corneille's Polyeucte had faced the misgivings of the soul and the weaknesses of the flesh with equal rigour. The Violaine of *L'Annonce faite à Marie*, the Sygne of *L'Ôtage*, the Lumir of *Le Pain dur*, the Prouhèze and the Rodrigue of the *Soulier de satin*, and of course the heroine of *Jeanne au bûcher*, are not mere sketches of ideal sanctity, but full-blooded human beings; and it is this combination of human frailty and deep fervency that makes the picture of their unbreakable moral courage so convincing. At the same time the material world is evoked in a spirit of defiance or derision; and the Claudel of *Le Soulier de satin*, for instance, revels in a kind of huge, grotesque humour which a fastidious taste may find somewhat heavy.

The most frequent note, however, is one of tragedy, at the various levels of life, in a romantic past or a grim present; and the play which most effectively conveys it, with a poignancy felt by the most sophisticated reader, is the 'mystery', *L'Annonce faite à Marie*. Here, as in all his better moments, Claudel manages by sheer force of emotion to raise the most simple, idiomatic French to a sustained pitch of strength and beauty. At times he yields to artistic caprice, and in his disdain of academic formality indulges in a phraseology which is too loose, or it may be, too direct, to be grammatical, but this is forgotten in the flow of his truly robust as well as highly poetical style. The 'verset', which is his almost constant form, is not felt by him as verse, but as a natural rhythm, imitating with the slightest degree of artifice the cadence of breathing and the spontaneous measure of eager speech. Whitman had instinctively discovered such a semi-metrical form; Péguy and T. S. Eliot have approximated to it. It sets an example that has been, and probably will again be followed, for it suits our age, transcending equally the *vers libre* and the *prose rythmée* of the moderns.

CHAPTER LXI

The Subconscious

ON the eve of the 1914–18 war the only persons in France who were acquainted with the work of Freud were mental specialists. The initiation of the general public began in 1922, when the first translation was published.

But before psycho-analysis was known, it was already becoming usual to explore the more secret places of the soul; the attention of writers and readers had been directed to a degree of penetrative analysis beyond the attempts of previous centuries. Romanticism had dwelt on emotion, passion, and the imaginative elements of the mind; it had ceased to demand or expect the clearness of classical psychology, and a shade of obscurity in the findings of analysts, once a sign of incomplete elucidation, had almost become a mark of profundity. The realists had set about the study of man in a determined fashion, bent to see through superficial conventions to a truth of instinct and impulse that was dark, often unsavoury, and somehow in the dependence of the body. To the symbolists actual life was full of subtle impressions, moods, and dreams, in which the secrets of our being, and a fate that took us away from the concurrence, and indeed the ken, of our reason, lay dormant. The Bergsonian doctrine had altered the whole course of philosophical reflection, with the result that the focus of personality was no longer the intelligence, but intuition and feeling; and the most precious intimations of our experience, the immediate data of the consciousness, were at best half-conscious, and revealed only to the philosopher's probing. Thus the world of the soul was the domain of all that was fleeting and indefinite. Bergsonism began to tell upon French literature somewhat earlier than psychoanalysis. It is admitted that Proust was indebted to Bergson before he knew Freud, and that the latter influenced him very little, if at all; and at another stage in this long progress towards a fuller realization of the realms within, a place should be found for Alain Fournier's *Le Grand Meaulnes*.

Proust's[1] exceptionally high reputation rests practically on one vast, massive novel, occupying some sixteen volumes, and unique in the wealth of its original features.

A novel we may call it, since the name has ceased to have any very definite meaning; but the spirit of the story would be more exactly defined if we regarded it as an autobiography, the record of a life which at the same time reflects the manners of the whole age constituted by the last thirty years of the nineteenth century and the first decade of the twentieth. The usual precautions are taken to avoid wounding susceptibilities; the names of the characters and places mainly concerned in the action are changed; the narrator's identity is left a blank; but the general outline of social development is accurate and the richness of a slightly obsolescent culture, and some of its inner symptoms of decay, are powerfully illustrated. The successive periods of the author's existence, his spiritual growth, are the framework upon which everything is dependent. His personality emerges clearly beneath the light veil that covers it: a sickly boy, all sensibility and nerves; then a reflective, brooding man, mixing uneasily with the world, drawn by the lure of successive loves, until his failing strength reduces him to the retirement of semi-invalidism and to the labours of composition. A vast section of society is depicted by this shrewd observer. He is keenly aware of the habits, the dress, gestures, and language of each layer; dwelling with a special intimacy of knowledge on the nobility, the wealthier bourgeoisie, and the professional classes. He hardly penetrates the fringe of the people except that his old woman servant, Françoise, is granted a full portrait, of admirable truth and flavour.

The deliberate, protracted story of an individual life, from early childhood to complete maturity, is saved from any charge of egotism

---

[1] Marcel Proust, born in Paris, 1871, of a well-to-do family, was delicate from childhood. As a young man he did for a time mix with the world, and he published essays (*Les Plaisirs et les jours*, 1896; *Pastiches et mélanges*, 1914, &c.) and translated Ruskin; but after 1909 he withdrew into retirement, and devoted his remaining strength to his long serial novel, finally named *A la recherche du temps perdu*, which came out in instalments till his death, 1922, and for some years afterwards: *Du côté de chez Swann*, 1913, revised text, 1917; *A l'ombre des jeunes filles en fleurs*, 1918; *Le Côté de Guermantes*, 1920; *Sodome et Gomorrhe*, 1922; *La Prisonnière*, 1924; *Albertine disparue*, 1925; *Le Temps retrouvé*, 1927. Most of these titles cover more than one volume in the now current edition (16 volumes). An earlier, unfinished novel, *Jean Santeuil*, was published in 1952.

by the central character's eager interest, which he communicates to us, in his material surroundings, and in the relatives, friends, and acquaintances who swarm over the four to five thousand pages of the work. But most of all it is saved by a repeated thrill of wonder and anguish which, from having been his main emotion, becomes an impersonal sense of universal experience, in which the riddle of human destiny is summed up—man's allegiance to time.

The title chosen for the whole work reveals this obsession with time. Proust is vividly alive to the miracle of memory, which for a while at least re-creates an image, a bloodless ghost of the past. But though, when we fasten desperately on the shadows of our consciousness, we can only draw from them an abstract and discoloured copy of what was, it is also true that at privileged, unpredictable moments the glorious authenticity of our forgotten experience itself may flash upon our minds. Impressions and emotions will then recur to us with the fresh, total authority of what was not dead, but only hidden away in the night of sense. The scent of a flower, the taste of a fruit, will suddenly replunge us into the very reality of our young life. On this wonderful power of involuntary memory, a half-mystical doctrine and cult of our rejuvenation through the resurgence of *le temps perdu* may be based; except that such bright, illuminating revelations, akin to ecstasy in their nature, are to be enjoyed, not exactly 'searched' for; we must take them as they come, though to some extent we may put ourselves in a state of grace, and wait for the 'spark from heaven'. Proust's philosophy at bottom is not very different from that of Arnold, and Wordsworth:

> One moment now can give us more
> Than years of toiling reason. . . .

These views are not refined to a properly metaphysical quality. Proust only suggests to us, by the whole tenor of his work, an intensified perception of time's practical identity with the very stuff of consciousness. As it was with Bergson, to him remembrance is, indeed, not a faculty of the soul, but an aspect of the soul itself.

Proust's strange book is put together in a peculiar way. Successive episodes are treated under separate and symbolic titles, their series forming a relatively coherent but imperfectly unified whole. Many passages bear obvious marks of haste and unfinished revision. Into the first draft of each part, additions have been worked at different times, with the result that the author reveals himself in at least two different moods. The one chiefly apparent in the initial volume, *Du côté de chez Swann*, and parts of the others, is a warm, lovely, wistful evocation of scenes, landscapes, and characters from the enchanting book of years, and of moments of emotion in the life of the hero. At such times the style is glowing and impressionistic, full of charm and poetry. But, and with increasing frequency as the work proceeds, the writer's attitude changes and becomes one of cool, disillusioned, and somewhat bitter interest in the vagaries of the world and the complexities of conduct. Here it is no longer the poet who speaks, but the analyst of thought and behaviour, whose object is not to move, but to instruct. The style is forceful, precise, and rather austere, animated only by a kind of subdued excitement, akin to that of the impassioned moralist. In spite of their interest, these argumentative digressions will strike many readers as somewhat heavy.

Yet few will not feel that these passages of meditative wisdom have much to do with the story's extraordinary hold upon us. They convey a treasure of clear-sighted penetration unrivalled in the long list of French moral inquiries. The special circumstances of Proust's life, his habit of penetrating to the hidden motives of conduct, have given his glance an acuteness, and his phrasing a firm accuracy, beyond all that classical or post-classical psychology could offer. His aim is definitely to descend to the last obscure layers of the mind, where the habits and rules of our mental being are shrouded in darkness. The subconscious is his chosen field; and without calling attention to the parallelism of his search with that of psycho-analysis, his work is in fact a signal proof of the direction in which, under many influences, contemporary thought had been moving. He was especially preoccupied with the realm of feeling, and he has given us ·a commentary upon love, its various shades, its incipient and declining stages, as close and shrewd as any professional treatise. A pessimistic strain is implied in this dissection; and indeed the whole subject of human passion, with Proust, takes on a somewhat morbid complexion, for the hectic intensity of his awareness is part and parcel of his abnormal life and his exceptional experience. For this reason the realism of some of his themes, though kept within bounds, will be found unpleasant by not a few. He is, as it were, under the maleficent spell of certain aspects of the unhealthy life of the senses; and although he is aware to the utmost degree of what he is about, we too are aware, as we watch him, of the threat that the privilege of playing with fire may imply to normal sanity, and we are aware, also, that we have before our eyes the germ of unbalance in genius.

On the other hand, Proust's work also has the qualities we more usually look for in fiction. Not only is the unnamed narrator's personality thrown open to us with a degree of convincing minuteness only autobiography can reach, but the wealth of first- or second-rate characters, mostly drawn themselves from actual observation, is worthy of the best achievements in the novel or drama.

From these outstanding literary merits Proust's style detracts as much as it adds to them. A complex of temperament and motives, among which the instinctive search for intellectual connexions between facts and the desire for complete sincerity of statement are conspicuous, has deflected his favourite mode of writing to a periodic, often rambling and even loosely constructed style. The main idea is expressed, then confirmed, explained, or qualified throughout a series of clauses which demand continuous, slow attention. The paragraphs are endless; parentheses and dashes flourish; some sentences run to extraordinary length. The result is a reflective and guarded utterance, that presents every thought as a synthesis of balanced, positive and negative elements. The impression thus created, though predominantly one of honesty and intelligence, is not unmixed with the fatigue due to constant effort. At times, however, when this manner is more lightly and happily handled, it has a fine vigour and amplitude of range; and the very careful rhythm often found at the end of paragraphs can have all the beauty of poetic numbers. Proust's style frequently displays the two further charms of irony and humour. But the master's touch, in spite of all blemishes, lies in the quality of his phrasing, raised above the common level of language by the aptness and suggestive force of every word. *A la recherche du temps perdu* contains imperfections that the author had no time to weed out, and it is unequal and at times unwieldy; but it remains a work of unquestionable power and originality, one of the dominating influences on twentieth-century fiction. In it the richness of a slightly obsolescent culture, and some of its inner symptoms of possible decay, are illustrated.

SURREALISM

The 'surrealist' movement is the last definite phase so far in the development of French literature. It began about the end of the First World War, and fell at the beginning of the Second into a state of suspended animation, from which it has not risen, though its influence is still widely felt.

Its leaders refused to let themselves be fitted into any pattern of literary evolution which might be held to link the present with the past. But the evidence is irresistible, that they continued, and brought to apparently the final stage, a process of liberation which had begun long before them. Romanticism had been a form of revolt; so were naturalism and symbolism. In all three, literary motives were prominent, and moral ones rather less conspicuous. The surrealist rebellion was not primarily artistic; it had its immediate roots in the circumstances of the time, and so assumed from the beginning the character of a social and philosophical insurrection.

It sprang directly from the war and from the shock to the thinking mind of the cruelties and horrors let loose upon the world. Indignation, despair, a feeling of helplessness in the clutch of a fate which, engineered by the accumulated errors of ages, seemed like a cosmic decree, violently wrenched a number of young men from that concurrence with the existing spiritual order, out of which the normal acceptance of facts grows. The political aspect of the desired revolution was not, however, immediately apparent. The first point on which unanimity was reached was the desirability of a complete break with intellectual and aesthetic tradition, after which the wreckage of the pre-existing art and literature would have to be cleared away. Next, since the edifice raised by the effort of thought had proved untenable, the elements of a new construction had to be looked for in the deeper instincts of the mind; and until another hierarchy could be built, anarchy was better than a rotten discipline. Turning their backs upon a lying civilization, the chiefs of the movement clung to what could be regarded as the only untainted powers in man, his primitive forces. So at bottom the main urge of surrealism was only the last wave of the tide that had risen with Rousseau, and again and again, in successive floods, swept through the nineteenth century.

'Dadaism' was the initial form of the crusade. A group of refugees in Zürich, when Switzerland received the waifs of the warring world, sought for a symbol of their disdain and hatred of the normal attempts of intelligence. A dictionary was opened at random and the word chanced upon, 'Dada', was hailed as the fit name for a programme of which the spirit was arbitrariness and irrationality, and the paramount aim destruction. The pretence of thinking logically and writing grammatically had clogged literature with commonplaces and stereotyped phrases. The free play of haphazard inspiration would purify language and renovate poetry. At the peace the 'Dadaists' transferred their activities to France under their leader Tristan Tzara, born in 1896, a Rumanian (*Sept manifestes Dada*, 1924). Their incoherent utterances failed to win much credit; Dadaism became merged in surrealism, and Tzara wrote a little more intelligibly.

The search for a definite doctrine was more serious with the central movement. While claiming absolute originality, its leaders acknowledged precursors in, for example, Nerval, Rimbaud, and Lautréamont, who had all three experimented with language and verse. They also owned to the influence of Guillaume Apollinaire, 1880–1918, the writer who first employed the word *surréaliste*; a subtle heir of symbolism, who could conjure up a secret magic from the most commonplace objects, and invest legend with mysterious reality (*Alcools*, 1913; *Les Mamelles de Tirésias*, 1917). But the avowed prophet, who had added new realms to inspiration, was Freud. The gospel now proclaimed, coolly and defiantly, was largely one of obedience to the subconscious. By all methods—automatic writing, trances, dreams, chance meetings, and accidents—our hidden impulses were to be consulted and the unknown made to speak. The new faith was sceptical and pessimistic, a kind of mysticism, as it were, of negation, except in so far as it strengthened that one traditionally mistrusted element of our deeper selves, desire. Its over-simplified, almost puerile, denial of all the rules of reasonable composition might have seemed to offer little promise. But the surrealist theories were not peculiar to literature alone. They, or something very like them, could be found in the work of the 'Cubists' and the abstract painters. Picasso, Braque, Derain, showed by their example that the times were ripe for audacious thrusts beyond the habits of the eye and the mind, and owed their altered vision of form and colour, suggestive of a new world, to the free play of their subconscious instincts.

The surrealists were on the whole too obscure to be successful as poets. Exception may be made for Pierre Reverdy, born 1889, whose *Épaves du ciel*, 1924, were a happy combination of the matter-of-fact and the illogical; for René Char, whose *Le Marteau sans maître*, 1934, and *Seuls demeurent*, 1943, were far above the common level of the group; and for Paul Éluard, 1895–1953, who, being a true poet, was not a systematic surrealist. The flow of his verse may be disrupted, though even this returns occasionally to almost regular measure, but its essential unity is almost invariably recreated by the quality of genuine poetic magic.

But the works that will probably survive are pamphlets, satires, stories—written in a prose that is vigorous, eloquent, and often more intrinsically poetic than the poems. The theorist and legislator of the movement, André Breton, born 1896, identified himself with its progress; he kept his band together, excommunicated not a few, adopted others, and so managed that surrealism, in spite of many youthful excesses, preserved some show of dignity. He led his flock to the communist fold (1931), and, when communism had shown its distrust, led it back: *Manifeste du surréalisme*, 1924; *Second manifeste du surréalisme*, 1930; *Les Vases communicants*, 1932. His *Nadja*, 1932, is a strange story, steeped in a sense of disquieting wonder. Others who may be mentioned with him include Louis Aragon (*Les Cloches de Bâle*, 1934) and Philippe Soupault, both born in 1897. After an attempt at orthodox communism the former broke with the party and wrote nationalist poetry.

The blunt, clear-cut energy of its pronouncements was to be expected in a doctrine that in several respects raised the cult of violence to the height of a principle. The tone may become monotonous in the long run, but it is essentially lively and makes these surrealist pamphlets pleasant reading: for instance Breton's *Manifeste du surréalisme*. But their dogmatic assurance fails to cover the weakness of the argument. 'Une monstrueuse aberration', Breton wrote, 'fait croire aux hommes que le langage est né pour faciliter leurs relations mutuelles.' However tempting a few artists may have found this highly original notion of language as the instrument of purely irrational and musical evocations, the mass of readers will demand, even from surrealist poetry, a modicum of assimilable communication. The very frequent absence of this has deprived surrealism of any action upon the general public. If art and life are to be regenerated, the regeneration must be effected by other methods than the banning of all previous culture. Yet, if to all practical purposes the movement has failed, and few of its works have become a permanent part of French literature, its lingering impact upon our time can by no means be disregarded.

CHAPTER LXII

The Literary Scene

CONTEMPORARY French literature does not lack writers of promise and distinction, but they hail from every point of the artistic horizon, and defy attempts to group them by aesthetic tendencies. In the circumstances this survey must be content with the old division between kinds, for all that its value is more than ever relative.

I. POETRY

Surrealism caused an agitation in French poetry which has not yet subsided. At the present day only a minority of the younger poets use fixed forms. Experiments are made again and again with all the varieties of unmetrical verse, including paragraphs of more or less rhythmical prose, and every degree of assonance. They often reveal talent, and a good deal of verbal music; but the authors themselves seem unconvinced, and no formula gains ascendancy. Too many of them are inclined to consider that only rare, subtle, and most often obscure themes are fit subjects for versified expression. Their intentions are understood and enjoyed by some, but the reading public as a whole remains passive. In the circumstances it is not surprising that poetry that is humorous or *fantaisiste* should show so much vitality, and such poets as Jacques Prévert and Henri Michaux are a testimony to its popularity.

Yet serious verse-writing is far from being a lost art. During the surrealist offensive, even humour and fancy had often been cloaks for a delicate sensibility and perceptiveness. Whether in metrical form or in prose, the evocations and effusions of Max Jacob (1876–1944), Francis Carco (born 1886), Léon-Paul Fargue (1878–1947), Pierre-Jean Jouve (born 1887), had shaded off from irony to mysticism; while the solitary and impressive figure of Saint-John Perse (Alexis Léger, born 1887) was being watched by a discerning few.

There are, however, indications, among the uncertainties and controversies of the present, that a compromise may yet be possible between the free, supple form which modernity seems to demand, and the fact that the poet's necessity is to communicate his mood, and that he can only succeed in this if he makes himself accessible. One such sign may be found in the work of Jules Supervielle (born 1884, in South America of French parents), a poet of independent inspiration. He represents no doctrine, no dogma, but lets his heart and senses respond to the calls of the universe, simply, tenderly, and soothingly. His overflowing humanity is unsophisticated; and at a time when sophistication reigns supreme it may signify a rebirth of poetry. The note sounded by Patrice de la Tour du Pin (born 1911) is fresh and somewhat similar. He betrays some of the hesitancy of the young, but has created harmonies, pure and wild, that can stir old emotions with convincing sincerity. His prosody, however relatively free, carries on the essential tradition of romantic lyricism. The work of Pierre Emmanuel (born 1916) suggests that in a new age, which once more sets store by logical thought, the themes which inspired Victor Hugo and Leconte de Lisle may again become matter for poetry. His dense and philosophical thought is most often cast in almost regular moulds.

2. THE NOVEL

The bulk of the creative literary instinct still finds its vent in the novel, of all forms the most universally affecting and the least determined. A selection from the enormous output of the period must be tentative and largely arbitrary.

The striking personality of George Bernanos, 1888–1948, is still living to us; he owed his impressiveness largely to his visionary power and remarkably intense gift of presentation. That his violent religious and political emotions implied a certain unbalance was apparent from the first; but *Sous le soleil de Satan*, 1926, and the *Journal d'un curé de campagne*, 1936, stirred their readers lastingly. An equally intense atmosphere of drama and anguish pervades the novels of André Malraux, born 1901 (*La Condition humaine*, 1933; *L'Espoir*, 1938). They are painful reading, but their high purpose and the despair felt by a lucid intelligence at seeing a confused, blood-stained world give them a nobility and eloquence all their own. The

energy of Henry de Montherlant, born 1896, and his scornful search
for sensation, are something very different, and make him a link
with masters of the recent past, Barrès, Nietzsche, Gide. He has no
sore social conscience to torment him, but obeys his own haughty
and egotistic impulses. He describes adventures of the heart and
senses, and the heroism he evokes is a virile type which for him is to
be found in the arenas of Spain (*Les Bestiaires*, 1926; *Célibataires*,
1934; *Olympiques*, 1938). He owes his reputation to his careful and
forcible style rather than to the vagaries of an inconsistent doctrine.
Those who appreciate a classical quality in writing admit the quiet
claim of Marcel Jouhandeau, born 1888, to their esteem. Like
Bernanos, he is a believer, keenly aware of the immanent evil of our
hearts. He does not exteriorize the drama of life, but traces it through
the silence of complicated, mysterious passions (*Chaminadour*, 1934;
Chroniques maritales, 1938). Another analyst is Jacques Chardonne,
born 1884, who has unveiled gently but pitilessly the humdrum
mediocrities to which romantic unions often lead (*L'Épithalame*,
1921; *Bonheur de Barbézieux*, 1938; *Chimériques*, 1948). His exquisitely
written stories exude, not ironical pessimism, but a clear-sighted
sanity.

A certain similarity, due to their meditative spirit and a talent
which aims high but does not court popularity, exists in the work of
three writers: Jacques de Lacretelle, born 1888, Jean Schlumberger,
born 1877, and Roger Martin du Gard, born 1881. The novels of the
first (*Silbermann*, 1922; *Les Hauts-Ponts*, 1932–6) are austere studies
of psychological and social cases, lucid and sad, written with great detachment and restraint. The second, in *Le Camarade infidèle*, 1922, and
Saint-Saturnin, 1931, studied the problems of the family and of groups
in a spirit of searching, scrupulous penetration, and with pathos,
poetry, and humour. He is a gifted, if slightly laboured, writer. The
third is the author of *Jean Barois*, 1913, and *Les Thibault*, eleven
volumes, 1922–40, works which, in manner and outlook, somewhat
resemble the naturalistic novels, but with a more sober brooding
upon a complex world, where science itself has ceased to be hopeful.
He is a vigorous and attentive writer, bent upon his self-imposed
and successful task of mirroring the broad image of a period. His
picture of a blind society rushing headlong into the inferno of the
1914–18 War is one of great dramatic force.

Earnestness is equally conspicuous in the work of George Duhamel, born 1884, whose position in the literary world has for many years been one of high official distinction. One source of his strength is his wide knowledge and experience of life. He studied medicine, and before 1914 formed one of the 'Groupe de l'Abbaye', a small band of artists founded on principles of voluntary labour, and with a common tie in their sense of social responsibility. During the 1914–18 war he was an army surgeon. The subdued pathos of his *Vie des martyrs*, 1917, a book that related the sufferings of the wounded soldiers, and in which art wisely abdicated before the poignancy of facts, won him a wide public that has remained faithful. His creative instinct has found many outlets, particularly in the novels which he has produced with the easy, regular abundance of a fertile mind. Two among these are particularly impressive: the series in five volumes, 1920–32, which revolves round the very striking figure of *Salavin*, a representative of the weakened humanity produced by our urban civilization; and the *Chronique des Pasquier*, in ten volumes, 1933–41, the full, many-sided history of a typical middle-class family. It paints the problems of our age with a frank, courageous touch that omits none of their mixed tragedy and comedy; but the dignity of man is preserved by the portraits of some noble characters, and the realistic method is enlivened by a discreet note of moral faith. The ample canvas, the balance of the various parts, and the art which distinguishes the whole, bid fair to keep these books lastingly alive. The first volumes, largely autobiographical, are particularly happy examples of a charming mixture of verisimilitude and humour. *Le Notaire du Havre* and *Le Jardin des bêtes sauvages* are worthy of being compared with the best Dickens.

Jules Romains, born 1885, sowed his wild oats with *unanimisme*, a doctrine emphasizing the collective element in all artistic expression. His first prose and verse illustrated it; with Duhamel and a few companions, he tried to live up to it at the 'Abbaye'. The attempt failed, but Romains never explicitly disowned its principles. After this sacrifice to idealism, his career bore the marks of a coolly realistic spirit. He has made his mark in several fields, but chiefly as a novelist. Its twenty-seven volumes make *Les Hommes de bonne volonté*, 1932–41, easily the longest of the various *chroniques* or *romans-fleuves* fashionable in modern literature. The work is a survey of the French and European world during the first quarter of the twentieth century. It is loosely assembled, and its parts are of unequal interest; but the amplitude of its scope is striking, and the vast whole is the achievement of a clear and robust mind. The interrelations and parallel developments of many groups, classes, ideas, economic trends, and political and military events, weave a tangled but fairly coherent web, studded or held together by the careers and destinies of representative individuals, among whom the most prominent are the author's brother Normaliens. The 1914–18 war, which is the central episode, and two volumes, *Prélude à Verdun* and *Verdun*, are treated in genuinely epic fashion. Such aspects of those years, and such milieux as Romains knew intimately, are convincingly described; others are clever figments, the artificiality of which can hardly be hidden by the talent of the sociologist and satirist. The style has animation, and at times even an imaginative, poetical force; but it can be clogged by a fondness for dissertation. Erotic episodes are too complacently introduced. The most valuable feature of the work is its insistence on man's persistent courage and elementary goodness, qualities which make the story of so many unseemly incidents and public disasters still inspiriting.

Intelligence, again, is the main gift of André Maurois, born 1885, who is also, among other things, a brilliant 'intermediary' between France and England. He is a writer of supple talent, with many and varied successes to his credit, not least his novels. These treat contemporary problems, including the delicate ones of love, marriage, and the family, with keen observation and judicious and tactful moralizing: *Climats*, 1928; *Le Cercle de famille*, 1932. Indeed the ethical point of view, a constant feature, gives many of these books a discreetly didactic turn. Maurois's first success was a humorous, charming study of British military psychology, *Les Silences du Colonel Bramble*, 1918. Humour is not absent from his more serious works, but the solid worth of such essays as *Aspects de la biographie*, 1928 (a corrective to a somewhat misleading *Vie de Shelley*, 1923), or *Histoire d'Angleterre*, 1937, is the fruit of reflection and careful documentation.

François Mauriac, born 1885, occupies a place of his own among French novelists. If his originality has an edge which is not always relished, his distinction is generally acknowledged, and by more than

The Literary Scene

a few admirers he is openly preferred to the other living masters of his craft. The choice may to some extent be due to the fact that his inspiration and indeed his whole vision of life are suffused with a profound sense of religion. But with Mauriac this eager spirituality is the unforced outcome of a deep intuition of the all-but-universality of evil, as seen by the more pessimistic doctors of the Church. Thus the foundation of faith does not grant him its usual reward of peace, but a tragic sense of the fickleness of our hearts and the fragility of our decisions. A native of the south-west of France, he has described its land and life graphically, using its hot, brooding stretches of moor and pine as settings for stories of vice and passion, secret tragedies that fester under the veil of middle-class respectability. His compressed, straightforward technique is far closer to tradition than to the new-fangled methods of the novel. Flaws have been detected in the structure of his books; and at times he certainly does sweep difficulties aside with the ruthless indifference of the idealist; but his strength lies elsewhere than in construction. His grip upon the psychology of sin has allowed him to create unforgettable characters which range through all the shades of fallen human nature. The impressive quality, indeed the very core of his manner and style, is the classical economy with which he can lay bare the workings of the soul. This, even more than his moving energy and his poetical, evocative phrasing, causes him to be regarded as one of the finest contemporary French prose writers (*Génitrix*, 1923; *Le Désert de l'amour*, 1925; *Thérèse Desqueyroux*, 1927; *Le Nœud de vipères*, 1932).

Many of the present-day French novels are of regionalist inspiration. Jean Giono, born 1895 (*Colline*, 1928), and Henri Bosco, born 1887 (*Le Mas Théotime*, 1946), write of Provence, its hilly vineyards, sun, enchantment, and mysteries; André Chamson, born 1900, has chosen the Cévennes (*Roux le bandit*, 1925); Henri Pourrat, born 1887, describes the rocky slopes of the Auvergne, where life is hard but robust (*L'Homme à la bêche*, 1939–41). These authors, and others like them, have discovered new and refreshing sources of fiction in places remote from the industrialized cities, where the spirit of old France is best preserved. Their studies of nature and of rustic life and character have the added charm of sincerity.

3. THE STAGE

In spite of the popularity of the cinema, the contemporary French stage still shows a great deal of vitality. Features of the period are the number of new plays, and the boldness of experiments. After the strict discipline of the old classical drama, followed by a long era of revolt and progressive enfranchisement, complete freedom has at last been won. Temperaments express themselves, and techniques are tried, with no apparent limit but the public's willingness to endure experiment. The work of Antoine, Paul Fort, and Lugné-Poë during the previous generation (see above, Part IX, Chapter LVII) has been continued and advanced by a series of reformers and leaders; among whom Jacques Copeau, 1879–1949, was a particularly interesting example of initiative and impulse. His playhouse, the Vieux Colombier, opened in 1913, was closed for financial reasons after nine years, but it had raised the whole art and atmosphere of playwriting to a higher level of spirituality and dignity. The lavishness of modern staging had been checked, and stress laid resolutely on the emotional and aesthetic values which simpler devices could serve without endangering their purity. Copeau formed disciples, and left behind him a school and a tradition. Parallel efforts were those of Charles Dullin at the Atelier, of Louis Jouvet at the Comédie des Champs-Élysées; of Georges Pitoëff and Jacques Hébertot, who did much to spread the vogue of foreign dramatists in France. Gaston Baty, at the Théâtre Montparnasse, struck out on independent lines, emphasizing the part to be played by scenic effects as an element in a general suggestion of poetry. Meanwhile a thoughtful player, Jean-Louis Barrault, was finding new meaning in the classics and reviving their appeal.

What strikes us during these intense and adventurous years is that the theatre is no longer regarded as a world by itself, the mystery of which must be practised and learnt precisely and exclusively. Its purpose is to create illusion which can only be effective in so far as it succeeds; and it is by no means unusual for writers who have already proved their worth as novelists or essayists to turn to playwriting, and sometimes with very considerable success. The most signal instance of that versatility is, of course, Jean Giraudoux (see above, Chapter LX). But Jules Romains, Schlumberger, Martin du Gard,

Duhamel, Montherlant, Mauriac, and others, have been more or less fortunate.

Psychological analysis and the subconscious, so conspicuous in the novel, have also made their influence felt in the drama. *Le Feu qui reprend mal*, 1921, and *Martine*, 1922, by Jean-Jacques Bernard, born 1894, are minute, pitiless studies of feelings too secret and painful not to fear the light of glib utterances. Henri-René Lenormand, 1882–1951, devoted himself more fully to the exploration of unexpressed and largely inexpressible moods (*Simoun*, 1920; *Le Mangeur de rêves*, 1922; *L'Homme et ses fantômes*, 1924). These obscure data of our inner lives are so elusive that drama frequently abandons the traditional attempt to convey them by words, leaving them to be deduced, as often as not, from the very hesitations of the speakers; and the paradoxical charge of making dialogue a matter of silences might apply to Lenormand no less than to Bernard. But over and above an appeal to unheard melodies his power lies in creating the anguished sense of tragedy that Maeterlinck before him had made his own.

There are, again, other dramatists whose manner is fully explicit, such as Paul Raynal, born 1890, whose *Tombeau sous l'Arc de Triomphe*, 1924, relieved some of the stirrings of the inter-war conscience, by exploding the cheap fiction of enforced and joyful sacrifice. Jean Sarment, born 1892, gave a new lease of life to poetic drama with *Le Pêcheur d'ombres*, 1921, and *Je suis trop grand pour moi*, 1924. The charm of *Jean de la Lune*, 1929, by Marcel Achard, born 1899, lies in its tenderness, fancy, and humour. Armand Salacrou, born 1900, has several successes to his credit, all widely divergent, and revealing fertile invention and a bold sense of dramatic grouping both in space and in time: *L'Inconnue d'Arras*, 1935; *Un Homme comme les autres*, 1936; *La Terre est ronde*, 1938.

While problem plays are officially discredited, philosophical drama has lately reasserted itself, before audiences too keenly aware of our moral uncertainties not to enter with sympathy into vividly presented debates of ideas. Gabriel Marcel, born 1887, has successfully conquered a public for plays of this type (*Le Quatuor en fa dièse*, 1925; *Un Homme de Dieu*, 1925; *Le Dard*, 1937). His characters communicate their own life and contrast to the conflicting theories and points of view they represent, and so add to their significance. Two *breadth of vein?*

further dramatists of ideas, Sartre and Camus, are discussed below (pp. 449–50). The comedies of Jules Romains (see above, Part IV, Chapter XXIII: *Cromedeyre le vieil*, 1920; *Knock*, 1923; *Donogoo*, 1930) and Marcel Pagnol, born 1895 (*Marius, Fanny, César*, 1928–31), were talented and brilliantly successful. But while the former has a Molièresque breadth of vein, the latter's clever mixture of realism and convention headed from the first for the cinema.

Among the younger playwrights, Jean Anouilh, born 1910, has created what may be a durable impression with his *pièces roses* and *pièces noires*. Despite these labels the rose-pink of his optimism is singularly less evident than the heavy tinge of almost bitter reflection (*Le Voyageur sans bagage*, 1936; *Le Rendez-vous de Senlis*, 1937; *Antigone*, 1943). His note is typical of a sad, anxious age, which sums up in itself all the uncertainties of past generations and adds to them the more searching disenchantment born of tragic experience.

4. EXISTENTIALISM

It is not yet possible to say whether existentialism will take its place among the successive influences by which French thought has been moulded. But since the war of 1939–45 it has been the most active movement in philosophy, with a presence felt in literature.

It would not be appropriate here to trace it to its distant origins. Its name must be interpreted in the light of the stress laid on the idea and the fact of existence. For many centuries philosophers had been striving to seize and define the essence of things, an effort that demanded the highest exertions of man's mind and which had been the supreme undertaking of reflection since the time of Plato. The world of appearances was to be made to yield its secret, and a more or less transcendent reality to be grasped beyond the reach of the senses. When existence was substituted for essence, the change was significant. A traditional search that had been the watchword of all idealism was, if not dropped, at least relegated to second place. A genuine metaphysics was still possible, but only through the study of the concrete facts perceived in our experience, which can be summed up under the name of 'the human condition'. This phrase implies a gloomy, almost a pessimistic cast of thought; and the leaders of the movement recognized their kinship with the moralists of the French seventeenth century. What they chiefly demanded of man was the courage to see things as they are, and to build life upon the freedom of a being who exists for a while, he knows not how or why, but who can at least stamp his existence with the choice of his will. Thus existentialism is modern and realistic. The lesson it teaches is one of complete independence from the authoritative formulas of intellectual, social, and political doctrines, a 'liberty' that each individual is to enjoy and to leave other men to enjoy, whatever their nation or their class. One form of existentialism, with Gabriel Marcel, clings to religious faith, but the majority of existentialists exclude all theistic speculation from their matter-of-fact investigation of what is.

It belonged to Jean-Paul Sartre, born 1905, to popularize the main tenets of what might be called a philosophical abdication of traditional philosophy. Instead of Kierkegaard's anguish, his mood was a cool determination to blink no reality. Fiction (*La Nausée*, 1938; short stories, *Le Mur*, 1939; and a group of three novels, *Les Chemins de la liberté*, 1945-9), gave concrete expression to a doctrine expounded in *L'Être et le néant*, 1943. Such watchwords as *l'absurdité*, *l'authenticité*, *l'engagement* have struck root even in the language of the lay public; while the technique of simultaneous presentation, a fashion spread by many examples, native or foreign, was vigorously illustrated. Vigour is indeed an undeniable merit of Sartre's writing; but the more than naturalistic coarseness of his pictures and his pitiless insistence on the distresses of the body have roused a not unjustifiable revolt in various quarters. Signs are not wanting of a gradual humanization of the writer's mood (*L'Existentialisme est un humanisme*, 1946). Meanwhile Sartre's fine sense of the theatre has also brought him success as a dramatist: *Les Mouches*, 1943, *Huis clos*, 1943, *Morts sans sépulture*, 1946, *Les Mains sales*, 1948. His plays are typical of the ease with which modern French drama moves among the many sources open to it, such as symbolism, psychology, history, and philosophical disquisitions on man's behaviour, and draws impressive effects from all.

Albert Camus, born 1913, has progressed from his first sympathy with the movement towards a more independent standing. This thoughtful and earnest writer shares the moral uneasiness of existentialism, but he is more directly anxious to provide a working compromise for a helpless generation. His novels, among them *La Peste*,

1947; his plays: *L'État de siège*, 1948; his essays: *Le Mythe de Sisyphe*, 1942, have secured him an audience. The weight and the spirituality of his manner contribute to his prestige; but the imperfect treatment he has given to a finely conceived ethical and historical treatise, *L'Homme révolté*, 1951, has added a note of reserve to yesterday's glowing estimate of his promise.

Conclusion

FRENCH literature from its beginnings until the present day has developed with remarkable consistency along a path indicated by the national instinct. The inevitable ups and downs have been less pronounced than in other comparable fields. The strongly original feature of this artistic achievement is that at a point well beyond halfway it presented a marked deflexion from what might have been considered, on the strength of the previous stages, its natural course. The present study has attempted to straighten out this apparent deviation to a more regular curve. After aiming for seven centuries at the formal perfection and substantial balance of classicism, France to all practical purposes realized this ideal, and almost immediately began to drift away from it. The explanation did not lie simply in the exhaustion resultant from a trying effort, and the weakening of overtaxed faculties. French literature did not fall into decay at the end of the classical age, for it possessed in store other powers than those upon which it had yet mainly lived. The seeds of romanticism had lain dormant all through its youth and early maturity. Conversely, the immediately subsequent periods revealed a latent craving for measure, equilibrium, and lucidity, associated in varying combinations with sensibility and imagination. The era of pure simple values was followed by one more complex, that was different, but not necessarily inferior. Just as the Victorian age is now developing a claim to consideration as one of the two chief phases of English literature, the French nineteenth century bids fair to equal, in the judgement of time, the legitimate prestige of the seventeenth. If for a while artistic unity was to some extent endangered there was compensation for the loss in a fuller range of effects. Even the agitated temper of our present age has not entailed any falling off from the relatively stable synthesis of the great romantics; and the most representative writers of the twentieth century, in their diversity and unevenness, have not perceptibly lowered the high-water mark of French literature.

Is this quality of consistency likely to endure? The answer must be that the fate of France's literature is, after all, bound up with her national existence; and that whatever surprises the coming decades may spring upon Europe and the world, there is little reason to fear lest the vitality of France should be unable to cope with the perils visible above the horizon of the present. The survival of nations is made up of the repeated miracle of a natural rejuvenescence from year to year.

Leaving out these incalculable factors, it is easy to notice, and possible to exaggerate, some signs of strain and of flagging freshness in a stream of literary invention that has been running for ten centuries. Nervous exhaustion and the exaggerated self-consciousness of the French have continually been pointed out by observers, native or foreign; but fresh outbursts of spiritual strength have time and again given the lie to such pessimistic warnings. The vigour of artistic creation is apparently inexhaustible in a people who are still a focus of new painting, new music, and the latest writing, and one of the world's most active centres of influence. That the luxuriant past, the prolonged expenditure of substance, in the history of French literature should provoke some heart-searching among psychologists and sociologists is only natural. But so far anxiety has not been justified; nor, should it ever be confirmed, would there be any conceivable remedy. It is improbable that human groups as yet have mastered the secrets of their moral well-being with sufficient clarity, or that they have reached a sufficient degree of self-discipline to take in hand the preservation of their mental health. While civilizations now know that they are mortal, it is still far from established that they can be made immortal by their own exertions. But if France in art, as in many other things, is living dangerously, a critic of her output can only regard it as practically certain that her resilience will be maintained; that her future will equal her past, and that the stream that has flowed so long and so abundantly will never fail.

The widespread uneasiness of our time may be only a passing cloud, that tomorrow will forget. But while conjecture is obviously rash and prophecy most imprudent, it is permissible to point out some potential sources of danger. The bane of French literature at the present time is more than ever the attraction of Paris and the large cities, the prestige of fashions and coteries, the excessive submission to ill-digested influences, national or foreign, and the ever-increasing sophistication of the young—none of these evils except the last can in any way be called new. A return from the over-centralized culture of our age to a more spontaneous and natural life, would be all in the interest of art, but the barriers to such a change are evident. The result is an ever-increasing gulf between the preciousness and obscurities of schools, theories, or techniques and the conservative tastes, or the timid perceptions, of the general public. It is no illusion of the middle-aged or the ageing that in all kinds of writing, and especially poetry, as in the fine arts, the need is for a return to plainer sanity, but the possibilities of change are too few, the symptoms too slight, to allow of any confidence.

Whatever may be amiss in principle, the fertility of the coming years seems to be assured. Men and women in all parts of France devote themselves, with varying degrees of success, to writing— some to while away the time, some to awaken sympathy, some to achieve fame. The tide of new print is not perceptibly abating; and there are just as many writers of genuine talent. A complete psychological cycle having apparently run itself out with gradually shortening periods, could another begin, and if so, on what basis? We do not know; the only safe inference is that the variety of the human mind is far greater than the power of logic. What might the literature of tomorrow be? We cannot guess. But our trust in an unforeseeable future rests on the sense of a spiritual will to live.

Index

This index contains the names of the writers, thinkers, and artists appearing in the text or in the notes, as well as those of the critics and commentators referred to.

Terms applying to institutions or groups that acquired a very special meaning in the history of French culture and literature are also included, together with titles of anonymous works, or works of doubtful authorship, or works written in collaboration. All these appear in italics.

The principal page references are printed in heavy type.